Residents of
MECKLENBURG COUNTY
NORTH CAROLINA
1762–1790

by
Kathleen Marler

CLEARFIELD

Copyright © 2005 by Kathleen Marler
All Rights Reserved.

Printed for
Clearfield Company by
Genealogical Publishing Co.
Baltimore, Maryland
2005

Reprinted for
Clearfield Company by
Genealogical Publishing Co.
Baltimore, Maryland
2007

ISBN-13: 978-0-8063-5285-5
ISBN-10: 0-8063-5285-X

Made in the United States of America

Introduction

The individuals named in this book were compiled mainly from Mecklenburg County Deeds Vol. One (July 1778 to March 1779), Vol. Two (Sept. 1779 to Oct 1782), and Vol. Three (Oct. 1782 to Sept. 1786) and will books A, B, and C. The years shown prior to 1790 represent a land sale or purchase, though in some instances an individual is only named as a witness, but this serves as proof of his presence in Mecklenburg County prior to the 1790 Federal Census. When a year is shown, such as 1774 - deed, this means that individual was mentioned as a previous land owner of that tract of land. No references are available for the original deed for that transaction. The water course named in the deed book is included with an individual to show his location in the county. The 1790 Federal Census enumeration is shown as 1790 - 124 00 - twp 2, naming the township the individual lived in. Other sources include *Decedents for Whom Loose Estates Papers Are Extant* by Herman W. Ferguson, *The 1778 Petition to the General Assembly,* early militia records, and cemetery records. The numbers listed below are for the various cemeteries, which are referenced in parentheses next to an individual's name. When an individual's death is shown as "died before 1783," for example, it was taken from references in the deed books.

1-Philadelphia Presbyterian

2-Steel Creek

3-Pleasant Hill

4-Settlers

5-Rocky River Presbyterian

6-Hopewell Presbyterian

7-Spears

8-Paw Creek Presbyterian

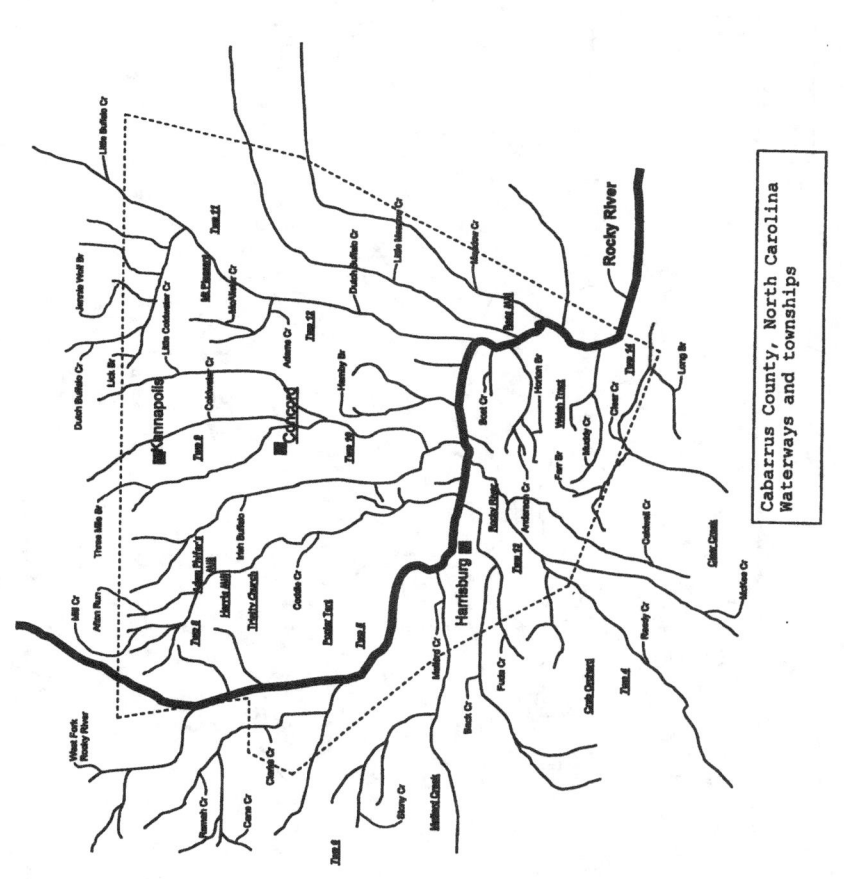

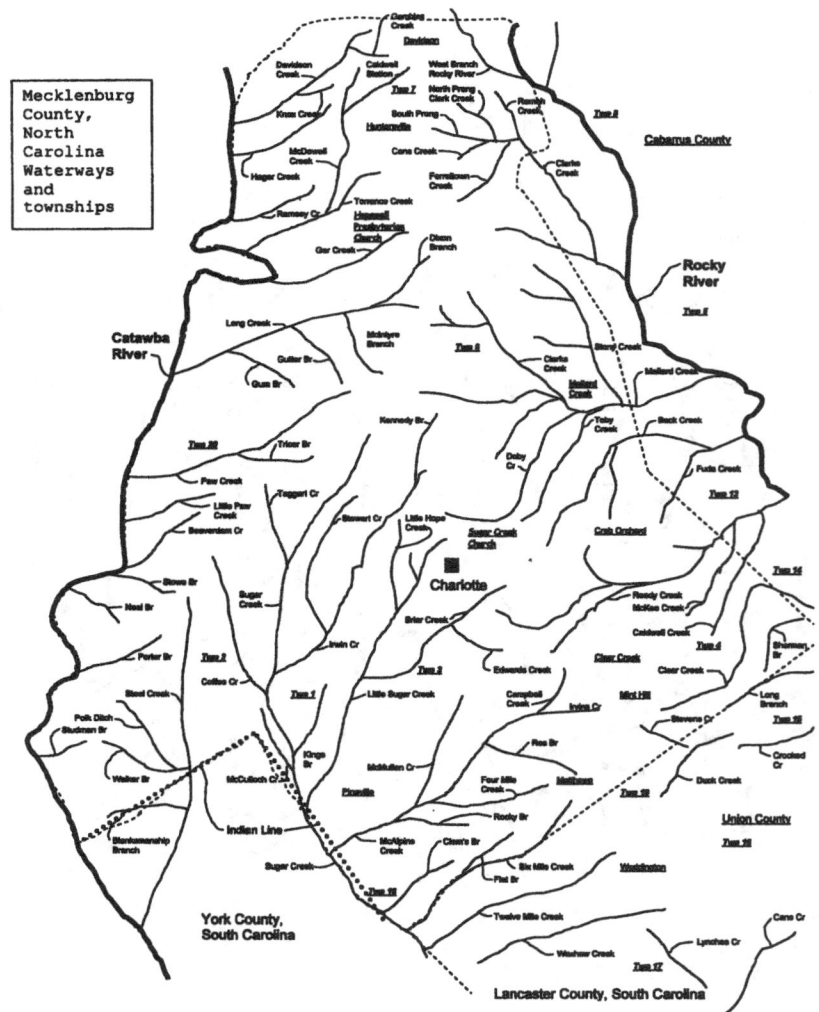

Residents of Mecklenburg County, North Carolina 1762-1790

Abernathy, Miles
    1790 - Will probated in Lincoln Co., NC
    Children: Robert, William, Charles, Julian, Miles,
    Sarah, Nathan, and Lucy Cox.
Abernathy, Miles & Usley Bracher
    1781 - married in Lincoln Co. Oct 6, 1781, bondsmen were
    Vincent Cox and John Abernathy.
    1790 - 124 00 - twp 6
    1800 - 71101-10010 - Lincoln County
    A Miles Abernathy is buried in the James Abernathy
    Cemetery in Gaston County, no dates.
Abernathy, Robert
    1772 - Robert's will was probated in Lincoln Co.
    Children: Miles ?
Abernathy, Robert
    1779 - witnessed deeds between Robert Scott and James
    Houston on Six Mile Creek and Twelve Mile Creek (twp
    16), bk 10, pg 317 and bk 10, pg 333.
    Moved to Lincoln Co., NC
Abots, Absolum
    1793 - Account ledger of John Melchor's store.
Adams, Charles & Mary
    1785 - deed on Crywell's Branch of Twelve Mile Creek
    1790 - 325 00 - twp 16
    1800 - Mecklenburg County
    Children: Samuel (Martha Gibbons), Agness
Adams/Adden, William
    1766 - listed in the militia company of Capt. Adam
    Alexander of Clear Creek.
    William was a signer of the petition to pardon the
    Cabarrus Black Boys in 1775.
    1777 - deed to James Carruth from William Adams and
    James Stafford, on Reedy Creek, a branch of Rocky River,
    bk 10, pg 254.
    1778 - deed to George Davis on Reedy Creek, bk 10, pg
    256.
    1793 - Account ledger of John Melchor's store.
Adelman, George
    1790 - 101 00 - twp 11
Agner, Jacob
    1784 - deed on Dutch Buffalow Creek
    Listed in Mecklenburg County Record of Accounts, pg 3
Alcorn, James & Katharine
    1771 - Tryon County Court Minutes 1769-1779, by Brent
    Holcomb, deed from James Armour, and James & Katharine
    Alcorn to William Armstrong for 400 acres, Test: Francis
    Armstrong, pg 63.
Aldridg, Isham
    1790 - 102 00 - twp 6
    An Isham Aldridge married Diannah Parker in Wilkes Co in
    1792, Isaac Walker bondsman.
Aldridg, William

1790 - 132 00 - twp 6
A Prince William Aldridge married Mary Ann Coons in
Wilkes Co. in 1793, Isaac Walker bondsman.
Aledge, Caleb
   1786 - indenture between John & Ann Thomson and Caleb
   Aledge for land on Richardson Creek, bk 12, pg 602.
Alexander, Aaron
   1771 - Aaron's will was probated in Mecklenburg Co.
   Children: David, Mary, Aaron, John B.
Alexander, Abihah
   1790 - 215 00 - twp 5
Alexander, Able
   1780 - witnessed deed from Isaiah Chittin to Zebulon
   Alexander on Sugar Creek, bk 10, pg 420.
   1790 - 222 00 - twp 1
   Son of Zebulon and Jane Alexander.
Alexander, Abner
   1779 - grant from North Carolina on Sugar Creek, bk 10,
   pg 489.
   1790 - 113 00 - twp 20
   1800 - Mecklenburg County
   Children: Lavinia (John Bigham)
   Son of Lavinia who died in 1810.
Alexander, Abraham & Dorcas
   1767 - Militia, Mecklenburgh Regiment (Captain)
   1786 - Abraham's will was probated in Mecklenburg Co.
   1790 - 313 08 - twp 3
   1800 - Dorcas' will was probated in Mecklenburg Co.
   Children: Joab, Cyrus, Isaac, Elizabeth (William
   Alexander), Abraham, Nathaniel, Ezra, Marcus
   Abraham was born in 1718.
Alexander, Abraham & Mary Sample
   1773 - bk 12, pg 468
   1775 - Abraham was one of the signers of the Mecklenburg
   Declaration of Independence on May 20, 1775.
   1777 - Commisioner of Mecklenburg County.
   1785 - deed on Coddle Creek from his father, John
   Alexander, bk 12, pg 538.
   1790 - 112 00 - twp 5
   1800 - Mecklenburg County
   Trustee of Liberty Hall
   Abraham died in Iredell County in 1829 at the age of 67.
   Son of Dorcas Alexander.
Alexander, Adam, Col & Mary (1)
   1766 - listed in the militia company of Capt. Adam
   Alexander of Clear Creek.
   1767 - Militia, Mecklenburgh Regiment (Captain)
   1775 - Adam was one of the signers of the Mecklenburg
   Declaration of Independence on May 20, 1775.
   1778 - witnessed a deed between David Oliphant, by
   Thomas Polk, attorney, and William Ross for land on
   Clear Creek, bk 11, pg 229.

Residents of Mecklenburg County, North Carolina 1762-1790

1779 - witnessed a bond between James Ross and James Carruth for land on Reedy Creek, bk 11, pg 108.
1780 - deed on Clear Creek, bk 11, pg 70.
1772 - witnessed deed of gift, along with Oliver Wiley, from John Carruthers to his daughter Mary Carruthers, bk 11, pg 109.
1790 - 313 05 - twp 14
Adam was a trustee for the congregation of Rock Springs in 1780.
Adam was born in 1728, died in 1798.
Alexander, Adlai
1781 - witnessed a deed between James Alexander and Hugh Neely for land on Mallard Creek, bk 11, pg 113.
Son of John & Susanna Alexander
Alexander, Amos & Susannah
1784 - mentioned in a deed to William Ramsey the Catawba River, bk 12, pg 158.
1790 - 143 06 - twp 7
1800 - Mecklenburg County
Children: Josiah Martin, Mary, Ephraim, Eli, Rebecca, Ezekiel, Minty
Son of Hezekiah & Mary Sample Alexander.
Alexander, Andrew & Sarah
1782 - Andrew's will was probated in Mecklenburg Co.
Alexander, Andw
1779 - deeds on the north side of Rocky River, bk 12, pg 50.
1783 - witnessed an indenture between Robert Hope and Zacheus Wilson, bk 12, pg 303.
1785 - witnessed an indenture between William Alexander and John McCaughey for a tract of land the north fork of Stoney Creek, bk 12, pg 485.
1790 - 130 06 - twp 5
Alexander, Andrew, Junr
1790 - 200 09 - twp 4
1800 - Cabarrus County
Alexander, Archibald
1779 - Bill of sale for one negro named Dinah from William Killingsworth of Craven Co., SC
1785 - witnessed deed between John Baxter and Josiah Harrison on Sugar Creek, being tracts originally granted to Ezekiel Alexander, part granted to Brice Miller then conveyed to Andrew Baxter, bk 12, pg 544.
Alexander, Aron & Eleanor
1779 - witnessed an indenture, along with Ezekiel and Will Polk, between John Johnston and Samuel McCleary for a tract of land joining Hugh Harris, bk 11, pg 173.
1790 - 234 01 - twp 7
1800 - Mecklenburg County
Children: Thomas, Agness, Matthew, Frank, Jesse
Aron's will was probated in 1806.
Alexander, Arthur & Margaret

Residents of Mecklenburg County, North Carolina
1762-1790

1763 - Arthur's will was probated in Mecklenburg Co. Children: Elias, Mary
Alexander, Azariah(8)
Azariah was born May 8, 1780, died Feb 5, 1854.
Alexander, Benjamin & Susannah
    1774 - sold 170 acres on both sides of Back Creek to James Scott, Test: John Garrison and Thomas Alexander, bk 10, pg 149.
    1779 - deed to Benjamin and William Alexander from John Garrison for 180 acres on both sides of Mallard Creek, Test: William Hutchison and Thomas Alexander, bk 11, pg 14.
    1779 - grant from North Carolina to Benjamin for 91 acres on Mallard Creek beginning on William Alexander's line, no. 19. (no book or page number)
    1782 - Benjamin sold a tract in SC on the east side of Broad River on Bell Creek-a branch of Bullock's Creek to Joseph Elliott, Jr., Test: John McNitt Alexander, bk 11, pg 100.
    1790 - 225 00 - twp 5
Alexander, Benjamin, Jr.
    1790 - 201 00 - twp 4
    1800 - Cabarrus County
    Reel 2, Box 3 - 1835 (Loose Estate Papers)
Alexander, Catherine
    1775 - Catherine's will was probated in Mecklenburg Co.
Alexander, Charles
    1776 - in Capt. Charles Polk's Light Horse Company.
    1779 - deed on King's branch of Sugar Creek, middle branch of Stone Creek.
    1790 - 143 00 - twp 3
    1800 - Mecklenburg County
    Son of Charles & Jean Alexander
Alexander, Charles, Capt & Jean
    1767 - Militia, Mecklenburgh Regiment (Lieutenant)
    1776 - in Capt. Charles Polk's Light Horse Company.
    1775 - Charles was one of the signers of the Mecklenburg Declaration of Independence on May 20, 1775.
    1776 - witnessed an indenture, along with William Heaslet, between William Alexander and Samuel Hemphill for a tract of land on a large branch of Stoney Creek, bk 11, pg 49.
    1777 - mentioned as an adjoining land owner on Sugar Creek along with Zebulon and Thomas Alexander, and James and William Yandel, bk 10, pg 94.
    1779 - grant for 100 acres on the middle fork of Stone Creek, beginning at Samuel Hemphill's corner, no. 53 (no book or page number).
    1782 - 108 acres on the south side of Rocky River to William S. Alexander, Test: John Baxter and J.T.R. Alexander, bk 11, pg 89.
    1790 - 314 06 - twp 20

Residents of Mecklenburg County, North Carolina   5
1762-1790

1800 - Mecklenburg County
Children: Jean, Cassandra, Charles, Adam, George, Peggy
Alexander, Daniel & Prudence
   1776 - Daniel's will was probated in Mecklenburg Co.
   Children: Margaret, James, William, Stephen, Josiah,
   Hezekiah
Alexander, Daniel
   1774 - mentioned as an adjacent land owner to Benjamin
   Alexander, and James Scott on Back Creek, bk 10, pg 151.
   1776 - deed
   1790 - 122 00 - twp 3
Alexander, Daniel
   1790 - 112 00 - twp 7
   1800 - Mecklenburg County
   Son of William & Rebecca Alexander
Alexander, David & Elizabeth
   1779 - deed from John Tool to David for 400 acres on the
   north branch of the Catawba River, Test:John Smith, Aron
   Alexander, and Thomas Shields, bk 11, pg 174.
   1790 - 504 02 - twp 7
   Children: Joel, Thomas, David, James, Ephraim, Mary,
   Sarah, Isaac, Fanny.
   Signer of 1778 Petition
   1796 - David's will was probated in Mecklenburg Co.
Alexander, Ebenezer
   1774 - deed for 300 acres from Ebenezer to Thomas Harris
   on Lacolet(Pacolet) River, South Carolina, next to
   George Alexander, bk 10, pg 428
   1790 - Iredell County ?
Alexander, Eli
   1790 - 123 01 - twp 20
Alexander, Elias & Agnes
   1776 - deed from Elias to Samuel Graham, Test: James
   Graham, and Will Reed, bk 10, pg 11.
   1790 - 112 00 - twp 4
   1800 - Mecklenburg County
   Son of Ann Alexander ?
Alexander, Elijah
   1776 - witnessed a deed, with William Reed and Abner
   Alexander, for 50 acres on McMichael's Creek from
   Augustine Culp to John Wilson, bk 11, pg 222.
   1790 - 123 00 - twp 4
   1800 - Mecklenburg County
   Son of William & Rebecca Alexander
   Elijah moved to Maury Co., TN
Alexander, Evan
   1783 - witnessed deed, with Adam and Isaac Alexander,
   between Oliver Wilie and Jacob Self for 12 acres on the
   south side of Clear Creek, bk 12, pg 214.
   1790 - 100 00 - twp 14
   1800 - Mecklenburg County
Alexander, Ezekiel

Residents of Mecklenburg County, North Carolina
1762-1790

No date - Ezekiel mentioned in a deed as the original
land owner of a tract on Sugar Creek close to the Indian
line, bk 12, pg 544.
Alexander, Ezekel & Rachel
    1790 - 100 02 - twp 4
    Children: Susannah Johnston, Minty
Alexander, Ezekel, Jr
    1790 - 101 00 - twp 4
Alexander, Ezekel, Esq
    1790 - 423 013 - twp 4
Alexander, Ezekel, Sr & Martha
    1780 - mentioned as an adoining land owner in a grant
    from North Carolina to Nathaniel Johnston on both sides
    of Long Creek, bk 12, pg 41.
    1783 - deeds
    1790 - 134 02 - twp 6
    1800 - Mecklenburg County
    Children: James Taylor, Ezekiel, Wallace, Sarah Robison,
    Deborah Robison (One of the Robinson's was Ezekiel)
    Ezekiel died in Mecklenburg Co., NC Aug 22, 1810.
    Wallace Alexander moved to Lincoln Co. where his will
    was probated in 1802.
Alexander, Ezra & Mary (Polly)
    1800 - Mecklenburg County
    Children: Parmenas, Augustus, Absolom, William, John,
    Elim, James, Agness
Alexander, Ezra, Sr.
    1775 - Ezra was one of the signers of the Mecklenburg
    Declaration of Independence on May 20, 1775.
    1790 - not shown in census
    1800 - Mecklenburg County
    Children: Eleanzer, James (Martha Rogers), Dorcas,
    Augustus, Paris, Redemption, Polly Ann
    Son of Abraham & Dorcas Alexander.
Alexander, Francis
    1790 - 112 00 - twp 9
    1800 - Mecklenburg County
Alexander, George, Col
    1778 - deed to Samuel Linton for 40 acres on Rocky River
    joining James Brown and Charles Harris' land, Test:
    Robert Cowdon and Alexander Brown, bk 10, pg 314.
    1790 - 315 011 - twp 5
Alexander, George, Jr
    1785 - Coddle Creek near the meeting house and the
    school house, bk
    1790 - 111 00 - twp 4
Alexander, George
    1790 - 112 00 - twp 20
Alexander, Hezekiah
    1778 - McCalpin's Creek (twp 15), lot 62 on the east
    side of Tryon Street in Charlotte.

1779 - mentioned as adjacent land owner in a grant from
North Carolina to Robert Smith for 77 acres on the south
side of McCalpins Creek, bk 10, pg 508.
Hezekiah was born 1728 in PA, died July 16, 1801, buried
in Sugar Creek Church Cemetery.

Alexander, Hezekiah & Mary Sample
1773 - witnessed a deed with Joseph Young from James
Alexander to John McKnitt Alexander for 5 acres that was
a part of Jeremiah Joy's barony, bk 10, pg 190.
1775 - Hezekiah was one of the signers of the
Mecklenburg Declaration of Independence on May 20, 1775.
1790 - 102 01 - twp 5
Children: William Laird (Elizabath Alexander), James R.,
Silas, Hezekiah, Amos, Joel B. (Cynthia Morrison),
Oswald, Esther (? Garrison), Kezia, Mary (? Polk)
Mary Sample was the daughter of William Sample.
Hezekiah died Aug 8, 1796.
Mary died Sept 30, 1803.

Alexander, Hezekiah & Patsy
1780 - mentioned as an adjacent land owner, as well as
Moses Andrews, in a grant from North Carolina to James
Wilson near the mouth of Fumler's Branch of Coddle
Creek, bk 12, pg 193.
1785 - mentioned as an adjacent land owner, as well as
Moses Andrews and Stephen Alexander, in a deed from
James Wilson to Martha Moffitte on Coddle Creek; Test:
Anthony Ross and Henry Short, bk 12, pg 558.
Son of Hezekiah & Mary Sample Alexander.

Alexander, Isaac
1778 - deed on Mallard Creek
1790 - 100 01 - twp 3
Trustee of Liberty Hall
Son of James & Elizabeth Alexander
One of the Isaac Alexander's was a commissioner of the
town of Charlotte in 1777.

Alexander, Isaac & Margaret P. Campbell
1778 - deed on Sugar Creek
1783 - deed to William Rowan for 106 acres on Mallard
Creek Test: William and Ezekiel Alexander and George
Ross, bk 11, pg 284.
1790 - 000 10 - twp 7
1800 - Mecklenburg County
Wife - Margaret P. Campbell, daughter of Isaac Campbell

Alexander, James
1767 - Militia, Mecklenburgh Regiment (Ensign)
1773 - James to John McKnitt Alexander, 5 acres that was
part of Jeremiah Joy's barony, Test: Joseph Young and
Hezekiah Alexander, bk 10, pg 190.

Alexander, James R.
1782 - deed from Joseph McKinly to James R. Alexander
for 115 acres originally deeded to James Bigger on the

Catawba River above the mouth of Crowder's Creek, bk 11, pg 280.
1790 - 103 00 - twp 2

Alexander, James, Doc. & Elizabeth
Children: Issac
1775 - witnessed a deed, with William Alexander, from Robert Smith, Sr. to Robert Smith, Jr. on the north side of Rocky River next to Charles Harris, bk 12, pg 595.
1778 - Signer of 1778 Petition
1779 - grant from North Carolina to James Alexander on Mallard Creek, bk 10, pg 530. Bordering Mathew Robinson and James Harris.
1781 - deed on Mallard Creek from James to Hugh Neely, bk 11, pg 113. Bordering Mathew Robinson, Test: Adlai Alexander.
1782 - grant from North Carolina to James for 220 acres on the north side of Rocky River next to Andrew Alexander and James Blythe, bk 12, pg 44.
1783 - mentioned in a deed to William Alexander, Sr. on Mallard Creek next to Mathew Robison, bk 12, pg 142.
1790 - 101 01 - twp 4
Wife - daughter of John & Susannah Alexander

Alexander, James & Jane
1781 - Jane witnessed a deed, with William Bean Alexander, from John McKnitt Alexander to John Neil for 96 acres on the Reedy Branch of Long Creek, bk 11, pg 78.
James died before 1783.

Alexander, James & Rachel
1779 - James' will was probated in Mecklenburg Co.
Children: Moses

Alexander, Jeremiah
1774 - witnessed a deed from the commissioners of Charlotte to John and William Patterson, Jr. for lots 195 and 198 on the north side of Tryon St., bk 10, pg 109.

Alexander, Joab & Hannah
married about 1794
1800 - Mecklenburg County
Son of Abraham & Dorcas Alexander.

Alexander, Joel
1790 - 101 00 - twp 7
1800 - Mecklenburg County
Son of Hezekiah & Mary Sample Alexander

Alexander, John McKnitt & Jane Bane, Margaret
1771 - John McLilley to John McKnitt Alexander, 200 acres on the eastern branches of Mallard Creek near Moses Alexander, bk 11, pg 192.
1773 - James Alexander, of Cecil County, MD to John McKnitt Alexander, five acres in what is part of Jeremiah Joy's barony. Witnesses: Joseph Young, Hezekiah Alexander, bk 10, pg 190.

1775 - John was one of the signers of the Mecklenburg Declaration of Independence on May 20, 1775.
1777 - witnessed a deed between Robert Harris, Sr. and John Henderson, Jr. on the head waters of Rocky River in the Welsh Tract. Abraham Alexander also a witness.
1781 - Clerk of court
1780 - deed from John to John Huggins on Garr Creek, witnesses Archibald Young, James Moore, bk 12, pg 424.
1779 -deed from John & Mary Buchannan on both sides of Garr Creek joining Richard Stephenson and Jeremiah Joy, witnesses: Hezekiah Alexander and Samuel Buchannan, bk 12, pg 474.
1782 - grant from North Carolina to John for 130 acres on the Meadow Branch of Mallard Creek, bk 12, pg 34.
1783 - witnessed a deed from Robert Robison, Sr. and John Robison for land on Reedy Creek in township 4, bk 11, pg 234.
1785 - power of attorney from James Moore of Hampshire Co., VA, to John McKnitt Alexander for sale of tract on McDowell Creek (twp 7), witnesses: James Knox, Margaret Alexander, bk 12, pg 563.
1790 - 301 016 - twp 6
Children: William Bane (Violet Davidson)
John died July 10, 1817, age 84, buried in Hopewell Church Cemetery.

Alexander, John M.L.
1761 - Jean Sample Person and John M.L. Alexander were administrators of the estate of Joseph Sample. In 1761 they sold 200 acres of Joseph Sample's estate on McCalpin's Creek to John Flenikin, bk 10, pg 392.

Alexander, John & Susannah
1778 - Signer of 1778 Petition
1790 - 104 00 - twp 4
Children: Asnath, Mathilda, Susanna, Adlai, son-in-law-James Alexander.
Son of James Alexander
John died in 1805.

Alexander, John
1767 - Militia, Mecklenburgh Regiment (Ensign)
1784 - between Rockey River and Coddle Creek. Children: Abraham
1784 - grant to Joseph Young mentions John Alexander as an adjoining land owner on Coddle Creek, bk 12, pg 155.
1784 - John Alexander, Sr. to James Smith on both sides of Coddle Creek containing 127 acres, Test: William Young and Benjamin Patten, bk 12, pg 457.
1785 - John Alexander gave his son Abraham a tract of land that was granted to John in 1765 on both sides of Coddle Creek, bk. 12, pg 538.
1790 - should be in twp 5

Alexander, John W. (Whitt ? or McNitt ?)

1763 - witnessed a deed between Daniel England and
Joseph Young on Coddle Creek, bk 10, pg 126.
1768 - mentioned as the grantee of 200 acres on Mallard
Creek near Nathaniel Johnston in 1768.
Alexander, Joseph
    1779 - grant from North Carolina on Coddle Creek near
Stephen Alexander, James Wilson, and Charles Caldwell,
bk 10, pg 523.
Alexander, Josiah & Elizabeth
    1776 - Josiah's will was probated in Mecklenburg Co.
    Children: Josiah, Deborah, Mary, Elizabeth, Squire
Alexander, Josiah & Mildred
    1783 - deed
    1790 - 132 02 - twp 8
    1800 - Cabarrus County
Alexander, Judith
    1790 - 111 00 - twp 2
Alexander, Levine/Lavinia
    1790 - 302 00 - twp 20
    1800 - Mecklenburg County
    Children: Abner, Ezra, Zadock, Dorcas, Sidney, Polly,
Loveday, Absolom
Alexander, Mathew
    1784 - witnessed a bill of sale from William and John
Gardner to Samuel Linton.
    Mathew lived near Col. George Alexander, in the area
that was twp 5 in 1790.
Alexander, Moses
    1765, 1770, 1774, 1779 - mentioned in deed on Mallard
Creek, near Adam Meek, David Garrison, and John McKnitt
Alexander.
    1790 - 372 01 - twp 5
    1800 - Cabarrus County
    Children: Moses, Sarah ? (William Callon)
Alexander, Moses
    1790 - 100 00 - twp 5
    1800 - Cabarrus County
    Son of Moses ?
Alexander, Moses
    1790 - 201 00 - twp 7
Alexander, Moses
    near Meadow Branch on the south side of Clear Creek.
Alexander, Nathaniel (doctor)
    1777 - trustee for the Presbyterial Congregation of
Rocky River, bk 10, pg 206.
    1779 - witnessed a deed with Andrew Alexander between
John Disart and Robert Craighead on Mallard and Stoney
Creek, bk 10, pg 398.
    1783 - deed to Moses Meek, Jr. for 110 a. on Stoney
Creek adjoining Joseph Mitchel, witnesses: William Lock,
Richard Smith, bk 12, pg 305.

Residents of Mecklenburg County, North Carolina 1762-1790

    1784 - mentioned as a neighbor in a grant to Robert Cowden for a tract between Rockey River and Coddle Creek, bk 12, pg 156.
    1784 - mentioned as Dr. Nathaniel as a neighbor in a grant to James Smith on a tract between Rocky River and Coddle Creek, bk 12, pg 149.
    Children: Elizabeth ? (George Harris)
Alexander, Nathaniel & Jenny
    1767 - Militia, Mecklenburgh Regiment (Colonel)
    1768 Twelve Mile Creek
    1779 - deed mentioning a tract on Twelve Mile Creek, originally granted to Nathaniel Alexander in 1753, bk 10, pg 309.
    1796 - Nathaniel's will was probated in Mecklenburg Co.
Alexander, Phineas
    1779 - mentioned as an adjacent land owner in a grant to William Dunn on King's branch of Sugar Creek near Charles Alexander, Ezekiel Polk, John Baird, and Alexander McClellan, bk 10, pg 502.
    1780 - Big Sugar Creek, King's branch of Sugar Creek.
    1782 - deed from Zebulon Alexander to Phineas for 111 acres on the south side of Sugar Creek, bk 11, pg 171.
    1783 - witnessed deed with John Barnett between John Barnett and Samuel Elliott on Sugar Creek, bk 12, pg 278.
    1790 - 134 00 - twp 1
    1800 - Mecklenburg County
    Son of Zebulon and Jane Alexander.
Alexander, Robert
    1788 - Loose estate papers
Alexander, Samuel & Sarah
    1784 - Samuel's will was probated in Mecklenburg Co.
Alexander, Samuel
    1773 - deed from Caleb Barr to Samuel for 32 acres in the Welch tract, Test: Samuel Pickence (Pickens) and Jacob Barr, bk 11, pg 164.
    1781 - deed from John Dysart to Samuel for 167 acres in the Welch tract on the south side of Rocky River in twp 4, Test: Thomas Nickel and James Patton, bk 11, pg 137.
    1786 - Welch tract (later, part of Cabarrus County)
Alexander, Samuel
    1790 - 202 00 - twp 20
    1800 - Mecklenburg County
Alexander, Stephen, Capt
    1779 - deed from Joseph Scott to Stephen for 215 acres on the south side of Coddle Creek, Test: John and Robert Allison, bk 10, pg 407.
    1785 - mentioned as an adjacent land owner to James Wilson, Hezekiah Alexander and Moses Andrews on the south side of Coddle Creek, bk 12, pg 558.
    1790 - 207 02 - twp 8
    1800 - Cabarrus County

Residents of Mecklenburg County, North Carolina
1762-1790

Alexander, Thomas, Capt
    1784 - witnessed a deed from John Brevard of Rowan County to James Williamson of twp 16 in 1790, for land on the braches of Rocky River, bk 12, pg 547.
    1790 - 133 06 - twp 4
    1800 - Mecklenburg County
    Wife - Jane Morrison, daughter of Neil Morrison
    Thomas was born in 1753 according to 1840 pension list and a Revolutionary Soldier, Major Thomas Alexander died Dec 28, 1844, age 92 according to The Charlotte Journal dated Jan 17, 1845.
    Son of Aaron & Eleanor Alexander.

Alexander, Thomas
    1774 - witnessed a deed, with John Garrison, from Benjamin Alexander to James Scott on both sides of Back Creek, adjoining Daniel Alexander, bk 10, pg 151.
    1777 - mentioned as an adjacent land owner to Zebulon and Charles Alexander, James and William Yandel, Peter Johnston, and Isaiah Fitten on Sugar Creek, bk 10, pg 94.

Alexander, Will
    1777 - witnessed deeds for Mathew and Francis Lock for land on Buffalo Creek and Coddle Creek(twp 9 in 1790) with James and Griffith Rutherford and William Sharpe, bk 12, pg 250 & 252.

Alexander, William Lee & Elizabeth
    1790 - 132 04 - twp 13
    Wife: Elizabeth
    Children: Sally (Archibald Henderson), Fanny, Nathaniel Washington, Erasmus
    Brother of Gov. Nathaniel Alexander
    William was born Nov 1, 1765, died March 16, 1806, buried in Smith Family Cemetery, Cabarrus Co.
    Elizabeth was born Aug 30, 1770, died March 30, 1808, buried in Smith Family Cemetery, Cabarrus Co.

Alexander, William & Margaret
    1775 - witnessed deed on Rocky River between Robert Smith, Jr. and Sr., bk 12, pg 595.
    1776 - William to Samuel Hemphill, 300 acres on Stoney Fork of Mallard Creek, Test: Charles Alexander and William Heaslet, bk 11, pg 49.
    1779 - grant to William from North Carolina for 147 acres on the south side of Mallard Creek, bk 10, pg 521.
    1783 - witnessed a deed between Hannah and Elinor Clark for 84 acres in twp 5, bk 12, pg 315.
    1785 - tract on a large branch of Stoney Fork of Mallard Creek.
    William may have been a Signer of 1778 Petition.
    1785 - 100 acres on the north fork of Stoney Creek to John McCaughey. Witnesses were Charles and Andrew Alexander, and J.M. Garrison, bk 12, pg 485.

Residents of Mecklenburg County, North Carolina 1762-1790

1785 - witnessed an indenture, along with Andrew Alwxander and J.M. Garrison, between Benjamin Alexander and John McCaughey for a tract of land on Back Creek, bk 12, pg 487.
1790 - 235 01 - twp 5
Alexander, William Bean & Violet
    1777 - Clerk of court
    1781 - lived on Long Creek
    1790 - 313 00 - twp 6
    Wife - Violet Davidson, daughter of John Davidson
Alexander, William, Jr.
    1790 - 213 00 - twp 1
Alexander, William, Capt B. & Sarah
    1782 - deeds on both sides of Caldwell branch, a branch of Mallard Creek.
    1783 - grant from North Carolina for 46 acres on Mallard Creek next to James Alexander and Mathew Robison, bk 12, pg 142.
    The William on Caldwell branch was a blacksmith.
    1790 - 242 09 - twp 4
    Wife - Sarah
    William was born 1751, died Oct 26, 1826
    Sarah died Nov 27, 1799
    Both are buried in Rocky River Presbyterian Church Cemetery.
Alexander, Wm, Sr & Rebecca
    1790 - 332 011 - twp 4
    Children: Elijah, William (Elizabeth Fish), Daniel, Josiah (Agnes Patterson), Rebecca (Charles Richmond)
Alexander, William & Mary
    1765 - mentioned in a deed; land conveyed to him on May 6, 1765 on Sugar Creek by Henry Eustace McCulloh, bk 10, pg 267.
    1771 - William was one of the Cabarrus Black Boys.
    1778 - deed from William to Robert Arthur for 240 acres on Sugar Creek, bk 10, pg 267.
    William & Mary were living in Rowan Co. in 1778.
Alexander, William & Agnes
    1772 - William's will was probated in Mecklenburg Co.
Alexander, Zebulon & Jane
    1782 - Zebulon to Phineas Alexander, 111 acres on the south side of Sugar Creek, bk 11, pg 171.
    1784 - Zebulon's will was probated in Mecklenburg Co.
    Zebulon and Jane lived in the area of Mecklenburg County that was in township 2 in 1790.
    Children: Phineas, Abel, Zebulon, Zenos, Mary (? Irwin, Ruth (John McRee), Hannah (? Greer), Tirzah, Martha, Deborah
Alexson, Peter
    1791 - Loose estate papers
Algia/Elga, Francis & Mary (see Elga)
    1792 - Francis' will was probated in Mecklenburg Co.

Allen, Alexander, Jr. & Margaret
    1790 - 142 00 - twp 13
    1782 - grant for 180 acres on Flag Run, a branch of
    Footy Creek, beginning on Robert Harris' corner, bk 12,
    pg 164.
    Children: Eleanor (? Duckworth), Ann (? Harris),
    Margaret (? Duckworth), Robert
    John & William Duckworth were in Burke Co. in 1790.
Allen, Alexander, Sr.
    1790 - 132 00 - twp 13
Allen, Andrew
    1790 - 132 00 twp 17
Allen, George & Sarah
    1770 - George's will was probated in Mecklenburg Co.
Allen, George
    1784 east side of Cataba adjoining the Tuckasuga Ford.
Allen, George, Sr.
    1790 - 010 01 - twp 4
    1800 - Mecklenburg County
Allen, John
    1770 - Long Creek.
    1786 - Loose estate papers
    Named in the estate of William Sample.
Allen, John & Sarah
    1778 - deed to William Eadger for 280 acres on a branch
    of Long Creek, bk 10, pg 88.
    1779 - witnessed a deed from David Reed to Nicholas
    Gibbony on Sugar Creek, bk 10, pg 412.
    1790 -334 00 twp 1
Allen, John & Agnes Sample
    1774 - deed to James Osburne for 160 acres on Rockey
    River adjoining John Frohook, bk 10, pg 111.
    1776 - John's will was probated in Mecklenburg Co.
    1790 - 012 06 - twp 4
    1800 - Mecklenburg County
    Children: Margaret ? (Alexander Cathey)
    John was a shoemaker.
Allen, Samuel & Patience
    1778 - deed to James McKee on the east side of Cataba on
    Beaver Dam Creek, bordered by John Giles and John Davis,
    Test: William Berryhill, Robert Irwin, and Thomas Greer.
    bk 11, pg 110.
    Samuel was a wheelwright.
Allen, Thomas
    1790 - 212 00 - twp 12
    1793 - Account ledger of John Melchor's store.
Allen, Thomas
    1790 - 000 10 - twp 17
Allen, William
    1778 - witnessed a deed from Robert and John Allison to
    John McClure on Long Creek and the Catawba River,
    beginning near Jeremiah Joy's line, bk 10, pg 92.

Residents of Mecklenburg County, North Carolina 1762-1790

Allet, Benjamin B.
    1778 - witnessed a deed from James Way to Robert Arthur on Four Mile Creek joining Henry Downs and Thomas Harris, bk 10, pg 73.
Allison, Andrew & Margaret
    1760 - conveyed a tract of land in Rowan Co. on the branches of Davidson and Back Creeks, no book and page number. Original grant to Andrew was in 1759.
Allison, Archabeld & Elizabeth(2)
    1790 - 313 00 - twp 1
    1800 - Mecklenburg County
    Children: Andrew, Sarah (? Berryhill), Elizabeth (? Oliphant).
Allison, David
    1786 - witnessed an indenture from Joseph Graham, sheriff, to Robert Smith, on Coldwater and Buffalo Creek, bk 12, pg 616.
    1790 - 100 00 - twp 1
    Children: Margaret (Valentine Hipp), Mabel (Andrew Hipp) David's will was probated in 1800.
Allison, John, Esqr.
    1778 - Robert and John Allison to John McClure on Long Creek and the Cataba River, bk 10, pg 92.
    1779 - witnessed a deed, with Robert Allison, from Joseph Scott to Stephen Alexander on the south branch of Coddle Creek, bk 10, pg 407.
    1781 - witnessed a deed from William Hayns to Jacob Self for 70 acres in twp 14, bk 11, pg 93.
    1781 - witnessed a deed, with Joseph Self, from William Hayns to William Mitchel for a tract of land on Muddy Creek, bk 11, pg 95.
    1785 - David Wilson to John Allison, 83 acres on ? adjoining John Farr, Ephraim Farr's old line, and Nathaniel Ervin's old line, bk 12, pg 52
    1790 - 313 05 - twp 9
Allison, Joseph
    1790 - 103 00 - twp 1
Allison, Robert
    1778 - Robert and John Allison to John McClure on Long Creek and the Cataba River, bk 10, pg 92.
    1785 - deed from Alexander Mitchel for 418 acres on both sides of a branch of Sugar Creek beginning on the Barony line, bk 12, pg 462.
    1790 - 134 03 - twp 1
Allison, Robert
    1778 - witnessed a deed, with John Hamilton, and Robert Hope, from Joseph Patterson to Robert Harris for 312 acres on Rocky River, adjoining Samuel Pickens and Thomas Shields, bk 11, pg 287.
    1779 - witnessed a deed, with John Allison, from Joseph Scott to Stephen Alexander on the south branch of Coddle Creek, bk 10, pg 407.

1800 - Cabarrus County
This Robert could be the one above, but the land locations suggest two Roberts, though there is only one Robert Allison in the 1790 and 1800 census.

Allison, Thomas
1776 - witnessed a deed from James Todd to John Todd on the head branches of Sugar Creek, bk 10, pg 21.
1778 - witnessed a deed from Robert and John Allison to John McClure on Long Creek and the Cataba River, bk 10, 92.
1782 - witnessed a deed from William Berryhill and Thomas McDowel to James Clark for 120 acres on Sugar Creek, adjoined by William Clark, bk 11, pg 183.

Almond, Nathan
1792 - Account ledger of John Melchor's store.

Almond, Richard
1793 - Account ledger of John Melchor's store.

Anderson, James
1784 - James' will was probated in Mecklenburg Co.

Anderson, John
1754 - named as land owner of a 225 acre tract on Long Creek that was conveyed by his heirs to Rev. Alexander Craighead on May 17, 1754, bk 10, pg 252.

Anderson, John
1765 - grant to John for land on Long Creek, no book or page number.
1781 - mentioned in a deed as an adjoining land owner to Gideon Thomson, William Lawing and Andrew McKee in the area of twp 2 or 3, bk 12, pg 444.

Anderson, Robert
1779 - witnessed a deed, with Robert Harris, from Henry Shute to Joseph Ross on the north side of Rocky River, bk 10, pg 354.
1782 - witnessed a deed, with Anthony Ross, from Isaac Sellars to John Adam Miller for 165 acres on the north side of Rocky River, adjoining Joseph Ross, bk 11, pg 231.
1790 - 205 00 - twp 8

Andrews, Moses
1769 - deed from John Mitchell to Moses for 130 acres, part of a tract originally granted to Ambrose Harding in 1763, bk 10, pg 180.
1780 - named as an adjoining land owner along with Hezekiah Alexander on Coddle Creek in a grant from North Carolina to James Wilson, bk 12, pg 193.
1790 - 112 00 - twp 8

Andrews, Robert
1784 - named as an adjoining land owner of Ephraim Farr, Hugh Hambleton, and John Graham on Rockey River, bk 12, pg 178.
1790 - 227 0 - twp 8

Andrews, William(5) & Elizabeth Morrison

Residents of Mecklenburg County, North Carolina 1762-1790

1790 -102 00 - twp 13
Wife - Elizabeth Morrison, daughter of Robert & Sarah Morrison.

Andrew, William & Barbara(5)
William was born Aug 13, 1758, died March 13, 1806. Barbara died July 1, 1800.

Apple, John
1778 - Signer of 1778 Petition

Appleton, William
1779 - named as an adjacent land owner to Thomas McCall, William Ligget, and John Ray on Findley's Creek, a branch of Twelve Mile Creek, no book or page number.
1790 -222 00 - twp 16

Archabeld, Robert, Rev
Pastor of Rocky River Presbyterian Church from 1778 to about 1792.
1779 - deed from William McWhirter to Robert, bk 11, pg 37.
1784 - named as an adjoing land owner of John Wallace on Wolf Meadow branch, a branch of Coddle Creek, bk 12, pg 183.
1790 -113 04 - twp 4

Armour, Andrew
1761 - mentioned in a deed as the original land owner of 212 acres granted to Andrew on the upper edge of the Mill Creek of the Cataba River, bk 10, pg 230.
1764 - deeds to James Armour on the south side of Catawba River between Croders Creek and Allison Creek, Test: Samuel Bigham, Moses Ferguson, Robert Leeper, Vol. 1, pg 550 & 592.

Armour, James
1753 - mentioned as the patentee of 640 acres on the Catawba River, Vol 1, pg 592.
1762 - Loose estate papers
1764 - mentioned in a deed from Andrew Armour to James Armour as deceased, Vol 1, pg 550.

Armour, James & Jean/Jennet
1765 - deed to Andrew Armour on the Catawba River for 640 acres, Test: Moses Ferguson and Robert Harris, Vol 2, pg 573.
1771 - from Tryon County Court Minutes by Brent Holcomb, a deed from James and James & Katharine Alcorn to Wm. Armstrong for 400 acres, Test: Francis Armstrong, pg 63.
1774 - Jean Armour's Creek is mentioned in a deed from Samuel McCrume to Stephen McCortle on the Catawba River, bk 10, pg 133.
1777 - mentioned in a deed as the original land owner of 315 acres on the Cataba near Mill Creek, bk 10, pg 230. James died before May 1769. The widder Armour is mentioned in a deed from Thomas Polk to John White, bk 4, pg 542.

Armstrong, John

Residents of Mecklenburg County, North Carolina
1762-1790

Armstrong, John
    1768 - Loose estate papers
    1790 - 101 00 - twp 9
Armstrong, John, Jr
    1790 - 000 10 - twp 9
Armstron, Matthew & Lily
    1779 - Matthew's will was probated in Mecklenburg Co.
Armstrong, Mathew & Mary Beaty
    1782 - Loose estate papers for Mathew
    Mary was the daughter of John Beaty.
Armstrong, Robert & Agnes Beaty(2)
    1780 -
    1790 - 114 00 - twp 13 (widow)
Armstrong, Robert
    1780 - witnessed a deed from William Barnett to William Daviss along the NC/SC line, bk 10, pg 445.
Arthur, Robert & Sarah
    1778 - deed from James Way to Robert for 227 acres on Four Mile Creek, joining Henry Downs and Thomas Harris, bk 10, pg 73.
    1778 - deed from William & Mary Alexander to Robert for 240 acres on Sugar Creek, bk 10, pg 267.
    1779 - mentioned as an adjoining land owner of John Sharpe and James Sharpe on Sugar Creek, bk, 10, pg 494.
Asburn, Alexander & Agnes (see Osbourne)
Ashley, John & Sarah
    1774 - deed from John Cole to John Ashley of Tryon Co., NC, 300 acres on both sides of Richardson's Creek, bk 10, pg 178
    1775 - deed from John to Reese Shelby for 300 acres on Richardson's Creek, bk 10, pg 177.
    John & Sarah were living in Tryon Co., NC in 1775.
    1790 - 124 00 - twp 12
Ashmore, James
    1771 - James was one of the Cabarrus Black Boys.
Ashmore, Walter
    1798 - Loose estate papers
Atkins, James
    1792 - Account ledger of John Melchor's store.
Atkins, Samuel
    1790 - 125 00 - twp 5
Aubin, Richard
    1778 - witnessed a deed from Thomas Thomson to Samuel Brown on the north side of the Cataba River on the head of Rockey River, bk 10, pg 365.
Aurey/Ourey/ Ury, Martin
    1790 - 123 00 - twp 11
Avent, James
    1790 - 116 05 - twp 15
    Son of Solomon Avant ?
Avery, Waitstill & Leah

Residents of Mecklenburg County, North Carolina   1762-1790

1769 - witnessed a deed from David Rees to James Rees on Caddle Creek, bk 10, pg 147.
1775 - Waitstill was one of the signers of the Mecklenburg Declaration of Independence on May 20, 1775.
1777 - deed from the commissioners of Charlotte to Waitstill for lots 73, 105, 235, 236, 327, 328, 329, 330, 331, 332, 333 in Charlotte, bk 10, pg 61.
1786 - witnessed a deed from Joseph Graham, sheriff, to Robert Smith at a public auction for a tract of land on Coldwater Creek Buffalo Creek, bk 12, pg 616.
Waitstill was an attorney and took oath of office in Tryon Co., NC. In 1777 he was elected the first Attorney General of North Carolina.
He moved to Burke Co., NC in 1781.
Wife - Leah Frank
Children: Isaac T., female (William W. Lenoir), female (Thomas Lenoir), female (? Poor)

Ayres, Thomas & Mary
1776 - Thomas' will was probated in Mecklenburg Co.

Baggs/Biggs/Beggs/Bugg, Archibald
1786 - Loose estate papers
Children: William ?

Bailey, Francis
1790 - 115 02 - twp 7

Bailey, Joseph
1790 - 112 00 - twp 14

Bailey, Richard
1790 - 133 00 - twp 4

Baird, John
1779 - mentioned as an adjoining land owner of William Dunn, Ezekiel Polk, Alexander McClelan, Phineas Alexander, and Charles Alexander on King's branch of Sugar Creek, bk 10, pg 502.

Baker, Absolom
1784 - deed from John Willis to Absalom for 200 acres on Buffalow Creek adjoining Martin Phifer and John Baker, bk 12, pg 449.

Baker, Christopher
1790 - 233 03 - twp 9

Baker, George & Rachel
1790 - 143 00 - twp 1
Children: Rebecca Mitchell (wife of John Mitchell), Jonathan, Aaron, Michael, Abel, Jacob, George, Rachel, Hannah, Elizabeth
George died in May 1815.

Baker, James
1780 - mentioned as an adjoining land owner of John Means, James White, Walter Farr, and William McWhirter on Wolf Meadow branch of Coddle Creek, bk 12, pg 77.

Baker, John

1782 - mentioned as an adjoining land owner of Samuel
Sensell, John Colebrook (Holbrook) on a branch of
English Buffalo Creek, bk 12, pg 65.
1784 - English Buffalow Creek
1778 - Signer of 1778 Petition.
1790 - 154 03 - twp 9
Baker, Joshua
1790 - 113 00 - twp 9
Baker, Michael
1777 - Loose estate papers
Balch, Amos
1778 - Signer of 1778 Petition
Balch, Hezekiah James & Martha
Both Poplar Tent Presbyterian Church and Rocky River
Presbyterian Church claim Hezekiah as their pastor from
1769 to 1776.
1775 - Hezekiah was one of the signers of the
Mecklenburg Declaration of Independence on May 20, 1775.
1776 - deed to James Walker for 88 acres on a ridge
between English Buffalo Creek and Caddle Creek, Test:
William Scott and John White, bk 10, pg 221.
1777 - witnessed a deed from David Garrison, Sr. to
David Garrison, Jr. on Mallard Creek, bk 10, pg 7.
Wife - Martha
Hezekiah died in 1776, and is buried in Poplar Tent
Presbyterian Church Cemetery.
Balch, John
1793 - Loose estate papers
Balch/Batch, Thomas
1790 - 133 00 - twp 4
Balch/Batch, William
1778 - witnessed a deed from John & Martha Rodgers to
Hugh Rodgers on English Buffalo Creek, bk 10, pg 337.
1779 - deed to John Carothers for 35 acres on the head
spring of Muddy Creek, Test: Hugh and Joseph Rodgers, bk
10, pg 372.
Baldwin, Joel(4) & Mary ?
1776 - Joel died Oct 21, 1776 at the age of 26, his will
was probated in Mecklenburg.
Children: Samuel, Jessie, Caleb
Baldwin, Mary
1779 - deed from George Greer to Mary for lot 92 in
Charlotte, Test: Thomas Henderson and Robert Barlned,
Jr., bk 10, pg 344.
Baldyoung, Archer
1780 - witnessed a deed from John McKnitt Alexander to
John Huggins for land on Garr Creek joining Richard
Stephenson and Jeremiah Joy, bk 12, pg 424.
Baley, Samuel
1790 - 134 04 - twp 4
Bankson, Andrew
1792 - Account ledger of John Melchor's store.

Barbrick, Christian
 1783 - deed from William Ross to Christian Barbarick of
 Rowan Co. for 300 acres on Coldwater Creek adjoining
 John McCoy and John Neichler, Test: Joseph Shinn, Robert
 Patterson, and James Ross, bk 12, pg 360.

Barbrick, Leonard
 1779 - deed from George & Catherine Goodnight to Leonard
 for 100 acres on both sides of Coldwater Creek,
 adjoining Henry Fisherman and Dobb's line, Test: Martin
 Fifer and Jason Frissell, bk 11, pg 10.
 1790 - 115 00 - twp 10

Barett, John
 1776 - witnessed a deed, with Charles Alexander and Will
 Reed, from John Dermond to John Wilson for 133 acres on
 the northwest side of McMichael Creek, bk 11, pg 246.
 1777 - unfinished two story house on lot adjoining No.
 73 in Charlotte, bk 10, pg 61.

Barett/Barrett, William & Margaret
 1778 - William's will was probated in Mecklenburg Co.
 Children: Abraham

Bargar, John & Anna
 1785 - deed to Frederick Beck for 202 acres on the east
 side of Dutch Buffalow Creek, Test: Joseph Shinn, and
 Samuel and Daniel Luther, bk 12, pg 501.

Barker, Daniel
 1779 - witnessed a deed, with Ruth Barker, from John
 Powell to William Barker for 70 acres on the north side
 of Muddy Creek in the Welch Tract, bk 10, pg 384.

Barker, Ephraim
 1779 - witnessed a deed, with William Lusk, from Thomas
 Polk, attorney for David Oliphant, to William Barker for
 30 acres on Muddy Creek, bk 10, pg 433.

Barker, Ruth
 1779 - witnessed a deed, with Daniel Barker, from John
 Powell to William Barker for 70 acres on the north side
 of Muddy Creek in the Welch Tract, bk 10, pg 384.

Barker, Samuel
 1773

Barker, William
 1779 - deed from John Powell for 70 acres on the north
 side of Muddy Creek in the Welch Tract, Test: Daniel and
 Ruth Barker, bk 10, pg 384.
 1779 - deed from Thomas Polk, attorney for David
 Oliphant, for 30 acres on Muddy Creek, bk 10, pg 433.

Barkley, Eleanor
 1783 - bill of sale to William Penney for three negroes,
 viz, Moses, a negro boy, Lizzy, a wench, and Lucy, a
 wench, Test: John Morton, Robert Scott, and David
 Templeton, bk 12, pg 243.

Barnet, Abraham & Mary

1781 - deed from Abraham and Samuel Barnet to Robert
Crocket for 250 acres on both sides of Long Creek
joining Samuel Sprott, and David McCord, bk 12, pg 476.
1784 - deed to Joseph Graham for 16 acres known as the
Lower Fishery, bk 12, pg 499.
Son of William Barnett ?

Barnet, Hugh & Susannah
1779 - mentioned in a grant to Edward Meloney as an
adjoining land owner on Sugar Creek with William
Houston, and David Crockett, bk 10, pg 487.
Children: Robert, James, Hannah (Michel Henderson),
Margaret, Elizabeth, Agness, Mary Dorcus, John, Hugh,
Ann
Hugh's will was probated in 1786.

Barnet, Hugh
1779 - witnessed a deed between James McClure and Aron
McWhirter on Twelve Mile Creek, bk 12, pg 329.
1779 - witnessed a deed, with Samuel Knox, from George
Nickelson to Margaret Wilson for lot 129 and 137 in
Charlotte, bk 11, pg 28.
1790 - 315 00 - twp 19
Children: Abel, Sarah, Ruth (? McWhirter), Hugh,
Moses, Mary

Barnet, John, Jr. & Rosannah
1781 - deed from James Fleniken to John for 172 acres on
both sides of McCalpins Creek, adjoining Thomas Drumond
and Test: William Reed, David Flaniken, and John Clark,
bk 11, pg 81.
1783 - deed to Samuel Elliott for 179 acres on Sugar
Creek, bk 12, pg 278, Test: Phineas Alexander and John
Barnet.
1790 - 103 00 - twp 2
Children: Ann, Mary, Kezia, Elizabeth, Jannet, Robert,
William, John, Joseph

Barnet, John, Sr. & Ann
1780 - witnessed a deed from William Barnett to William
Daviss along the wagon road on the line between North
and South Carolina, bk 10, pg 445.
1780 - mentioned in a grant to David Litham as an
adjoining land owner along with William Davies on Waxhaw
Creek, bk 10, pg 507.
1780 - mentioned as adjoining in a grant to William Moor
on Cane Creek, bk 12, pg 26.
1790 - 103 01 - twp 2
Wife - Ann Spratt, daughter of Thomas Spratt
Children: Mary (? Jack), Ann (? Elliott), John,
Susannah (? Smart), William (Jane Jack)

Barnet, John
1772 - witnessed a deed from Thomas Polk to James Moore
on the south branch of Steel Creek adjoining John Henry,
Samuel Knox, and Samuel Davis, bk 10, pg 137.

Residents of Mecklenburg County, North Carolina
1762-1790

    1779 - grant to John for 30 acres on Sugar Creek adjoining Francis Ross and Martha McNeal, bk 10, pg 526.
    1790 - 113 00 - twp 20
Barnett, Moses & Martha
    1798 - Loose estate papers for Moses
Barnet, Robert
    1790 - 133 00 - twp 16
Barnet, Robert, Jr. & Jennet Todd
    1786 - deed to David Kenneday for 7 acres on Sugar Creek, Test: William Reed, bk 12, pg 586.
    1789 - Sugar Creek
    1790 - 111 02 - twp 1
    Children: Marcus, James G. (Deborah Montgomery), David Edwin (Rebecca Montgomery), Robert Franklin (Mary Sample), Amos (Catherine Porter), Jenny, Polly
Barnet, Robert, Sr. & Catherine
    1773 - witnessed a deed from Alexander McKee to William Berryhill on Sugar Creek, bk 11, pg 129.
    1790 - 134 00 - twp 2
Barnet, James
    1782 - grant to James and William Barnet for 228 acres on Big Sugar Creek, bk 12, pg 76.
Barnet, Samuel
    1781 - deed from Abraham and Samuel Barnet to Robert Crocket for 250 acres on both sides of Long Creek joining Samuel Sprott, and David McCord, bk 12, pg 476.
Barnet, Thomas & Ann
    1782 - named as one of the chainbearers of a tract of land on Kings branch of Sugar Creek, bk 12, pg 234.
    1783 - named as an adjoining land owner to Robert Wilson, William Bigham, and John McDowel on Sugar Creek, bk 12, pg 107.
    Thomas was born in 1759 in Orange Co., NC and moved to Mecklenburg County in 1799.
    Wife - Ann Graham, dau of James & Mary Barber Graham.
    Children: Nancy (Isaac Price), Ann, Thomas, Sarah (Charles Elms), Elizabeth, John, George, Susan
    Thomas had a brother named John Barnett.
    Son of William Barnet
Barnett, William & Jane
    Children: Annie (James Jack), Samuel (Eliza Joyner, Elizabeth Worsham),
Barnett, William & Mary
    Mary died Oct 4, 1764.
Barnett, William, Jr. & Mary McRee
    1780 - deed to William Daviss for 13 acres along the Waggon Road on the line between North and South Carolina, bk 10, pg 445.
    1782 - grant to William and James Barnet for 228 acres on Big Sugar Creek, bk 12, pg 76.
    1782 - mentioned in a grant to Ezekiel Polk as an adjoining land owner on Sugar Creek along with Robert

McCleary, bk 12, pg 43.
William died Aug 23, 1785, and Mary died Apr 11, 1785.
Barnett, William, Sr. & Margaret
    1769 - grant from King George III for a tract on Kings branch of Sugar Creek, no book or page number.
    1775 - mentioned as an adjoining land owner of Thomas Ferguson, George Cahoon, John Henry, and Edward Williams on Steel Creek, bk 10, pg 251.
    Children: Thomas, William (Mary McRee), Samuel, Abraham (Mary Brownfield), Mary (? Elliot), Ruth, Ann, James, Elizabeth, Margaret
    1778 - William's will was probated in Mecklenburg County.
Barnheart/ Barenhart, Charles
    1784 - mentioned as an adjoining land owner to Jacob Dean, Peter Ross, Jacob Faget, and Michael Fogelman near Hamby's Run, a branch of Rocky River, bk 12, pg 137.
    1790 - 354 00 - twp 12
    1794 - Account ledger of John Melchor's store.
    1800 - Cabarrus County
Barnhart, John "Christian" & Mary Elizabeth
    1784 - grant to Christian for 45 acres on Little Coldwater Creek adjoining John Blackwater, and Adam Bower, bk 12, pg 191.
    Coldwater Creek next to Christian Goodknight
    1790 - 101 00 - twp 10
    Wife - Mary "Elizabeth" Barringer, daughter of Matthias Barringer
    Christian was born April 5, 1719, died Aug 10, 1799, buried in Old Coldwater Church Cemetery.
    Elizabeth was born Aug 26, 1724, died Aug 24, 1798, buried in Old Coldwater Church Cemetery.
Barnhart, Christian, Jr.
    1790 - 113 00 - twp 10
    1800 - Cabarrus County
Barnhart, George & Patsy (Martha)
    1790 - 102 00 - twp 10
    1800 - Cabarrus County
    Wife - Martha "Patsy" Reed, daughter of John & Sarah Kiser Reed.
Barnhart, Henry
    1779 - deed for lots 169 and 177 in Charlotte, Test: George Rice and Joseph Robison, bk 11, pg 136.
    1790 - 123 00 - twp 3
Barnhart, Mathias
    1778 - Signer of 1778 Petition
Barnhart, Mathias
    1790 - 121 00 - twp 10
    1800 - Cabarrus County
Barnhill, Robert
    1790 - 112 00 - twp 14
    1800 - Mecklenburg County

Pension denied - no proof of service.
Barns, Robert
    1779 - mentioned in a grant to Alexander McClellan as an adjoining land owner along with James Flanigan, Archibald McNeal, and Samuel Linton, no book or page number given, and no watercourse named.
Barns, Sarah
    1779 - Indenture of Mary Barns to Andrew Walker, Mary not yet 18.
    Children: Mary
Barns, Thomas
    1774 - witnessed a deed, with William McWhorter and John Means, from Robert and Elizabeth Campbell to William Means on Coddle Creek, bk 12, pg 237.
Barns, William
    1790 - 154 00 - twp 9
Barr, Caleb
    1773 - deed to Samuel Alexander for 32 acres in the Welch tract, Test: Samuel Pickence and Jacob Barr, bk 11, pg 164.
Barr, Esther
    1777 - Loose estate papers
Barr, Jacob
    1773 - witnessed a deed from Caleb Barr to Samuel Alexander in the Welch tract, bk 11, pg 164.
Barr, James & Elizabeth
    1781 - deed from James Barr and Margaret Wallace to John Levison for 200 acres on the south side of Rockey River at the Baroney line, adjoining James Dysart, Test: Robert Harris, John Davidson, and Thomas Mitchel, bk 11, pg 79.
    1785 - deed to James McKnight for 53 acres on the south side of Rockey River, Test: George Ross, and Joseph Graham, bk 12, pg 559.
    1785 - deed to James McRight for 293 acres on the north side of Lewis branch, Test: Joseph Graham, and George Ross, bk 12, pg 574-B.
    James was one of the executors of the estate of Joseph Wallace.
    James died Dec 17, 1802, and is buried in Blackstock Cemetery.
Barr, Nathan
    1775 - witnessed a deed, with Charles Miller, Jr., and Thomas Crawford, from Robert Crawford to Hugh White on Warsaw Creek, adjoining William Beard, and John Currey, bk 10, pg 33.
Barr, Widow
    1765 - Loose estate papers
Barret, John (see Barett)
Barringer, Adam
    1790 - 203 00 - twp 10
Barringer, George & Molly

1767 - Militia, Mecklenburgh Regiment (Lieutenant)
1768 - tract conveyed to George for 26 acres on Dutch Buffalo Creek that he sold to John Culp in 1774, Test: Mathias and John Barringer, bk 12, pg 375.
1782 - mentioned as an adjoining land owner on Dutch Buffalo Creek in a grant to John Lewis Beard, bk 12, pg 114.
1783 - Dutch Buffalo Creek

Barringer, John
1774 - witnessed a deed from George & Molly Barringer to John Culp for 26 acres on Dutch Buffalo Creek, bk 12, pg 375.
1783 - deed to Matthias Barringer for 250 acres on the east side of Dutch Buffalow Creek, and another tract of 50 acres both adjoining George Barringer, Test: John Kobb, and Adalyh Nussman, bk 12, pg 332.
1784 - grant to John for 477 acres on Dutch Buffalo Creek, bk 12, pg 123.
Children: Mathias

Barringer, John & Christiana
1790 - 154 02 - twp 12
1800 - Cabarrus County
Wife - Christiana Killian
Children: George, John, Paul, Elizabeth (3rd wife of John Peck)
Son of John Paul and Anna Eliza Eisman Barringer.
Christiana was born Feb 20, 1755, died Jul 16, 1832, buried in St John's Evangelical Lutheran Church Cemetery
John was born June 22, 1752, died Aug 25, 1817, buried in St John's Evangelical Lutheran Church Cemetery.

Barringer, John, Jr. & Ann
Wife - Ann Catherine Moyer
Childern: Nathaniel H. (Susanna Faggart), Martin (Sally Moose)

Barringer, John Paul & Anna
Wife - Anna Eliza Eisman
Children: John (Christiana)
John was born June 4, 1721 in Germany, died Jan 1, 1807, buried in St John's Evangelical Lutheran Church Cemetery.
Son of Wilhelm & Paulina Behringer, who died in Aug 1748 while on their way to America.

Barringer, Matthias
1783 - Dutch Buffalow Creek
1774 - witnessed a deed from George & Molly Barringer to John Culp for 26 acres on Dutch Buffalo Creek, bk 12, pg 375.
1782 - mentioned as an adjoining land owner on Dutch Buffalo Creek in a grant to John Lewis Beard, bk 12, pg 114.
1790 - 336 02 - twp 11
Children: Mary Elizabeth (Christian Barnhardt)

Residents of Mecklenburg County, North Carolina
1762-1790

Son of John Barringer.
Barringer, Paul & Anna Eliza
   1784 - grant to Paul for 50 acres on the east side of Dutch Buffalow Creek, bk 12, pg 130.
   1784 - grant to Paul for 88 acres on the west side of Dutch Buffalo Creek, bk 12, pg 135.
   1784 - grant to Paul for 600 acres on both sides of Paul's Run Branch of Dutch Buffalow Creek, bk 12, pg 148.
   1784 - deed from James White, Jr. to Paul for 178 acres on both sides of Dutch Buffalo Creek, adjoining Mathias Beaver, Test: Adolph Niesmann, and Phillip Littigar, bk 12, pg 395.
   1784 - deed from Thomas Polk to Paul for 262 acres on both sides of Dutch Buffalo Creek, Test: Ezekiel Polk, and John Hamilton, bk 12, pg 398.
   1790 - 144 013 - 12
   1800 - Cabarrus County
   Wife - Anna Eliza Eisman
Barry/Berry, Adam
   1795 - Account ledger of John Melchor's store.
Barry/Berry, George
   1790 - 102 00 - twp 9
Barry/Berry, Jacob
   1784 - mentioned as an adjoining land owner of Christian Goodman on Dutch Buffalo Creek, bk 12, pg 161.
Barry/Berre, Matthew
   1794 - Account ledger of John Melchor's store.
Barry/Berry, Richard & Ann
   1762 - witnessed a deed, with Thomas Price, from Reese & Sarah Price to Matthew Knox, Vol 1, pg 80.
   1764 - witnessed a deed, with Martin Fifer, from Arthur & Justina Dobbs to Arthur McKay for a tract on both sides of Connerford branch and Great Coldwater Creek, bk 10, pg 404 and Three Mile Creek, bk 10, pg 435.
   1767 - Militia, Mecklenburgh Regiment (Captain)
   1775 - Richard was one of the signers of the Mecklenburg Declaration of Independence on May 20, 1775.
   1777 - mentioned as an adjoining land owner to Robert Bell, and Robert Henderson, on the Cataba River, bk 10, pg 40.
   1779 - witnessed a deed, with Benjamin Wilson, and William Henderson, from Archibald Henderson to John Henderson, bk 12, pg 427 & 429, no watercourse named.
   1790 - 406 00 - twp 7
   1800 - Mecklenburg County
   Wife - Ann Price
Barry/Berry, William
   1781 - witnessed a deed, with John McNitt Alexander, from James Knox to Benjamin Knox on the south fork of McDowell Creek, bk 11, pg 82.
Barlow, Amrose

1790 - 124 00 - twp 4
Bartley, Daniel
  1790 - 116 00 - twp 8
Barton, John
  1778 - witnessed a deed, with Duncan Ocheltree, from
  Thomas Polk to Robert Graham on a ridge between Sugar
  Creek and McMichael Creek, beginning by the Spring
  Branch, bk 10, pg 31.
Basdill, Reuben
  1790 - 133 03 - twp 16
Bassett, Fracis
  1778 - witnessed a deed, with Jacob Ormond, from Michael
  Siggett, Jr. to David Ore (Orr) on Henley's Fork of
  Twelve Mile Creek, bk 10, pg 37.
  1778 - witnessed a deed, with James Douglas, and John
  Haggins, from William Haggins to William Givens on
  McCorkle's branch of Twelve Mile Creek, adjoining
  Grifforth Rutherford, bk 10, pg 49.
Batch/Balch, Hezekiah James & Martha
  1776 - deed to James Walker for 88 acres on a ridge
  between English Buffalow and Coddle Creek, Test: William
  Scott, and John White, bk 10, pg 221 & 223.
Batey, Samuel (see Samuel Baley)
  1790 - 134 04 - twp 4
Batey, Walter
  1790 -215 02 - twp 19
Batey, William
  1790 - 111 00 - twp 4
Bawyers, Adam (see Adam Bower)
Baxter, Andrew
  1775 - Andrew's will was probated in Mecklenburg Co.
  Children: Francis (this could be Frances, and his
  wife?), Andrew, James, John
Baxter, Andrew
  1774 - land on Sugar Creek conveyed to Andrew in Oct
  1774 from Brice Miller, original grantee, bk 12, pg 544.
  1774 - deed to John Baxter for 90 acres beginning at the
  Indian line, originally granted to Brice Miller, bk 10,
  pg 153, Test: Patrick Jack, and James Simson.
  1777 - deed to Andrew for lots 146 and 154 in Charlotte,
  bk 11, pg 7.
Baxter, James
  1785 - witnessed deed from John Baxter to Josiah
  Harrison on Sugar Creek, bk 12, pg 544.
  1790 - 104 01 - twp 20
Baxter, John & Jean Potts
  1774 - deed to Josiah Harrison on Sugar Creek. Original
  grantees - part, Brice Miller, part Ezekiel Alexander,
  then to Andrew Baxter, bk 12, pg 544.
  1774 - deed from Andrew Baxter to John for 90 acres
  beginning at the Indian line, originally granted to

Brice Miller, Test: Patrick Jack, and James Simson, bk 10, pg 153.

Bays, James
1784 - witnessed a deed from John, Samuel, David, and James Flanigan to John Smith for a tract on the north side of McCalpins Creek, adjoining Abraham Miller, bk 12, pg 587.
1790 - 323 00 - twp 20

Beach, Justice
1783 - deed from William Lawing to Justice, Test: Daniel Landers, and John McKnitt Alexander for 125 acres on the Cataba River, bk 12, pg 208.
1784 - witnessed a deed, with William Ramsey, from John Johnston to Edward Stockes for a tract on the ridge between Long Creek and Thompson Branch, bk 12, pg 267.
1790 - 234 00 - twp 6

Beaker, John
1779 - mentioned as an adjoining land owner of Robert Beaker, and Edward Givens on the Cataba River and on both sides of Davidson's Creek, bk 11, pg 44.

Beaker, Robert & Sarah
1779 - deed to Edward Givens for 313 acres on the Catawba River and on Davidson's Creek joining Edward Givens, bk 11, pg 44.
Robert & Sarah were from Henry Co., VA in 1779.

Bean, Daniel & Sarah Ross
1790 -111 00 - twp 14
Married in Mecklenburg County in 1789.

Bean, James
1790 - 132 00 - twp 1

Bean, Robert
1790 - 341 00 - twp 13
Robert's will was proven in April 1801.

Bean, William
1779 - Campbell's Creek, Clear Creek
1790 - 314 00 - twp 14

Beard, John Lewis
1782 - grant for 150 acres on a branch of Dutch Buffalow Creek, adjoining George Barringer, and Mathias Barringer, bk 12, pg 114.

Beard, William
1775 - mentioned as an adjoining land owner to Robert Crawford, Hugh White, and John Currey on Warsaw (Waxhaw) Creek, Test: Nathan Barr, Charles Miller, Jr., and Thomas Crawford, bk 10, pg 33.
1783 - witnessed a deed from John McFarlin to Robert Mitchel, bk 12, pg 362.

Beatchey, James
1785 - named as an ajoining land owner to George Karriker, and John George William on a branch of Rockey River, Test: Lewis Wilhelm, Qudray Wilonlee, and Paul Farrow, bk 12, pg 592.

Beaty, Abel
    Children: James, William
    Abel and Thomas signed a declaration in Tryon Co., NC in 1775.
    Abel and Thomas Beaty were the sons of John Beaty who settled in western Mecklenburg County in 1749.
Beaty, Charles
    1764 - Charles' will was probated in Mecklenburg Co.
    Children: Abel, John
Beaty, Francis
    1762 - original grantee for a tract on Paw Creek, no book or page number given, mentioned in deed bk 12, pg 387.
    1762 - named as the original grantee of a tract on the Catawba River, no book or page number given, mentioned in deed bk 10, pg 40.
    1763 - mentioned as the original grantee for a tract on Beaverdam Creek of the Catawba River, granted to Francis on Dec 21, 1763, bk 11, pg 158.
    Francis sold land to John Todd near the Gum Branch of Long Creek, mentioned in bk 11, pg 103, but no bk, page number or year are given.
    1773 - Francis' will was probated in Mecklenburg Co.
    Children: Thomas, James, Robert, Hugh, John, Francis, Wallace, female (Robert Grey), Agnes (Robert Armstrong)
Beaty, Francis
    1774 - Loose estate papers
Beaty, James & Mary Hunter
    1782 - deed from Thomas and William Beaty for 273 acres on the Cataba River joining Beaty Ford, Test: Jean Graham and John Long, bk 12, pg 489.
    James, Thomas, and William were all of Lincoln Co., NC in 1782.
    Mary was the daughter of John Hunter, Sr.
    James was the son of Abel Beatey.
Beaty, John, Jr. & Mary
    1782 - grant to John from North Carolina for 40 acres on Sugar Creek, adjoining Nathaniel Erwin, and Alexander Staret, bk 12, pg 175.
    1784 - grant to John for 25 acres on Reedy branch of Sugar Creek, adjoing Moses' Steel's old corner, bk 12, pg 176.
    1790 - 124 09 - twp 1
    1800 - Mecklenburg County
Beaty, John, Sr.(2)
    1782 - mentioned in a deed as an adjoining land owner on Sugar Creek, along with William Irwin, and Alexander Starret, bk 12, pg 38.
    Children: James, Lydia (? Spencer)
    1790 - 235 00 - twp 1
    1800 - Mecklenburg County
Beaty, John

John owned land on the west side of the Catawba River in
1749.
Children: Abel, Thomas, Mary (Matthew Armstrong)
Beaty, Samuel & Elizabeth
1779 - deed from Joseph Mitchell to Samuel for 115 acres
on Rockwide Creek, bk 10, pg 449.
Children: Abby, Mily, Martha, Agness, Nathan, William,
Anderson
Son-in-law: James Hill
Beaty, Thomas
1782 - deed to William and James Beaty on the Catawba
River joining Beaty Ford, Test: John Long, Jean Graham,
bk 12, pg 489.
of Lincoln Co., NC in 1782.
Thomas died in 1787.
Children: John, Thomas, William
Beaty, William
1779 - mentioned as an adjoining land owner to Thomas
Neely on the head branch of Reedy Creek, no book or page
number given.
1782 - Cataba River joining Beaty Ford
of Lincoln Co., NC in 1782.
Beaver/Bever, Daniel
1790 - 121 00 - twp 12
1793 - Account ledger of John Melchor's store.
Beaver/Bever, Mathias & Susan ?
1781
Mathias died before 1782, and Susan Beaver was one of
the executors of his estate, along with Mathias Beaver
and Jacob Jeem.
Children: Daniel ?, Christopher ?, Mathias ?
Beaver, Mathias
1782 - deed to Jacob Jeem and Susan Beaver for 146 acres
on both sides of Dutch Buffelow Creek, Test: John
Barringer, and George McKee, bk 11, pg 162.
Beck, Fredrick
1785 - deed from John & Anna Bargar to Frederick for 202
acres on Dutch Buffelow Creek, Test: Joseph Shinn,
Samuel and Daniel Luther, bk 12, pg 501.
1790 -138 00 - twp 11
1800 - Cabarrus County
Belk, Britain
1782 - witnessed a deed, with James Belk, from William
Sheperd to John Belk on Stroud's Fork of Lynch's Creek,
bk 11, pg 131.
1783 - witnessed a deed, with John Belk, Sr., from David
Griffith to James Belk for 100 acres on Leintraces
(Lynches) Creek, bk 11, pg 224
Belk, Darling
1785 - witnessed a deed, with John Belk and John
Thompson, from Drury & Martha Thompson, of Camden
District, South Carolina, to Charles Cook on Little

Ritchardson's Creek beginning on Charles Cook's corner on the county line, bk 12, pg 600.
1790 - 132 00 - twp 17
1800 - Mecklenburg County
Son of John & Mary Ann Belk

Belk, James
1783 - deed from David Griffith to James for 100 acres on Leintraces (Lynches) Creek, Test: Britain Belk and John Belk, Sr., bk 11, pg 224
Son of John & Mary Ann Belk
1784 - witnessed a deed, with John Belk, from George & Lese Miller, of Camden District, South Carolina, to Tobias Ramsey on Linches Creek, bk 12, pg 379.
James was born Feb 4, 1765.

Belk, John, Esqr. & Mary Ann
1782 - deed from William Sheperd to John, sadler, for 200 acres on Stroud's fork of Lynch's Creek, Test: James and Britain Belk, bk 11, pg 131.
1783 - witnessed a deed, with Britain Belk, from David Griffith to James Belk for 100 acres on Leintraces (Lynches) Creek, bk 11, pg 224
1783 - witnessed a deed from John Thompson to Charles Cook on Ritcheson Creek, bk 11, pg 292.
1784 - witnessed a deed, with James Belk, from George & Lese Miller, of Camden District, South Carolina, to Tobias Ramsey on Linches Creek, bk 12, pg 379.
1784 - witnessed a deed, with James Doster, from David & Hannah Griffith to Larence Shanepaker for 200 acres on Polecat Branch of Linchous (Lynches) Creek, bk 12, pg 270.
1790 - 101 08 - twp 17
1800 - Mecklenburg County
Children: John, Darling, Nancy (? McCorkle), Frances (? Montgomery), James, Gracey (William Calvert)

Belk, John
1783 - witnessed a deed, with William Waddle, from Denis & Mary McFall to Joseph Wilson for land on McDowell's Creek, bk 12, pg 497. (This could be John Bell instead of Belk. John Belk lived at the opposite end of the county and a John Bell lived in the same township with Joseph Wilson and William Waddle.)

Bell, James
1790 - 222 00 - twp 8
1800 - Cabarrus County

Bell/Beel, John & Rachel
1781 - deed from David Davis to John for 134 acres originally granted to Joseph Hobbs in 1769, Test: Samuel Blyth, and John Wiete, bk 11, pg 102.
1790 - 100 00 - twp 7
1800 - Mecklenburg County

Bell, Robert

1774 - deed from Abraham & Jannet Miller to Robert for 155 acres on McCalpin Creek, Test: James Boyas and John Hanna, bk 10, pg 18.
1777 - deed from Robert & Isbell Henderson to Robert for 79 acres on the Catauba River, adjoining Robert Henderson, and Richard Barry, Test: John, William, and Archibald Henderson, bk 10, pg 40.

Bell, Walter
1784 - deed to George Davies for 300 acres on Caudle (Coddle) Creek, adjoining Samuel Ziklegg, and William Hall, Test: Thomas and Robert Benson, bk 12, pg 351.
1790 - 100 00 - twp 7

Benham, Daniel
1790 - 134 01 - twp 20

Benninger, Martin
1770 - Loose estate papers

Benson, James
1778 - deed from James & Mary Harris, Sr. for 153 acres in the Welch tract, Test: James Neal, and Thomas Benson, bk 10, pg 289.

Benson, Robert
1784 - witnessed a deed, with Thomas Benson, from Walter Bell to George Davies on Coddle Creek, bk 12, pg 351.
1790 - 102 00 - twp 8

Benson, Thomas
1778 - witnessed a deed from James & Mary Harris, Sr. to James Benson for 153 acres in the Welch tract, bk 10, pg 289.
1784 - witnessed a deed, with Robert Benson, from Walter Bell to George Davies on Coddle Creek, bk 12, pg 351.
1790 - 122 00 - twp 8

Berger, George Henry
1775 - witnessed a deed, with John Sheppard, from Samuel Suther, minister of Orange Co., NC, to Christian Goodman for 125 acres on Dutch Buffalo Creek, adjoining George Tucker, bk 10, pg 26.

Berger, John
1790 - 133 00 - twp 11

Berryhill, John & Elizabeth Allison
1790 -333 00 - twp 1

Berryhill, Joseph & Hannah(2)
1781 - Joseph's will was probated in Mecklenburg Co. Children: Andrew, Joseph

Berryhill, Samuel
1778 - Samuel's will was probated in Mecklenburg Co. Children: John

Berryhill, Wm(2)
1773 - deed from Alexander McKee to William for 150 acres on Sugar Creek, adjoining Robert Walker, Test: Joseph Montgomery, and Robert Barnet, bk 11, pg 129.

1782 - deed from Alexander McKee to William for 200 acres on Sugar Creek, adjoining William Clark, Test: John Bigham, and James Clark, bk 11, pg 157.
1782 - deed from William and Thomas McDowell to James Clark for 120 acres on Sugar Creek formerly owned by Alexander McKee, Test: Thomas Allison, and Will Reed, bk 11, pg 183.
1784 - witnessed a deed, with William McCafferty, and James Tagert, from Isaac & Elenor Williams to George Hutchison for 100 acres on Sugar Creek, adjoining Adam Caruther, James Taggert, Thomas Polk, and David Hays, Sr., bk 12, pg 437.
1778 - witnessed a deed, with Robert Irwin, and Thomas Greer, from Samuel & Patience Allan to James McKee on Beaverdam Creek of the Cataba River, bk 11, pg 110.
1790 - 104 01 - twp 1
1800 - Mecklenburg County

Best, Bostian
1761 - Bostian's will was probated in Mecklenburg Co.

Best/Bost, John
1790 - 112 00 - twp 11

Bets, William
1779 - named as an adjoining land owner on Six Mile Creek to John Potts, and William Courtney, Test: William Courtney and Michael Dely, bk 12, pg 248.

Bewhannon, John
1785 - witnessed a deed, with Arthur Jamison, from Andrew Dune to Robert Dune for 136 acres on Long Creek, bk 12, pg 541.

Bger ?/Byer, John
1778 Signer of 1778 Petition

Bickens/Pickens, William
1780 - witnessed a deed, with John Davis, from Joseph & Agnes Ewart to Alexander Robison on Rockey River, adjoining Benjamin Brown, bk 10, pg 440.

Bickerstaff/Beggerstaff, Samuel & Elizabeth ?
1764 - Samuel's will was probated in Mecklenburg Co. Children: Eason, Benjamin, Samuel

Biggar, James
1763 - grant to James dated Sept 21, 1763, mentioned in a deed from John & Catherine Biggar to Rev. William Tenant, bk 10, pg 84.

Biggar, John & Catherine
1777 - deed to John Turner of Craven Co., SC for 220 acres on the Catawba River adjoining Adam Calhoon, and David McMicken, Test: William Harris, Samuel Chambers, and Joseph Waddle, bk 11, pg 141.
1782 - named as an adjoining land owner to James & Sunah Brown, and Charles & Samuel Calhoon, on the Cataba River opposite the mouth of Crowder Creek, Test: Walter Davis, and Robert & Jack Mulligan, bk 11, pg 166.

Biger, John

1785 - named as an adjoining land owner on Rockey River to George Garmon, George Kizer, John Finney, and Peter Reap, Test: Michael Garmon, and Adam Alexander, bk 12, pg 484.

Biggers, Joseph
1783 - named as an adjoining land owner of David McKinley, and Hugh Campbell on Anderson Creek, bk 12, pg 109.
1790 - 315 00 - twp 13
1800 - Cabarrus County

Biggers, Moses
1765 - mentioned as original greantee in a deed from James & Sunah Brown to Charles & Samuel Calhoon on the Cataba at the mouth of Crowder's Creek, bk 11, pg 166.

Biggers, Robert & Catherine Thompson
Married in Mecklenburg County in 1788.
1790 - 102 00 - twp 9

Biggart, Samuel
1767 - Loose estate papers

Bigham, Andrew & Agnes Patterson(2)
1790 - 302 00 - twp 20
Andrew died June 3, 1788, age 63
Agnes died Sept 27, 1805, age 73

Bigham, Hugh
1781 - deed from Samuel Bigham Sr. for 200 acres on Sugar Creek joining William Bowman, John Taylor, and William Porter, Test: Will Reed, John Payton, bk 11, pg 155.
1790 - 101 00 - twp 2

Bigham, Hugh & Mary(3)
1765 - Hugh died in 1765, Mary died in 1772.
Children: Joseph (died as a child)

Bigham, James, Jr.
1790 - 222 00 - twp 2

Bigham, James, Sr. & Elizabeth(2)
1790 - 113 00 - twp 2
Children: Margaret
James died Nov 10, 1790, age 71

Bigham, John & Mary Greer(2)
1782 - mentioned as an adjoining land owner of Hector & Margaret McLane, William Cooper, Francis Herron, William McDowel, and James Sprott on King's Branch of Sugar Creek, bk 12, pg 234.
1783 - witnessed a deed, with James Wilson, from George & Margaret Cahoon to James Green on the south side of Sugar Creek adjoining Robert Wilson, and Zacheus Wilson, bk 12, pg 218.
1790 - 233 04 - twp 2
1800 - Mecklenburg County

Bigham, John
1775 - witnessed a deed, with James Tate and Robert Maxwell, from Samuel Knox to Thomas Ferguson on the

Cataba River on the waters of Steel Creek, adjoining
William Barnett, George Cahoon, John Henry and Edward
Williams, bk 10, pg 251.
1790 - 152 00 - twp 3
Bigham, Joseph
Revolutionary Soldier - died Sept 15, 1840, age 80
according to The Charlotte Journal dated Oct 1, 1840.
Bigham, Moses
1785 - deed from Samuel & Deborah McCleary for 56 acres
on Big Sugar Creek adjoining Robert McCrees, Hugh
Harris, and the Cataba Indian lands, Test: Ezekiel Polk,
and John Pelly, bk 12, pg 447.
Bigham, Robert, Jr.(2)
1790 - 112 00 - twp 2
1800 - Mecklenburg County
Children: Jane (James Turner), Robert
Brother: Joseph
Son of Robert Bigham
Bigham, Robert, Sr.(2)
Robert died Oct 7, 1777, age 65. He immigrated from
Ireland in 1768.
Bigham, Robert
1780 - mentioned as an adjoining land owner to John &
Samuel Bigham, and Robert Maxwell on Steel Creek, bk 10,
pg 439.
Bigham, Samuel, Sr. & Mary
1764 - witnessed a deed, with Moses Ferguson, and Robert
Leeper, from Andrew Armour to James Armour on the
Catawba River between Croders Creek and Allison Creek,
Vol 1, pg 550.
1774 - deed to John Whiteside for 217 acres on Steel
Creek, adjoining Samuel Knox, and Dinnes McCormick,
Test: Thomas McGee, and William Reed, bk 10, pg 411.
1780 - deed to John Porter for 180 acres on the north
fork of Steel Creek, adjoining John & Robert Bigham, and
Robert Maxwell, Test: Robert Hunter, Samuel Bigham, and
Alexander Porter, bk 10, pg 439.
1781 - north fork of Steel Creek, Sugar Creek
1790 - 201 00 - twp 2
1800 - Mecklenburg County
Bigham, Samuel, Jr. & Nancy L. McKnight
1780 - witnessed a deed, with Robert Hunter and
Alexander Porter, from Samuel Bigham, Sr. and John
Porter on Steel Creek, bk 10, pg 439.
1790 - 144 00 - twp 2
1800 - Mecklenburg County
Wife - Nancy L. McKnight
Bigham, William, Jr & Sarah
1775 - deed to Thomas Spencer for 15 acres on the north
part of Steel Creek, Test: Robert Wilson, and James
Turner, bk 10, pg 171. (Signed deed as Will.)
1779, 1780 - north part of Steel Creek, Sugar Creek

1790 - 214 00 - twp 2
Bird, William
    1774 - mentioned as an adjoining land owner to Joseph &
    Nancy Greer, Robert Crawford, and John Curry on Waxhaw
    Creek, bk 10, pg 246.
Bishop, Henry
    1782 - Loose estate papers
Bitty, John
    1779 - witnessed a deed, with Ezekiel Polk, from
    Nathaniel Cook to John Wilson on Sugar Creek, bk 10, pg
    301.
Black, Ezekel &   ?   McCombs
    1790 - 112 02 - twp 15
    1800 - Mecklenburg County
    Ezekiel's wife was a daughter of James & Mary McCombs.
    Revolutionary Soldier - died July 17, 1837, age 81
    according to The Charlotte Journal dated July 28, 1837.
Black, George
    1785 - witnessed a deed, with Thomas Morrow, from Jacob
    Self to Henry Ford for 78 acres on both sides of Clear
    Creek, bk 12, pg 513.
Black, James
    1775 - deed to George Cathey for 200 acres on the north
    side of the Cataba River, part of a grant to John Cowan
    in 1754, Test: William Moore, George Cathey, and Robert
    Cain, bk 10, pg 51.
Black, James
    1778 - witnessed a deed, with William Balch, from John &
    Martha Rodgers to Hugh Rodgers on English Buffalo Creek,
    bk 10, pg 337.
    1779 - deed from Thomas Polk, attorney for David
    Oliphant, to James for 159 acres on Anderson Creek,
    Test: Thomas Rodgers, and John Dickson, bk 10, pg 313.
    1790 - 202 00 - twp 13
Black, James
    1790 - 235 00 - twp 19
    1800 - Mecklenburg County
Black, John
    1790 - 103 00 - twp 13
Black, John & Mary
    1779 - grant to John for 150 acres on Beard's branch of
    McCalpin's Creek (twp 15), bk 10, pg 522.
    1779 - grant to John for 146 acres on McCalpin's Creek
    beginning at Thomas Gribble's old corner, bk 10, pg 536.
    1782 - deed to Abraham Miller for 122 acres on
    McCalpin's Creek, including the forks, Test: William
    Query, and Thomas Black, bk 11, pg 105.
    1785 - deed from William & Sarah Ervin/Erwin to John for
    100 acres on McCalpin's Creek, Test: Samuel Black, and
    Thomas Ervin, bk 12, pg 441.

1785 - witnessed a deed, with Samuel Black, from William
& Sarah Irwin to Thomas Irwin for 126 acres on
McCalpin's Creek, bk 12, pg 453.
1790 - 216 02 - twp 15
1800 - Mecklenburg County
Children: John, Martha (Daniel McAuley), William,
Samuel, Elizabeth (? Robinet), Rosannah (John
Walker), Margaret (Rodrick McAuley), Esther (James
Walker), Jane (John Witherspoon), Deborah (? Bays)
Black, John
1764 - deed from the heirs of Rachel Price on McDowell's
Creek that John sold to John Jetton on Aug 12, 1766, no
book or page number given, mentioned in a deed from John
Jetton to Lewis Jetton, bk 12, pg 555.
Black, Robert & Eleanor Russell
1762 - marriage bond
Black, Samuel & Jane
1785 - witnessed a deed, with Thomas Ervin, from William
& Sarah Ervin/Erwin to John Black on McCalpin's Creek,
bk 12, pg 441.
1785 - witnessed a deed, with John Black, from William
& Sarah Irwin to Thomas Irwin for 126 acres on
McCalpin's Creek, bk 12, pg 453.
1786 - witnessed a deed, with Johanas Jegler, from
Paulser & Franney Ness to Paul Furrow (Furr ?) for 90
acres on both sides of Dutch Buffalo Creek, bk 12, pg
580.
1790 - 101 00 - twp 15
1800 - Mecklenburg County
Black, Thomas
1772 - Thomas' will was probated in Mecklenburg Co.
Children: William, Thomas, John
Black, Thomas
1782 - witnessed a deed, with William Query, from John
Black to Abraham Miller on McCalpin's Creek, bk 11, pg
105.
Black, Thomas, Capt.
1790 - 145 00 - twp 7
Black, Thomas
1790 - 122 00 - twp 10
1800 - Cabarrus County
Black, William
1763 - William's will was probated in Mecklenburg Co.
Children: William, John
Black, William
1783 - witnessed a deed, with Richard Smith, from
Nathaniel Alexander to Reuben Meek for 100 acres on
Rockey River, on both sides of the Wagon Road that leads
to John McKnitt Alexander, adjoining Adam Meek, bk 12,
pg 307.
1790 - 213 07 - twp 5
Black, William

Residents of Mecklenburg County, North Carolina 1762-1790

1775 - William's will was probated in Mecklenburg Co. Children: Eleanor, Frances, William
Black, William, Jr.
   1790 - 103 00 - twp 19
Black, William, Sr.
   1767 - Militia, Mecklenburgh Regiment (Ensign)
   1778 - mentioned as an adjoining land owner to William Holland, Andrew Stinson, and Joseph Sample on McCalpin's Creek, Test: Abraham Miller, and Thomas Mann, bk 10, pg 378.
   1779 - witnessed a deed, with George Montgomery, from John & Ann Johnston to John Smith on McCalpin's Creek, bk 10, pg 390.
   1790 - 202 01 - twp 15
   William owned land on McCalpin's Creek (twp 15).
Black, William & Mary
   1771 - deed from Abner & Justina Nash for 95 acres in the Welch Tract on the south side of the middle fork of Beaver Pond Creek, Test: Clement Nash, bk 10, pg 166.
   1778 - deed to Thomas Black for 110 acres originally belonging to George Augustine Selwyn, Test: Samuel Fleniken, William Pickens, and John Smith, bk 10, pg 362.
   1790 - 132 00 - twp 13
   Signer of 1778 Petition.
Blackwater/Blackwelder, John
   1784 - named as an adjoining land owner to Christian Barnhart, and Adam Bower on Little Coldwater Creek, bk 12, pg 191
   Son of Caleb & Betsey Blackwelder.
Blackwelder/Blackwater, Caleb & Elizabeth Phifer
   1784 - named as an adjoining land owner to Mathias Moyer and John Misenheimer on Adam's Creek, bk 12, pg 188.
   1778 - Signer of 1778 Petition
   1790 - 114 00 - twp 12
   Wife - Elizabeth(Betsey)Phifer, sister of Martin Phifer. Children: Catherine, Issac (Mary Phifer), John, Jacob, Martin, Rachel, Daniel
   Son of Johannas & Elizabeth Maushardt Blackwelder
   Betsey was born April 4, 1724, died 1794, buried in St John's Evangelical Lutheran Church Cemetery.
Blackwelder, Charles
   1790 - 123 00 - twp 10
Blackwelder, Isaac & Mary Phifer
   1790 - 142 00 - twp 12
   1800 - Cabarrus County
   Wife - Mary Phifer
   Son of Caleb & Betsey Blackwelder.
   Revolutionary Soldier - died Nov 17, 1843 in Cabarrus County, NC, age 86 according to The Charlotte Journal dated Nov 24, 1843.
Blackwelder, Jacob

1790 - 111 00 - twp 12
1800 - Cabarrus County
Son of Caleb & Betsey Blackwelder.
Blackwelder, Jno Adam & Catron
 1790 - 101 00 - twp 10
 Son of Johannas & Elizabeth Maushardt
Blackwelder, John
 1790 - 116 00 - twp 10
Blackwelder, Martin
 1790 - 111 00 - twp 12
 1793 - Account ledger of John Melchor's store.
 1800 - Cabarrus County
 Son of Caleb & Betsey Blackwelder.
Blackwood, James
 1790 - 224 01 - twp 2
Blackwood, John(2)
 John died Sept 10, 1779, age 85.
Blackwood, Thomas & Sophia Gardner
 1790 - 103 01 - twp 6
 Children: Margaret, Hannah
Blackwood, William
 1780 - deed from James Brown to William for 250 acres on Gum Branch of Long Creek, being the tract granted to Walter Davis in 1764 and joins the land Francis Beaty sold to John Todd, Test: Joseph Kerr, and John Todd, bk 11, pg 103.
 1790 - 125 02 - twp 6
Blair, John
 1778 - Loose estate papers
Blair, John & Jane(2)
 John died Sept 1823, Jane died Sept 5, 1832, age 70. Both were born in Scotland.
Blair, William & Sarah Douglas
 William was a signer of the petition to pardon the Cabarrus Black Boys in 1775.
 1790 - 335 00 - twp 15
 1800 - Mecklenburg County
Blaster/Plaster, Abraham
 1790 - 201 00 - twp 12
 1793 - Account ledger of John Melchor's store.
 1800 - Cabarrus County
Blaster/Plaster, John
 1793 - Account ledger of John Melchor's store.
Bleckley, Thomas
 1778 - Signer of 1778 Petition
Blewer, John
 1779 - witnessed a deed from Jacob Myer to Boltes Neas on Dutch Buffalo Creek, bk 10, pg 409.
Blue, Stephen
 1790 - 123 00 - twp 17
 1800 - Mecklenburg County
Blythe, James

Residents of Mecklenburg County, North Carolina   41
1762-1790

    1780 - named as an adjoining land owner ro John & Jean Wear, Thomas Walker, and William Graham on the Cataba River, bk 10, pg 456.
    1782 - grant from North Carolina to James for 297 acres on the north side of Long River adjoining Robert Campbell and Robert Erwin, bk 12, pg 45.
    1790 -163 00 - twp 16
    1800 - Mecklenburg County
Blythe, Richard
    1790 - 102 00 - twp 7
Blythe, Samuel & Elizabeth
    1777 - witnessed a deed, with William Graham, and William Bowen, from Robert & Hannah Erwin to John Wier/Wear, on the Cataba River adjoining John Price, and Alexander Cathey, bk 10, pg 230.
    1781 - witnessed a deed, with John Wiete, from David Davis to John Beel/Bell, bk 11, pg 102.
    1790 - 020 011 - twp 7
    Children: James, Richard, Jean, Ann, Elizabeth, Mary, Samuel
    Grandson: William Conner
    Samuel's will was probated in 1796.
Boal, James
    1768 - named as the original land owner of a tract on the head branches of Mallard Creek and Long Creek, granted Dec 22, 1768 and by him conveyed to John Boal and Thomas McLure, and by them to Robert McCleary on April 17, 1771, bk 12, pg 257.
Boal, John
    1769 to 1771 - land owner on the head branches of Mallard Creek and Long Creek near David & Jane Russell, and Robert & Elizabeth McCleary, bk 12, pg 257.
Bogarn/Boger, Jacob
    1784 - named as adjoining land owner on Blackwater Run, a branch of Dutch Buffalow Creek, neighboring Christopher & Tobias Goodman, bk 12, pg 165.
    1790 - 133 00 - twp 11
    1800 - Cabarrus County
Boger, Daniel
    1790 - 123 00 - twp 11
    1800 - Cabarrus County
    Children: Martin (Mary A.)
    1793 - Account ledger of John Melchor's store.
Boger, Peter
    1773 - deed from Jacob Swink to Peter for 122 acres on both sides of Shenawolf branch of Rocky River, Test: James Killpatrick and Michael Goodnight, bk 10, pg 106.
    1790 - 125 00 - twp 11
    1800 - Cabarrus County
Boiser, Boston
    1764 - Loose estate papers
Boloson, Isack

1793 - Account ledger of John Melchor's store.
Bonds, George
    1790 - 232 00 - twp 16
    1800 - Mecklenburg County
Bonds, Samuel
    1780 - deed from Linard Green to Samuel for 68 acres
    beginning on the south bank of Rockey River, Test:
    William Haynes and Jacob Self, bk 11, pg 9.
    1793 - Account ledger of John Melchor's store.
Booker, Joseph
    1790 - 125 00 - twp 9
Booth, William
    1764 - mentioned as land owner in a deed dated 1774 for
    a tract of 214 acres on Lodle (Coddle) Creek which he
    conveyed to Daniel & Martha England in 1773, bk 10, pg
    126.
Bor ? , James
    1778 - Signer of 1778 Petition
Bordon, Edmond
    1767 - grant from Henry Estes McCulloch on Back Creek,
    no book or page number given, mentioned in a 1785 deed
    from Benjamin & Susanna Alexander to John McCughey, bk
    12, pg 487.
Bost, Elias & Katherine
    1778 - Signer of 1778 Petition
    1790 -133 00 - twp 12
    Elias was born 1748, died Oct 12, 1822, buried in St
    John's Evangelical Lutheran Church Cemetery.
    Katherine was born June 1753, died Aug 26, 1826, buried
    in St John's Evangelical Lutheran Church Cemetery.
    Children: William (Elizabeth ?), Daniel (Elizabeth
    Nussman), Solomon (Milly Faggart), John H., Margaret
    (Jacob Faggart, Jr.), Mary Elizabeth (Daniel Faggart)
Bost, George & Hannah
    1790 - 231 00 - twp 12
    Wife - Hannah Gregory
    George died 1808, buried in St John's Evangelical
    Lutheran Church Cemetery.
    Hannah died 1843, buried in St John's Evangelical
    Lutheran Church Cemetery.
Bost, Jacob & Catherine
    1790 - 115 00 - twp 12
    1794 - Account ledger of John Melchor's store.
    Jacob was born Jan 1, 1753, died Sept 25, 1830, buried
    in St John's Evangelical Lutheran Church Cemetery.
    Catherine was born Feb 2, 1759, died March 21, 1841,
    buried in St John's Evangelical Lutheran Church
    Cemetery.
Bost, John
    1778 - Loose estate papers
Bost, John
    1790 - 112 00 - twp 11

Residents of Mecklenburg County, North Carolina   43
1762-1790

Bost, Johannes & Susannah
   Wife - Susannah Catherina
   Children: William, Anna Maria, Leonhardt, Maria
   Catharina, John, Elias, Margaretha, Barbara, Elizabeth,
   Jacob, George, Dorothy, Christina, Margaret
Bost, Solomon & Milly
   Children: Nelson (Julia A.)
Bostian, Matthias & Sarah
   1784 - deed from Adam & Cathey Moyar for 200 acres on
   Rocky River on Little Coldwater Creek, about a mile
   above John Young's land and joining Gov. Dobbs upper
   line, Test: Joseph Shinn, and Jason Frizell, bk 10, pg
   421.
   1784 - deed to Henry Farr for 100 acres on Coldwater
   Creek, adjoining Gov. Dobbs about a mile above John
   Luther's land beginning on Paul Harrins' corner, Test:
   Joseph Shinn, and Jacob Crider, bk 12, pg 459.
Bostion, Jonas
   1790 - 105 00 - twp 12
   1800 - Cabarrus County
Bouchfriend, George
   1790 - 102 00 - twp 5
   1800 - Cabarrus County
Bourns/Burns, Robert
   1770 - witnessed a deed, with Isaac Jetton, to John
   Davies for lot 74 in Charlotte, bk 11, pg 18.
Bowey, Conrad
   1765 - Loose estate papers
Bowen, William
   1777 - witnessed a deed, with William Graham and Samuel
   Blythe, from Robert & Hannah Erwin to John Wier on the
   Cataba River and Mill Creek, bk 10, pg 230.
Bower, Adam & Elinor
   1779 - deed from Martin Phifer to Adam for 164 acres on
   Great Coldwater Creek, a draft of Rockey or Johnson
   River, Test: Jason Frissell, bk 10, pg 465.
   1782 - deed from Adam & Elinor to Martin Phifer, Sr. for
   5 acres on Coldwater Creek at the Coldwater meeting
   house, beginning below the spring, Test: Joseph Shinn,
   bk 11, pg 135.
   1784 - named as an adjoining land owner to Christian
   Barnheart and John Blackwater/Blackwelder on Little
   Coldwater Creek, bk 12, pg 191.
Bower/Brower, George
   1792 - Account ledger of John Melchor's store.
Bowman, Andrew & Margaret
   1775 - Andrew's will was probated in Mecklenburg Co.
Bowman, Margaret
   1784 - Loose estate papers
Bowman, Samuel

1781 - named as an adjoining land owner to Samuel
Bigham, Sr., John Taylor, William Porter, and James
McKee on Sugar Creek, bk 11, pg 160.
1790 - 115 03 - twp 8

Bowman, William
1781 - named as an adjoining land owner to Samuel
Bigham, Sr., Hugh Bigham, John Taylor, and William
Porter on Sugar Creek, bk 11, pg 155.

Boyce, John
1795 - Loose estate papers

Boyd, Hugh Colloden
1781 - witnessed a deed, with Mat Troy, from Peter
Johnston to Andrew McKee for a tract of land joining
Gideon Thomson, William Lawing, and John Anderson, bk
12, pg 444.

Boyd, John
1769 - named in a deed, no book or page number given.

Boyd, Robert
1769 - named in a deed, no book or page number given.
1792 - Loose estate papers

Boyrs, James
1767 - named as the original land owner of a tract
containing 100 acres on Sugar Creek deeded from Robert
Walker, Jr. to John Green on April 5, 1784, bk 12, pg
337.

Boyer, James & Margaret
1773 - deed to John McDowel for 150 acres on Sugar Creek
adjoining Thomas Polk, and Alexander McKee, Test: James
& Joseph Tagert, bk 10, pg 319.

Boyes/Boys, James & Margaret
1774 - witnessed a deed, with John Hanna, from Abraham &
Jannet Miller to Robert Bell on McCalpin Creek, bk 10,
pg 18.
1779 - grant to James for 130 acres on McCalpin's Creek
adjoining Hezekiah Alexander(twp 15), bk 10, pg 518.
1779 - witnessed a deed, with John Morris, and William
Kerr, from Francis Johnston and Agnes Henderson to
Prudence Hays, widow of William Hays, for 32 acres on
McCalpin's Creek, bk 11, pg 64.
1800 - Mecklenburg County
Children: Samuel, John, Sarah
James' nuncupative will is dated Oct 1803.

Boyse, John
John's will was probated in Oct 1794.
Brothers: David, James, Robert, William

Boyse, William
Named in his brother John's will as living in
Mecklenburg County in 1793.

Boyett, William
1783 - named as an adjoining land owner of Walter
Smiley, John Chamberlain, and George Townsend on
Buffalo Creek, bk 12, pg 118.

Residents of Mecklenburg County, North Carolina
1762-1790

Bracken, Solomon & Elizabeth Gibbons
    Elizabeth was the daughter of William & Jannett Gibbons.
Bradford, David
    1779 - Loose estate papers
Bradford, James
    1790 - 000 10 - twp 8
Bradford, Mary
    1790 - 213 00 - twp 8
    1800 - Cabarrus County
Bradly, Elijah
    1779 - Power of attorney from Henry Bradly, of York Co.,
    PA, father of Elijah, to Benjamin Alexander, bk 10, pg
    452.
    In custody of James Bradly of Mecklenburg Co.
Bradley, Francis
    1780 - killed in the Revolution
    Brother of Esther Bradley Price, wife of Isaac Price.
Bradley, Hannah
    1779 - Loose estate papers
Bradly, Henry
    1779 - Power of attorney to Benjamin Alexander while in
    York Co., PA to take possesion of his estate, "and bring
    it about to answer some good ends to me or to my
    children", bk 10, pg 452.
Bradly, James
    1777 - deed to Benjamin Bryan for a tract on both sides
    of the south fork of Crooked Creek, Test: Joseph Harris,
    and Joseph Harris, Jr., bk 10, pg 228.
    1782 - grant for 37 acres on the east side of Rockey
    River, bk 12, pg 58.
Bradly, Joshua
    1779 - Power of attorney from Henry Bradly, of York Co.,
    PA, father of Joshua, to Benjamin Alexander, bk 10, pg
    452.
    In custody of James Bradly of Mecklenburg Co.
Bradley, Jonas & Winifred
    1778 - Jonas' will was probated in Mecklenburg Co.
Bradley, Widow
    1790 - 114 00 - twp 6
Bradshaw, James (5)
    1768 - deed from Hugh Edgar for 63 acres on Rockey
    River, Test: Robert Harris, and Robert Harris, Jr., bk
    10, pg 118.
    1782 - grant for 150 acres on Hanbey's Run, a branch of
    Rockey River, bk 12, pg 63.
    1790 - 246 00 - twp 13
    1800 - Cabarrus County
    James was born 1742, died Feb 19, 1809 and is buried in
    Rocky River Presbyterian Church Cemetery.
    Children: James Watson (Sarah Morrison)
Bradshaw, Josiah
    1790 - 215 01 - twp 6

Residents of Mecklenburg County, North Carolina
1762-1790

Bradshaw, Samuel
　1790 - 102 00 - twp 15
Bradshaw, Widow
　1790 - 121 00 - twp 15
Braley, Thos C
　1790 - 000 10 - twp 4
Brandon, James
　1773 - witnessed a deed, with Daniel Little, Thomas
Polk, from Henry Eustace McCulloch to John Nicholson, bk
10, pg 46.
Brandon, John
　1790 - 132 00 - twp 14
Breden, Isaac
　1782 - grant for 154 acres on Rockey River near the head
of Meadow Spring, adjoining William Winchester, and
Charles Dacton, bk 12, pg 171.
Brevard, Alexander & Rebecca
　About 1790, Alexander moved to Lincoln Co., NC.
　Wife: Rebecca Davidson, daughter of Maj. John Davidson.
Brevard, Benjamin
　1774 - deed from John, Jean, Robert & Benjamin Brevard
to Andrew Downes for 350 acres adjoining Samuel Young,
Test: James Maxwell, bk 10, pg 183.
　1790 - Iredell County ?
Brevard, E.
　1779 - witnessed a deed, with William Barker, from
Thomas Polk, attorney for David Oliphant, for 16 acres
on Anderson's Creek, bk 10, pg 460.
Brevard, E.A., Col
　Born 1787, died 1854 - Lincoln County
Brevard, Ephraim, Dr.
　1782 - Loose estate papers
Brevard, Ephraim
　1774 - deed for lot 15 in Charlatte, Test: Robert Irwin
and Hezekiah Alexander, bk 10, pg 192.
　1775 - Ephraim was one of the signers of the Mecklenburg
Declaration of Independence on May 20, 1775.
　1777 - witnessed a deed, with Alexander Long, from
George Cusick to John Davison on the north side of the
Cataba River, originally granted to Andrew Cathey, bk
11, pg 93A.
　1777 - witnessed deed, with Thomas Harris, to John Foard
for lots 49 & 50 in Charlotte, bk 10, pg 44.
　1779 - witnessed a deed, with John Alexander, from
Thomas Polk to Robert McElrath for a lot in Charlotte,
bk 11, pg 127.
　1779 - witnessed indenture between Thomas Polk and
Robert McElwrath for lot #1 in the town of Charlotte.
John Alexander was also a witness, bk 11, pg 127, and
lot #5, bk 11, pg 145.
　Trustee of Liberty Hall
　Wife - a daughter of Col. Thomas Polk

Children: Martha (? Dickerson)
Brother: Adam
Son of John Brevard
Ephraim was born in MD in 1744.
Brevaird, Joel
  1779 - deed to James Jack for lot 165 in Charlotte, bk 10, pg 300.
Brevard, John & Jean
  1774 - deed from John, Jean, Robert & Benjamin Brevard to Andrew Downes for 350 acres adjoining Samuel Young, Test: James Maxwell, bk 10, pg 183.
  1784 - deed from John & Jean to James Williamson on the branches of Rockey River, originally granted to John in 1751, Test: Thomas Alexander, and John Gillespie, bk 12, pg 547.
  1785 - deed from William McCree to John Brevard, John Dickey and William Sharp, of Rowan County, executors of the LWT of Brigadier William Davidson, deceased, for the legatees of William Davidson, for a tract of land on the branches of Davidson and Back Creek in Rowan County, bk 12, pg 574.
  1790 - Iredell County ?
  Children: Ephraim, Adam, Jane (Ephraim Davidson), Mary (William Davidson)
Brevard, Robert
  1774 - deed from John, Jean, Robert & Benjamin Brevard to Andrew Downes for 350 acres adjoining Samuel Young, Test: James Maxwell, bk 10, pg 183.
  1790 - Iredell County ?
Brevard, Zebulon
  1777 - witnessed a deed, with John Jetton, Jr. and Lewis Jetton, from John Jetton to Isaac Jetton for 188 acres adjoining Abram Jetton and Hugh Lawrin, bk 12, pg 494.
  1778, 1779, 1781 land joining John Morrow and Andrew Downs, Coddle Creek
  1790 - Burke County ?
Briance, William
  1784 - witnessed a deed, with Robert Ervin, from James & Jean Davis to Walter Phair/Pharr for 114 acres on the south side of Rocky River, originally conveyed to Samuel Crawford, bk 12, pg 550.
Briges, James
  1790 - 414 00 - twp 12
  1800 - Cabarrus County
Brineger/Pasenger, Erasmus
  1790 - 211 00 - twp 11
  1800 - Cabarrus County
Britain/Britton, James & Jemima
  1766 - listed in the militia company of Capt. Adam Alexander of Clear Creek.
Brodinax, John
  1790 - 133 016 - twp 7

Broom, John & Sarah
   John died 1795 in Mecklenburg County.
Brown, Alexander
   1778 - Witnessed a deed, with Robert Cowdon, from George
   Alexander to Samuel Linton on Rockey River, joining
   James Brown and Charles Harris, bk 10, pg 314.
   1778 - Signer of 1778 Petition
Brown, Benjn
   1773 - deed to John Lockhart for 170 acres, Test: Robert
   Smith, bk 10, pg 276.
   1780 - named as an adjoining land owner to Joseph &
   Agnes Ewart, and Alexander Robison, Test: John Davis and
   William Pickens, bk 10, pg 440.
   1790 - 223 01 - twp 8
   1800 - Mecklenburg County
   Children: Joseph, Mary, Fanny, John, Ann, Jean, William
   Benjamin's property adjoined Alexander & Rachel
   Robinson, and they are mentioned in his will.
Brown, Benjamin & Jean Ross
   Children: Nancy Beard Brown
   Jean's brothers were John and George.
   Benjamin wrote his will in 1795.
Brown, Daniel
   1785 - witnessed a deed, with William Polk, and John
   Nelson, from Joseph Graham, sheriff, to Samuel Martin
   for 91-1/2 acres on Tryon Creek in a judgement against
   William McCafferty, bk 12, pg 567.
Brown, David
   1790 - 313 00 - twp 1
Brown, David
   1796 - Loose estate papers
Brown, Jacob
   1785 - witnessed a deed, with Ad Osborn, from William
   McCree to John Brevard, John Dickey and William Sharp of
   Rowan County, bk 12, pg 574.
Brown, James
   1773 - witnessed a deed, with Robert Smith, Jr. for a
   tract on Rocky River, originally Test: John Frohock, and
   Moses Alexander, bk 10, pg 160.
   1778 - named as an adjoining land owner to George
   Alexander, Samuel Linton, and Charles Harris, Test:
   Robert Cowdon and Alexander Brown, bk 10, pg 314.
   1790 - 123 01 - twp 5
   1800 - Mecklenburg County
Brown, James
   1780 - deed to William Blackwood for 250 acres on the
   Gum branch of Long Creek, Test: Joseph Kerr, and John
   Todd, bk 11, pg 103.
   1790 - 141 00 - twp 14
Brown, James & Susannah
   1778 - deed to Charles and Samuel Calhoon for 400 acres
   on the east side of Cataba River at the mouth of

Crowder's Creek, Test: Walter Davis, and Robert & Jack
Mulligan, bk 11, pg 166.
1790 - 211 00 - twp 20
1800 - Mecklenburg County
Brown, John
 1778 - witnessed a deed, with Richard Aubin, from Thomas
& Mary Thomson to Samuel Brown on the north side of the
Cataba River on the head of Rockey River, bk 10, pg 365.
Brown, John & Sarah
 1790 - 302 00 - twp 17
 Children: Walker, William, Lydy, Ann, Sarah, Charity,
Jacob, Jonathan, Alan
Brown, Patrick & Mary
 1790 - 402 00 - twp 1
 1800 - Mecklenburg County
 Children: Margaret, Robert, Eleanor, Mary, James, Agnes,
William
Brown, Richard
 1790 - 000 10 - twp 2
 Son of Robert Brown.
Brown, Robert
 1769 - Robert's will was probated in Mecklenburg Co.
 Children: Richard
Brown, Robert
 Robert died 1795
 Siblings: William, David, Margaret, Elizabeth, Martha
Brown, Samuel
 1778 - deed from Thomas & Mary Thomson to Samuel for 240
acres on the north side of the Cataba River on the head
of Rockey River, bk 10, pg 365.
 1790 - 122 00 - twp 8
Brown, Samuel & Margaret
 1772 - Samuel's will was probated in Mecklenburg Co.
Brown, William & Margaret
 1790 - 133 00 - twp 12
Brown, William & Margaret (Moore ?)
 1780 - named as an adjoining land owner and witnessed a
deed from William Hugans to William Merchant on Meekels'
Creek, bk 11, pg 148.
 1790 - 126 00 - twp 20
 Children: Martha, Mary, Elizabeth, Margaret (? Shaw),
William, David, John, Rachel (? Swann)
Browfield, John
 1778 - witnessed a deed, with William Motheral and
Thomas Burnett, from Robert & Margaret McKnight to James
McKnight on a creek where Armour's road crosses, bk 10,
pg 42.
 1782 - witnessed a deed between Zebulon Alexander and
Phineas Alexander on the south side of Sugar Creek, bk
11, pg 171.
Brownfield, Robert & Jenny Stuart

1779 - witnessed a deed, with Matthew McClure, to John Foard for lots 85 and 93 in the town of Charlotte, bk 10, pg 368.
1790 - 101 00 - twp 2
Children: William (Peggy Giles), Isabella, Margaret (Robert McKnight), Ann, John, Robert
Brother: Charles

Brownfield, William & Peggy
1790 - 133 00 - twp 2
1800 - Mecklenburg County
Wife - Margaret Giles

Bruster, James
1790 - 223 05 - twp 18

Bryan, Benjamin, Jr.
1777 - deed from James Bradley to Benjamin for a tract on both sides of the south fork of Crooked Creek, Test: Joseph Harris, and Joseph Harris, Jr., bk 10, pg 228.

Bryan, Kiah
1790 - 101 00 - twp 14

Bryan, Mathew
1790 - 254 00 - twp 1
1800 - Mecklenburg County

Bryance, Henry
1790 - 100 00 - twp 10

Bryance, Henry, Jr.
1790 - 123 00 - twp 10
1800 - Cabarrus County

Bryance, William
1790 - 122 00 - twp 10
1794 - Account ledger of John Melchor's store.

Bryson, Hugh
1790 - 244 00 - twp 7
Hugh's wife was the sister of Thomas Davidson.

Buam, James
1790 -

Bucklaw, Garrot
1766 - listed in the militia company of Capt. Adam Alexander of Clear Creek.

Buckalow/Bucklaw, George
1766 - listed in the militia company of Capt. Adam Alexander of Clear Creek.
1782 - deed to Tunas Hogland for 36 acres on McCalpin's Creek, adjoining James McClure, and James Clark, Test: James Walker, and Robert Donalson, bk 12, pg 508.

Bucklaw, James
1766 - listed in the militia company of Capt. Adam Alexander of Clear Creek.

Buccalo/Burealo/Bucklaw, Jonathan
1766 - listed in the militia company of Capt. Adam Alexander of Clear Creek.

1775 - deed from William Smith to Jonathan for 58 acres
on McCalpin's Creek, Test: John Ford, and Zebulon
Robinett, bk 10, pg 174.
1776 - in Capt. Charles Polk's Light Horse Company.
1776 - McCalpin's Creek
The widow Buckalew was adjoining Frederick Shaver on
McCalpin's Creek in 1783, bk 12, pg 106.
Bucklaw, Richard
1766 - listed in the militia company of Capt. Adam
Alexander of Clear Creek.
Buchanan, John & Mary
1779 - deed to John McKnitt Alexander on both sides of
Garr Creek, adjoining Richard Stephenson and Jereemiah
Joy, Test: Hezekiah Alexander and Samuel Buchannon, bk
12, pg 474.
1780 - deed to John McKnitt Alexander on both sides of
Goose Creek for a meeting house and graveyard, Test:
Hezekiah Alexander and Samuel Buchanan, bk 11, pg 87.
1783 - east side of Cataba on both sides of Long Creek
about half a mile west of Toole's road. Gum Creek.
Dividing ridge between Four Mile Creek and McCalpin's
Creek (twp 15).
1785 - witnessed a deed, with Arthur Jamison, from
Andrew Dun to John Dun on Long Creek, bk 12, pg 519.
1785 - witnessed a deed, with Arthur Jamison, from
Andrew Dune to Robert Dune on Long Creek, bk 12, pg 541.
Buckhannon, Samuel
1779 - witnessed a deed from John & Mary Buchannon to
John McKnitt Alexander on Garr Creek, bk 12, pg 474.
1783 - witnessed a deed from John & Mary Buchanan to
John McKnitt Alexander for 145 acres on Goose Creek, bk
11, pg 87.
1780 - grant to Samuel for 20 acres on the head waters
of Crocket Creek, bk 12, pg 100.
    head waters of Beard's branch, a branch of McCalpin's
Creek (twp 15)
1790 - 322 00 - twp 15
Buckhannon, Robert & Tracy
1790 - 324 00 - twp 5
1800 - Mecklenburg County
Children: Charles, Edward, George W., Rachel, Jean,
Ruth, Robert
Bugg/Bagg/Bogg, William
1790 - 123 00 - twp 14
Burnet, John
1775 - named as the land owner of a tract originally
granted to James McClelland in 1754. John conveyed it to
John McDowel, then John McDowel conveyed it to Joseph
Wallace in 1775. Test: Benjamin Walace, and Robert
Dowel, bk 10, pg 286.
Burnet, Thomas

1778 - witnessed a deed, with William Motheral and John
Brownfield, from Robert & Margaret McKnight to James
McKnight on a creek where Armour's road crosses, bk 10,
pg 42.
Burnet, William
1773 - named as the owner of a corner lot in Charlotte
on the west side of Tryon Street, bk 10, pg 36.
Burns, Andrew & Susannah
1778 - mentioned as an adjoining land owner to David
Smith, Robert Smith, and William Johnston, on Rockey
River, bk 10, pg 541.
1778 - deed to Robert Smith, Jr. for 172 acres on Rockey
River adjoining James Wallace, and William Gardner,
Test: John Smith, and Martha Smith, bk 10, pg 82.
Mentioned in the estate papers of Nicholson Ross.
Burns, Isaac
1776 - Loose estate papers
Burns, James & Penelope C.(5)
1790 - 216 00 - twp 13
1800 - Cabarrus County
Burns, Peter
1783 - grant for 100 acres on Coddle Creek and Wolf
Meadow Branch joining Hugh Caruthers, and William Means,
bk 12, pg 151.
Burns, Robert
1786 - Loose estate papers
Bush, John, Jr.
1792 - Account ledger of John Melchor's store.
Bush, Richard
1793 - Account ledger of John Melchor's store.
Bussard, John & Ann
1782 - deed to John Barriger for 202 acres on the east
side of Buffalow Creek, commonly called Dutch Buffalow,
adjoining Fight Gorright, bk 11, pg 125.
1790 - 203 01 - twp 11
Byars, David
1774 - witnessed a deed for lot 156 in Charlotte to John
Work, bk 10, pg 217.
Caegle, Henry
1790 - 141 00 - twp 14
1800 - Cabarrus County
Cagle/Kagel, George & Margaret
1777 a branch of Dutch Buffalow Creek
1793 - Account ledger of John Melchor's store.
Blacksmith
Cagle/Kagel, George, Jr.
1793 - Account ledger of John Melchor's store.
Cahoon/Calhoon, George
1775 - named as an adjoining land owner to Thomas
Ferguson, Samuel Knox, William Barnett, John Henry, and
Edward Williams on Steel Creek, bk 10, pg 251.
Caigle, Charles

Residents of Mecklenburg County, North Carolina 1762-1790

1790 - 235 00 - twp 12
Caigle, Charles, Jr.
    1790 - 101 00 - twp 12
Caigle, John
    1790 - 236 00 - twp 12
    1800 - Cabarrus County
Cain, Hugh
    1776 - Loose estate papers
Cain, Robert
    1775 - Witnessed a deed, with George Cathey, and William Moore, from James Black to George Cathey on the north side of the Cataba River. Originally granted to John Cowan in 1754, bk 10, pg 51.
Cairns/Carnes, Alexander
    1779 - grant to Alexander for 190 acres on Waxhaw Creek adjoining James Waugh, and George McWhorter's old line, bk 10, pg 524.
    1780 - witnessed a deed, with Henry Foster, from George & Elizabeth McWhirter to Dennis Titus of Camden District, SC, for a tract on Warshaw/Waxhaw Creek, adjoining Samuel Macloveny, bk 10, pg 447.
    1786 - witnessed a deed, with Archibald Cowait, and John Lithem, from John & Catherine Nutt to Robert Orr and Thomas Lackey for 300 acres on Waxhaw Creek, adjoining Alexander Carns, Rebecca Moor, William Davis, Robert Crocket, and James Lashley, bk 12, pg 609.
    1786 - deed from Denis & Mary Fittes to Alexander for 44 acres on Waxhaw Creek, Test: James Epelman, Thomas Lackey, and Samuel Farr, bk 12, pg 612.
    1790 - 145 03 - twp 17
    1800 - Mecklenburg County
Cairns, Daniel
    1777 - deed from Daniel Cairns of Mecklenburg Co., NC to Archibald Cowsert of Craven County, SC, for and in consideration of the sum of two hundred and seventy pounds South Carolina currency to him in hand paid by Cowsert, for a tract of land containing 125 acres lying in both the counties above mentioned, being part of William King's tract, lying on both sides of the Waggon Road and on the north side of Waxaw Creek, Test: John Nutt, J. Miller, and Catherine Nutt, bk 10, pg 207.
    1790 - 214 00 - twp 17
Caldwell, Alexander & Sallie
    Pastor of Rocky River Presbyterian Church from 1793 to 1797.
    Wife - Sallie Davidson, daughter of John Davidson.
Caldwell, Charles
    1779 - adjoining land owner to Joseph Alexander, Stephen Alexander, and James Wilson on Coddle Creek, beginning at a steep bank near Stephen Alexander, bk 10, pg 523.

1785 - adjoining land owner of John Wilson, Dr. Thomas
Donnell, John Donnell, and Joseph Campbell on Coddle
Creek, bk 12, pg 533.
1790 - 101 02 - twp 5
Children: David, Charles, Martha
Charles' will was probated in April 1792 in Mecklenburg.

Caldwell, Daniel & Jean Morrison
1790 - 141 00 - twp 13
1800 - Mecklenburg County
Wife - Jean Morrison, daughter of Robert & Sarah
Morrison.

Caldwell, David, Capt.
David was a signer of the petition to pardon the
Cabarrus Black Boys in 1775.
1779 - adjoining land owner of Evan Shelby, and James
Ross, Test: James Stafford, and James Stafford, Jr. on
Caldwell's Beaverdam Branch of Rockey River, bk 12, pg
211.
1780 - David's will was probated in Mecklenburg Co.
(Loose estate papers)
Children: William, Ann

Caldwell, David, Jr.
1786 - Loose estate papers

Caldwell, David
1790 - 100 00 - twp 5

Caldwell, James
1766 - listed in the militia company of Capt. Adam
Alexander of Clear Creek.
1775 - James was a signer of the petition to pardon the
Cabarrus Black Boys.

Caldwell, John & Elizabeth
John was a signer of the petition to pardon the Cabarrus
Black Boys in 1775.
1782 - grant for 134 acres on Anderson Creek, bk 12, pg
67.
1782 - named as an adjoining land owner to Archibald
White, Sr. on Anderson Creek, bk 12, pg 59.
1784 - deed to William and Adam Edgar for a 200 acre
tract, and a 134 acre tract on Anderson Creek, Test:
Samuel and Archibald White, bk 12, pg 401.

Caldwell, John & Eleanor
1768 - Loose estate papers

Caldwell, Robert
1790 - 102 00 - twp 13
1800 - Mecklenburg County
Wife - Pheobe Morrison, daughter of Robert & Sarah
Morrison.
Children: John (Mary Allen), Robert (Serena Houston),
Daniel (Isabella E. Shields), Margaret (Joshua Teeter),
James (Polly Dixon), Silas (Matilda Evaline Query, Lyde
Cochran), William (Elizabeth E. Query)
Robert died Nov 6, 1832, buried in Spears Graveyard.

Residents of Mecklenburg County, North Carolina 1762-1790

Caldwell, Robert
    1780 - adjoining land owner to George McWhirter, Dennis Titus, Samuel Macloveny, and Samuel Wylie on Warshaw Creek, bk 10, pg 447.
    1754 - granted 517 acres on Warshaw Creek on Feb 23, 1754, no book or pg number given, only mentioned in the above deed.

Caldwell, Samuel, Capt. & Abigail Alexander
    1793 - married May 8, 1793, John McKnitt Alexander, bondsman; 2nd wife - Elizabeth
    Wife - Abigail B. Alexander, daughter of John McKnitt Alexander,
    Children: Jane Bane, David Thomas
    Abigail died before 1807 and her children were named in her father's will.
    Elizabeth died 1825.
    Samuel died 1826, age 57.

Caldwell, Thomas, Capt.
    1775 - Capt. John Springs company

Caldwell, William & Agness Givens
    1778 - Signer of 1778 Petition.
    1790 - 142 04 - twp 7
    Agness was the daughter of Edward, Jr. & Agness Gibbons.

Caldwell, William
    1779 - witnessed a deed, with James Morrison, from John & Adam Miller to William Bean on Campbell's Creek and Clear Creek, bk 11, pg 68.

Calhoon, Adam
    1777 - named as an adjoining land owner to John Turner, John & Catherine Bigger, and David McMicken, bk 11, pg 141.
    1782 - witnessed a deed, with William McKinley, and James Miller, from Joseph & Elizabeth McKinley to John Carruthers, bk 11, pg 149.

Calhoon/Calhoone, Charles
    1778 - deed from James & Susannah Brown to Charles & Samuel Calhoon for 400 acres on the Cataba River opposite the mouth of Crowder's Creek and joining John Bigger, bk 11, pg 166.
    1783 - deed to John Thompson for a tract of land on both sides of Benet's fork of Ritcheson's Creek about half a mile above the old Indian path, Test: Robert Irwin, Thomas Greer, and George Calhoon, bk 11, pg 257.
    1790 - 115 03 - twp 2
    1800 - Mecklenburg County

Calhoun/Cahoon, George & Margaret(2)
    1775 - named as an adjoining land owner to Thomas Ferguson, Samuel Knox, William Barnett, John Henry, and Edward Williams on Steel Creek, bk 10, pg 251.
    1783 - deed to James Green for 150 acres on Sugar Creek, next to Zacheus Wilson, and Robert Wilson, Test: John Bigham, and James Wilson, bk 12, pg 218.

1783 - witnessed a deed from Charles Calhoon to John
Thompson on Benet's fork of Ritcheson's Creek, bk 11, pg
257.
1790 - 101 00 - twp 2
George died June 8, 1795 at the age of 83.

Calhoon, Samuel
1778 - east side of Cataba River at the mouth of
Crowder's Creek
1790 - 135 03 - twp 2
1800 - Mecklenburg County

Callahan/Calland, William
1782 - grant for 100 acres on Rockey River, adjoining
James White, bk 12, pg 84.
1790 - 301 02 - twp 13
1800 - Cabarrus County

Camble, James, Jr.
1778 - Signer of 1778 Petition

Cambler, Robert (See Robert Campbell)

Campbell, Alexander & Peggy
1780 - grant for 34 acres on Campbell's Creek, a branch
of McCalpin's Creek, adjoining Margaret Wilson, bk 12,
pg 17.
1790 - 112 02 - twp 4
1800 - Mecklenburg County
Children: Isaac, Peggy (? Miller)
Grandson: Alexander Campbell Miller

Campbell, Alexander
1780 - grant for 39 acres on Sugar Creek adjoining John
Allen, bk 12, pg 24.

Campbell, Andw(5)
1778 - Signer of 1778 Petition
1790 - 122 00 - twp 13
Son of James Campbell.
Andrew died in 1796 at the age of 41.

Campbell, Archibald & Elizabeth
1782 - Archibald's will was probated in Mecklenburg Co.

Campbell, Daniel
1781 - died on an expedition to South Carolina.

Campbell, Hugh
1782 - named as an adjoining land owner to John
Campbell, and Joseph Bigham on Reedy Creek and Anderson
Creek, bk 12, pg 31.

Campbell, James
1764 - mentioned in a deed from Andrew Armour to James
Armour as an adjoining land owner on the south side of
the Catawba River between Croders Creek and Allison
Creek, Vol 1, pg 550.
1778 - Signer of 1778 Petition
1783 - James' will was probated in Mecklenburg Co.
Children: Andrew

Campbell, James
1790 -115 00 - twp 10

Residents of Mecklenburg County, North Carolina 57
1762-1790

Children: Jean, James
James died in 1800, Let. Test. to Aaron Townsend,
William Townsend security. Jean was bound to Lewis
Townsend, James was bound to Archibald McLarty.
(Cabarrus County court records)

Campbell, Jennett
   1799 - Loose estate papers
Campbell, John
   1767 - named as land owner in 1767 of a tract on the
   head branches of Sugar Creek that he deeded to Robert
   Crocket, bk 11, pg 271.
Campbell, John
   1782 - grant for 230 acres on Reedy Creek and Anderson
   Creek adjoining Hugh Campbell, and Joseph Bigham, bk 12,
   pg 31.
Campbell, Joseph
   1785 - named as an adjoining land owner to John Wilson,
   Thomas Donnell, and Charles Caldwell on Coddle Creek, bk
   12, pg 533.
Campbell, Murdock
   1793 - Account ledger of John Melchor's store.
Campbell, Robert & Jannet(2)
   1782 - named as an adjoining land owner to James Blythe,
   and Robert Erwin on the north side of Long River, bk 12,
   pg 45.
Campbell, Robert(2)
   1775 - witnessed a deed, with Ebenezer Newton, from
   James Johnson to William Gardner on Sugar Creek, bk 10,
   pg 191.
   1784 - deed from Bruce Levingston to Robert for 130
   acres on King's branch of Sugar Creek, adjoining Tobe
   Campbell, Test: Abraham and Henry Levingson, bk 12, pg
   289.
   1790 - 116 00 - twp 1
   1800 - Mecklenburg County
Campbell, Robert & Elizabeth
   Robert was a signer of the petition to pardon the
   Cabarrus Black Boys in 1775.
   1779 - deed to William Means for 61 acres on Coddle
   Creek and the waters of Rocky and Johnston's Rivers,
   Test: William McWhorter, John Means, and Thomas Barns,
   bk 12, pg 237.
Campbell, Thomas
   1778 - Signer of 1778 Petition
   1790 - 100 00 - twp 9
   1794 - Account ledger of John Melchor's store.
Campbell, Tobe
   1784 - named as an adjoining land owner to Bruce
   Levingson, and Robert Campbell on King's Branch of Sugar
   Creek, bk 12, pg 289.
Cance, David

1783 - witnessed a deed, with Benjamin Knox, from George Cathey to William Moore on a branch of McDowell's Creek, bk 11, pg 276.

Cannon, James & Ann Black
1790 - 101 03 - twp 9
1800 - Cabarrus County
James & Ann were married in 1790, John Allison, bondsman.

Cannon, James, Sr.
1790 - 111 00 - twp 6

Cannon, James
1784 - Loose estate papers

Cannon, John
1778 - deed from John Todd, Jr. for 120 acres on the head branches of Sugar Creek, Test: Samuel Martin, and John Alexander, bk 10, pg 346.
1790 - 311 00 - twp 6

Cannon, Joseph
1790 - 115 00 - twp 6
1800 - Mecklenburg County
Son of Margaret Cannon

Cannon, Margret
1790 - 112 02 - twp 6
Children: Rachel (? Sharp), Thomas A., Joseph, Margaret (? Sharp)

Caple/Kepple, Peter
1790 - 212 00 - twp 11
1800 - Cabarrus County

Carlock/Garlock, David
1793 - Account ledger of John Melchor's store.

Carney, Patrick
1790 - 000 10 - twp 4

Carpenter, Christian
1767 - Militia, Mecklenburgh Regiment (Lieutenant)

Carpenter, Jonathan
1793 - Account ledger of John Melchor's store.

Carr/Kerr, Patrick
1769 - witnessed a deed, with Samuel Wilson, from John & Elizabeth Mitchell to Jonathan Newman on the south side of Clark's Creek, originally granted to Jeremiah Joy, bk 10, pg 169.
1769 - witnessed a deed, with Joseph Patterson, from John & Elizabeth Mitchell to Moses Andrews, originally granted to Ambrose Harding, bk 10, pg 180.

Carr/Kerr, Robert
1773 - deed from Robert to Benjamin Walace for 125 acres on Long Creek, Test: Robert Carr, and Joseph Kerr, bk 10, pg 124.
1777 - witnessed a deed, with Hezekiah Alexander, from Richard Stevenson to John McNitt Alexander, and Robert Ewart, on Garr Creek, including Hopewell Meeting House and graveyard, adjoining Jeremiah Joy, and John

Buchanan, bk 12, pg 472. (For the express purpose of building Hopewell Presbyterian Church)

Carragan, Thomas
   1790 - 101 00 - twp 15

Carragan, Henry
   1798 - Loose estate papers

Carrigan/Carriger, Hugh & Mary
   1772 - deed to John Ramsey for 60 acres on Whetstone Branch, adjoining John Quirry, Test: Francis Glass, and William Ramsey, bk 10, pg 103.
   1783 - named as an adjoining land owner to Robert Harris, and John Hud on Goose Creek, bk 12, pg 152.

Carrigan/Kergin, James
   1773 - deed from John McConey for 50 acres for the sum of one shilling, Test: Witt Carragin, and John Tanner, bk 10, pg 182.
   1790 - 204 02 - twp 8
   1800 - Cabarrus County

Carrigan, William/Witt
   1773 - witnessed a deed, with John Tanner, from John McConey to James Kergin for 50 acres, bk 10, pg 182.
   1790 - 000 10 - twp 15

Carriger/Carringer, Andrew & Eleanor Kiser
   1784 - grant for 200 acres between Phillip Carringer's two entries, bk 12, pg 185.
   1790 - 133 00 - twp 12
   1800 - Cabarrus County

Carriger/Carrigan/Kerriker, George & Susan
   1790 - 134 00 - twp 12
   1800 - Cabarrus County

Carriger/Carrigan, Phillip, Jr
   1790 - 121 00 - twp 12
   1800 - Cabarrus County

Carriger/Carrigan, Phillip, Sr
   1784 - named as an adjoining land owner to John Chamberlain, and Andrew Carringer, bk 12, pg 185.
   1790 - 201 00 - twp 12
   1800 - Cabarrus County

Carriker/Karriker, George & Susan
   1785 - deed to John George William for 100 acres on a branch of Rocky River, adjoining Peter Reas, James Cuntress, and James Beatchey, Test: Lewis Wilham, Qudray Wilonlee, and Paul Farrow, bk 12, pg 592.
   1783 Goose Creek

Carrins, Daniel
   1783 - grant for 50 acres on the dividing ridge between Twelve Mile Creek and Waxhaw Creek, adjoining Moses McCanter, and Benjamin Ford, bk 12, pg 112.

Carroll, James
   1790 - 102 00 - twp 1

Carroll, John

Residents of Mecklenburg County, North Carolina
1762-1790

1779 - deed to Joseph Carroll for 100 acres on Sugar Creek, Test: William Hayns, and John Nicholson, bk 10, pg 324.
Heir of Samuel Carroll

Carroll, Joseph
1779 - deed from John Carroll for 100 acres on Sugar Creek, Test: William Hayns, and John Nicolson, bk 10, pg 324.
1790 - 322 03 - twp 1

Carroll/Caryl, Samuel
1771 - Loose estate papers
1771 - Samuel's will was probated in Mecklenburg Co.
Children: Samuel, Joseph, John

Carruth, James(2)
1775 - James died Sept 2, 1775, age 31, and his will was probated in Mecklenburg Co.
Children: John, Adam

Carruth, James
1778 - named as an adjoining land owner to William Adams, and George Davis on Reedy Creek, bk 10, pg 256.
1779 - bond between James Ross and James for 593 acres where James Ross lives on Reedy Creek, to be peaceably turned over by James Ross by Oct 6, 1779, Test: Adam Alexander, bk 11, pg 108.

Carruth, James
1774 - Loose estate papers

Carruth, John & Rosanna Gingles
1784 - grant to John for 90 acres on Huggin's Run, a branch of Reedy Creek, bk 12, pg 195.
Wife: Rosanna Gingles, daughter of Samuel & Margaret McAllister Gingles.
John was the son of Walter & Sarah Allison Carruth.
John died in 1828 in TX
Rosanna died in 1816 in Blount Co., TN

Carruth, John & Elizabeth Cathey
1784 - witnessed a deed, with Robert Irvin, and John Hana, from John Sloan to Jesse Clark, on a branch of Sugar Creek between Isaac Williams and Robert Walker, and James Tagart's land, bk 12, pg 466.
Elizabeth was the daughter of George Cathey.

Carruth, Robert
1777 - witnessed a deed, with James Houston, to Andrew Baxter for lot 146 and 154 in Charlotte, bk 11, pg 7.

Carruth, Walter & Sarah Allison
1783 - deed to Henry Vernor for 215 acres on Paw Creek, Test: John Green, and James Sloan, originally granted to Francis Beaty in 1762, bk 12, pg 387.
Children: John (Rosanna Gingles)
Of Lincoln Co., NC in 1783
Son of James & Margaret Law Carruth.

Carruthers, Adam

1784 - named as an adjoining land owner to Isaac Williams, George Hutchison, James Tagart, Thomas Polk, and David Hays, Sr. on Little Sugar Creek, Test: William McCafferty, James Tagart, and William Berryhill, bk 12, pg 437.

Carruthers, Andw & Sarah(2)
    1778 - deed from Caleb & Barbara Phifer to Andrew for 65 acres, Test: Hugh McCree, Martin Phifer, and Archibald White, bk 10, pg 462.
    1778 - Signer of 1778 Petition
    Children: James, Robert, Andrew, John, William, Samuel, Ezekiel, Archibald, Margaret (Samuel Sloan), Isabella (Absolam Woodard), unborn child
    Mentioned in the estate papers of Nicholson Ross in 1774.
    Andrew died in Cumberland Co., PA in 1783.
    Sarah died in Mecklenburg Co., NC, Sept 16, 1798.

Carruthers, Andrew
    1790 - 318 01 - twp 9
    Son of Andrew & Sarah Carruthers.

Carruthers, Elias
    before 1790

Carruthers, Hugh
    1763 - named as the previous owner of a tract above the mouth of the 8th fork of the Catawba River, bk 11, pg 33.

Carruthers, Hugh
    1782 - Hugh's will was probated in Mecklenburg Co.
    Children: James, Hugh

Carruthers, Hugh
    1774 - witnessed a deed, with James Kile, from Isaac & Rebecca Sellers to John Davis on the south side of Rocky River, adjoining William White, bk 10, pg 188.
    1782 - named as an adjoining land owner to John Russle on Coddle Creek, bk 12, pg 85.
    1782 - named as an adjoining land owner to William Scott, David Purvine, John Rodgers, and James Walker, bk 12, pg 71.
    1783 - named as an adjoining land owner to Peter Burns, and William Means on Coddle Creek and Wolf Meadow Branch, bk 12, pg 151.
    1790 - 132 00 - twp 13
    1796 - bondsman for Sarah Carithers and James Morrison.
    1800 - Cabarrus County

Carruthers, James
    1780 - deed from John Driskell to James for 140 acres on Caldwell Creek, originally conveyed to Abner Nash, then Andrew Greer, Robert Harris, then to John Driskell, Test: Francis Ross, and William Scott, bk 11, pg 54.
    1790 - 114 00 - twp 13 (neighboring Hugh Carruthers)

Carruthers, James
    1779 - Reedy Creek

Residents of Mecklenburg County, North Carolina
1762-1790

1774 - bought land in Mecklenburg Co. from John
Carothers of Cumberland Co., PA, Test: James & Agnes
Pulley, adjoining Robert Carothers, bk 10, pg 157.
1790 - 232 02 - twp 2 (neighboring John & Robert
Carruthers)

Carruthers, John & Sarah
Wife - Sarah
Children: Robert, James, John, William, Andrew, Samuel,
Ezekiel, Archibald, Margaret, Isabella

Carruthers, John & Sarah
1790 - 333 00 - twp 8
Children: Mary
1800 - Cabarrus County

Carruthers, John & Mary Vance, Esther Sample(2)
1782 - witnessed a deed, with Isaac Price, on the Cataba
River above the mouth of Crowder's Creek adjoining John
Bigger, bk 11, pg 280.
1782 - deed from Joseph & Elizabeth McKinley to John for
100 acres on the Cataba River adjoining Daniel Williams,
and James McCall, originally granted to John Bigger, bk
11, pg 149.
1784 - named as an adjoining land owner to James McCall,
and Phebe Williams, bk 12, pg 177.
1790 -132 00 - twp 2
Wife - Mary Vance, dau of David & Ruth Wilson Vance.
Children: David (Nancy Knox), John,
John died Feb 28, 1838, age 83

Carruthers, John & Elinor (Shelby ?)
1766 - listed in the militia company of Capt. Adam
Alexander of Clear Creek.
1772 - deed of gift to daughter, Mary, for one negro man
named Siris, her own mare, and one large red cow, Test:
Adam Alexander, and Oliver Wiley, bk 11, pg 109.
1779 - deed from William Balch for 35 acres on the head
spring of Muddy Creek, originally conveyed to Abner
Nash, then Andrew Greer, then Robert Harris, Thomas
Rodgers, then to William Balch, Test: Hugh and Joseph
Rodgers, bk 10, pg 372.
1782 - deed of gift from John to his daughter, Isobel,
for one negro girl, named Philis, one mare and saddle,
and one black heifer three yrs old, Test: Adam
Alexander, and Oliver Wiley, bk 11, pg 115.
1782 - deed of gift from John to his daughter, Sarah,
one negro girl named Jude, one mare and saddle, and one
black heifer three yrs old, Test: Adam Alexander, and
Oliver Wiley, bk 11, pg 116.
1782 - deed of gift from John to his wife, Elinor, for
the plantation, etc., Test: Adam Alexander, and Oliver
Wiley, bk 11, pg 117.
1782 - deed of gift from John to his daughter, Mary, 105
acres on Anderson Creek, Test: Adam Alexander, and
Oliver Wiley, bk 11, pg 118.

Children: Mary, Isobel, Sarah
Carruthers, John
   1790 - 102 07 - twp 14
   1800 - Mecklenburg County
Carruthers, Robert C. & Margaret(5)
   1771 - Robert was one of the Cabarrus Black Boys.
   1779 - deed from Thomas Polk, attorney for David
   Oliphant, for 37 acres on the dividing ridge between
   Henderson's and Caldwell's Creeks, Test: Thomas
   McFadden, and Henry Rock, bk 10, pg 432.
   1790 - 336 00 - twp 13
   Margaret died Aug 12, 1794
Carruthers, Robert
   1790 -125 01 - twp 2
Carson, Jane
   1790 - 002 00 - twp 7
Carson, John & Sally
   1779 - witnessed a deed, with William Johnston, from
   John Garrison to Samuel Hemphill for lots 201, 204, 330,
   331, 335, and 336 in Charlotte, bk 11, pg 16.
   1779 - named as an adjoining land owner to David Reed,
   Nicholas Gibbony, Henry Varner, and Samuel Kearth on
   Sugar Creek, Test: John Allen, and John McDowell, bk 10,
   pg 412.
   1790 - 100 00 - twp 1
   1800 - Mecklenburg County
   John died in 1812.
Carson, Thomas(2)
   Thomas died in 1776, at the age of 45.
Carter, Charles
   1793 - Account ledger of John Melchor's store.
Carter, Henry
   1776 - in Capt. Charles Polk's Light Horse Company.
Carter, Jacob
   1793 - Account ledger of John Melchor's store.
Carter, Samuel, Jr.
   1793 - Account ledger of John Melchor's store.
Carter, Samuel, Sr.
   1793 - Account ledger of John Melchor's store.
Carver, (see Larver)
Case, Henry
   1785 - Loose estate papers
Casey, Jacob
   1790 - 115 00 - twp 12
Casey/Carey, Mary
   1790 - 101 00 - twp 8
Casiah, Dunning
   1766 - listed in the militia company of Capt. Adam
   Alexander of Clear Creek.
Casiah, Sandiver
   1766 - listed in the militia company of Capt. Adam
   Alexander of Clear Creek.

Casper, Peter & Ann Mary
    1786 - named in a deed, no book or page number given.
Caster, John
    1790 - 102 00 - twp 10
Castillo, Miles & Hannah
    1790 - 124 00 - twp 1
    1800 - Mecklenburg County
    Hannah died Oct 1805.
Castle, Thomas
    1792 - Account ledger of John Melchor's store.
Caswell/Ciswell, Andrew
    1767 - Militia, Mecklenburgh Regiment (Lieutenant)
Cathey, Alexander & Margaret Allen
    1777 - named as adjoining land owner to John Price, and
    John Weir, beginning at the upper edge of the Mill
    Creek, originally granted to Andrew Armour in 1761.
    1790 - 213 00 - twp 1
    1800 - Mecklenburg County
    Pension denied 1838 - no proof of marriage or service.
Cathey, Andrew(2)
    1753 - deed to George Cusick for 200 acres on the north
    side of the Cataba River, no book or page number given.
    1783 - named as adjoining land owner to William
    Patterson, John L. Davis, Ambrose McKee, and Richard and
    David Robison , bk 11, pg 301.
    Children: George, John, Andrew, Archibald
    Andrew died Jan 20, 1785 at the age of 64, and his will
    was probated in Mecklenburg Co. in 1786.
    Son of George and Jean Cathey.
Cathey, Andrew
    1790 - 101 00 - twp 2
    Son of Andrew Cathey.
Cathey, Archabeld, Capt/Col & Mary
    1777 - Loose estate papers
    1790 - 113 011 - twp 7
    1800 - Mecklenburg County
    Children: John, Nancy
Cathey, Esther(2)
    1790 - 235 00 - twp 1
    1800 - Mecklenburg County
    Esther died Aug 1825, dau of George and Jean Cathey.
Cathey, George & Frances Henry(2)
    1749 - named as the grantee of a tract later owned by
    Mathew Toole, then John Toole who in 1779 sold it to
    David Alexander, on the south side of the north branch
    of the Cataba River, bk 11, pg 174.
    1790 - 313 05 - twp 1
    Francis Cathey died Dec 17, 1798, age 74.
Cathey, George
    1775 - witnessed a deed, with William Moore, and Robert
    Cain, from James Black of Rowan Co., NC to George Cathey

Residents of Mecklenburg County, North Carolina 65
1762-1790

for 200 acres on the north side of the Cataba River, bk
10, pg 51.
1790 - 203 05 - twp 2
Cathey, George, Sr & Margaret(2)
1775 - deed from James Black of Rowan Co., NC to George
for 200 acres on the north side of the Cataba River,
Test: George Cathey, William Moore, and Robert Cain, bk
10, pg 51.
1777 - deed from George & Margaret of Burke Co., NC to
Hugh Lucas for 200 acres on the north side of the Cataba
River, Test: Joseph Jack, James McMahan, and J.
McDowell, bk 10, pg 242.
1778, 1783, south fork of McDowell's Creek
George died May 25, 1801 at age 77.
Cathey, Jeane(2)
1777 - Loose estate papers
Jeane died March 12, 1777 at age 85.
Widow of George Cathey.
Cathey, John
1788 - Loose estate papers
Cathey, John, Jr
1779 - named as adjoining land owner to William Waddle,
and   ? Miller, bk 12, pg 4.
1782 - Loose estate papers
Cathey, Josiah
1778 - Loose estate papers
Cathey, Josiah(2)
Josiah died Sept 26, 1788 at age 29, son of George
Cathey.
Cathey, Mary(2)
Mary died Aug 1802.
Caughon, George
1780 - deed from James Maxwell to George for 115 acres
on Rocky River, Test: John Hagler, and Joyauurn Goylorw
(in Dutch), bk 12, pg 226.
Caule, William
1783 - witnessed a deed, with Adam Meek, from Thomas &
Mary Harris to William Means for 428 acres adjoining
James Way, bk 12, pg 255.
Cerlaugh/Carlock, George
1790 - 114 00 - twp 10
1800 - Cabarrus County
Cerlock/Carlock, Frederick & Clary
1784 - grant for 200 acres on a branch of Coldwater
Creek adjoining Isaac Lofton & William Waggoner, bk 12,
pg 196.
Children: Rachel (?   Williams)
Chainey, William & Elizabeth Hargett
1790 - 142 00 - twp 16
1800 - Mecklenburg County
Chamberlain, John

1784 - grant for 170 acres on the west side of Coldwater Creek above the mouth of Voil Branch running with William Voil's line, bk 12, pg 184.
1790 - 117 00 - twp 10
1800 - Cabarrus County

Chambers, James
1790 - 111 00 - twp 19

Chambers, Samuel
1777 - witnessed a deed, with William Kerr, and Joseph McKinley, from John & Catharine Biggar to Rev. William Tenant of Charlestown, SC, for 300 acres opposite the mouth of Crowder's Creek on the Cataba River, bk 10, pg 84.

Chapple, William
1785 - Loose estate papers

Charles, Henry
1790 - 101 00 - twp 15

Charles, John
1783 - named as an adjoining land owner to John Meisenheimer, William Leopard, Jacob Richey, Jacob Hough, and Michael Cline on Dutch Buffalow Creek, bk 12, pg 147.
Meeting House Branch.

Cheek, Silas
1790 - 100 09 - twp 2
1800 - Mecklenburg County

Chittin/Fitten, Isaiah
1777 - deed from Peter Johnston for 160 acres on Sugar Creek adjoining Zebulon, Thomas, and Charles Alexander, James Yandel, and William Yandel, Test: Will Reed, Dan Ocheltree, and Adam Stuart, bk 10, pg 94.
1780 - deed to Zebulon Alexander for 200 acres on Sugar Creek adjoining Phineas Alexander, Test: Phineas and Abell Alexander, and Robert Cunningham, bk 10, pg 420.

Christenberry, Moses
1790 - 101 00 - twp 7
Children: Daniel F. ? (Daniel was born Aug 9, 1793)

Christenberry, Nicholas & Ann
1790 - 213 00 - twp 7
1800 - Mecklenburg County

Christman, George
1790 -111 00 - twp 11

Christman, George
1790 - 111 00 - twp 12

Christman, Michael
1768 - named as the grantee of 125 acres on Dutch Buffalo Creek, no book or page number given, bk 10, pg 26.
1783 - named as an adjoining land owner to John Michael & Margaret Clonts, and Christian Goodman on the waters of Rocky River on a branch of Dutch Buffalo Creek,

adjoining Gasper Saxer, Test: John Leopard and George
Soatman, bk 12, pg 293.

Chronicle, William
   1784 - named as the owner of a tract on the Cataba River
adjoining the Tuckasuga Ford, originally granted to
Joseph Harding, then to George Allen, William Chronicle,
William Barnett, Sr., Abraham Barnett, then to Joseph
Graham in 1784, bk 12, pg 499.
   William died Oct 7, 1780, in the battle of King's
Mountain.
   Half brother of James McKee.

Clain, George
   1790 - 122 00 - twp 12

Clarey/McClarey, Wm
   1790 - 200 00 - twp 1
   1800 - Mecklenburg County

Clark, Benjamin
   1790 - 114 00 - twp 7
   1800 - Mecklenburg County

Clark, Cornolus
   1766 - listed in the militia company of Capt. Adam
Alexander of Clear Creek.

Clark, James
   1780 - named as an adjoining land owner to William
Johnston, and William McClure on Mallard Creek, bk 12,
pg 91.
   1790 - 100 00 - twp 6
   1800 - Mecklenburg County

Clark, James & Lucy
   1766 - listed in the militia company of Capt. Adam
Alexander of Clear Creek.
   1771 - deed from Abner Nash to James for 173 acres in a
tract known as the Welch Tract on the head branch of
Rockey River, Test: Clement Nash, bk 10, pg 387.

Clark, James & Hannah
   1782 - witnessed a deed, with John Bigham, from
Alexander McKee to William Berryhill on Sugar Creek, bk
11, pg 157.
   1782 - deed from William Berryhill and Thomas McDowel to
James for 120 acres on Sugar Creek, Test: Thomas
Allison, and Will Reed, bk 11, pg 183.
   1782 - named as an adjoining land owner to George
Buckalow, Tunas Hogland, and James McLure on McCalpin's
Creek, Test: James Walker, and Robert Donalson, bk 12,
pg 508.
   1783 - Hannah sold 84 acres to Elinor Clark, widow of
John Clark in what was twp 5 in 1790, Test: Samuel
Pickens, and William Alexander, bk 12, pg 315.
   James died before 1783.

Clark/Glark, Jesse

1783 - named as an adjoining land owner to Robert
Walker, Jr., John Green, William Clark, and John Walker,
bk 12, pg 331.
1783 - deed from Jonas Clark to Jesse for 120 acres on
Sugar Creek, Test: Samuel Martin, and Robert Walker,
adjoining William Clark, bk 11, pg 254.
1784 - deed from John Sloan for 200 acres on a branch of
Sugar Creek joining Isaac Williams, Robert Walker, James
Tagart, David Hays, Thomas Polk, and Alexander McKee,
Test: Robert Irvin, John Hana, and John Carruth, bk 12,
pg 466.
1790 - 232 02 - twp 1
1800 - Mecklenburg County
Son of William & Susannah Clark.

Clark, John & Elinor
1777 - named as the original grantee of a tract on the
Northwest branch of Twelve Mile Creek, bk 10, pg 202.
1779 - witnessed a deed, with William Cochran, from
David Rea to Andrew Rea, Archibald Crocket, and John
Flenniken on Four Mile Creek, bk 11, pg 25.
1781 - witnessed a deed, with William Reed, and David
Flaniken, from James Fleniken to John Barnett on
McCalpins Creek, bk 11, pg 81.
1783 - deed from Hannah Clark, widow of James Clark, to
Elinor, widow of John Clark, for 84 acres, Test: Samuel
Pickens, and William Alexander, bk 12, pg 315.
Children: Thomas
John died before 1783.
1790 - 101 00 - twp 5 (Eliner)

Clark, Jonas
1783 - deed to Jesse Clark for 120 acres on Sugar Creek
Test: Samuel Martin, and Robert Walker, adjoining
William Clark, bk 11, pg 254.

Clark, Joseph
1790 - 102 00 - twp 7
1800 - Mecklenburg County

Clark, Mary
1780 - witnessed a deed from Robert & Hannah Craighead
to Joseph Mitchel on Rockey River, bk 11, pg 197.

Clarke, Robert R.
1790 - 133 00 - twp 1
1800 - Mecklenburg County

Clark, Thomas
1784 - named as an adjoining land owner to Thomas Polk,
and Andrew Dune on both sides of Long Creek, Test:
Robert Dunn, and Andrew Lawing, bk 12, pg 283.

Clark, Thomas
1773 - named as a land owner on the Northwest branch of
Twelve Mile Creek originally granted to his father, John
Clark on March 31, 1753, bk 10, pg 202.
Son of John Clark.

Clark, William

1772 - William's will was probated in Mecklenburg Co.
Children: William, Joseph, Benjamin
Clarke, William & Susannah(2)
    1772 - deed from Henry Eustace McCulloh to William for 102 acres on Sugar Creek, adjoining John McClure, Test: Richard Mason, and William Patterson, bk 10, pg 238.
    1779 - witnessed a deed, with John Cochran, from David Rea to Andrew Rea, Archibald Crocket, and John Flenniken on Four Mile Creek, bk 11, pg 25.
    1783 - named as an adjoining land owner to Robert Walker, Jr., John Green, Jesse Clark, and John Walker, bk 12, pg 331.
    1790 - 303 03 - twp 1
    William died May 2, 1791 at the age 70.
    Susannah died Sept 6, 1791, age 64.
Clause, Michael
    1782 - named as an adjoining land owner to Jacob Phifer, and Paul Dupley on Dutch Buffalo Creek, bk 12, pg 93.
Clay, Isham
    1790 - named in a deed, no book or page number given.
Clay, James
    1790 - 111 00 - twp 14
Clayton, James
    1790 - 000 10 - twp 1
Clegg, Samuel
    1764 - named in a deed, no book or page number given.
Clemments, Samuel
    1790 - 000 10 - twp 11
Clemons, Andrew M
    1767 - Loose estate papers
Cleymon, Richard
    1790 - 116 00 - twp 19
Cleymon, Simon
    1790 - 114 00 - twp 19
Cline/Klein, George
    1794 - Account ledger of John Melchor's store.
Cline, Michael & Catherine
    Wife - Catherine Shuffert, daughter of George & Gertrude Hubener Shuffert.
    Son of Moritz & Anna Catherina Marzloff Klein.
    Michael died 1782, buried in Old Coldwater Church Cemetery.
    Catherine was born Nov 14, 1734, died March 11, 1798, buried in Old Coldwater Church Cemetery.
Cline, Michael
    1783 - named as an adjoining land owner to John Meisenhimer, William Leopard, Jacob Richey, Jacob Hough, and John Charles, bk 12, pg 147.
    1784 - grant for 150 acres on a branch of Coldwater Creek, adjoining Jacob Misenhimer, and Martin Stought, bk 12, pg 192.
    1790 - 105 00 - twp 12

Cliver/Clavin, George
    1790 - 123 00 - twp 3
Clonts, George
    1790 - 113 00 - twp 11
    1800 - Cabarrus County
Clonts, Jeremiah
    1790 - 132 00 - twp 11
    Jeremiah was born 1756 according to 1840 pension list.
Clontz, John Michael & Margaret
    1768 - patent for 200 acres on Rocky River and Dutch
    Buffalo Creek, no book or page number given.
    1783 - deed for 200 acres to Christian Goodman on the
    waters of Rocky River on a branch of Dutch Buffalo
    Creek, adjoining Gasper Saxer, Test: John Leopard and
    George Soatman, bk 12, pg 293.
Clots, Tobias
    1790 - 102 00 - twp 12
    1800 - Cabarrus County
    Children: Tobias (Elizabeth Peck)
Coak, Charles
    1790 - 106 03 - twp 17
Coak, Robert
    1790 - 102 00 - twp 17
Coan, Lewis
    1790 - 103 00 - twp 12
Coates, Jonathan
    1777 - witnessed a deed, with Nathaniel From, and
    Alexander Karrel, from Capt. James Pettigrew to George
    Greer for lots 34 and 92 in Charlotte, bk 10, pg 275.
Coble, Peter
    1790 - 104 00 - twp 11
Coburn, Samuel
    1779 - named as adjoining land owner to Thomas Shields,
    John Tool, and David Alexander on the south side of the
    north branch of the Catawba River, bk 11, pg 173.
Cochran, Benjamin W.
    1771 - Benjamin was one of the Cabarrus Black Boys.
    1783 - named as an adjoining land owner to John Robb,
    and Phillip Miller on Clear Creek, Test: Adam and Evan
    Alexander, bk 12, pg 222.
    1790 - 142 00 - twp 13
    1800 - Cabarrus County
Cochran, Benjn
    1790 - 101 00 - twp 7
Cochran, James & Mary
    1783 - deed from James to George Helms for 200 acres on
    both sides of Stuart's fork of Richardson's Creek, Test:
    William and Amelia Madelph. Bk 12, pg 505.
Cochran, John
    1779 - witnessed a deed, with William Cochran, from
    David Rea to Andrew Rea, Archibald Crocket and John
    Flenniken on Four Mile Creek, bk 11, pg 25.

1790 - 103 00 - twp 16
Cochran, John & Dorcas
    Wife - Dorcas Harris
    No date - witnessed a bill of sale, along with James
    Finley, from James Harris to James Maxwell, bk 10, pg
    318.
    1790 - 121 01 - twp 13
    1800 - Cabarrus County
Cochran, Paul
    1784 - named as an adjoining land owner to David Davis
    on, bk 12, pg 172.
    1790 - 242 00 - twp 13
Cochran/Coughran, Robert (M)
    1777 - witnessed a deed, with Henry Fleming, from Thomas
    & Elizabeth McQuown to their son, Alexander McQuown, for
    132 acres on both sides of Coddle Creek, adjoining James
    Neel, bk 10, pg 234.
    1779 - grant for 300 acres on Footy/Fuda Creek, bk 10,
    pg 515.
    1790 - 126 00 - twp 13
    1800 - Cabarrus County
Cochran, Robert
    1790 - 213 00 - twp 1
Cochran, Thomas
    1786 - Thomas' will was probated in Mecklenburg Co.
    Children: John, William, Robert
Cochran, Thomas, Jr.
    1790 - 157 00 - twp 16
Cochran, Thomas, Sr.
    1780 - grant for 20 acres on both sides of Soder Branch
    of Twelve Mile Creek, adjoining James Way, and William
    Houston, bk 12, pg 162.
    1790 - 221 01 - 16
Cochran, Wm
    1779 - witnessed a deed, with William Cochran, from
    David Rea to Andrew Rea, Archibald Crocket and John
    Flenniken on Four Mile Creek, bk 11, pg 25.
    1790 - 201 00 - twp 13
    1800 - Cabarrus County
Cochran, William
    1790 - 133 00 - twp 1
Coffey, John & Hester Givens/Gibbons
    Hester was the daughter of William & Jannett Gibbons.
Coile/Corle, John
    1790 - 123 00 - twp 12
Cole, John & Mary
    1774 - deed from John & Mary of SC, to John Ashley of
    Tryon Co., NC for 300 acres on Richardson's Creek
    beginning on the east side of the Indian path, Test:
    Rees Shelby, and Henry Hargitt, bk 10, pg 178.
Coleman, Jacob
    1786 - Loose estate papers

Coleman, Mark
    1790 - 165 00 - twp 10
    1800 - Cabarrus County
Coleman, Nicholas
    1780 - witnessed a deed, with Jason Frissel, from Martin Fifer to Peter Sell for 190 acres on Little Coldwater Creek adjoining Jacob Seah, bk 11, pg 74.
Coleman, Nicholas & Margaret
    Wife - Margaret Franks, daughter of Jacob & Susannah Roan Franks.
Colledge, Henry
    1785 - deed from Dunnon and Mary Corion for 28 acres on the head waters of Cane Branch, Test: George Garman, and Samuel Larking, bk 12, pg 536.
    1790 - 102 00 - twp 14
    1800 - Cabarrus County
Collins, Seth
    1779 - witnessed a deed, with John Alison, from Jonathan & Rebecka Newman to Robert Hope for one tract containing 380 acres on Rockey River, and another containing 29 acres on Clarks Creek, bk 11, pg 46.
Colt, James
    1778 Signer of 1778 Petition
Conder, George
    1782 - named as an adjoining land owner to Mitchael Winecoff, William Irwin, and James Russell on Three Mile Branch of Coldwater Creek, bk 12, pg 113.
Conger, John
    1774 - mentioned in the estate papers of Nicholson Ross.
Conger, Jonathan
    1774 - mentioned in the estate papers of Nicholson Ross.
Conkrite, Harkles/Hardy
    1783 - named as an adjoining land owner to James Scott, on both sides of Three Mile Branch of Coldwater Creek, bk 12 pg 170.
Conner, James & Lillis
    Wife - Lillis Wilson, daughter of Samuel & Mary Winslow Wilson.
    Children: Henry Workman, Margaret Jack (J. Franklin Brevard)
Conner, James
    1790 - 300 04 - twp 7
    1800 - Mecklenburg County
    Brothers: Charles, Henry
    One of the Conners was married to a daughter of Samuel Blythe and had a son named William Conner.
Conner, William
    1790 - 121 00 - twp 7
Contz, Lewis
    1790 - 124 00 - twp 15
Conway, Mary

1774 - deed from Mary and Catharine Hoiy, heirs of the estate of Eloner McDowel, to Mathew Lock of Roan/Rowan Co., NC, for 640 acres on Rockey River and Buffalo Creek, Test: Alexander Martin, and Griffith Rutherford, bk 10, pg 144.

Cook, Abraham
   1778 - deed from William Haggins to Abraham for 202 acres on Waxhaw Creek and Twelve Mile Creek, Test: Joseph Douglas, William Givens, and Henry Hurst, bk 10, pg 394.

Cook, Benjamin
   1779 - witnessed a deed, with Jarnet Cook, from John Curry to Edward Curry for 200 acres on both sides of Cain Creek near Waxhaw Creek, bk 11, pg 181.
   1784 - deed from Benjamin, of Craven Co., SC to Jack Liget of Mecklenburg Co., NC, for 250 acres on the head of the Mile Branch of Two Mile Creek, adjoining Robert McClure, witnessed Joshua Yarbrough, and Sylvanus Phillips, bk 12, pg 443.

Cook, Charles
   1783 - deed from John & Ann Thompson to Charles for 150 acres on Little Ritcheson Creek, a branch of Big Ritcheson Creek, Test: John Belk, Sr., and John Libley, bk 11, pg 292.
   1785 - deed from Drury & Martha Thompson to Charles for 195 acres on both sides of Little Richardson's Creek on the county line, Test: John Belk, John Thompson, and Darsen Belk, bk 12, pg 600.
   1790 - 106 03 - twp 17

Cook, Isaac
   1783 - Witnessed a deed, with Farmer Davis, to James Jack for lot 25 in Charlotte, bk 11, pg 294.
   1783 - witnessed a deed, with Farmer Deavers, from James Jack to James Orr for lot 25 in Charlotte, bk 11, pg 269.
   1790 - 223 08 - twp 3
   1800 - Mecklenburg Count

Cook, Jacob
   1783 - named as an adjoining land owner to Paul Walter, and Nicholas Cook on Coldwater Creek, bk 12, pg 139.
   1790 - 133 00 - twp 12
   Jacob died before Jan 1800 according to Cabarrus court records.

Cook, James
   1782 - deed to Andrew Walker for 200 acres on the north fork of Waxhaw Creek adjoining William McCorlis, Test: William Cry, and John McCullah, bk 11, pg 126.

Cook, James
   1790 - 254 06 - twp 7

Cook, Jarnet

1779 - witnessed a deed, with Benjamin Cook, from John
Curry to Edward Curry for 200 acres on both sides of
Cain Creek near Waxhaw Creek, bk 11, pg 181.
Cook, John
1780 - grant for 15 acres on Mallard Creek, adjoining
Alexander Wallace, and Michael Henderson, bk 12, pg 138.
1780 - named as an adjoining land owner to Alexander
Wallace, Michael Henderson, Mathew Robison, William
Hemphill, and Thomas Frohock, bk 12, pg 120.
Cook, Joseph
1790 - 105 02 - twp 20
Cook, Nathaniel
1774 - deed from William Starret to Nathaniel for 50
acres on Sugar Creek, adjoining Nathaniel Irwin, and
Andrew Sprott, Test: Thomas Polk, and William Manson, bk
10, pg 370.
1779 - deed to John Wilson for 43 acres on Sugar Creek
adjoining Thomas Polk, Test: Ezekiel Polk, and John
Bitty/Beaty, bk 10, pg 301.
Cook, Nicholas
1783 - named as an adjoining land owner to Paul Walter,
and Jacob Cook on Coldwater Creek, bk 12, pg 139.
1790 - 302 00 - twp 10
Cook, Nicholas, Jur.
1790 - 111 00 - twp 10
Cook, Robert
1790 - 102 00 - twp 17
Cook, William
1778 - named as an adjoining land owner to William
Haggins, and Abraham Cook, on Waxhaw and Twelve Mile
Creek, bk 10, pg 394.
Coon, Nicholas
1783 - named as adjoining land owner to Nicholas Walter,
John Ross, Paul Walters, and Mathias Mitchel on a branch
of Coldwater Creek, bk 12, pg 126.
Cooper, Doctor
1790 - 112 00 - twp 1
Cooper, John(2)
1790 - 202 00 - twp 1
John died April 11, 1801 at the age of 80.
Cooper, John
1790 - 122 00 - twp 8
Cooper, Joseph
1790 - 000 10 - twp 3
1800 - Mecklenburg County
Cooper, Joseph
1793 - Account ledger of John Melchor's store.
Cooper, William
1782 - deed from Hector & Margaret McLane to William for
a tract on both sides of King's branch of Sugar Creek,
adjoining Francis Herron, William McDowel, John Bigham,

Residents of Mecklenburg County, North Carolina   75
1762-1790

and James Sprott, Test: Isack Herron, and John and
Robert Hunter, bk 12, pg 234.
Cope, Nicholas
   1785 - named in a deed, no book or page number given.
Copeland, Dennis
   1790 - 123 00 - twp 8
Corcham/Corum, William & Abigail
   1794 - Loose estate papers
Coreham/Corum, Robert
   1795 - Loose estate papers
Corle, John
   1790 - 123 00 - twp 12
Corion/Corsiak, Dunnon & Mary
   1785 - deed to Henry College for 28 acres on the head of
   Cane Branch, Test: George Garman, and Samuel Larking, bk
   12, pg 536.
   mentioned in the estate papers of Nicholson Ross 1774.
Corzine, George
   1783 - named as an adjoining land owner to John
   Setsinger, Alexander Ferguson, John Weyle, James
   Morrison, and John Shaver, on Coldwater and Buffalow
   Creeks, bk 12, pg 150.
   1790 - 315 00 - twp 10
   1800 - Cabarrus County
   Children: George, Rachel, Abigail (all under age in
   1798)
   George died before 1798, Eli Corzine was security for
   his will.
Corzine, George, Jr.
   1786 - named as an adjoining land owner to Robert Smith,
   John Wilie, Alexander Ferguson, and James Morrison on
   Coldwater Creek and Buffalo Creek, Test: David Allison,
   and Waitstill Avery, bk 12, pg 616.
   1790 - 124 00 - twp 10
   1800 - Cabarrus County
Corzine, John & Leah Shinn
   1776 - Loose estate papers
Corzine, John & Mary
   1776 - Buffalow Creek
   Children: George, Samuel, William, 7 unnamed daughters.
Corzine, John
   1776 - John's will was probated in Mecklenburg Co.
   Children: John, Samuel, George, William
Corzine, Levil
   1790 - 134 00 - twp 10
   1800 - Cabarrus County
   Son of Nicholas Corzine
Corzine/Crozine, Nicholas
   1769 - Nicholas' will was probated in Mecklenburg Co.
   1769 - Loose estate papers
   Children: Levoy, Nicholas, George
   Brother: George

Corzine, Nicholas
    1790 - 114 00 - twp 10
    1800 - Cabarrus County
    Son of Nicholas Corzine
Corzine, Samuel
    1790 - 113 00 - twp 10
    1800 - Cabarrus County
    Son of John & Mary Corzine
Cothran, Henry
    1790 - 101 00 - twp 11
Coul/Caul, James
    1790 - 000 10 - twp 15
Courtney, William
    1779 - named as an adjoining land owner to James & Margaret Potts, William Potts, Hugh McLile, Archibald Crocket, Zeph John, and John Potts on Six Mile Creek, bk 12, pg 248.
    (William was unable to appear in court to make oath as witness to a deed between James and John Potts by reason of age and bodily infirmity and other disposition in 1783.
    1790 - 201 00 - twp 16
Cowait, Archibald
    1786 - witnessed a deed, with Alexander Carns, and John Lithem, from John & Catherine Nutt to Robert Orr and Thomas Lackey for 300 acres on Waxhaw Creek, bk 12, pg 609.
Cowan, John & Margaret
    1754 - grant for 200 acres on the north side of the Cataba River, no book or page number given.
    Children: William, Hannah, Joseph, John, Mary
    1775 - John's will was probated in Mecklenburg Co.
Cowan, Joseph
    1754 - named as an original grantee, no book or page number given.
    son of John & Margaret Cowan.
Cowan, William
    1784 - Loose estate papers
Cowan, William
    1785 - died, unmarried
    son of John & Margaret Cowan.
Cowdon, Robert
    1778 - witnessed a deed, with Alexander Brown, from George Alexander to Samuel Linton for 40 acres on Rockey River, adjoining James Brown, and the late Charles Harris, bk 10, pg 314
    1784 - grant for 38 acres on the waters between Coddle Creek and Rockey River, adjoining John Alexander, Jr., Nathaniel Alexander, Ezekiel Sharp, and Arthur Donnelson, bk 12, pg 156.
Cowden, Samuel
    1782 - Samuel's will was probated in Mecklenburg Co.

Residents of Mecklenburg County, North Carolina 1762-1790

1783 - Loose estate papers
Children: Walter, John
Cowden, Walter
   1786 - Loose estate papers
   Son of Samuel Cowden.
Cowden, Widow
   1790 - 102 00 - twp 5
Cowen, John
   1776 - Loose estate papers
Cowen, Samuel
   1790 - Loose estate papers
Cown, Lewis
   1790 - 103 00 - twp 12
Cowsert, Archibald
   1777 - deed from Daniel Cairns to Archibald, of Craven Co., SC for 125 acres on the north side of Waxaw Creek, Test: John & Catherine Nutt, and J. Miller, bk 10, pg 207.
Cox, John
   1790 - 103 00 - twp 11
   1800 - Cabarrus County
Cox, Moses
   1790 - 102 00 - twp 11
   1800 - Cabarrus County
Cox, William
   1790 - 101 00 - twp 11
   1800 - Cabarrus County
Craig, John
   1790 - 102 00 - twp 15
Craige, Moses & Isabella
   1783 - grant for 129 acres on Twelve Mile Creek on the south side of Glady Fork, adjoining William Mathews, bk 12, pg 136.
   1790 - 224 00 - twp 16
   1800 - Mecklenburg County
Craighead, Alexander, Rev & Margaret ?
   1754 - mentioned in a deed from Robert & Hannah Craighead to John Long on Long Creek as the owner of the 225 acre tract in 1754, bk 10, pg 252.
   1765 - Alexander's will was probated in Mecklenburg Co. Children: James, Margaret, Robert, Thomas
   Wife: ? Richardson, daughter of William Richardson, paster of Waxhaw Presbyterian Church.
   Alexander was the first pastor of Rocky Springs Presbyterian Church from 1758 to 1766.
Craighead, Robert & Hannah
   1776 - deed to Thomas Polk for 500 acres on Indian Camp Creek, a branch of the Cataba River adjoining Matthew Tool , Test: Ezekiel Polk, and William Alexander, bk 10, pg 348.
   1779 - deed from John & Ruth Disart to Robert for 185 acres on Mallard Creek and Stoney Creek, adjoining

Robert Scott, Test: Nathaniel Alexander, and Andrew
Alexander, bk 10, pg 398.
1780 - deed to Joseph Mitchel for 100 acres on Rockey
River adjoining Adam Meek, Test: Mary Clark, and J.
Johnston, bk 11, pg 197.
1782 - named as an adjoining land owner to Job Williams
on Mallard Creek, bk 12, pg 92.
1783 - deed to Job Williams for 108 acres on both sides
of Stony Creek, Test: Samuel Patton, and Thomas
Faulkner, bk 12, pg 224.
1790 - 243 04 - twp 5

Crawford, David & Mary
David was born 1740, died Aug 6, 1820, buried in Poplar
Tent Presbyterian Cemetery
Mary was born 1745, died May 15, 1820, buried in Poplar
Tent Presbyterian Cemetery

Crawford, George
1766 - listed in the militia company of Capt. Adam
Alexander of Clear Creek.

Crawford, John
1790 - 101 00 - twp 14

Crawford, Joseph
1783 - Loose estate papers

Crawford, Robert
1775 - deed to Hugh White for 127 acres on both sides of
Warsaw/Waxhaw Creek adjoining William Beard, and John
Currey, Test: Nathan Barr, Charles Miller, Jr., and
Thomas Crawford, bk 10, pg 33.
1784 - named as an adjoining land owner to John, Robert,
and Elijah Crocket, Daniel Carns, and John Nutt on
Waxhaw Creek, Test: George Davidson, John Linn, and
Henry Leviston, bk 12, pg 419.

Crawford, Samuel
1778 - witnessed a deed, with William Shields, from
Robert & Hannah Craighead to John Long for 225 acres on
Long Creek, bk 10, pg 252.

Crawford, Thomas
1775 - witnessed a deed, with Nathan Barr, and Charles
Miller, Jr., from Robert Crawford to Hugh White on
Waxhaw Creek, bk 10, pg 33.

Crawl, John
1780 - grant for 100 acres on both sides of Carswell
Branch of Twelve Mile Creek, adjoining John Cry, bk 12,
pg 21.

Cray/McCray, William
1790 - 125 01 - twp 9
1800 - Cabarrus County

Creaton/Craton, James
1790 - 101 01 - twp 9
1800 - Cabarrus County

Creaton, William & Fanny
Wife - Fanny Reed, daughter of John & Sarah Kiser Reed

Creps/Cress, Phillip
    1790 - 124 01 - twp 11
Creps/Cress, Tobias
    1790 - 103 00 - twp 11
    1800 - Cabarrus County
Creson, Conrad
    1790 - 113 00 - twp 15
Cress, Henry
    Buried in St John's Evangelical Lutheran Church
    Cemetery, but dates and location have been lost.
Cress, Johann Nicolaus Dienrich & Catherine
    1781 - deed from Nicholas and George Owery to Martin
    Owery for 164 acres on a branch of Dutch Buffalow Creek,
    Test: Joseph Shinn, bk 11, pg 97.
    1783 - Nicholas' will was probated in Mecklenburg Co.
    Wife - Catherine Eberhard
    Children: Tobias, Phillip, Catherine, John Henry,
    Elizabeth Rosannah, Jacob, Mary, Ann Margaret, Sophia
    Nicholas was born May 12, 1721, died 1783, buried in St
    John's Evangelical Lutheran Church Cemetery.
Crider, Daniel
    1792 - Account ledger of John Melchor's store.
Crider/Drider, George
    1793 - Account ledger of John Melchor's store.
Crider/Criden, Jacob
    1784 - witnessed a deed, with Joseph Shinn, from John
    Willis to Absalom Baker on Buffalo Creek, bk 12, pg 449.
    1784 - witnessed a deed, with Joseph Shinn, from Mathias
    & Sarah Bostian to Henry Farr on Rocky River and
    Coldwater Creek, bk 12, pg 459.
Crimble, Murey
    1745 - received a land patent dated March 3, 1745 on
    Rockey River in the Great Tract, referred to in a deed
    from Abner Hash to David Oliphant, bk 10, pg 259.
Christman, Michael, Sr.
    1768 - Loose estate papers
Christman, Michael
    1783 - named as adjoining land owner to John Michael and
    Margaret Clontz, and Christian Goodman on Dutch Buffalo
    Creek, bk 12, pg 293.
Christman, George
    1794 - Account ledger of John Melchor's store.
    1790 - 111 00 twp 12
Christman, George
    1790 - 111 00 - twp 11
Chrocrft, George
    1778 - Signer of 1778 Petition
Criswell, John & Jean/Jane
    1773 - deed from John Jackson & Mary Moore for 165 acres
    on the Cataba River adjoining Joseph Hobbs, Test: Robert
    Waddle, William Graham, and Abel Duckworth, bk 10, pg
    90.

1777 - deed to William Laughland for a tract on the Cataba River, originally granted to Joseph Hobbs, Test: William Graham, and Abel Mankens, bk 10, pg 303.

Crockett, Andrew
  1786 - deed from Joseph Graham, sheriff, to Robert Smith, in a judgement against Andrew and John Letsinger for a tract of land on Coldwater and Buffalow Creek, bk 12, pg 616.

Crockett, Archibald & Mary
  1774 - deed to John Willson for 450 acres on Six Mile Creek, Test: Brice Miller, James Tate, and John McGown, bk 10, pg 130.
  1778 - witnessed a deed dated Jan 13, 1778, along with James Bratton, from James Potts to William and John Potts for 250 acres the Flat Branch of Twelve Mile Creek, no book or page number given, proven Jan 1778.
  1779 - named as an adjoining land owner to James and William Potts, Hugh McLile, and Zeph John on Six Mile Creek near Stillhouse Branch, bk 12, pg 272.
  1779 - witnessed a deed, with William Hanston, from Nathaniel Johnston of Rowan Co., NC to Hugh Crye of Mecklenburg Co., NC for 220 acres on the middle fork of Twelve Mile Creek, bk 10, pg 309.
  1779 - deed from David Rea to Andrew Rea, Archibald Crocket, and John Flenniken for 5 acres on Four Mile Creek, Test: John and William Cochran, bk 11, pg 25.
  1790 - 415 00 - twp 19

Crockett, David & Elizabeth
  1779 - named as an adjoining land owner to Edward Meloney, William Houston, and Hugh Barnet on Sugar Creek, bk 10, pg 487.
  1782 - deed to Joseph Galbreath for 50 acres on a branch of Sugar Creek adjoining James Reed, and Alexander Mitchel, Test: Moses Robison, and Edward Malony, bk 11, pg 91.
  1782 - deed from Hugh & Elizabeth Rondles to David for 50 acres on a branch of Sugar Creek adjoining James Reed, and Alexander Mitchel, Test: Andrew Henderson, and Edward Malony, bk 11, pg 98.

Crockett, Elijah
  Son of John Crockett

Crockett, John
  1784 - deed of gift to his sons, Robert and Elijah, two tracts on Waxhaw Creek, his old plantation, bk 12, pg 419.
  Children: Robert, Elijah.

Crockett, Robert
  1786 - named as as adjoining land owner to John & Catherine Nutt, Thomas Lackey, Alexander Carns, Rebeckah Moor, William Davis, and James Lashley on Waxhaw Creek, bk 12, pg 609.
  Son of John Crockett

Crockett, Robert & Rachel Kerr
    1767 - deeded 44 acres on the head branches of Sugar
    Creek, no book or page number given.
    1781 - deed from Abraham and Samuel Barnet to Robert for
    250 acres on Long Creek, adjoining Samuel Sprott, and
    David Miller, Test: William McCleary, and William
    Ritchey, bk 12, pg 476.
    1783 - deed to John McClure for 44 acres on the head
    branches of Sugar Creek, bk 11, pg 271.
    1783 - named as an adjoining land owner to Cerns
    Henderson on Sugar Creek, bk 12, pg 111.
    1790 - 117 00 - twp 6
Crockett, Robert
    1779 - witnessed a deed, with John McClanahan, from
    William Hambilton to William Ferril on the north side of
    Waxhaw Creek, adjoining John Rogers, bk 11, pg 67.
    1780 - named as an adjoining land owner to Joseph
    Douglas, John Wilson, and Michael Ligget, bk 12, pg 95.
    1784 - deed from William Hagens to Robert for 150 acres
    on Twelve Mile Creek, adjoining James McCorkle, Test:
    Joseph Douglas, bk 12, pg 382.
Crommer/Croner, Jacob
    1778 - Signer of 1778 Petition.
    1780 - deed from John & Catherine McCoy for 79 acres on
    Three Mile Creek, Test: Richard Trotter, and Martin Orr,
    bk 11, pg 66.
    1783 Three Mile Creek, near Umberford's Branch.
Crowell, George
    1793 - Account ledger of John Melchor's store.
Crowell/Croul/Crowl/Kroll, Peter & Catherine
    1790 - 202 00 - twp 12
    1794 - Account ledger of John Melchor's store.
Crowell/Croul, Peter
    Children: George, Dietrich, Simon, William (Wilhelm)
    1763 - Peter's will was probated in Mecklenburg County.
    1764 - Loose estate papers
Crowle, Samuel
    1790 - 223 00 - twp 14
Crowle, Samuel, Jr.
    1790 - 112 00 - twp 14
Crowell, Simon, Sr.
    1794 - Account ledger of John Melchor's store.
Crowmell/Cromwell, John
    1778 - Signer of 1778 Petition
    1782 - a branch of Reedy Creek called John Cromwell's
    branch was referred to in a grant to Robert McMurray, bk
    12, pg 14.
    1782 - named as an adjoining land owner to Robert
    Turner, James Morrow, William Taylor, and William
    Spears, bk 12, pg 78.
Crumel, James
    1790 - 112 00 - twp 13

Crumell, John
   1800 - Cabarrus County
   1778 - Signer of 1778 Petition
   1790 - 225 00 - twp 13
   1800 - Cabarrus County
Cruse, Adam
   1790 - 112 00 - twp 11
   1800 - Cabarrus County
Cruse, Andrew
   1790 - 111 00 - twp 11
   1800 - Cabarrus County
Cruse, William
   1790 - 133 00 - twp 12
Cry, Hugh & Elizabeth
   1779 - deed from Nathaniel/Nathan Johnston of Rowan Co., NC for 220 acres on Twelve Mile Creek, originally granted to Nathaniel Alexander, Test: William Hanston, and Archibald Crockett, bk 10, pg 309.
   1779 - deed to Jacob Seeres for 270 acres, Test: John McCorkle, and John Foster, bk 11, pg 96.
Crye, James
   1790 - 302 00 - twp 16
   1800 - Mecklenburg County
   Children: John, Samuel (never married), Sarah
Crye, John & Catherine Shimmin
   1780 - named as adjoining land owner to John Crawl/Crowell on Carswell branch of Twelve Mile Creek, bk 12, pg 21
   1790 - 312 00 - twp 16
   1800 - Mecklenburg County
   Children: William (Sarah Higgins), Sarah, Catherine (Joshua Gordon), Margaret (Thomas Walker), James, David (Jean Elliott), John Alexander, Isabella (William Craig)
   John died in 1794 in Mecklenburg County.
Crye, William
   1782 - witnessed a deed, with John McCullah, from James Cook to Andrew Walker for 200 acres on the north fork of Waxhaw Creek adjoining William McCorlis, bk 11, pg 126.
   1782 - witnessed a deed, with Andrew Walker, from Henry Hurst to John Galaspy of Guilford Co., NC, for 202 acres, no watercourse given, bk 12, pg 220.
   1785 - deed from William to Andrew Walker for 100 acres on a branch of Twelve Mile Creek called Crywell's branch, adjoining Robert Davis, and Charles Adams, Test: John Walker, and John Gillespie, bk 12, pg 518.
   1790 - 132 00 - twp 15
   Wife - Sarah Higgins, April 8, 1779
   Children: David, John, Samuel
   William was born 1754, died Aug 29, 1835
   Sarah was born 1762.
   Son of John & Catherine Crye.

William was born in the Isle of Man, raised in Chester Co., PA, moved to Mecklinburg Co. NC, then to Burke Co., NC, then to Granville Dist, SC, then to Burke Co. again, then on to Hale County in GA, and then to McMinn Co., TN

Cryor/Crider, George
    1780 - deed from George's father, Peter Cryer, for 33 acres on a branch of Rockey River, Test: Frederick Ciser, bk 12, pg 203.
    Son of Peter Crider.
Cryor, Peter
    1780 - deed to his son, George, for 33 acres on a branch of Rockey River, winessed by Frederick Kiser/Ciser, bk 12, pg 203.
    Children: George
Culp, Augustine
    1776 - deed to John Wilson for 50 acres on McMichael's Creek adjoining Samuel Jack, Test: William Reed, Elijah and Abner Alexander, bk 11, pg 222.
Culp/Koulp, Edward
    1783 - witnessed a deed from George Harris to William Reed on Crooked Creek, bk 12, pg 522.
Culp, George & Barbara
    Wife - Barbara Goodman
Culp/Kolp, John
    1774 - deed from George & Molly Barringer to John for 26 acres on Dutch Buffalo Creek, Test: Mathias and John Barringer, bk 12 , pg 375.
    1790 - 224 00 - twp 11
    1793 - Account ledger of John Melchor's store.
    1800 - Cabarrus County
Cummins/Commins, Benjamin
    1793 - Account ledger of John Melchor's store.
Cummins, Charles
    1771 - Charles' will was probated in Mecklenburg Co.
    Children: John, Francis
Cummins, John
    1790 - 102 00 - twp 1
    1800 - Mecklenburg County
Cuningham, Nathaniel
    1790 - 112 01 - twp 20
Cunningham, Robert
    1780 - witnessed a deed, with Phineas and Abell Alexander, from Isaiah Chittin to Zebulon Alexander on Sugar Creek bk 10, pg 420.
Cunningham/Coningham, Roger & Mary
    1790 - 212 00 - twp 19
    1800 - Mecklenburg County
    Wife - Mary
    Children: Mary, Margaret, Elenor, James, William, Robert
    Sons-in-law: John and James Sharp
Cunningham, Roger
    1808 - Loose estate papers

Residents of Mecklenburg County, North Carolina
1762-1790

Cuningham, William
    1790 - 123 00 - twp 20
Cuntress, James
    1785 - named as previous land owner of a tract
    containing 100 acres on Rockey River, neighboring George
    & Susan Karriker, John George William, Peter Reas, and
    James Beatey, bk 12, pg 592.
Curran, Mary
    1778 - Loose estate papers
Currethers, Edmund
    1790 - 111 00 - twp 1
Curry, Edward & Lucy
    1779 - deed from John Curry for 200 acres on Cain Creek
    near Waxhaw Creek, Test: Jarnet and Benjamin Cook, bk
    11, pg 181.
    1785 - deed to James Hagens of Camden Dist., SC, from
    Edward & Lucy of Georgetown Dist., SC for a tract on
    Cain Creek, granted to John Curry in 1769, Test: John
    and Samuel Hagins, bk 12, pg 604.
Currey, James & Margaret
    1790 - 143 00 - twp 19
    1800 - Mecklenburg County
    Children: Ann (died 1780, age 1), Robert, Allen, John,
    Henry, James, Nickson, daughter (Robert Sloan), daughter
    (William Gilmer), daughter (Alexander McGahey)
Curry, John
    1769 - named in a 1785 deed as the previous owner of a
    tract on Cain Creek, granted to John Curry in 1769, bk
    12, pg 604.
    1774 - named as an adjoining land owner to Joseph &
    Nancy Greer, Robert Crawford, and William Bird, bk 10,
    pg 246.
    1775 - named as an adjoining land owner to Robert
    Crawford, Hugh White, and William Beard on Warsaw/Waxhaw
    Creek, Test: Nathan Barr, Charles Miller, Jr., and
    Thomas Crawford, bk 10, pg 33.
    1779 - deed to Edward Curry for 200 acres on Cain Creek
    near Waxhaw Creek, Test: Jarnet and Benjamin Cook, bk
    11, pg 181.
    1784 - deed from John of Ritcherson, state of Georgia,
    to John Foster of Mecklenburg Co., NC, for 150 acres on
    the east side of Waxhaw Creek, Test: William Meyer, John
    McCannon, and Green Rives, bk 12, pg 579.
Cusick, George
    1753 - deed from Andrew Cathey for 200 acres on the
    north side of the Cataba River, no book or page number
    given.
    1777 - deed to John Davison for 200 acres on the north
    side of the Cataba River, Test: Ephraim Brevard, and
    Alexander Long, bk 11, pg 93A.
Cuthbertson, David, Jr.

1786 - deed from Robert Slavy/Slaven for 252 acres on
both sides of Crooked Creek, Test: Samuel Smith, and
John Cuthburtson, bk 12, pg 589.
1790 - 112 00 - twp 14
Cuthbertson, John
1786 - witnessed deed from Robert Slavy/Slaven to David
Cuthbertson, Jr. on Crooked Creek, bk 12, pg 589.
1790 - 113 00 - twp 14
Cuthbertson, Moses
1784 - Loose estate papers
Cuthbertson/Culbertson, William & Margaret
1790 - 235 00 - twp 15
Dacton, Charles
1782 - named as an adjoining land owner to Isaac Breden
and William Winchester on Rockey River near the head of
the Meadow Spring, bk 12, pg 171.
Daker, Christopher
1790 - 324 00 - twp 4
Daniel, Paul
1793 - Account ledger of John Melchor's store.
Children: Henry
Daniel, Susana
1782 - deed from William Hayns for 140 acres on Muddy
Creek, Test: John Nelson, and Daniel Methine, bk 11, pg
189.
1783 - deed to Robert John for 140 acres on Muddy Creek,
adjoining Thomas Mary, and William Michel, Test: Thomas
Morrow, Rees Shelby, and Daniel Metheny, bk 12, pg 287.
Darbey, Charles
1790 - 101 00 - twp 15
Darnell, Joseph & Winefred
1790 - 135 06 - twp 2
Wife: Winnefred Perry
Children: Joshua, Joseph R., John, William, Elizabeth (
? Smith), Winefred (? Smith), Jenny (?
Cunningham), Sukey (? Boyd), Polly (? Cothorn),
Patsy Darnall, Hannah (? Person)
1800 - Mecklenburg County
Joseph's will was probated in Nov 1812.
Darnell, William & Phillis
1790 - 154 00 - twp 2
Children: James and John (Polly ?), Polly (?
Alexander)
William's will was probated in Oct 1799.
Daugherty, David
1777 - deed from James & Mary Meek for 115 acres on
Rockey River adjoining Robert Harris, bk 10, pg 219.
1790 - 215 00 - twp 7
1800 - Mecklenburg County
Davidson, George
1780 - named as adjoining land owner to Sarah Gillian on
Twelve Mile Creek, bk 12, pg 23.

1784 - witnessed a deed of gift, along with John Linn, and Henry Leviston, from John Crocket to his sons, Robert and Elijah on Waxhaw Creek, bk 12, pg 419.

Davison, Isaac
1782 - witnessed a deed, with James Davison, from Andrew & Margaret Morison to John Davison on Rockey River, bk 12, pg 368.

Davidson, James
1782 - witnessed a deed, with Isaac Davison, from Andrew & Margaret Morison to John Davison on Rockey River, bk 12, pg 368.
Brothers: John, Samuel, Thomas

Davidson, John & Margaret
John was a signer of the petition to pardon the Cabarrus Black Boys in 1775.
1779 - John was a merchant.
1781 - witnessed a deed from James Barr and Margaret Wallace to John Levison on Rockey River, adjoining James Dysart, bk 11, pg 79.
1782 - deed from Andrew & Margaret Morison for 170 acres on Rockey River, Test: James and Isaac Davison, bk 12, pg 368.
1784 - deed to Robert Martin for 200 acres on Rockey River, adjoining James Dysard, Test: William Waddle, Sam Davidson, and John Wier, bk 12, pg 308.
1790 - 112 09 - twp 6
Wife - Margaret (Wilson ?)
Children: Mary, Sam Wilson Davidson, John

Davidson, John, Majr. & Violet
1767 - Militia, Mecklenburgh Regiment (Lieutenants)
1775 - John was one of the signers of the Mecklenburg Declaration of Independence on May 20, 1775.
1777 - deed from George Cusick for 200 acres on the north side of the Cataba River, sold to Cusick by Andrew Cathey in 1753, bk 11, pg 93A.
1784 - deed from Benjamin & Jemimah Knox for 206 acres on the south fork of McDowell Creek, adjoining Mathew McClure, Test: Samuel Davidson, and Joseph Fraser, bk 12, pg 353.
1790 - 226 026 - twp 7
Wife - Violet Wilson, daughter of Samuel & Mary Winslow Wilson, Sr.
Brothers: James, Samuel, Thomas
Children: Isabella (Joseph Graham), Rebecca (Alexander Brevard), Violet (William Bain Alexander), Elizabeth (William Lee Davidson), Mary (Dr. William McLean), Sallie (Alexander Caldwell), Margaret (Maj. James Harris), John (Sallie Brevard), Robert (Margaret Osbourne)

Davison, John
1778 - witnessed a deed, with Hugh Pollock, from William Givens to Robert Scott on Six Mile Creek, bk 10, pg 278.

1778 - John's will was probated in Mecklenburg Co.
Children: James, Samuel
Davidson, Samuel
    1784 - witnessed a deed, with Joseph Fraser, from
Benjamin & Jemimah Knox to John Davidson on the south
fork of McDowell Creek, originally granted to George
Cathey then to James Knox, bk 12, pg 353.
    1790 - 121 00 - twp 7
    Brothers: James, John, Thomas
Davidson, Sam
    1784 - witnessed a deed, with William Waddle, and John
Wier, from John Davidson to Robert Martin on Rockey
River, adjoining James Dysard, bk 12, pg 308.
Davidson, Thomas
    1790 - 100 00 - twp 7
    Wife - Sarah
    Children: Mary Long Davidson
    Brothers - James, John & Samuel
    Sister: female (Hugh Bryson)
    Thomas' will was probated in July 1800.
Davidson, William
    1780 - William's will was probated in Mecklenburg Co.
    1782 - Loose estate papers
    Children: Isaac
Davison, William Lee & Elizabeth
    1782 - deed for lot 52 in Charlotte, bk 10, pg 163.
    1785 - deed from William McCree to John Brevard, John
Dickey, and William Sharp, executors of the LW&T of
Brigadier William Davidson for 435 acres in Rowan County
on the branches of Davidson and Back Creek, adjoining
James McCullough, and Samuel Alison, bk 12, pg 574.
    Wife - Elizabeth Davidson, daughter of John Davidson.
Davies, Benjamin
    1795 - Account ledger of John Melchor's store.
Davies/Davis, David(2)
    1781 - deed to John Beel/Bell for 134 acres, Test:
Samuel Blythe, and John Wiete, bk 11, pg 102.
    David died Nov 18, 1776, at the age of 63.
Davies, George
    1784 - deed from Walter Bell for 300 acres on Coddle
Creek joining Samuel Ziklegg, and William Hall, Test:
Thomas and Robert Benson, bk 12, pg 351.
Davies, Hadawick (spinster)
    1784 - deed from Peter Johnston for 182 acres on
McCalpin Creek joining William Flanagan, and another
adjoining tract of 200 acres, and another adjoining
tract of 170 acres on McMichael's Creek, Test: James
Latta, and James Jackson, bk 12, pg 404.
Davies, James & Rebecca
    1767 - witnessed a deed, with

Children: Martha (? Craig), Sarah (? Nesbit), Jennet (? Baker), Rebecca (? Baker), Israel, Robert

Davies, John
    1770 - deed for lot 74 on south side of Tryon Street in Charlotte, Test: Isaac Jetton, and Robert Bourns, bk 11, pg 18.

Davies, Rebecca M.(2)
    Rebecca died March 1, 1784 at age 48.

Davies/Davis, Robert
    1782 - grant for 100 acres on Rockey River, adjoining William Waddlington, bk 12, pg 66.

Davies/Davis, Walter(2)
    1800 - Loose estate papers
    Walter died Dec 18, 1800 at age 65.

Davies/Davis, William
    1779 - named as adjoining land owner to David Litham, and John Barnett on Waxhaw Creek, bk 10, pg 507.
    1800 - Loose estate papers
    Children: Ann (? Porter), Andrew, William, John, female (James McEwen), Margaret (? Beaty), Betsy (? Scott), Mary

Davis, Andrew
    Andrew was one of the first settlers on Reedy Creek according to *Descendants of James & Jennet Morrison of Rocky River*.
    1790 - 306 00 - twp 13
    1800 - Cabarrus County
    Children: Robert

Davis, Andrew(2)
    1792 - Andrew died Feb 8, 1792 at the age of 21.

Davis, Daniel
    1789 - Loose estate papers

Davis, Daniel
    1790 - 000 10 - twp 7
    1800 - Mecklenburg County

Davis, David
    1776 - David's will was probated in Mecklenburg Co.
    Children: William, George

Davis, David & Jane
    1784 - grant for 40 acres on Rockey River adjoining Paul Cochran, bk 12, pg 172.
    1790 - 102 00 - twp 8
    Pension denied - no proof of identity with the soldier in the certificate of the comptroller of NC.

Davis, David
    1790 - 115 00 - twp 7
    1800 - Mecklenburg County

Davis/Deaver, Farmer
    1783 - Witnessed a deed, with Isaac Cook, to James Jack for lot 25 in Charlotte, bk 11, pg 294.

Residents of Mecklenburg County, North Carolina 1762-1790

1783 - witnessed a deed, with Isaac Cook, from James Jack to James Orr for lot 25 in Charlotte, bk 11, pg 269.

Davis, George
    1790 - 122 00 - twp 1
    1800 - Mecklenburg County
    Children: James C., Israel, Robert, William & John.

Davis, George
    1766 - listed in the militia company of Capt. Adam Alexander of Clear Creek.
    1774 - witnessed a deed, with Francis Newel, from William Spears to Thomas Davis on Reedy Creek, bk 10, pg 396.
    George was a signer of the petition to pardon the Cabarrus Black Boys in 1775.
    1778 - deed from William Adams for 130 acres on Reedy Creek, adjoining James Carruth, Test: Robert and William Harris, bk 10, pg 256.
    1782 - grant for 7 ½ acres on Reedy Creek, between Reedy Creek and McKee's Creek adjoining John Haggin, bk 12, pg 79.
    1782 - grant for 47 acres on Reedy Creek, adjoining Hugh Kimmonds, bk 12, pg 80.
    1782 - grant for 13 ¼ acres adjoining William Adams, bk 12, pg 82.
    1790 - 164 01 - twp 13
    1800 - Cabarrus County

Davis, Isaac
    1790 - 102 00 - twp 8

Davis, James & Margaret
    1765 - deed to John Davis for 230 acres on the south side of Sugar Creek, bk 11, pg 19.
    1765 - deed to John Davis for 260 acres on the south side of Sugar Creek, Test: Thomas Polk, and Will Polk, bk 11, pg 20.
    1782 - witnessed a deed, with Joseph Davis, from George Dods to Joseph Davis on Sugar Creek, bk 11, pg 154.
    1790 - 126 01 - twp 17
    1800 - Mecklenburg County

Davis, James & Jean
    1784 - deed to Walter Phair/Pharr/Farr for 114 acres on the south side of Rocky River, Test: William Briance, and Robert Ervin, bk 12, pg 550.
    1790 - 132 00 - twp 14

Davis, James
    1790 - 126 01 - twp 17

Davis, John L.
    1765 - deed from James & Margaret Davis for 230 acres on the south side of Sugar Creek, bk 11, pg 19.
    1765 - deed from James & Margaret Davis for 260 acres on the south side of Sugar Creek, Test: Thomas Polk, and Will Polk, bk 11, pg 20.

1779 - Cataba River
1782 - named as an adjoining land owner to Matthew &
David Roberson, and Thomas Greer, Test: William
Patterson, and Alexander Roberson, bk 11, pg 158.
1783 - named as an adjoining land owner to Richard and
David Robison, Ambrose McKee, and Andrew Cathey, Test:
Andrew Cathey, and William Patterson, bk 11, pg 301.
1790 - 312 00 - twp 2
1800 - Mecklenburg County

Davis, John, Sr.
1774 - deed from Isaac and Rebecah Sellers for 50 acres
on the south side of Rockey River formerly granted to
William White, Test: Hugh Carothers, and James Kile, bk
10, pg 188.
1780 - witnessed a deed, with William Bickens (Pickens),
from Joseph and Agnes Ewart to Alexander and Rachel
Robison on the branches of Rockey River, bk 10, pg 440.
1784 - witnessed a deed, with Benjamin Lewis, from
Joseph & Margaret Fraser to Samuel Davis, Jr. for 285
acres on Clark's Creek, adjoining Joseph Maxwell, and
David Smith, bk 12, pg 470.
1790 - 203 00 - twp 8

Davis, John
1774 - deed from John Rilliah for 193 acres on the ridge
between McMichael's Creek and McCalpin's Creek,
adjoining John Frohock, bk 10, pg 135.
1778 - witnessed a deed, with Hugh Pollock, from William
Givens to Robert Scott on Six Mile Creek, bk 10, pg 279.

Davis, Joseph(2)
1782 - deed from George Dods for 100 acres on Sugar
Creek, adjoining James Johnston, Test: Joseph and James
Davis, bk 11, pg 154.
Joseph died Aug 17, 1790 at age 30.

Davis, Martha
1778 - deed for lot 79 and lot 712 in Charlotte, Test:
Samuel McCleary, and William Hutchison, bk 11, pg 133.

Davis, Robert
1770 - Robert's will was probated in Mecklenburg Co.
Children: James, Robert, George, William

Davis/Davies, Robert
1766 - listed in the militia company of Capt. Adam
Alexander of Clear Creek.
1774 - Loose estate papers

Davis/Davies, Robert
1771 - Robert was one of the Cabarrus Black Boys.
1790 - 165 00 - twp 13
1800 - Cabarrus County
Son of Andrew Davis.

Davis, Robt
1778 - Signer of 1778 Petition
1785 - named as adjoining land owner to William and
Andrew Walker, Charles Adams, and William Crye on a

branch of Twelve Mile Creek called Crywell's branch, bk
12, pg 518.
1790 - 231 04 - twp 17

Davis, Samuel
1772 - named as an adjoining land owner to Thomas Polk,
James Moore, John Henry, and Samuel Knox on the head
waters of the south branch of Steel Creek, bk 10, pg
137.
1790 - 101 04 - twp 4
Samuel died Oct 22, 1790, buried in Steel Creek
Cemetery.
1790 - Loose estate papers

Davis, Samuel, Jr.(2)
1784 -deed from Joseph & Margaret Fraser for 285 acres
on Clark's Creek, adjoining Joseph Maxwell, and David
Smith, Test: Benjamin Lewis, John Davis, Sr. bk 12, pg
470.

Davis, Thomas
1778 - named as an adjoining land owner to William
Givens, and Robert Scott on Six Mile Creek, bk 10, pg
278.
1790 - 244 00 - twp 13
1800 - Cabarrus County

Davis, Thomas
1766 - listed in the militia company of Capt. Adam
Alexander of Clear Creek.
1777 - deed to Alexander Lewis for 45 acres on both
sides of Reedy Creek, deeded to Thomas by William
Spears, Test: Thomas Fadon (McFadden), and William
Newel, bk 10, pg 401.
1790 - 244 00 - twp 13
1800 - Cabarrus County

Davis, Walter
1764 - grant for 250 acres on the Gum branch of Long
Creek, no book or page number given.
1778 - witnessed a deed, with Robert and Jack Mulligan,
from James & Susannah Brown to Charles and Samuel
Calhoon on the Cataba River opposite the mouth of
Crowder's Creek, book 11, pg 166.
1790 - 345 08 - twp 2
Wife - Ann
Walter died in 1839 at the age of 71, buried at
Providence Church.

Davis, William
1780 - deed from William Barnett of Camden Dist., SC for
13 acres along the Waggon Road on the line between North
and South Carolina, Test: John Barnett, Jesse Price, and
Robert Armstrong, bk 10, pg 445.

Davis, William
1790 - 000 10 - twp 13

Dawson, James

1779 - witnessed a deed, with William Stephenson, from John and Joseph McDowel to Hugh Laurance on McDowel Creek, bk 10, pg 305.

Dean/Teem, Adam
1790 - 142 00 - twp 12
1794 - Account ledger of John Melchor's store.

Dean/Teem, Jacob
1784 - grant for 31 acres on Hamby's Run of Rockey River, adjoining Peter Ross, Jacob Faget, Michael Fogleman, and Charles Barnheart, bk 12, pg 137.
1790 - 201 00 - twp 12
1792 - Account ledger of John Melchor's store.

Deaton/Dorton, Mathew
1790 - 102 00 - twp 10

Deaver/Davis, Farmer
1783 - witnessed a deed, with Isaac Cook, to James Jack for lot 25 in Charlotte, bk 11, pg 294.
1783 - witnessed a deed, with Isaac Cook, from James Jack to James Orr for lot 25 in Charlotte, bk 11, pg 269.

Deasmond/Dermond, John
1776 - deed to John Wilson for 133 acres on the northwest side of McMichael Creek, Test: John Barett, Charles Alexander, and Will Reed, bk 11, pg 246.
1779 - grant for 34 acres on the east side of McMichle's Creek, adjoining Philip Meek, and John Wilson, bk 10, pg 495.
northwest side of McMichael's Creek.

Dearmond, Thomas
1769 - granted 182 acres on McCalpin's Creek that he later sold to Peter Johnston, referenced in bk 12, pg 404.
1772 - Loose estate papers

Debreel, Edward
1783 - named as a land owner on the Catawba River, bk 12, pg 208.

Delo/Dely, Michael
1779 - witnessed a deed, with William Courtney, from James and Margaret Potts to William Potts for 600 acres on the north side of Six Mile Creek joining Hugh McLile, and Archibald Crocket, bk 12, pg 272.
1779 - witnessed a deed, with William Courtney, from James and Margaret Potts to John Potts for 400 acres on Six Mile Creek joining John King, and William Courtney, bk 12, pg 248.

Delph, Peter & Eve
1777 - deed to Jacob Missonheimer for 150 acres on Lick branch of Buffalow Creek, Test: John Nichler, and Joseph Shenn (Shinn), bk 10, pg 240.

Demsey, John
1790 - 116 00 - twp 15

Dermond/Desmond, James

Residents of Mecklenburg County, North Carolina
1762-1790

1790 - 123 00 - twp 20
Derr/Dorr, Andrew
   1796 - Account ledger of John Melchor's store.
Derr/Dorr, Martin
   1793 - Account ledger of John Melchor's store.
Derr/Dorr, Phillip
   1793 - Account ledger of John Melchor's store.
Derr/Dorr, Ulrich
   1793 - Account ledger of John Melchor's store.
Desard, John
   1779 - named as an adjoining land owner to Job Williams on Stoney Creek beginning on the west side of the Waggon Road that goes from Charlotte to Salisbury, bk 10, pg 497.
Dickey, James
   1779 - named as an adjoining land owner to David Willson, John Farr, Ephraim Farr, and Nathaniel Erwin, bk 10, pg 503 and 504.
Dickey, John
   1785 - deed from William McCree to John Dickey, John Brevard, and William Sharp, for 435 acres in Rowan County on the branches of Davidson and Back Creeks, joining James McCullough, and Samuel Alison, Test: Ad Osborn, and Jacob Brown, bk 12, pg 574.
Dickson, Clebe
   1795 - Account ledger of John Melchor's store.
Dickson, James
   1778 - deed from John & Jane McCall for 93 acres on Clear Creek, Test: Samuel Montgomery, and John Wylie, bk 11, pg 56.
   1779 - deed from William Watson for 75 acres on Clear Creek, Test: John Jackson, David Moore, Andrew Moore, and Joseph Robbs, bk 11, pg 191.
   1790 - 112 00 - twp 14
   1793 - Account ledger of John Melchor's store.
Dickson, John
   1779 - witnessed a deed, with Thomas Rodgers, from Thomas Polk, attorney for David Oliphant, to James Black on Anderson Creek, bk 10, pg 313.
Dickson, Joseph
   1780 - witnessed a deed, with William Hutchison, from Moses Hutchison to Samuel Hart for lots 340, 341, and 342 in Charlotte, bk 11, pg 23.
Dillinger, Valintine
   1776 - Valentine's will was probated in Mecklenburg Co.
Dinkins, John & Polly
   1790 - 233 012 - twp 2
   1800 - Mecklenburg County
Dobbs, Alexander
   1754 - named as the original grantee of a tract on the north side of Cataba about 2 miles above the mouth of the 8th fork, bk 11, pg 33

Dobbs, Arthur & Justina
   1755 - Governor of the province of North Carolina,
   referenced in bk 12, pg 499, until 1785 when William
   Love's term began, see bk 12, pg 515.
   1764 - deed to Arthur McCay for 79 acres on both sides
   of Three Mile Creek, Test: Richard Berry, and Martin
   Fifer, bk 10, pg 435.
   1764 Little Coldwater Creek
   1784 - Governor Dobbs named as an adjoining land owner
   to William Penny, and James Ross on the west side of
   Buffalo Creek, Test: Samuel and John Moarton, bk 12, pg
   339.
Dodds, George
   1782 - deed to Joseph Davis for 100 acres on Sugar Creek
   adjoining James Johnston, Test: Joseph and James Davis,
   bk 11, pg 154.
   1784 Sugar Creek
Doherty/Daugherty, David
   1777 - Rocky River
   1790 - 100 00 - twp 7
   1800 - Mecklenburg County
Doherty, James
   1790 - 231 01 - twp 5
Doherty, James
   1790 - 001 00 - twp 9
Doherty, John
   1790 - Loose estate papers
Doherty, Widow (widow of John ?)
   1790 - 104 02 - twp 6
Dolin, Henry
   1790 - 123 00 - twp 11
   1800 - Cabarrus County
Donaldson, Andrew
   17?4 - Loose estate papers
Donaldson, Arthur
   1776 - Arthur's will was probated in Mecklenburg Co.
   1777 - Loose estate papers
   Children: Arthur, Ruth, Hannah
Donaldson, Arthur
   1784 - named as an adjoining land owner to Robert
   Cowden, John Alexander, Jr., Nathaniel Alexander, and
   Ezekiel Sharp on Coddle Creek and Rockey River, bk 12,
   pg 156.
   1790 - 125 00 - twp 15
   1800 - Cabarrus County
Donaldson/Donnelson, John
   1785 - witnessed a grant, along with Joseph Harris, to
   Emanuel Stephens on Crooked Creek, bk 12, pg 515.
   1785 - witnessed a deed, with Joseph Harris, from
   William Love to Manuel/Emanuel Stephens on Crooked
   Creek, bk 12, pg 527.

Residents of Mecklenburg County, North Carolina 1762-1790

1786 - witnessed a deed, with John Query, from Joseph and Jane Harris to Jonathan Query on Crooked Creek, bk 12, pg 591.
1790 - 125 00 - twp 15
Donaldson, Robert
1782 - witnessed a deed, with James Walker, from George Buckalow to Tunas Hogland on McCalpin's Creek, adjoining James McClure and James Clark, bk 12, pg 508.
1784 - Rob Donaldson witnessed a deed, with George McWherter, from William and Sarah Love to Emanuel Stephens on the south side of Crooked Creek, bk 12, pg 285.
1790 - 121 00 - twp 19
1800 - Mecklenburg County
Donaldson, William
1754 - named as original grantee of a tract on Six Mile Creek, no book or page number given.
Donnel, John
1785 - named in a deed from John Wilson to Dr. Thomas Donnel as the land owner of 50 acres he bought from William Wallace on Coddle Creek, bk 12, pg 533.
Donnell, Thomas, Dr.
1785 - witnessed a deed, with Thomas Harris, from David Wilson to John Alison, adjoining John Farr, and Nathaniel Ervin's old line, bk 12, pg 520.
Dorton, Charles
1790 - 162 00 - twp 13
1800 - Cabarrus County
Dorton, David(5)
David died Feb 9, 1847 at the age of 70.
Dorton/Deaton, Mathew
1790 - 102 00 - twp 10
Dorton, William
1784 - Loose estate papers
Dosber/Doster, James
1779 - grant to James on both sides of Richardson's Creek adjoining William Phillips, bk 12, pg 110.
1784 - witnessed a deed, with John Belk, from David and Hannah Griffith to Larence Shanepaker on the head of polecat branch of Linchous (Lynches) Creek, bk 12, pg 270.
1790 - 215 00 - twp 17
Doub, George
1792 - Loose estate papers
Douglas, James
1778 - witnessed a deed, with Francis Bassett, and John Haggins, from William Haggins to William Givens for 250 acres on McCorkle's branch of Twelve Mile Creek, bk 10, pg 49.
Douglas, Joseph & Margaret
1774 - Witnessed a deed from Joseph and Nancy Greer to Robert Crawford on Waxhaw Creek, bk 10, pg 246.

Residents of Mecklenburg County, North Carolina
1762-1790

1778 - witnessed a deed, with William Givens, and Henry Hurst, from Willliam Haggins to Abraham Cook for 202 acres between Waxhaw and Twelve Mile Creek, adjoining William Cook, bk 10, pg 394.
1779 - witnessed a bill of sale, along with William Haggons, and Moses Thomson, from William Killingsworth, of Craven Co., SC, to Archibald Alexander for one negro wench named Dinah, about 36 yrs old, bk 12, pg 381.
1779 - witnessed a deed, with William Reed, from Robert Graham to Robert Hays on Sugar Creek, bk 10, pg 340.
1780 - grant for 150 acres on the south side of Twelve Mile Creek adjoining John Wilson, Robert Crocket, and Michael Ligget, bk 12, pg 95.

Dove, Caleb
1790 - 114 00 - twp 12
1800 - Cabarrus County

Dove, George
1789 - Loose estate papers

Dow, John(8)
John died April 21, 1828

Dowel, Robert
1775 - witnessed a deed, with Benjamin Walace, from John and Elinor McDowel to Joseph Wallace, bk 10, pg 286.

Downs, Andrew & Anne
1774 - deed to John Morrow for 150 acres joining Zebulon Brevard, Test: John Maxwell, and Bartholomew Johnson, bk 10, pg 39.

Downs/Dawns, Henry
1772 - witnessed a deed, with James Tate, from James McClure to James Potts on the Flat Branch of Twelve Mile Creek, bk 10, pg 257.
1775 - Henry was one of the signers of the Mecklenburg Declaration of Independence on May 20, 1775.
1778 - named as an adjoining land owner to James Way, Robert Arthur, and Thomas Harrison Four Mile Creek, bk 10, pg 73.
1781 - witnessed a deed, with Thomas Downs, and John Robinson, from Robert Dunn to James Huston, bk 11, pg 248.
1790 - 200 03 - twp 19
Children: Thomas, Samuel, Jane (John ? Robinson), Milly (? Brewster)
Henry's will was probated Oct 1798.
Henry is buried in Providence Presbyterian Church Cemetery.

Downs/Dawns, Samuel
1790 - 102 01 - twp 19
1800 - Mecklenburg County
Son of Henry Downs

Downs/Dawns, Thomas

Residents of Mecklenburg County, North Carolina 1762-1790

1781 - witnessed a deed, with Henry Downs, and John Robinson, from Robert Dunn to James Huston, bk 11, pg 248.
1785 - witnessed a deed, with James Baxter, and Archibald Alexander, from John and Jean Baxter to Josiah Harrison on Sugar Creek, bk 12, pg 544.
1790 - 111 01 - twp 19
1800 - Mecklenburg County
Son of Henry Downs

Doyls, Thomas
1778 - Signer of 1778 Petition

Drennan, John
1779 - witnessed an indenture, along with John Walker, between Andrew Walker and Sarah Barns, mother of Mary Barns, bk 10, pg 310.

Driskel, John
1778 - deed from Robert Martin for 140 acres on Caldwell Creek, Test: William Driskel, and Robert Harris, Jr., bk 10, pg 5.
1780 - John Driskell, of Rowan Co., NC to James Carrothers of Mecklenburg Co., NC, 140 acres on Caldwell Creek, Test: Francis Ross, and William Scott, bk 11, pg 54.

Driskel, William
1778 - Signer of 1778 Petition
1778 - witnessed a deed, with Robert Harris, Jr., from Robert Martin to John Driskel for 140 acres on Caldwell Creek, bk 10, pg 5.

Drumond, Thomas
1781 - named as an adjoining land owner to James Fleniken, and John Barnett, Test: William Reed, David Fleniken, and John Clark, bk 11, pg 81.

Dry, Andrew & Barbara
Wife - Barbara Teem
Children: Daniel
Andrew was born March 26, 1762, died April 9, 1828, buried in St John's Evangelical Lutheran Church Cemetery.
Barbara was born July 14, 1765, March 19, 1848, buried in St John's Evangelical Lutheran Church Cemetery.

Dry, Charles & Christine
1790 - 123 00 - twp 12
Charles died before 1797. His estate settlement was by Owen Dry and divided between Charles' six children.

Dry, Eve
Eve was born Feb 1, 1757, died Nov 17, 1828, buried in St John's Evangelical Lutheran Church Cemetery.

Dry, Martin & Katherine
1790 - 222 00 - twp 11
1800 - Cabarrus County
Wife - Katherine Keppel
Children: Abraham (Mary Ann Harkey)

Martin was born July 10, 1759, died Dec 11, 1836, buried in St John's Evangelical Lutheran Church Cemetery.
Dry, Owen
    1790 - 133 00 - twp 12
    1800 - Cabarrus County
    Owen died March 5, 1820, buried in St John's Evangelical Lutheran Church Cemetery.
Dry, Phillip
    1790 - 101 00 - twp 12
    1800 - Cabarrus County
Duck, Abel
    1790 - 123 00 - twp 7
Duck, Absalom
    1790 - 131 00 - twp 7
Duck, George
    1790 - 142 00 - twp 7
Duck, George, Jr.
    1790 - 000 10 - twp 7
Duck, John
    1790 - 113 00 - twp 7
Duck, Simon
    1790 - 123 00 - twp 7
    1800 - Mecklenburg County
Duckworth, Abel Hankines
    1773 - witnessed a deed, with Robert Waddle, and William Graham, from John Jackson and Mary Moore to John Criswell on the Cataba River, bk 10, pg 90.
    1779 - witnessed a deed, with Simon Duckworth, from Gilbert & Margaret McNair to George Duckworth for 150 acres, being the same tract granted to Alexander Lewis in 1753, bk 11, pg 153.
Duckworth, George
    1779 - deed from Gilbert & Margaret McNair for 150 acres, being the tract granted to Alexander Lewis in 1753, Test: Simon Duckworth, and Abel Hankines Duckworth, bk 11, pg 153.
Duckworth, Simon
    1779 - witnessed a deed, with Abel Duckworth, from Gilbert & Margaret McNair to George Duckworth for 150 acres, being the same tract granted to Alexander Lewis in 1753, bk 11, pg 153.
Duckworth, William
    1772 - Loose estate papers
    Two of the Duckworth's married daughters of Alexander Allen, Jr.
Duff, Dennis
    Mentioned in the estate papers of Nicholson Ross 1774.
Dugal/McDugal, Thomas
    1790 - 100 00 - twp 7
Duglass, James, Esqr
    1778 -
    1790 - 133 01 - twp 15

Residents of Mecklenburg County, North Carolina 99
1762-1790

Duglass, Joseph & Margaret
    1774 -
    1779 -
    1780 - south side of Twelve Mile Creek
Duglass, Margaret
    1774 -
    Children: Thomas, Joseph, George, Margaret C. (?
    Canson), Jennette L. (? Lucas)
Dunbarr, Nathaniel
    1790 - 000 10 - twp 15
    1800 - Mecklenburg County
Dunlap, Gilbert
    1782 - named as an adjoining land owner to George
    Heloms, on Camp Branch of Richardson's Creek, bk 12, pg
    159.
Dunlap, Samuel
    1754 - named as a land owner along the Waggon Road on
    the line between North and South Carolina in 1754,
    adjoining William Davis, bk 10, pg 445.
Dunlap, William & Agnes Carnes
Dunn, Andrew
    1784 - deed from Thomas Polk for 660 acres on Long
    Creek, adjoining Thomas Clark, Gideon Thompson, and
    William Lawing, Test: Robert Dunn and Andrew Lawing, bk
    12, pg 283.
    1785 - deed to John Dun for 186 acres on Long Creek,
    originally granted to John Anderson in 1765, then to
    Thomas Polk, then Andrew Dunn, Test: John Buchannon, and
    Arthur Jamison, bk 12, pg 519.
    1785 - deed to Robert Dune for 136 acres on Long Creek,
    Test: John Bewhannon, and Arthur Jamison, bk 12, pg 541.
    1785 - deed to James Dunn for 186 acres on Long Creek,
    Test: John Buchannon, and Arthur Jamison, bk 12, pg 543.
    Brothers: Robert, James, John
    Sisters: Betty (? Jamison), Peggy (? Kincaid)
Dunn, Andrew & Mary
    1790 - 126 00 - twp 15
    Children: Andrew, James, Thomas, Jane (John Gibbons),
    Elizabeth (Thomas Spratt), Martha, Mary
    1800 - Mecklenburg County
    Andrew died in 1805, age 54, buried at Providence
    Church.
Dunn, Andrew, Sr. & Isabella
    1779 - Cataba River and Long Creek.
    1790 - 202 02 - twp 6
    Children: Robert, Andrew, James, Thomas, 6 daughters
    Andrew's will was probated Jan 1791.
Dunn, James & Elizabeth
    1781 - named as an adjoining land owner to Robert Dunn,
    and James Huston, bk 11, pg 248.
    1790 - 100 00 - twp 6
    Son of Andrew & Isabella Dunn

Dunn, James & Martha
　　1778 - named as as adjoining land owner to William
　　Givens, and Robert Scott,Test: Hugh Pollock, and John
　　Davies, bk 10, pg 279.
　　1790 -212 00 - twp 15
　　Children: Margaret, Martha, Elizabeth, James (Elizabeth)
　　James died Dec 1799, age 77, buried at Providence
　　Church.
Dunn, James
　　1800 - Loose estate papers
Dunn, John & Jane Elliot
　　1785 - deed from Andrew Dun for a tract on Long Creek,
　　Test: Arthur Jamison, John Buchannon, bk 12, pg 519.
　　Wife - Jane Elliott, daughter of George Elliott
　　Brother of Andrew Dunn.
Dunn, Robert & Ann
　　1781 - deed to James Huston for 112 acres, Test: John
　　Robinson and Thomas and Henry Downs, bk 11, pg 248.
　　1790 - 112 00 - twp 6
　　Brother of Andrew Dunn
　　Son of Andrew Dunn.
Dunn, Simon
　　1790 - 000 10 - twp 13
Dunn, William & Mary(2)
　　1779 - grant for 200 acres on King's branch of Sugar
　　Creek adjoining Ezekiel Polk, John Baird, Alexander
　　McClelan, Phineas Alexander, and Charles Alexander, bk
　　10, pg 502.
　　1790 - 124 00 - twp 2
　　1800 - Mecklenburg County
　　Children: Thomas, Hugh, Martha, Margaret.
　　William died May 15, 1809, at age 70.
Dunsmore, Mary(2)
　　died Oct 2, 1790 at age 75
Dupry, Paul
　　1773 - Loose estate papers
Dupley, Paul
　　1782 - named as an adjoining land owner to Jacob Phifer,
　　and Michael Clause on Dutch Buffalow Creek, bk 12, pg
　　93.
Duyne, Darby & Hannah
　　1787 - Darby's will was probated in Mecklenburg Co.
Dysart, Cornelius & Charity
　　Wife - Charity Jack, daughter of Patrick & Lillis McAdoo
　　Jack.
　　Children: James, Robert
　　Cornelius died soon after the Revolutionary War.
Dysart/Disart, James
　　1773 - deed to Ephraim Farr for 130 acres on Rockey
　　River adjoining Mitchel's Barony line, Test: David
　　Wilson, and   ?   Farr, bk 11, pg 169.

1781 - named as an adjoining land owner of James Barr, Margaret Wallace, and John Levison on Rockey River at the Baroney line, also called Mitchel's Barony line, bk 11, pg 79.
1783 - named as an adjoining land owner to Jacob Agner, and Thomas Polk on Dutch Buffalo Creek, bk 12, pg 389.
1784 - named as an adjoining land owner to Robert Martin on Rocky River, bk 12, pg 308.
Children: John

Dysart/Disart, John & Margaret
1779 - south side of Rocky River on the Welch tract.
1781 - John Dysert of Burke Co., NC to Samuel Alexander for 167 acres in the Welch tract on the south side of Rockey River, Test: Thomas Nickel and James Pattom, bk 11, pg 137.
Son of James Dysert.

Dysart/Disart, John & Ruth
1779 - named as an adjoining land owner to Henry and Ann Sadler, John McCandless, and Andrew Elliott on Mallard and Stoney Creek, bk 12, pg 614.
1779 - deed to Robert Craighead for 185 acres on Millard and Stoney Creeks, adjoining Robert Scott, and another tract for 180 acres, adjoining the above tract and beginning by the wagon road, Test: Nathaniel and Andrew Alexander, bk 10, pg 398.

Eadger, William
1778 - deed on Long Creek, bk 10, pg 88
1784 - deed on Anderson Creek, bk 10, pg 206.
Children: Adam.

Eafrit, Jacob
1790 - 112 00 - twp 12

Eager/Edgar, Adam
1777 - witnessed a deed, with Robert Harris, Jr., from Robert Harris and Nathaniel Alexander to Samuel White, for the use of the Presbyterian Congregation, bk 10, pg 206.
1784 - deed to Adam and William Edgar from John and Elizabeth Caldwell for 200 acres on Anderson Creek, Test: Samuel and Archibald White, bk 12, pg 401.
1790 - 213 03 - twp 13
Son of William.

Eager/Eadger, Hugh
1768 - deed to James Bradshaw for 63 acres on Rocky River, Test: Robert Harris, and Robert Harris, Jr., bk 10, pg 118.
1778 - witnessed a deed, with Joseph Kerr, from John and Sarah Allen to William Eadger for 280 acres on a branch of Long Creek, bk 10, pg 88.
1790 -124 00 - twp 13

Edgar, William

1778 - deed from John & Sarah Allen for 280 acres on a branch of Long Creek, Test: Joseph Kerr, Hugh Edgar, bk 10, pg 88.
1784 - deed to Adam and William Edgar from John and Elizabeth Caldwell for 200 acres on Anderson Creek, Test: Samuel and Archibald White, bk 12, pg 401.
Eagle, John
   1784 - named as an adjoining land owner to Jacob Teem, and Frederick Hertough on Hamby's Run of Rocky River, bk 12, pg 145.
   Children: Phillip
Eagle/Eagley, Phillip
   1790 - 123 00 - twp 10
Eakins, John
   1790 - 104 00 - twp 15
Easenhart/Earnhart, George
   1790 - 113 00 - twp 11
   1793 - Account ledger of John Melchor's store.
Easter, James
   1774 - witnessed a deed, with Samuel Jack, to William Davison for lot 52 in Charlotte, bk 10, pg 163.
Edminson, James
   1766 - listed in the militia company of Capt. Adam Alexander of Clear Creek.
Edmiston, John
   1790 - 124 00 - twp 5
Edwards, John
   1775 - John's will was probated in Mecklenburg Co.
   Children: John
Edwards, John & Penellopy
   1776 - Loose estate papers for John
   1778 - Loose estate papers for Penellopy
Eisenhart, Henrey
   1764 - Loose estate papers
Elga/Algia, Francis
   1790 - 121 00 - twp 1
   1800 - Mecklenburg County
   Wife - Mary
   Francis' will was probated in 1794.
Elkins, Shadrick
   1790 - 113 00 - 15
   1800 - Mecklenburg County
Elliot, Andrew & Esther
   1779 - named as an adjoining land owner to John McCandless, Henry and Ann Sadler, and John Disart on Mallard Creek, bk 12 pg 614.
   1781 - deed from Andrew & Ester, of Wake Co., GA, to Samuel Linton for 200 acres on Mallard Creek, Test: Arthur Elliot, and John Linton, bk 11, pg 29.
Elliott, Arthur

1781 - witnessed a deed, with John Linton, from Andrew &
Esther Elliot of Wake Co., GA, to Samuel Linton on
Mallard Creek, bk 11, pg 29.
Elliott, Edward
1780 - witnessed a deed, with Dun Ochiltree, from Robert
Elliot to James Jack on the west side of Sugar Creek, bk
11, pg 59.
Elliot, George
1790 - 333 03 - twp 6
1800 - Mecklenburg County
Children: Jane (John Dunn)
Elliott, James
1772 - James' will was probated in Mecklenburg Co.
Children: Robert, Isabella
Elliott, Joseph, Jr.
1782 - deed from Benjamin Alexander for a tract in SC on
the east side of Broad River on Bell Creek-a branch of
Bullock's Creek, Test: John McNitt Alexander, bk 11, pg
100.
Son of Joseph Elliot, Sr.
Elliott, Joseph, Sr.
1779 - Joseph's will was probated in Mecklenburg Co.
Children: Joseph
Elliott, Robert & Martha
1783 - named as adjoining land owner to William
Hutchison, Robert Elliott, and William Elliott on the
head waters of Sugar Creek, bk 11, pg 209.
Robert was mentioned in the estate settlement of William
Sample.
Elliott, Robert
1767 - grant on Sugar Creek, no book or page number
given, bk 11, pg 274.
1780 - deed to James Jack for 100 acres on the west side
of Sugar Creek, Test: Edward Elliot, and Dun Ochiltree,
bk 11, pg 59.
1782 - Loose estate papers
Children: William ?, Samuel ?
Elliott, Samuel
1780 - witnessed a deed, with James Jack from William
Elliot to Joseph Nicholson on Sugar Creek, bk 11, pg 73.
1783 - deed from John Barnett for 179 acres on Sugar
Creek, Test: Phineas Alexander and John Barnett, bk 12,
pg 278.
1783 - named as an adjoining land owner to James Jack,
and Phineas Alexander on Sugar Creek, bk 11, pg 274.
1790 - 234 01 - twp 3
1800 - Mecklenburg County
Elliott, Solomon
1772 - Solomon's will was probated in Mecklenburg Co.
Children: John
Elliott, Thomas

1783 - witnessed a deed, with Robert Irwin, from James
Jack to Phineas Alexander on Sugar Creek, bk 11, pg 274.
1790 - 302 02 - twp 3
Elliot, William
1779 - witnessed a deed, with Robert Abernathy, from
Robert Scott to James Houston on Six Mile Creek, bk 10,
pg 317.
1780 - deed to Joseph Nicholson for 158 acres on Sugar
Creek, Test: James Jack, and Samuel Elliot, bk 11, pg
73.
1782 - deed to James Witherspoon for lots 115 and 123 in
Charlotte, Test: Hugh Harris, and Robert McCleary, bk
11, pg 143.
1782 - named as an adjoining land owner to John Sample
on the head waters of Sugar Creek, bk 12, pg 189.
1783 - named as an adjoining land owner to Joseph
Nicholson, and William Hutchison on Sugar Creek, bk 11,
pg 209.
Son of Robert Elliot ?
Elliot, William
1790 - 000 10 - twp 6
Ellis, William
1779 - witnessed a deed, with Robert Abernathy, from
Robert Scott to James Houston on Twelve Mile Creek, bk
10, pg 333.
Emerson, Henry & Nancy
1790 -111 00 - twp 3
1800 - Mecklenburg County
Revolutionary Soldier - Henry was born in 1760 according
to an 1840 pension list, and he died Sept 5, 1842, age
84 according to The Charlotte Journal.
Nancy died in April 1846, age 81 according to The
Charlotte Journal dated May 1, 1846.
Emmerson, James
1790 - 114 04 - twp 7
1800 - Mecklenburg County
England, Daniel & Martha
1763 - deed to Joseph Young for 214 acres on Coddle
Creek, adjoining John Alexander, Test: John Griffee, and
John Whitt Alexander, bk 10, pg 126.
Epelman/Apelman, James
1786 - witnessed a deed, with Thomas Lackey, and Samuel
Farr, from Denis & Mary Fittes to Alexander Carns on
Waxhaw Creek, bk 12, pg 612.
Erwin, Christor/Christopher
1790 - 106 00 - twp 20
1796 - Loose estate papers
Erwin, Edward
1790 -115 00 - twp 6
1790 - Edward's will was probated in Mecklenburg Co.
Children: John, Robert
Erwin, Nathaniel

Residents of Mecklenburg County, North Carolina 1762-1790

   1779 - named as an adjoining land owner to David
   Willson, John Farr, Ephraim Farr, and James Dickey, bk
   10, pg 503 and 504.
Erwin/Irwin, Robert & Hannah
   1777 - deed to John Wier for 315 acres, adjoining John
   Price, and Alexander Cathey, originally granted to James
   Armour, and another tract of 212 acres joining the
   first, beginning at the upper edge of the Mill Creek,
   originally granted to Andrew Armour in 1761.
   1786 - deed from William Ervin for 124 acres on
   McCalpin's Creek, Test: John & Catherine Foard, bk 12,
   pg 576.
   1790 - 226 03 - twp 2
Erwin/Irwin, Robert
   1784 - witnessed a deed, with William Briance, from
   James and Jean Davis to Walter Phair, on the south side
   of Rockey River, bk 12, pg 350.
   1790 - 122 01 - twp 5
   1800 - Cabarrus County
Erwin/Irwin, Samuel
   1790 - 111 01 - twp 7
Erwin/Irwin, Thomas
   1790 - 124 00 - twp 8
   1800 - Cabarrus County
Erwin/Irwin, Thomas
   1785 - witnessed a deed, with Samuel Black, from William
   & Sarah Erwin to John Black for 100 acres on McCalpin's
   Creek, bk 12, pg 441.
   1790 - 112 00 - twp 15
Erwin/Ervin, William & Sarah
   1779 - McCalpin's Creek (twp 15)
   1790 - 303 00 - twp 15
   1800 - Mecklenburg County
Erwin/Irwin, William, Jr.
   1790 - 111 00 - twp 15
Erwin, William
   1782 - named as an adjoining land owner to James Russle,
   James White, Michael Winecoff, and George McMaster on a
   draft of the three mill branches, bk 12, pg 86.
Espy, Samuel
   Wife - Elizabeth Sloan, Mary
   Samuel was born 1757, died Dec 29, 1838
   Elizabeth was born Nov 7, 1759, died Dec 23, 1812
   Mary was born 1774, died March 6, 1846
   All three are buried in Long Creek Presbyterian Church
   Cemetery, Gaston County.
Esselman/Emmerson, James
   1790 - 114 04 - twp 7
   1800 - Mecklenburg County
Evalt/Evatt, Jacob
   1790 - 222 00 - twp 11
   1800 - Cabarrus County

Evalt/Evatt, Michael
    1790 - 142 00 - twp 11
Evitts, William
    1790 - 213 00 - twp 7
Ewart, Joseph & Agnes
    1780 - deed to Alexander Robison for 106 acres on the branches of Rockey River adjoining Benjamin Brown, Test: John Davis, and William Bickens (Pickens), bk 10, pg 440.
    1790 - 234 00 - twp 6
    1800 - Mecklenburg County
Ewart, Robert & Margaret
    1777 - deed from Richard Stevenson to John McKnitt Alexander, of Mecklenburg and Robert Ewart, of Tryon County, on Garr Creek including Hopewell Meeting House, bk 12, pg 472.
    1781 - Robert's will was probated in Lincoln Co.
    Margaret died in 1805.
Ewart, Robert
    1764 - grant to Robert on the branches of Rockey River, no bk or page number given.
    Children: Joseph
    1764 - Robert's will was probated in Mecklenburg Co.
Ewart, Samuel
    1799 - Loose estate papers
Ewens, John
    1796 - Loose estate papers
Faden/McFaden, Thomas
    1777 - witnessed deed, with William Newell, between Thomas Davis and Alexander Lewis on both sides of Reedy Creek, bk 10, pg 401.
    1782 - grant from North Carolina on Anderson Creek next to William Newell, bk 12, pg 140.
    1782 - adjoining Francis Newell and Robert McEachin, bk 12, pg 46
    1790 - 111 00 - twp 13
Faggenwinter, Christian
    1790 - 101 00 - twp 10
Faggett, Jacob & Anna
    1777 - witnessed a deed, with Elias Foust, from Frederick Fisher, Jr. to Martin Fisher on the ridge between Coldwater and Adam's Creek, bk 10, pg 205.
    1784 - grant for 296 acres on Adam's Creek, adjoining Peter Hope, Michael Fogleman, and Martin Phifer, bk 12, pg 146.
    1790 - 223 00 - 12
    1794 - Account ledger of John Melchor's store.
    1800 - Cabarrus County
    Wife - Anna Maria Fisher
    Children: Jacob (Margaret Bost), Daniel (Mary Elizabeth Bost)

Jacob was born 1721, died aug 14, 1800, buried in St
John's Evangelical Lutheran Church Cemetery.
Anna was born 1736, died 1790, buried in St John's
Evangelical Lutheran Church Cemetery.
Faggett, Moses
   1790 - 124 01 - twp 17
Faggott, Valentine & Elizabeth
   1790 - 102 00 - twp 12
   1794 - Account ledger of John Melchor's store.
   1800 - Cabarrus County
   Wife - Elizabeth Smith, daughter of Henry & Mary Barbara
   Smith, married Jan 8, 1789.
   Children: Milly (Solomon Bost), Sophia (Jacob C.
   Goodman)
   Valentine was born Dec 4, 1763, died May 2, 1830, buried
   in St John's Evangelical Lutheran Church Cemetery.
   Elizabeth was born Nov 14, 1770, died Aug 17, 1846,
   buried in St John's Evangelical Lutheran Church
   Cemetery.
Faggart, Solomon & Sophia
   Children: William Ritz, George Ephraim, Elias Franklin,
   Henry Graber, Daniel Chalmers, Paul Alexander, John
   Caldwell, Margaret Adeline (Mathias J. Bost), Amilia
   Elizabeth
Faires, James & Margaret Alexander(4)
   James died in 1808.
   Brother: William Faires
   Sisters-Mary Wright, Ann Neaper, Jane Wilson, dec'd.
Fair, Walter(5)
   Walter died Dec 22, 1799 at the age of 59.
Farr/Pharr, Ephraim
   1773 - deed from James Dysart for 130 acres on Rockey
   River, Test: David Wilson, and ? Farr, bk 11, pg 169.
   1775 - witnessed a deed, with William Gardner, from
   Samuel Morton to John Farr for 118 acres on the ridge
   between Coddle Creek and Alton's Run adjoining John
   Frohock, bk 10, pg 173.
   1779 - named as an adjoining land owner to John Hughs,
   David Wilson, John McAbley, and Nathaniel Erwin on
   Coddle Creek, bk 10, pg 493 and 503.
   1778 - Signer of 1778 Petition
   1779 - grant for 150 acres on Coddle Creek, adjoining
   John Farr, John Hughes, and Archibald Houston, bk 10, pg
   517.
   1784 - Ephraim's will was probated in Mecklenburg Co.
   Children: Ephraim, James, Samuel
   1785 - Loose estate papers
Farr, Ephraim
   1784 - deed from Martin Phifer, Sr. for 300 acres on
   Caudle Creek adjoining David Templeton, Test: Archibald
   Houston, Richard Trotter, and William Fraser, bk 12, pg
   366.

1784 - grant for 30 and 5/10 acres on Rockey River joining Hugh Hambleton, deceased, Robert Andrews, and John Graham, deceased, bk 12, pg 178.
1785 - deed to Archibald Houston for 150 acres, half of the 300 acre tract granted to Ephraim in 1779, adjoining John Hughes, Test: David Wilson, bk 12, pg 481.
1785 - deed to John & William Hamilton for 130 acres joining Mitchel's Barony line, Test: Joseph Sharp, and David Wilson, bk 12, pg 531.

Farr, Henry
1784 - deed from Mathias & Sarah Bostian for 100 acres on Coldwater Creek, adjoining John Luther, Governor Dobbs, and Paul Harrin, Test: Joseph Shinn, and Jacob Crider, bk 12, pg 459.

Farr, John & Margaret
1771 - witnessed a deed, with Alexander Wallace, from John McLilley to John McKnitt Alexander on the eastern branches of Mallard Creek, adjoining Moses Alexander, bk 11, pg 192.
1775 - deed from Samuel Morton for 118 acres on the ridge between Coddle Creek and Alton's Run, adjoining John Frohock, bk 10, pg 173.
1777 Coddle Creek
1778 - Signer of 1778 Petition.
1779 - named as an adjoining land owner to Nathaniel Erwin, bk 10, pg 503.
1790 - 156 00 - twp 10

Farr, Margt
1790 - 202 06 - twp 8
Widow of John

Farr, Samuel
1779 - near Waxhaw Creek
1786 - witnessed a deed, with James Epelman, and Thomas Lackey, from Denis & Mary Fittes to Alexander Carns on Waxhaw Creek, bk 12, pg 612.
Children: Samuel, James B., Elizabeth, Margaret (? Reid), Hannah A. (? Farr)

Farr/Pharr, Samuel
Children: Catherine (? Nicholson), Samuel, Sarah (? Rogers), Walter Franklin, Hugh S., Jane (? McCacheron)
Samuel was born April 10, 1777, died May 16, 1844, buried in Pharr Family Cemetery, Cabarrus Co.

Farr/Phair, Walter
1780 - named as an adjoining land owner to John Means, James White, James Baker, William McWhirter, and Mr. Archibald on Wolf Meadow Branch of Coddle Creek, bk 12, pg 77.
1784 - deed from James & Jean Davis for 114 acres on the south side of Rockey River, being the place conveyed for Samuel Craford, Test: William Briance, and Robert Ervin, bk 12, pg 550.

1790 - 254 01 - twp 10
1800 - Cabarrus County
Children: John, Samuel, Robert
Walter's will was proven in April 1801.

Farrior, Henry
   1769 - Henry's will was probated in Mecklenburg Co.
   Children: John, Paul

Farris, John
   1780 - deed from James Sawyer for 400 acres on Sugar Creek adjoining Moses Steel, witnessed Moses Swann, and David Hayns, bk 11, pg 122.

Farris, Walter
   1782 - named as adjoining land owner to John and William Means on Coddle Creek, bk 12, pg 75.

Farrow, Paul
   1785 - witnessed a deed, with Lewis Wilham, and Quadray Wilonlee, from George & Susan Karriker to John George William for 100 acres on a branch of Rockey River including Peter Rea's and James Cuntress' improvements, adjoining James Beatchey, bk 12, pg 592.

Faulkner, Thomas
   1783 - witnessed a deed, with Samuel Patton, from Robert & Hannah Craighead to Job Williams on both sides of Stoney Creek, bk 12, pg 224.

Ferguson, Alexander & Mary
   1775 - named as an adjoining land owner to Robert Russell, Sr., James Russel, and David Purviance on the west side of Buffalow Creek, bk 12, pg 445.
   1783 - named as an adjoining land owner to John Setsinger, George Crozine (Corzine), John Weyle (Wylie), John Shaver, and James Morrison on Coldwater and Buffalow Creek, bk 12, pg 149.
   1790 - 142 03 - twp 13
   1800 - Cabarrus County
   Children: Robert
Alexander died 1801.

Ferguson, Moses & Martha(2)
   1764 - witnessed deeds, with Samuel Bigham, and Robert Leeper, from Andrew Armour to James Armour on the south side of Catawba River between Croders Creek and Allison Creek, Vol. 1, pg 550 & 592.
   1770 - deed from Moses & Martha (of Tryon Co., NC), and Samuel & Mary Knox (of Meck. Co., NC), to Francis and Joseph Johnston, for 400 acres on east side of Catawba and SE side of path leading from Jean Armour's to the Catawba Nations, Test: Thomas Neely, Hugh Neely, and Alexander Johnston, Vol 5, pg 198.
Martha died Oct 27, 1778 at the age of 58.

Ferguson, Samuel
   1781 - deed for 100 acres and personal property to his daughter, Agnes, Test: Samuel Martin, Hugh Pollock, and Thomas Harris, bk 11, pg 259.

1786 - Samuel's will was probated in Mecklenburg Co.
Children: Agnes, Alexander, Mattie

Ferguson, Thomas & Eleanor(2)
   1775 - deed from Samuel Knox on Steel Creek joining William Barnett, George Cahoon, John Henry, and Edward Williams, Test: James Tate, Robert Maxwell, and John Bigham, bk 10, pg 251
   1790 - 233 012 - twp 2
   Thomas died Jan 20, 1795 at age 66 and his will was probated in Mecklenburg Co.
   Children: William, unnamed daughter who married Joseph Wilson.
   Grandchildren: Eleanor Wilson, Martha Wilson, Thomas Wilson, David Wilson, Robert Wilson.

Ferguson, Widow
   1790 - 002 05 - twp 10

Ferguson, William & Mary Bigham(2), Sarah Moore
   1790 - 100 00 - twp 2
   1800 - Mecklenburg County
   Children: Polly, Martha, Sarah, Jane Elizabeth, Thomas, William, Alexander, John.
   Son of Thomas & Eleanor Ferguson.
   Mary died Feb 6, 1795.

Ferrier, Thomas
   1778 - Signer of 1778 Petition.

Ferrill, Gabriel
   1790 - 112 00 - twp 6
   1800 - Mecklenburg County

Ferrill, John
   1790 - 121 00 - twp 6

Ferrill, William
   1779 - deed from William Hambilton for 100 acres on Waxhaw Creek, adjoining John Rogers, Test: John McClanahan, and Robert Crocket, bk 11, pg 67.

Ferril, William
   William's parents were neighbors of James & Frances Sloan, William Brown, and the Christenberry's. before 1800 according to the pension papers of James Sloan.

Fesperman, Fredrick
   1790 - 104 00 - twp 11
   Son of Frederick & Christina Fesperman

Fesperman/Festerman, Henry
   1782 - Loose estate papers

Fesperman, Henry & Christina
   1790 - 101 00 - twp 11
   1791 - Loose estate papers
   Wife - Christina
   Children: Michael, John, Frederick, Henry (dec'd), Margaret (Henry Ritchie)
   1791 - Henry's will was written, and probated in Mecklenburg Co., buried in St John's Evangelical Lutheran Church Cemetery.

Residents of Mecklenburg County, North Carolina 1762-1790

Fesperman, John
   1794 - Account ledger of John Melchor's store.
Fesperman, Michael
   1790 - 145 00 - twp 11
   1800 - Cabarrus County
   Son of Frederick & Christina Fesperman
Fesperman, Michael
   Son of Henry & Christina Fesperman
   Michael was born 1740, died 1806, buried in St John's Evangelical Lutheran Church Cemetery.
Fifer, see Phifer
File, George
   1778 - Signer of 1778 Petition
   1784 - named as an adjoining land owner to Henry Soceman, and George Sticklether on Dutch Buffalow Creek, bk 12, pg 131.
File, John
   1794 - Account ledger of John Melchor's store.
Fincher, James
   1790 - 142 00 - twp 16
   1800 - Mecklenburg County
Fincher, Jonathan
   1790 - 236 00 - twp 16
   1800 - Mecklenburg County
Fincher, Richard
   1790 - 124 00 - twp 16
Findly/Finly, John
   1781 - named as an adjoining land owner to Archibald Ramsey, John Tanner, and John Mitchel on Coddle Creek, Test: William Ramsey, and Isabel Robison, bk 11, pg 85.
   1790 - 101 00 - twp 17
   1800 - Mecklenburg County
Fine, John
   1778 - Signer of 1778 Petition.
Fink, David
   1790 - 122 00 - twp 12
   1800 - Cabarrus County
Fink, George
   1790 - 101 00 - twp 12
   1794 - Account ledger of John Melchor's store.
Finley, Alexander
   1779 - witnessed a deed, with Margaret McCurdy, from Michael Liggett to Grace Harrison for one negro woman named Levinia, bk 11, pg 31.
Finley, Charles
   1790 - 000 10 - twp 16
   Son of James Finley
Finley/Findley, James
   1779 - named as the land owner of a tract on Caldwell's Creek, sold to him by Abner Nash, no book or page number given, bk 10, pg 351.
   1790 - 102 00 - twp 16

Children: William, Charles, James, George, Jannett, Martha (Daniel Robertson), female (Wm. Chapel) James witnessed a bill of sale, along with John Cochran, between James Harris and James Maxwell, bk 10, pg 318, no date given.

Findley, John
  1766 - listed in the militia company of Capt. Adam Alexander of Clear Creek.
  1776 - in Capt. Charles Polk's Light Horse Company.

Finley, Thomas
  1766 - listed in the militia company of Capt. Adam Alexander of Clear Creek.
  1783 - deed to Hugh Patterson for 189 acres on Rockey River adjoining James Dysart, Test: Samuel Killough, and James Stephenson, bk 12, pg 393.
  Son of James Finley

Finley, William
  1790 - 000 10 - twp 16
  Son of James Finley

Finney, Alexander
  1780 - witnessed a deed, with Margaret McCurdy, from Adam Alexander to Samuel Montgomery on Clear Creek, bk 11, pg 70.

Finney/Fenney, Eleanor
  1783 - grant for 91 acres on Four Mile Creek, bk 12, pg 629.
  Children: Elizabeth, Catron (? Moore), Mary (? Gallbreath), Susannah (? Morgan)

Finney, James
  1783 - witnessed a deed, with William Miller, from Robert McGinty to William Kennedy on McCalpin's Creek, bk 12, pg 491.
  1784 - named as an adjoining land owner to James & Elizabeth Maxwell on Rockey River bk 12, pg 364.

Finney, John & Rachel
  1785 - named as an adjoining land owner to George Garmon, George Kizer, John Letsinger/Setsinger, Peter Reap, and John Biger, Test: Michael Garmon, and Adam Alexander, bk 12, pg 484.
  Children: Mary (? Long), Rachel (? Winchester), Thomas, Alexander, John

Fisher, Charles
  1790 - 101 00 - twp 17
  1800 - Mecklenburg County
  Children: William, John, Frederick, Paul, Mary (? Starnes)

Fisher, Frederick, Sr.
  1767 - deed to Martin Fisher for 149 acres on the ridge between Coldwater and Adam's Creek, no book or page number given, bk 10, pg 205.
  Children: Martin

Fisher, Frederick, Jr. & (Dutch ?)

1777 - deed to Martin Fisher for 149 acres on the ridge
between Coldwater and Adam's Creek being the land that
was granted to Martin Fisher, by Frederick Fisher, Sr.
in 1767, and from Martin Fisher to Frederick Fisher, Jr.
in 1774, bk 10, pg 205.
1790 - 122 00 - twp 17
1800 - Mecklenburg County

Fisher, George
1790 - 201 00 - twp 15
1800 - Mecklenburg County

Fisher, John
1790 - 122 00 - twp 17
1800 - Mecklenburg County
Children: Rosetta (Tobias Miller)

Fisher, Lewis & Christina
1790 - 104 00 - twp 12
1800 - Cabarrus County
Children: John (Elizabeth Cline)
Christina was born Jan 1, 1768, died Sept 9, 1845,
buried in St John's Evangelical Lutheran Church
Cemetery.

Fisher, Martin
1767 - deed from Frederick Fisher, Sr., for 149 acres on
the ridge between Coldwater and Adam's Creek, no book or
page number given, bk 10, pg 205.

Fisher, Paul & Mary
1790 - 101 00 - twp 17 (near Waxhaw Creek)
1800 - Mecklenburg County
Children: Martin, William, Sylvanus, Rachel, Mary,
Arnold, unborn child.

Fisher, William
1790 - 112 00 - twp 17
1800 - Mecklenburg County

Fisherman, Henry (See Henry Fesperman)
Fitten, Isaiah (see Isaiah Chitten)
Fittes, Dennis & Mary
1786 - deed to Alexander Carns for 44 ¼ acres on Waxhaw
Creek, Test: James Epleman, Thomas Lackey, and Samuel
Farr, adjoining George McWhorter, bk 12, pg 612.

Flenniken, Charles
1790 - 101 00 - twp 6
1800 - Mecklenburg County

Fleniken, David
1781 - witnessed a deed, with William Reed, and John
Clark, from James Flaniken to John Barnett, bk 11, pg
81.
1784 - deed from John, Samuel, David and James
Flenniken to John Smith for 198 acres on McCalpin's
Creek, Test: James Bays, and John Kirkpatrick, bk 12, pg
587.
1790 - 183 00 - twp 20
1800 - Mecklenburg County

Flannigan, Dennis
   1779 - grant for 100 acres on both sides of Crooked
   Creek, bk 10, pg 492.
Flenniken, James
   1779 - James' will was probated in Mecklenburg Co.
   Children: David
Flaniken, James
   1779 - named as an adjoining land owner to Alexander
   McClellan, Robert Barns, Archibald McNeal, and Samuel
   Linton, no book and page number given, and no
   watercoarse named.
   1781 - deed to John Barnett for 172 acres on both sides
   of McCalpin's Creek, adjoining Thomas Drumond, Test:
   William Reed, David Faniken, and John Clark, bk 11, pg
   81.
   1782 - grant for 100 acres on Medon's Branch of Rockey
   River, bk 12, pg 37.
   1782 - named as an adjoining land owner to Samuel
   Linton, Alexander McClellan, and John Bigham on King's
   Branch of Sugar Creek, bk 12, pg 108.
   1784 - see David Fleniken.
   Son of William Flaniken.
Flenikin, John
   1761 - deed from John M.L. Alexander and Henry and Jane
   Person, for Joseph Sample, deceased, for 200 acres on
   McCalpin's Creek, bk 10, pg 392.
   1775 - John was one of the signers of the Mecklenburg
   Declaration of Independence on May 20, 1775.
   1779 - witnessed a deed, with Thomas Harris, from John
   Smith to Andrew Neel on Twelve Mile Creek, bk 11, pg 52.
   1780 - witnessed a deed, with John Stewart, from Robert
   & Sarah Arthur to James Kenedy on Four Mile Creek, bk
   11, pg 2.
   1784 - see David Fleniken.
   John is buried in Providence Presbyterian Church
   Cemetery.
Flenniken, Samuel
   1774 - witnessed a deed from John Allain to James
   Osburne on the waters of Rockey River and the Cataba
   River, adjoining John Frohock, bk 10, pg 111.
   1778 - witnessed a deed, with William Pickens, and John
   Smith, from William Black to Thomas Black, bk 10, pg
   362.
   1779 - grant for 100 acres on Four Mile Creek and
   McCalpin's Creek, bk 10, pg 534.
   1780 - named as an adjoining land owner to Neal Morrison
   on McCalpin's Creek, bk12, pg 99.
   1784 - see David Fleniken.
Flaniken/Flanagan, William
   1781 - named as land owner of 172 acres on both sides of
   McCalpin's Creek, bk 11, pg 81.
   1780- McCalpin's Creek (twp 15)

1784 - named as an adjoining land owner to Peter
Johnston, Hadawick Davies, and William Yandle on
McCalpin's Creek, bk 12, pg 404.
Children: James
Flaugh/Flough/Flow, David
1766 - listed in the militia company of Capt. Adam
Alexander of Clear Creek.
1790 - 235 00 - twp 14
1792 - Loose estate papers
Fleming, Allison
1784 - witnessed a deed, with John Fleming, and John
Houston, from George Fleming, of Rowan Co., NC to
Mitchell Fleming, of Mecklenburg Co., NC, for 205 on
Coddle Creek, adjoining David Templeton, David Houston,
Thomas McQuown, Henry Henry, bk 12, pg 344.
Fleming/Flemen, James & Margaret
1783 - deed to Paul Fifer for 100 acres on the Meadow
Branch of Rockey River adjoining Douglas Winchester,
Test: Archibald White, and John Hagler, bk 12, pg 216.
Fleming, John
1779 - named as the previous land owner of a tract of
land John sold to George McWhirter, no watercourse or
other dates given, bk 11, pg 37.
1783 - witnessed a deed, with Alexander McEwin, and Hugh
Rodgers, from William & Jane Ross to Seth Rodgers for a
tract of land adjoining William White, and William Hays,
bk 11, pg 290.
1784 - witnessed a deed, with Allison Fleming, and John
Houston, from George Fleming, of Rowan Co., NC to
Mitchell Fleming, of Mecklenburg Co., NC, for 205 on
Coddle Creek, adjoining David Templeton, David Houston,
Thomas McQuown, Henry Henry, bk 12, pg 344.
Fleming, George
1784 - deed to Mitchell Fleming for 205 acres on Coddle
Creek adjoining David Templeton, David Houston, Thomas
McQuown, Henry Henry, bk 12, pg 344.
George was living in Rowan Co., NC in 1784.
Fleming, Henry
1777 - witnessed a deed, with Robert Cochran, from
Thomas and Elizabeth McQuown to Alexander McQuown, their
son, for 132 acres on Coddle Creek, granted to Thomas in
1752, adjoining James Neel, bk 10, pg 234.
Flemming, Mitchell
1784 - deed from George Fleming for 205 acres on Coddle
Creek adjoining David Templeton, David Houston, Thomas
McQuown, Henry Henry, bk 12, pg 344.
1790 - 122 00 - twp 8
1800 - Cabarrus County
Flinn, Nicholas
1785 - Nicholas' will was probated in Mecklenburg Co.
Children: Rebecca, Jane
Flouck, Jacob

1778 - Signer of 1778 Petition
Flough, David (See David Flaugh/Flow)
Fogelman, Christian
    Christian was born March 11, 1774, died Sept 29, 1812,
    buried in St John's Evangelical Lutheran Church
    Cemetery.
Fogleman, Melchor
    1790 - 323 00 - twp 12
    1800 - Cabarrus County
Fogleman, Michael
    1784 - named as an adjoining land owner to Jacob Dean,
    Jacob Fagot, Peter Ross, and Charles Barnheart on
    Hamby's Run of Rockey River, bk 12, pg 137.
    1784 - named as an adjoining land owner to Jacob Fagot,
    Peter Hope, and Martin Phifer on Adam's Creek, bk 12, pg
    146.
Foil, George
    1790 - 321 00 - twp 11
Foil, John
    1790 - 104 00 - twp 12
Folk, William
    1790 - 101 00 - twp 12
    1793 - Account ledger of John Melchor's store.
    1800 - Cabarrus County
Forbers/Forbes, Hugh & Mary McCorkle
    1790 - 103 00 - twp 16
    Wife - Mary McCorkle, daughter of John & Margaret
    McCorkle.
    Hugh was born in 1757 according to 1840 pension list.
Forbes, Justin
    1774 - witnessed a deed, with Robert Gawin, from Samuel
    and Rachel McCrume to Stephen McCortle on Jean Armour's
    Creek, bk 10, pg 133.
Ford, Benjamin
    1783 - named as an adjoining land owner to Daniel
    Carnins on the dividing ridge between Twelve Mile Creek
    at Waxhaw Creek, bk 12, pg 112.
Ford, Daniel
    1780 - witnessed a deed, with William Hutchison, from
    Patrick McDonnel to Alexander Sterron for lots 204, 335
    & 336 in Charlotte, bk 11, pg 130.
    1784 - Daniel owned a lot in Charlotte that was sold at
    public auction to satisfy a debt, bk 12, pg 321.
    Judgement obtained against Daniel for a debt due to
    Thomas Polk in 1784.
Ford, Harblin
    1790 - 151 00 - twp 15
Ford, Henry
    1785 - deed from Jacob Self for 78 acres on both sides
    of Clear Creek, Test: George Black, and Thomas Morrow,
    bk 12, pg 513.
    1786 - Henry's will was probated in Mecklenburg Co.

Residents of Mecklenburg County, North Carolina 1762-1790

Children: John
Ford, John
    1777 - witnessed a deed, with John Nicholson, from Thomas Richey to Joseph Nicholson on Haw Creek, bk 10, pg 14.
    1777 - witnessed a deed, with John Nicholson, from Thomas Richey to Joseph Nicholson on Sugar Creek, adjoining Cubert Nicholson, bk 10, pg 9.
    1782 - Loose estate papers
Ford/Foard, John
    1777 - lots 49 and 59 on the east side of Tryon Street, Test: Ephraim Brevard, and Thomas Harris, bk 10, pg 44.
    1778 - witnessed a deed, with Ezekiel Polk, from William and James McCafferty to Thomas Polk for lot 9 fronting Trade Street in Charlotte, bk 10, pg 66.
    1779 (April 13) - deed for lots 85 and 93 in Charlotte, Test: Robert Brownfield and Matthew McClure, bk 10, pg 368.
    1779 (April 15) - deed to Ochilltree Martin and Company for lots 85 & 93 in Charlotte, Test: John Allen and Margaret Jack, bk 10, pg 350.
Ford, John & Catherine
    John was one of the signers of the Mecklenburg Declaration of Independence on May 20, 1775.
    1775 - witnessed a deed, with Zebulon Robinett, from William and Catherine Smith to Jonathan Buckaloe on McCalpin's Creek, bk 10, pg 174.
    1778 - John & Catherine witnessed a deed from John Robinett to Joseph Robb on the ridge between McCalpins Creek and Goose Creek, bk 10, pg 330.
    1779 - witnessed a deed, with Joseph Robb, from Robert Galbreath to Emanuel Stephens on Crooked Creek, bk 10, pg 358.
    1779 - grant for 100 acres on the dividing ridge between Clear Creek and McCalpin's Creek, bk 11, pg 121.
    1785 - witnessed a deed from Thomas Gribble to James Hood, Sr. on McCalpin's Creek, bk 12, pg 434.
    1790 - 102 07 - twp 15
    1798 - John's will was probated in Mecklenburg Co.
    1798 - Loose estate papers for John.
    Children: Zebulon, Elizabeth (? Morris)
    A John Ford was a trustee for the congregation of Rocky Spring in 1780.
    1805 - Loose estate papers for Catherine.
Ford/Foard, Zeblin/Zebulon/Harblin & Elizabeth
    1790 - 151 00 - twp 15
    1800 - Mecklenburg County
    1813 - Loose estate papers
    Son of John & Catherine Ford
Ford, Widow (Rebeckah)
    1790 - 114 00 - twp 14
    1800 - Cabarrus County

Children: John
Forney, Jacob & Mariah
    1767 - Militia, Mecklenburgh Regiment (Captain)
    Wife - Mariah Bergner
    Children: Abram (Rachel Gabriel), Jacob (Mary Corpening), Peter (Nancy Abernathy), Catherine (Abram Earnhardt), Elizabath (John Young), Christina (David Abernathy), Susan (John D. Abernathy)
    Jacob moved to Lincoln Co., NC
Forrister, Owen
    1779 - deed from Mannie Justice for 200 acres on the Long Branch of Coldwater Creek, Test: James Hurt, and Jason Frizell, bk 10, pg 385.
Forsyth, Robert
    1790 - 334 00 - twp 7
Forsyth, Hugh
    1783 - grant for 101 acres on the Cedar Fork of Twelve Mile Creek, bk 12, pg 154.
    1790 - 123 00 - twp 16
Foster, Henry
    1780 - witnessed a deed, with Alexander Cairns, from George and Elizabeth McWherter to Dennis Titus of Camden Dist., SC, on Warshaw (Waxhaw) Creek, bk 10, pg 447 & bk 11, pg 307.
Foster, James
    1772 - witnessed a deed, with John Barnet, from Thomas Polk to James Moore on the head waters of the south branch of Steel Creek, bk 10, pg 137.
    1773 - witnessed a deed, with Samuel Jack, to Joseph Nicholson for lot 6 on the south side of Tryon Street in Charlotte, bk 10, pg 53.
    1778
    1784 - James owned a lot in Charlotte that was sold at public auction to satisfy a debt in 1784.
Foster, John
    1777 - witnessed a deed, with William Osburn, from James and Sarah Lynn to John Osborn, bk 10, pg 214.
    1779 - witnessed a deed, with John McCorkle, from Hugh & Elizabeth Cry to Jacob Seeres for 270 acres, bk 11, pg 96.
    1784 - deed from John Curry for 150 acres on the east side of Waxhaw Creek, Test: William Meyer, John McCannon, and Green Rives, bk 12, pg 579.
    1790 - 101 04 - twp 17
Foust, Elias
    1777 - witnessed a deed, with Jacob Fagott, from Frederick Fisher, Jr. to Martin Fisher on the ridge between Coldwater and Adams Creeks, bk 10, pg 205.
Fowler, John
    1790 - 212 00 - twp 16
Frank, Jacob & Susannah

1782 - named as an adjoining land owner to Mathias
Mitchel, and James Ross on Little Coldwater Creek, bk
12, pg 144.
1787 - grant for 200 acres on Cumberford's Branch of
Coldwater Creek joining Nicholas Coleman, Jacob Ross,
John Long, and Joseph Shinn.
Wife - Susannah Roan, daughter of Henry & Elizabeth
Roan.
Children: Elizabeth (George Phifer), Isabella (Mathias
Mitchler, Jr.), Margaret (Nicholas Coleman), Frederick,
Catherine (John Reidling), Jacob, John, Joseph (Millison
Gisserd), Susannah (Daniel Harke/House), Mary (Daniel
Blackwelder)
Jacob died before 1794 in Cabarrus County.

Franklin, James
1764 - James's will was probated in Mecklenburg Co.
Children: James, Joseph, William, Andrew

Frazer, James & Mary ?
1787 - James' will was probated in Mecklenburg Co.
Children: James, Samuel

Frazer/Fraser, James
1790 - 100 00 - twp 6

Fraser/Frazer, Joseph & Margaret
1784 - witnessed a deed, with Samuel Davidson, from
Benjamin & Jemimah Knox to John Davidson on the south
fork of McDowell's Creek, bk 12, pg 353.
1784 - deed to Samuel Davis, Jr. for 285 acres on
Clark's Creek beginning on the Barony line adjoining
Joseph Maxwell, and David Smith, Test: Benjamin Lewis,
and John Davis, bk 12, pg 470.
No date - grant to Joseph Frazer, No. 139, bk 12, pg 56,
no other details.
1790 - 143 00 - twp 6
1800 - Mecklenburg County

Frazer, Samuel
1790 - 102 00 - twp 6

Frazer, William
1784 - witnessed a deed, with Archibald Houston, and
Richard Trotter, from Martin Phifer, Sr. to Ephraim Farr
on Caudle Creek, bk 12, pg 366.
1790 - 136 00 - twp 9
1800 - Cabarrus County

Fredrich, Philip
1766 - listed in the militia company of Capt. Adam
Alexander of Clear Creek.

Freeman, Allen, Jr.
1790 - 102 00 - twp 14
1793 - Account ledger of John Melchor's store.
Son of Allen & Barbara Freeman.

Freeman, Allen, Sr. & Barbara
1780 - deed from John and Elinore Polk on Clear Creek,
Test: William and Charles Polk, bk 10, pg 442.

1790 - 133 012 - twp 14
1800 - Mecklenburg County
Children: Gideon, William, Allen, Isham, Charles, Nancy
(? Wagstaff), Sarah, Susannah (? Garmon), Jemima,
Peggy
Freeman, Charles
1792 - Account ledger of John Melchor's store.
Freeman, Clebe
1793 - Account ledger of John Melchor's store.
Freeman, David & Jane Hayes
1790 - 325 00 - twp 1
1800 - Mecklenburg County
Children: James, Reuben, Michael, Sarah (?
Bigham), Ann (? Berryhill), Jemima (? Stephenson),
step-daughter Elizabeth Hayes
Freeman, Elyburn
1790 - 102 00 - twp 14
Freeman, Gidion
1790 - 114 01 - twp 14
Son of Allen & Barbara Freeman.
Freemond, Jacob
1782 - named as an adjoining land owner to Jane Rodgers
on Twelve Mile Creek, bk 12, pg 39.
Freeman, Mary(2)
1779 - Mary died Feb 13, 1779 at the age of 30.
Freeman, Michael
1790 - 104 01 - twp 1
1800 - Mecklenburg County
Son of David & Jane Hayes Freeman.
Freeman, Reuben & Nancy(2)
1790 - 101 00 - twp 1
1800 - Mecklenburg County
Mentioned in the estate of Wm. Sample.
Son of David & Jane Hayes Freeman.
Freeman, Widow
1790 - 034 00 - twp 14
Freeman, William
1790 - 114 00 - twp 14
1793 - Account ledger of John Melchor's store.
Son of Allen & Barbara Freeman.
Frizell, Jason
1777 - witnessed a deed, with Caleb Phipher, and
Archibald Houston, from Martin and Catherine Phipher to
Robert Morton on Coddle Creek, adjoining Archibald
Templeton, ? McCulloh, and John Frohock, bk 10, pg 69.
1777 - witnessed a bond, along with Charles Reese,
between Catherine Phifer, widow of John, and John
Barringer, bk 10, pg 198.
1777 - witnessed a deed, with Joseph Shinn, from Adam
and Cathey Moyar to Mathias Boston on Little Coldwater
Creek, bk 10, pg 421.

1779 - witnessed a deed from Martin Phifer to Adam Bower on Great Coldwater Creek, bk 10, pg 465.
1779 - witnessed a deed, with James Hurt, from Mannie Justice to Owen Forrister on the Long Branch of Coldwater Creek, bk 10, pg 385.
1779 - witnessed a deed, with John March, from Mounce Justice to Andrew McClenhan on the Long Branch of Coldwater Creek, bk 10, pg 431.
1779 - witnessed a deed, with Martin Fifer, from George & Catherine Goodknight to Leonard Barbrick on Coldwater Creek, adjoining Henry Fisherman, bk 11, pg 10.
1780 - witnessed a deed, with Nicholas Coleman, from Martin Phifer to Peter Sell on Little Coldwater Creek adjoining Jacob Seah, bk 11, pg 74.
1780 - witnessed a deed, with Henry Sensill, from Hance & Mary Justice to Samuel Sensill on Cuflon Creek, adjoining John Phifer, John Baker, John Armstrong, William Houston, and James McDowell, bk 11, pg 4.

Frohock, John
1765 - witnessed a deed, with Moses Alexander, from Robert Smith to Henry Eustace McCulloh for 218 acres on Rockey River, bk 10, pg 160.
1775 - named as an adjoining land owner to Samuel Morton, and John Farr on Coddle Creek and Alton's Run, Test: Ephraim Farr, and William Gardner, bk 10, pg 173.
1777 - named as an adjoining land owner to Martin Phifer, Robert Morton, Archibald Templeton, and Henry Eustace McCulloh on Coddle Creek, bk 10, pg 69.

Frohock, John
1774 - named as an adjoining land owner to John Rilliah, and John Davis on McMichael and McCalpin Creeks, bk 10, pg 135.

Frohock/Fowhawk, Thomas
Attorney for Henry Eustace McCulloh - bk 10, pg 46.
1779 - named as an adjoining land owner to John & Prudence Smith, John King, John Johnston, and James Osburn on McCalpin's Creek, Test: Robert & William Smith, bk 12, pg 280.
1779 - named as an adjoining land owner to John Smith, and John Johnston on McCalpin's Creek, bk 10, pg 528.
1780 - named as an adjoining land owner to Alexander Wallace, John Cook, Michael Henderson, Mathew Robison, and William Hemphill on Mallard Creek, bk 12, pg 120.
McCalpin's Creek (twp 15) and the Waggon Road.

From, Nathaniel
1777 - witnessed a deed, with Jonathan Coates, and Alexander Karrel, from Capt. James Pettigrew to George Greer for lots 34 and 92 in Charlotte, bk 10, pg 275.

Fruseland/Frieseland, George
1790 - 113 00 - twp 12
1793 - Account ledger of John Melchor's store.

Furr/Flinn?, Henry & Catherine

1790 - 113 00 - twp 10
Wife - Catherine Pless
Children: Elizabeth (? Phillips), Paul M., daughter
(Peter Earnhardt), John, Rachel (? Misenheimer),
Rosena (? Eagle), Sophia (? Eagle), Daniel, Henry,
Tobias (Rosena or Sopia was married to John Eagle)
Furrer, Heinrich (Henry Furr) & Rosena
    1769 - Henry's will was probated in Mecklenburg County.
    Wife - Rossena
    Children: John, Paul
Furr, Jacob
    1785 - Loose estate papers
Furr/Forr, John
    1790 - 262 03 - twp 12
    1793 - Account ledger of John Melchor's store.
    1800 - Cabarrus County
Furr, Paul & Mary
    1790 - 134 01 - twp 12
    1800 - Cabarrus County
    Children: Paul, Daniel, Leonard, Rosena (? Klutts),
    Mary (? Ury), Sally (? Heilick), Elizabeth (?
    Furr), Catherine (Christopher Osbourne)
Furrow, Paul
    1786 - deed from Paulser & Franney Ness for 90 acres on
    both sides of Dutch Buffelow Creek, subdivided from
    Paulser's plantation, Test: Samuel Black, and Johanas
    Jegler, bk 12, pg 580.
Gaby/Galey, Benjamin
    1789 - Loose estate papers
Gabie, Robert
    1766 - Robert's will was probated in Mecklenburg Co.
    Children: John, Joseph
    1766 - Loose estate papers
Galbreath, John
    1776 - in Capt. Charles Polk's Light Horse Company.
Galbreath, Joseph
    1782, 1787 branch of Sugar Creek
    Son of Joseph Galbreath, Sr.
Galbreath, Joseph, Sr.
    1779 - deed from John & Jane Hall for 13 acres on Goose
    Creek, bk 10, pg 328.
    1782 - deed from David & Elizabeth Crocket for 50 acres
    on a branch of Sugar Creek adjoining James Reed, and
    Alexander Mitchel, Test: Moses Robison, and Edward
    Malony, bk 11, pg 91.
    1782 - witnessed a deed, with John McGinty, from William
    & Margaret Query to David Whipple on Goose Creek, bk 11,
    pg 151.
    Children: Robert, John, Joseph (One of them married Mary
    Finney)
Gailbraith, Martha
    1790 -132 00 - twp 6

Residents of Mecklenburg County, North Carolina
1762-1790

Galbraith/Gailbraith, Robert
   1776 - in Capt. Charles Polk's Light Horse Company.
   1777 - deed from William & Agness Henderson for 70 on both sides of Crooked Creek, Test: John Harris, and Josham Irvin, bk 10, pg 291.
   1779 - deed to Emanuel Stephens for 70 acres on Crooked Creek that was conveyed to Robert by William & Agness Henderson in 1777, bk 10, pg 358.
   1790 - 205 00 - twp 19
   Son of Joseph Galbreath, Sr.

Galbreath, William
   1776 - 2nd Sergeant in Capt. Charles Polk's Light Horse Company.

Galliway/Galloway, Thomas
   1790 - 152 00 - twp 5

Galloway, James
   1778 - Loose estate papers

Gantt, Thomas (See Thomas Gent)

Gantt, William (See William Gent)

Garber, Leonard & Rosanna
   1786 - Loose estate papers
   Children: Samuel, Leonard, Sarah, Elizabeth, Magdalene, Margaret, Rosanna.

Gardner, James
   1778 - Signer of 1778 Petition
   1782 - named as an adjoining land owner to Adam Meek on Mallard Creek, bk 12, pg 5.
   1790 - 116 02 - twp 5

Gardner, John & Elizabeth
   1784 - bill of sale, with William Gardner, to Samuel Linton, for a negro fellow, Test: Robert Smith, and Mathew Alexander, bk 12, pg 380.
   1790 - 112 00 - twp 5
   John was born in 1764 according to 1840 pension list.

Gardner, William
   1775 - deed from James Johnson for 73 acres on Sugar Creek, Test: Robert Campbell, and Ebenezer Newton, bk 10, pg 191.

Gardner, William
   1775 - witnessed a deed, with Ephraim Farr, from Samuel Morton to John Farr for 118 acres on the ridge between Coddle Creek and Alton's Run, adjoining John Frohock, bk 10, pg 173.
   1778 - named as an adjoining land owner to Andrew & Susannah Burns, Robert Smith, Jr., and James Wallace, Test: John & Martha Smith, bk 10, pg 82.
   1779 - named as an adjoining land owner to Andrew Burns, David & Mary Smith, Robert Smith, and William Johnston on Rockey River, bk 10, pg 541.
   1779 - grant for 37 acres on Coddle Creek, bk 10, pg 492.

1784 - named as an adjoining land owner to David & Mary Smith, and Samuel Killough on Rockey River, bk 12, pg 327.
1784 - bill of sale, with John Gardner, to Samuel Linton, for a negro fellow, Test: Robert Smith, and Mathew Alexander, bk 12, pg 380.
1790 - 224 00 - twp 5
1800 - Cabarrus County

Garmon, George
1784 - George's will was probated in Mecklenburg Co. Children: George, Isaac

Garmon, George & Jane
1784 - grant for 40 acres on Meadow Creek, bk 12, pg 134.
1785 - deed to George Kizer for a tract of land on both sides of Rockey River, adjoining John Finney, John Biger, and Peter Reap, Test: Michael Garmon, and Adam Alexander, bk 12, pg 484.
1785 - witnessed a deed, with Samuel Larking, from Dunnon & Mary Corion to Henry Colledge on the head of Cane Branch, bk 12, pg 536.
1790 - 111 08 - twp 14 (widow)
1798 - Loose estate papers

Garmon, George
1793 - Account ledger of John Melchor's store.

Garmon/Gammon, Michael
1779 - witnessed a deed, with William Polk, from Thomas Polk to William Hayns on Muddy Creek, bk 10, pg 311.
1784 - grant for 30 acres on the west side of Rockey River adjoining Christopher Osburn, bk 12, pg 157.
1790 -117 09 - twp 14
1800 - Cabarrus County

Garmon/Gammon, William
1779 - named in a deed, no book or page number given.

Garner, Ann(2)
Ann died Sept 15, 1778 at age 25.

Garrett, Daniel
1778 - Signer of 1778 Petition

Garrett/Garrot, Thomas
1766 - listed in the militia company of Capt. Adam Alexander of Clear Creek.
1790 - 105 00 - twp 17

Garrett, William
1790 - 104 00 - twp 17

Garrison, Adam & Anney
1778 - deed to Henry Kent for a tract on Rockey River, Test: Robert Sholty, and George Green, no book or page number given.

Garrison, Agnes(2)
Agnes died Aug 10, 1774 at age 27.

Garretson, Arthur

1812 - Seventh Company detached from the First
Mecklenburg Regiment.
Garrison, Arthur
  1769 -
  1779 -
  1782 - grant for 29 acres on both sides of Sugar Creek,
  adjoining Col. Polk, bk 12, pg 81.
  1784 - deed to Richard Mason on Middle Branch, a branch
  of Sugar Creek for 186 acres beginning on top of a ridge
  thirty-five rods from the town of Charlotte, adjoining
  John Sample, Test: Robert Scott, George Rice, and David
  Mason, bk 12, pg 313.
  Arthur was mentioned in the estate settlement of Wm.
  Sample.
Garrison, David, Sr. & Sarah
  1765 - grant for 152 acres from Henry Eustace McCulloh,
  no book or page number given, bk 10, pg 7.
  1767 - Militia, Mecklenburgh Regiment (Lieutenant)
  1777 - deed to David Garrison, Jr. for 152 acres on the
  north side of Mallard Creek, Test: John Garrison, and
  James Balch, bk 10, pg 7.
  1790 - 135 00 - twp 5
Garrison, David & Mary
  1774 - deed to Adam Meek for 70 acres on the west side
  of Mallard Creek joining Moses Alexander, Test: John
  Garrison and David Garrison, Jr.
  1782 - named as an adjoining land owner to Adam Meek and
  James Gardner on Mallard Creek, bk 12, pg 5.
  1790 - 135 00 - twp 5
Garrison, John M. or W. & Hannah
  1774 - witnessed a deed, with Thomas Alexander, from
  Benjamin & Susannah Alexander to James Scott on both
  sides of Back Creek, adjoining Daniel Alexander, bk 10,
  pg 151.
  1777 - deed from Alexander & Sarah Mitchel for 50 acres
  on a branch of Sugar Creek adjoining James Reed, Test:
  Richard Robinson, and A. McKee, bk 10, pg 23.
  1779 - deed to Hugh Rondles for 50 acres on a branch of
  Sugar Creek joining James Reed, and Alexander Mitchell,
  beginning by the mill dam, bk 11, pg 94.
  1779 - deed to Samuel Hemphill for lots 201, 204, 330,
  331, 335, 336 in Charlotte, Test: John Carson, and
  William Johnston, bk 11, pg 16.
  1779 - deed to Benjamin & William Alexander for 180
  acres, including a mill, on Mallard Creek, Test: William
  Hutchison and Thoomas Alexander, bk 11, pg 14.
  1785 - witnessed a deed, with Charles and Andrew
  Alexander, from William & Margaret Alexander to John
  McCaughey on a small branch of Stoney Creek, the north
  fork, adjoining James Hunter, bk 12, pg 485.
  1785 - witnessed a deed, with Andrew and William
  Alexander, from Benjamin & Susanan Alexander to John

McCaughey for 400 acres on Back Creek adjoining Evan
Shelby, Edmond Bordon, and Henry Mitchel, bk 12, pg 487.
1790 - 112 01 - twp 6
1800 - Mecklenburg County
Garrison, Samuel R. & Martha Morrison
1790 - 112 04 - twp 7
Martha was the daughter of Robert & Abigail Morrison.
Samuel & Martha moved to Bedford Co. TN with other
members of the Morrison family.
Garrison, Sarah
Children: Mary, Nancy, Sarah, Jenny, James, Arty
Gaseway, John
1790 - 142 00 - twp 9
Gaston, Thomas
1790 - 120 00 - twp 20
Gent, Thomas
1794 - Loose estate papers
Gent, William
1794 - Loose estate papers
Gerster, Henry
1793 - Account ledger of John Melchor's store.
Gibbeney/Gibbony, Nicholas(2)
1779 - deed from David Reed for 200 acres on Sugar Creek
adjoining Henry Varner, Samuel Kearh, and John Carson,
Test: John Allen, and John McDowell, bk 10, pg 412.
1790 - 124 06 - twp 1
1800 - Mecklenburg County
Children: David ?
Nicholas was born in 1741, died 1821.
1821 - Loose estate papers
Gibbons/Givvens, Edward & Mary
1779 - deed from Robert & Sarah Beaker for 313 ½ acres
on Davison's Creek adjoining John Beaker, Test: John
Patterson, and Edward Givens, Jr., bk 11, pg 44.
1790 - 202 011 - twp 7
Gibbons/Givens, Edward, Jr. & Agnes
1779 - witnessed a deed, with John Patterson, from
Robert & Sarah Beaker to Edward Givens on Davidson
Creek, adjoining John Beaker, bk11, pg 44.
Children: Edward, Mary (Samuel Givens), Margaret (Moses
White), Agness (William Caldwell)
Givens, Edward
1779 - Edward's will was probated in Mecklenburg Co.
Children: Samuel, Edward
Givens, Edward
1791 - Edward's will was probated in Mecklenburg Co.
Children: Michael, Jacob, Ruth ?
1792 - Loose estate papers
Gibbens/Givvens, John & Mary McCall
1779 - deed from William & Rachel Robison for 200 acres
on Four Mile Creek near Providence, a tar kiln branch

and both sides of the old sawmill path, Test: Archibald
Crockett, John McCulloh, and John Wilson, bk 11, pg 298.
1790 - 142 00 - twp 16
1800 - Mecklenburg County
Mary was the daughter of Francis McCall.
Gibbons/Givvins, John, Sr. & Jane Dunn
1790 - 201 00 - twp 7
Jane was the daughter of Andrew & Mary Dunn.
Gibbons/Givvins, Jno Ruther
1790 - 143 00 - twp 7
1800 - Mecklenburg County
Gibbons/Givens, John
1782 - Loose estate papers
1790 -121 00 - twp 16
1800 - Mecklenburg County
Wife: Mary McCall, daughter of Francis McCall.
Gibbons/Givvins/Gibbens, John, Jr.
1790 - 122 00 - twp 7
Gibbons/Givvins, Samuel & Mary Givens
　　1777 - witnessed a deed, with Thomas Givens, from John &
　　Sarah Hobbs to Lewis Jetton on McDowell's Creek, bk 10,
　　pg 24.
　　1777 - witnessed a deed, with Lewis Jetton, from Joseph
　　& Sarah Hobbs to Thomas Givens for 150 acres on
　　McDowell's Creek, bk 10, pg 269.
　　1790 - 121 00 - twp 16
　　Mary was the daughter of Edward, Jr. & Agnes Gibbons.
　　Children: Martha (Samuel Adams)
　　Samuel was born in 1763 according to an 1840 pension
　　list.
　　Revolutionary Soldier - died April 16, 1846 in Union
　　Co., NC, age 85 to 90 according to The Charlotte Journal
　　dated May 1, 1846.
Gibbons/Givens, Thomas
　　1777 - deed from Joseph & Sarah Hobbs for 150 acres on
　　McDowell's Creek, adjoining Charles Moses, John McDowel,
　　and John Miller, Test: Lewis Jetton, and Samuel Givens,
　　bk 10, pg 269.
　　1777 - witnessed a deed, with Samuel Givens, from John &
　　Sarah Hobbs to Lewis Jetton on McDowell's Creek, bk 10,
　　pg 24.
　　1783 - Loose estate papers
Gibbons/Givins/Gibbons, William & Jannet
　　1780 - grant for 100 acres on Givens Mill Branch, a
　　branch of Twelve Mile Creek, bk 12, pg 19.
　　1790 - 114 00 - twp 16
　　Children: Samuel, William, Martha, Elizabeth (Solomon
　　Bracken), Sarah (Robert Ramsey), Agness (Hans McCain),
　　Hester (John Coffey)
　　William's will was probated in April 1798.
Gibbons/Givens, William & Sarah

1778 - deed from William Haggins for 250 acres on
McCorkle's Branch of Twelve Mile Creek, adjoining
William Haggins, and Griffith Rutherford, Test: James
Douglas, and John Haggins, bk 10, pg 49.
1778 - deed to John Thompson for 300 acres joining
Mathew McCorkel, Test: John and Benjamin Walace, bk 10,
pg 285.
1778 - witnessed a deed, with Joseph Douglas, and Henry
Hurst, from William Haggins to Abraham Cook between
Waxhaw Creek and Twelve Mile Creek, adjoining William
Cook, bk 10, pg 394.
1790 - 114 00 - twp 16

Gibbons/Givens, William & Jannet
1778 - deed to Robert Scott for 143 acres on Six Mile
Creek adjoining James Dunn, Test: Hugh Pollock, and John
Davies, bk 10, pg 279.

Gibson, George
1789 - Loose estate papers

Gibson, John
1790 - 134 02 - twp 6

Gilbert, Barbara
1767 - Loose estate papers

Gilbert, Jamson
1793 - Account ledger of John Melchor's store.

Gilbert, John
1793 - Account ledger of John Melchor's store.

Giles, Edward, Esqr.
1779 - witnessed a deed from Nathaniel Gilmore to Robert
Smith on Rockey River, bk 10, pg 374.
1779 - grant for 102 acres on Mallard Creek, adjoining
William Alexander, and Moses Alexander, bk 10, pg 514.
1790 - 424 00 - twp 5

Giles, John & Ann(2)
John died Dec 13, 1777 at the age of 50.
Ann died Dec 13, 1777 at the age of 66.
Children: Susannah, Sarah, Mary (William Henderson, Sr.)

Giles, Nathaniel
1790 - 113 00 - twp 5

Gillan/Gillin, Francis
1777 - Loose estate papers

Gillan, John
1790 - 103 00 - twp 2

Gillen, Sarah
1780 - grant for 100 acres on Twelve Mile Creek
adjoining George Davidson, bk 12, pg 23.

Gillaspie, Andw
1790 - 101 00 - twp 17

Gillaspie, Charles
1790 - 111 00 - twp 18

Gillaspie, Isaac

1778 - witnessed a deed, with Thomas Gilespy, from
George Cathey to James Knox on the south fork of
McDowel's Creek, bk 11, pg 211.
Gillaspie, Jacob
  1790 - 101 00 - twp 16
Gillaspie, James
  1790 - 122 02 - twp 7
  1800 - Mecklenburg County
Gillaspie, James
  1790 - 114 00 - twp 8
Gillaspie/Galaspy, John
  1784 - witnessed a deed, with Thomas Alexander, from
  John & Jean Brevard to James Williamson on a branch of
  Rockey River, bk 12, pg 547.
  1785 - near Twelve Mile Creek
  1790 - 144 00 - twp 18
Gillaspie, Joseph & Ruth
  1783 - deed to John and Tunas Hood for 53 acres on both
  sides of Goose Creek, Test: Benjamin McKenzy, bk 12, pg
  206.
  1790 - 302 01 - twp 7
  Children: James, John Joseph, Jacob,
  Alexander, William, Martha Williamson
  Ruth died May 29, 1811, C, pg 126
Gilleland, John
  1790 - 204 00 - twp 8
Gillett, Aron
  Aron was a physican.
  1782 - Power of attorney to Samuel Martin and William
  Polk, bk 11, bp 187.
Gilmer, John
  1772 - John's will was probated in Mecklenburg Co.
  Children: James
Gilmore, Archabeld
  1781 - deed from John Houston for 140 acres on a branch
  of Coddle Creek called Hugh Parks Creek, adjoining James
  Templeton, Test: John Tanner, and Hugh Rodgers, bk 10,
  pg 444.
  1790 - 101 00 - twp 8
  1800 - Cabarrus County
Gilmore, Margret (widow of James ?)
  1790 - 123 00 - twp 2
  Children: Josiah, Mary, Nathaniel, William
Gilmore/Gilmor, James(2)
  James died Oct 8, 1784, age 40.
Gilmore, James
  1790 - Loose estate papers
Gilmore/Gilmor, James & Margaret(2)
  1780 - grant for 100 acres on both sides of Rockey River
  adjoining Jonathan Newman, and Nathaniel Gilmore, bk 12,
  pg 90.
  James died Oct 8, 1784 at the age of 40.

Margaret died March 30, 1815 at the age of 63.
Gilmore, John & Mary
   1769 - named as an adjoining land owner to John &
   Elizabeth Mitchell, and Jonathan & Rebecca Newman on the
   south side of Clark's Creek, Test: Samuel Wilson, and
   Patrick Carr, bk 10, pg 169.
   1779 - named as an adjoining land owner to Jonathan &
   Rebecca Newman, and Robert Hope on the south side of
   Clark's Creek, a branch of Rockey River, Test: John
   Alison, and Seth Collins, bk 11, pg 46.
   Children: James, Nathaniel, Sarah, Agness, Susannah,
   March (dau.), Elizabeth
   1790 - 133 02 - twp 5 (Widow Gilmore, next to Nathaniel)
   1790 - Loose estate papers
Gilmore/Gilmor, Margaret(2)
   Margaret died March 30, 1805, age 63.
Gilmore, Nathaniel & Jane
   1779 - deed to Robert Smith for 22 acres on Rockey
   River, Test: Edward Giles, bk 10, pg 374.
   1780 - named as an adjoining land owner to James &
   Margaret Gilmore, and Jonathan & Rebecca Newman on
   Rockey River, bk 12, pg 90.
   1780 - grant for 38 acres on the south side of Rockey
   River adjoining Jonathan & Rebecca Newman, bk 12, pg 69.
   1781 - deed to Zacheus Wilson for 227 acres adjoining
   Robert Hayes, Test: John Smith, and Robert Harris, bk
   12, pg 317.
   1790 - 215 00 - twp 5
Gilmore, Patrick
   1790 - 171 00 - twp 7
   1800 - Mecklenburg County
Gilmore, William
   1790 - 103 00 - twp 2
Gingles, John & Rachel Morrison(7), Amelia Davis
   1790 - 101 00 - twp 13
   Children: Jenny, Margaret (James Semianes Russell),
   Samuel Harvey (Trizah Morrison), Mary (? Parks),
   Rachel (Samuel F. Morrison), Rosanna (William Pickens
   Morrison), Elizabeth (Peter Roland McCachern), James
   (Sarah Graves), John (Dorcas Morrison McGinnis, Martha
   Clementine Purviance, Elizabeth Brice Cochran Harris),
   William Lee (Rachel Russell), Charles Harrison (Mary
   Morrison), Malinda E. (Elam Harvey Davis), Harriet
   Wife: Rachel Morrison, daughter of James & Jennett Hall
   Morrison.
   John was the son of Samuel & Margaret McAllister
   Gingles.
Gingles, Samuel & Margaret McAllister
   1767 - named in a deed on Crowders Creek, no book or
   page number given.
   1777 - Loose estate papers
   Samuel died Jan 24, 1777.

Margaret died March 28, 1809.
Children: Rosanna (John Carruth), Isabella (Alexander
Austin), Mary (Alexander McCarter/McClarty), Samuel
(Elenor Beaty), James (Elizabeth ?), Adlai, Rachel
(John Harris), John (Rachel Morrison).

Gingles, Samuel & Eleanor Beaty
   1781 Duck Creek
   Wife: Elenor Beaty, daughter of Thomas & Agnes Houston
   Beaty.
   Children: David (Mary Rhyne), Adlai, Samuel, Thomas
   Hunter (Peggy B. Erwin), Edwin LeRoy (Delia Darwin),
   Minty Caroline, Margaret (Isaac Erwin), Charles
   Samuel was the son of Samuel and Margaret McAllister
   Gingles.
   Samuel and other family members moved to Lincoln Co., NC
   before 1800.

Givvins (see Gibbons)

Glark/Clark, Jessey
   1790 - 232 02 - twp 1
   1800 - Mecklenburg County

Glass, Francis
   1771 - witnessed a bond between Thomas Willson and James
   Willson, bk 10, pg 209.
   1772 - witnessed a deed, with William Ramsey, from Hugh
   & Mary Caragan to John Ramsey on Whetstone's Branch,
   adjoining John Quirry, bk 10, pg 103.
   1790 - 245 00 - twp 15

Glass, Robert
   1794 - Loose estate papers

Glass, Robert
   1771 - witnessed a bond between Thomas Willson and James
   Willson, bk 10, pg 209.
   1782 - named as an adjoining land owner to William &
   Margaret Query, and David Whipple on the middle fork of
   Goose Creek, bk 11, pg 151.
   1790 - 101 00 - twp 15
   1800 - Meckelburg County
   Children: Margaret (? Richardson), Elizabeth,
   Lawrence, Martha Glass, James

Glover, Ezekel
   1790 - 102 00 - twp 9

Glover, John
   1790 - 000 10 - twp 9

Glover, William
   1790 - 101 00 - twp 9
   1800 - Cabarrus County

Goforth, William
   1779 - deed from Alexander Wallace for a tract on
   Mallard Creek, Test: Nathaniel Irwin, and William
   Hemphill, bk 11, pg 305.
   1790 - 226 00 - twp 4
   1800 - Mecklenburg County

Residents of Mecklenburg County, North Carolina
1762-1790

Goldman, Henry, Sr.
    1781 - Henry's will was probated in Mecklenburg Co.
    Children: Henry, John, Charles, Elizabeth, Catharine,
    Rachel, Leah, Martha
    1781 - Loose estate papers
Gonder/Conder, George
    1790 - 244 00 - twp 10
Gonder/Conder, Lewis
    1790 - 200 00 - twp 15
    1800 - Mecklenburg County
Goodknight, George & Catherine
    1779 - deed to Leonard Barbrick for 100 acres on
    Coldwater Creek, joining Henry Fisherman, Test: Martin
    Fifer, Jason Fissell, bk 11, pg 10.
Goodknight, Michael
    1764 - deed to Michael Goodknight and Christopher Landis
    from James McClain for 190 acres on Three Mile Creek,
    Test: Martin Phifer, Moses Shiddel, bk 10, pg 155.
    1773 - witnessed a deed, with James Killpatrick, from
    Jacob Swink to Peter Boga on Shenawolf Creek, a branch
    of Rockey River, bk 10, pg 106.
Goodman, Christian
    1775 - deed from Samuel Suther, minister of Orange Co.,
    NC, for 125 acres on Dutch Buffalo Creek, adjoining
    George Tucker, Test: George Henry Berger, and John
    Sheppard, bk 10, pg 26.
    1778 - Signer of 1778 Petition.
    1783 - deed from John Michael and Margaret Clontz for
    200 acres on Dutch Buffalo Creek adjoining Gasper Saxer,
    and Michael Christman, Test: John Leopard, and George
    Soatman, bk 12, pg 293.
    1784 - grant for 250 acres at the head of a draft of
    Dutch Buffalo Creek adjoining Jacob Berry, bk 12, pg
    161.
Goodman, Christopher
    1784 - grant for 149 acres on both sides of Blackwater
    Run, a branch of Dutch Buffalow Creek, adjoining Jacob
    Bogarn, and Tobias Goodman, bk 12, pg 165.
    1790 - 222 00 - twp 11
Goodman, Christopher, Jr.
    1790 - 124 00 - twp 11
Goodman, Elizabeth
    1790 - 202 00 - twp 11
Goodman, George
    1790 - 104 00 - twp 11
    1800 - Cabarrus County
    Son of Michael Goodman.
Goodman, Jacob
    1782 - deed from Staphel & Catherine Goodman for 200
    acres on a branch of Dutch Buffalow Creek adjoining
    Waddle, Brandon, and Gov. Dobbs, Test: James Ross, bk
    12, pg 346.

Residents of Mecklenburg County, North Carolina   133
1762-1790

1790 - 124 00 - twp 11
Goodman, Jacob
   1790 - 124 00 - twp 9
Goodman, Michael
   1777 - deed from George & Margaret Cagle for 200 acres on a branch of Dutch Buffalo Creek adjoining Waddle, Test: Joseph Shinn, and James Ross, bk 12, pg 373.
   1777 - Michael's will was probated in Mecklenburg Co. Children: Christopher, Michael, Jacob, George, John
Goodman, Michael
   1785 - Loose estate papers
Goodman, Michael
   1790 - 101 00 - twp 11
Goodman, Michael, Jr.
   1790 - 124 00 - twp 11
Goodman, Staphel & Catron
   1782 - deed to Jacob Goodman for 200 acres on a branch of Dutch Buffalow Creek adjoining Waddle, Brandon, and Gov. Dobbs, Test: James Ross, bk 12, pg 346.
Goodman, Tobias
   1784 - named as an adjoining land owner to Christopher Goodman, and Jacob Bogarn on Blackwater Run, a branch of Dutch Buffalow Creek, bk 12, pg 165.
Goodnight, Christian
   1783 - grant for 212 acres on Coldwater Creek adjoining Christian Barnheart, bk 12, pg 190.
   1790 -
Goodnight, George & Catherine
   1779 - deed to Leonard Barbrick for 100 acres on both sides of Coldwater Creek, adjoining Henry Fisherman and Dobb's line, Test: Martin Phifer, and Jason Frissell, bk 11, pg 10.
Goodnight, Henry
   1778 - Signer of 1778 Petition
Goodnight, Michael
   1764 - deed from James & Ruth McClain to Christopher Landis and Michael Goodnight for 190 acres on Three Mile Creek, adjoining Joseph Rodgers, Test: Martin Phifer, and Moses Shiddel, bk 10, pg 155.
   1773 - witnessed a deed, with James Killpatrick, from Jacob Swink to Peter Bogar on Shenawolf Creek, a branch of Rockey River, bk 10, pg 106.
Gordin/Gordon, John
   1790 - 323 00 - twp 16
Gorright, Fight
   1782 - named as adjoining land owner to John & Ann Bussard, and John Barriger on Dutch Buffalow Creek, bk 11, pg 125.
Goth, William
   1783 - witnessed a deed, with Robert Morris, John McKnitt Alexander, and Joseph Rodgers, from Robert &

Elizabeth McCleary to David Russell on the head branch of Mallard Creek and Long Creek, bk 12, pg 257.

Gowan/Gawin, Robert
    1774 - witnessed a deed, with Justin Forbes, from Samuel & Rachel McCrume to Stephen McCortle, bk 10, pg 133.

Goylorw, Joyauurn (Dutch)
    1780 - witnessed a deed, with John Hagler, from James & Elizabeth Maxwell on Rocky River, bk 12, pg 226.

Graff, William
    1793 - Account ledger of John Melchor's store.

Graham, George & Lydia(4)
    1784 - witnessed a deed, with James Tagert, from Robert Walker, Jr. to John Green for 150 acres on Sugar Creek adjoining Thomas Polk, bk 12, pg 337.
    1785 - witnessed a deed, with James Robison, from Alexander Mitchel to Robert Alison on a branch of Sugar Creek, bk 12, pg 462.
    1790 - 122 04 - twp 1
    George died March 29, 1826 at age 68.
    Children: John, Mary (? Carruth), Betsy Caroline (? Bostick), Jane (? McRee)

Graham, James
    1776 - witnessed a deed, with Will Reed, from Elias & Agness Alexander to Samuel Graham, adjoining John Allen, bk 10, pg 11.
    1790 - 000 10 - twp 1

Graham, Jean
    1782 - witnessed a deed, with John Long, from Thomas Beaty to William and James Beaty, adjoining Beaty Ford, bk 12, pg 489.

Graham, John
    John died before 1784 and is named as an adjoining land owner to Ephraim Pharr, Hugh Hambleton, and Robert Andrews on Rockey River, bk 12, pg 178.

Graham, Joseph, Majr. & Isabealla
    1784 - witnessed a deed, with Robert Steven, from Mathew Miller to William Ramsey on Clear Creek, bk 12, pg 357.
    1784 - deed from Abraham & Mary Barnet for a tract adjoining the Tuckasuga Ford, and another tract known as the Lower Fishery, Test: David Allison, and Richard Houston, bk 12, pg 499.
    1785 - witnessed a deed, with George Ross, from James & Elizabeth Barr to James McKnight on Rockey River, bk 12, pg 559.
    1785 - witnessed a deed, with George Ross, from James & Elizabeth Barr to James McKnight on Lewis Branch of Rocky River, bk 12, pg 574-B.
    1790 - 112 08 - twp 1
    Sheriff of Mecklenburg in 1784.
    Wife - Isabella Davidson, daughter of John & Violet Wilson Davidson
    Buried in Lincoln County

Residents of Mecklenburg County, North Carolina   135
1762-1790

Graham, Richard & Agnes
   Children: James, Joseph, William
   Richard died in 1779.
Graham, Robert & Mary Craig
   Wife - Mary Craig
   Children: Samuel, Robert, John, Nancy Agnes, James, Margaret
   1779 - deed from Thomas Harris, Sheriff to satisfy a judgement against William Walker, on Sugar Creek, bk 10, pg 356.
   1779 - deed to Robert Hays for 116 acres on Sugar Creek adjoining William Wilson, James Wilson, and John McCluer, Test: William Reed, and Joseph Douglas, bk 10, pg 340.
   1782 - deed to John Springstreet for 200 acres on Sugar Creek adjoining David Garrison, Test: William Wilson, and Hugh Pollock, bk 12, pg 383.
Graham, Samuel
   1776 - deed from Elias & Agness Alexander for 200 acres adjoining John Allen, Test: James Graham, and Will Reed, bk 10, pg 11.
   1778 - deed from Thomas Polk for 145 acres on the dividing ridge between Sugar Creek and McMichael's Creek, beginning on the Spring Branch, Test: Duncan Ochiltree, and John Barton, bk 10, pg 31.
   1790 - 100 01 - twp 4
   1800 - Mecklenburg County
Graham, William
   1775 - William was one of the signers of the Mecklenburg Declaration of Independence on May 20, 1775.
   1790 - 102 00 - twp 20
Graham, William & Mary McKee
   Wife: Mary McKee, daughter of Alexander McKee.
   Children: Agnes, John
   1767 - William's will was probated in Mecklenburg Co.
Graham, William & Margaret
   1773 - witnessed a deed, with Robert Waddle, and Abel Duckworth, from John Jackson and Mary Moore to John Criswell, bk 10, pg 90.
   1777 - witnessed a deed, with Samuel Blythe, and William Bowen, from Robert & Hannah Erwin to John Wier at the upper edge of the Mill Creek, bk 10, pg 230.
   1777 - witnessed a deed, with Abel Mankens, from John & Jean Criswell to William Laughland, bk 10, pg 303.
   1780 - witnessed a deed, with Hugh Lucas, from John & Jean Wear to Thomas Walker, adjoining James Blyth, William Graham, and Alexander Lewis, bk 10, pg 456.
   1790 - 371 04 - twp 7
   1800 - Mecklenburg County
   Children: John, James, Richard(in TN), William, Samuel, Ezekiel, Alexander, Griffith, Joseph
Gray, David

1793 - Account ledger of John Melchor's store.
Gray, Jacob
   1790 - 311 00 - twp 16
Gray, James
   1794 - Account ledger of John Melchor's store.
Gray, Sampson
   1793 - Loose estate papers
Gray, Sherrod
   1790 - 122 02 - twp 16
   1800 - Mecklenburg County
Gray, Thomas & Nancy W.
   Pension denied July 7, 1838 - no proof of service.
Gray, William
   1794 - Account ledger of John Melchor's store.
Greber, Philip
   1793 - Account ledger of John Melchor's store.
Greber/Gerber, Samuel
   1795 - Account ledger of John Melchor's store.
Greble/Gribble, Thomas & Sarah Irwin
   1766 - listed in the militia company of Capt. Adam Alexander of Clear Creek.
   1779 - deed from Thomas and his wife, Sarah, to William Irwin on McCasan's Creek, Test: John Harris, bk 11, pg 40. Sarah's signature is Sarah Irwin, not Greble.
   1779 - named as as adjoining land owner to John Black on McCalpin's Creek, bk 10, pg 536.
   1783 - named as an adjoining land owner to Robert McGinty, William Kenedy, and William Miller, bk 12, pg 491.
   1785 - deed to James Hood, Sr. for 12 acres on McCalpin's Creek adjoining Tunas Hood, Test: John Foard, bk 12, pg 434.
   1790 - 125 00 - twp 15
   1800 - Mecklenburg County
Green, Aaron
   1794 - Account ledger of John Melchor's store.
Green, George
   1778 - witnessed a deed, with Robert Sholty, from Adam & Anney Garrison to Henry Kent on Rockey River, no book or page number given.
Green, Jacob
   1795 - Account ledger of John Melchor's store.
Green, James
   1783 - deed from George & Margaret Calhoon for 150 acres on Sugar Creek adjoining Robert and Zacheus Wilson, Test: John Bigham, and James Wilson, bk 12, pg 218.
Greene, John & Margaret
   1779 - witnessed a deed, with James Reed, from William McKinley and Joseph Scott to James Owens on Paw Creek, bk 10, pg 322.
   1783 - witnessed a deed, with James Sloan, from Walter Carruth to Henry Vernor on Paw Creek, bk 12, pg 387.

1784 - bill of sale from Robert Walker for a horse and 150 acres adjoining Jesse and William Clark, and John Walker, Test: James Tagert, bk 12, pg 331.
1784 - deed from Robert Walker, Jr. for 150 acres on Sugar Creek adjoining Thomas Polk, and James Boyce, Test: George Graham, and James Tagert, bk 12, pg 337.
1790 - 224 02 - twp 1
Children: Mary, John, Moses, Isaac, Tabitha, David Haynes Green, daughter who must have died between 1790 and 1794.
John's will was probated Oct 1794.
Green, Linard & Ann
1780 - deed to Samuel Bonds for 68 acres on the south bank of Rockey River, Test: William Haynes, and Jacob Self, bk 11, pg 9.
Green, Needom
1793 - Account ledger of John Melchor's store. (deceased)
Green, Richard
1794 - Account ledger of John Melchor's store.
Greer, Alexander & Mary Spratt(2)
Alexander died Sept 24, 1838 at the 58.
Mary died Feb 24, 1825 at age 44.
Alexander was the son of James Greer.
Greer, Andrew
1772 - named as land owner of a tract on the head spring of the Muddy Creek of Rockey River which he later sold to Robert Harris, who sold to Thomas Rodgers, who sold to William Balch, who sold to John Carothers in 1779, bk 10, pg 372.
1772 - named as land owner of a tract of land on Caldwell Creek which he sold to Robert Harris in 1775, bk 11, pg 54.
1779 - named as an adjoining land owner to William Balch, John Carothers, Thomas Rodgers, and Robert Harris on Muddy Creek, bk 10, pg 372.
Greer, George
1777 - deed for lots 34 & 92 in Charlotte, Test: Nathaniel From, Alexander Karrel, and Jonathan Coates, bk 10, pg 275.
Of Camden District, SC in 1779.
Greer, James(2)
James died June 29, 1784 at the age of 76.
Greer, James & Martha Grimes
1790 - 223 02 - twp 2
Greer, John H. & Margaret P. Rose
1790 - 111 00 - twp 19
1800 - Mecklenburg County
Greer, Joseph & Nancy
1774 - deed to Robert Crawford for 127 acres on both sides of Waxhaw Creek, adjoining William Bird, and John Curry, Test: Joseph and Margaret Duglas, bk 10, pg 246.

of SC in 1774.
Greer, Margaret
    Margaret died April 12, 1787 at the age of 76.
Grees, Nicholas
    1778 - Signer of 1778 Petition
Greer, Thomas & Susannah
    Children: Andrew Greer
Greer, Thomas & Hannah Alexander(2)
    Thomas died at the age of 84.
    Hannah died March 22, 1788, age 27.
    Children: Zenas Alexander (Mary McComb)
Greer, Thomas J. & Jane Springs(2), Mary H.(2)
    1782 - named as an adjoining land owner to Matthew,
    Alexander, and David Roberson on Beaver Dam Creek, bk
    11, pg 158.
    1778 - witnessed a deed, with William Berryhill, and
    Robert Irwin, from Samuel & Patience Allen to James
    McKee on Beaver Dam Creek adjoining John Giles, and John
    Davis, bk 11, pg 110.
    1782 - witnessed a deed, with Nathaniel Irwin, and John
    Brownfield, from Zebulon & Jane Alexander to Phineas
    Alexander, bk 11, pg 171.
    1783 - witnessed a deed, with Robert Irwin, and George
    Calhoon, from Charles Calhoon to John Thompson on
    Benet's fork of Ritcheson's Creek, bk 11, pg 257.
    1790 - 123 05 - twp 2
    Children: Thomas
    Jane died Dec 28, 1808.
    Mary H. died Nov 26, 1845 age 54.
Grier, Margaret
    Wife of Robert Grier, Sr. who died in Dallas Co., AL in
    Aug 1822.
    Children: Isaac, Robert, Mary Johnston, Betsy Grier,
    Peggy Key
Grier, William
    1790 - Loose estate papers
Gregory, Christian
    1790 - 133 00 - twp 11
    1793 - Account ledger of John Melchor's store.
Griffey/Griffith, Aron & Jane
    1790 Children: Eli, James, Grier, Jonathan, Jannet,
    Hannah, Polly, Peggy, Catherine, Rachel, Anna.
Griffee, John
    1763 - witnessed a deed, with John Whitt Alexander, from
    Daniel & Martha England to Joseph Young on Long Creek,
    bk 10, pg 124.
Griffin, Richard
    Richard was born in 1757 according to 1840 pension list.
Griffin, Thomas
    1793 - Account ledger of John Melchor's store.
Griffith, David & Catherine

1783 - deed to James Belk for 100 acres on the north
fork of Leintraces (Lynches) Creek adjoining Henry
Lewis, Test: John and Britain Belk, bk 11, pg 224.
Griffith, David & Hannah
    1784 - deed to Larence Shanepaker for 200 acres at the
head of Polecat Branch of Linchous (Lynches) Creek,
Test: John Belk, and James Doster, bk 12, pg 270.
Grimes, John
    1775 - named as the owner of a tract on the north side
of the Cataba River on the head of Rockey River, which
he sold to Thomas Thomson before 1778, bk 10, pg 365.
    1780 - witnessed a deed, with Alexander McEwen, and John
Houston, from William Penny, to William Ross on Coddle
Creek, bk 11, pg 111.
Groner, Jacob & Elizabeth
    Wife - Elizabeth
    Children: Jacob (Margaret Eagle, Catherine Dewalt)
    1790 - 312 00 - twp 10
    1800 - Cabarrus County
Guiliams, Travis
    1790 - 102 00 - twp 14
Gurley, Jacob
    1793 - Account ledger of John Melchor's store.
    1793 - Jacob settled the account of Benjamin Thomas at
John Melchor's store.
Gurley, James
    1791 - Account ledger of John Melchor's store.
Gusko, George Wm.
    1793 - Account ledger of John Melchor's store.
Hadden, George
    1790 - 121 00 - twp 19
Haddock, James
    1790 - 112 00 - twp 10
Hadley, Joshua
    1771 - Joshua was one of the Cabarrus Black Boys.
    1783 - grant for 350 acres on Buffalo Creek, adjoining
Walter Smiley and James Morrison, bk 12, pg 94.
    1784 - named as an adjoining land owner to John Shaver
on Coldwater Creek.
    1790 - 314 00 - twp 10
    1800 - Cabarrus County
Hagens, James
    1785 - deed from Edward & Lucy Curry of Georgetown Dist,
SC to James, of Camden Dist, SC, on Cain Creek,
witnessed by Samuel and John Hagins, bk 12, pg 604.
Haggins, John
    1773 - named as an adjoining land owner to Joseph
Kennedy, and Hannah McKee, bk 10, pg 122.
    1779 - deed to James Osmond and Robert Newton for 180
acres on Twelve Mile Creek adjoining Robert Ramsey,
Test: William Haggans, bk 11, pg 106.

1782 - named as an adjoining land owner to George Davis on Reedy Creek and McKee's Creek, bk 12, pg 79.

Hagens, William
    1778 - deed to William Givens for 250 acres on both sides of McCorkle's branch of Twelve Mile Creek, adjoining Griffith Rutherford, Test: James Douglas, Francis Bassett, and John Haggins, bk 10, pg 49.
    1778 - deed to Abraham Cook for 202 acres on Waxhaw Creek and Twelve Mile Creek, bk 10, pg 394.
    1779 - deed to John McCullough for 87 acres on Twelve Mile Creek, Test: Duncan Ochiltree, bk 10, pg 425.
    1779 - named as an adjoining land owner to Michael Ligget, bk 10, pg 498.
    1783 - deed with James Houston, to William Potts for 200 acres on Back Creek joining James Potts, Jacob Scroft, and William King, bk 12, pg 290.
    1792 - Loose estate papers

Hagler, Jacob
    1790 - 144 00 - twp 12
    1794 - Account ledger of John Melchor's store.

Hagler, John
    1780 - witnessed a deed from James Maxwell to George Caughon on Rocky River, bk 12, pg 226.
    1783 - witnessed a deed from James Flemen to Paul Fifer on Meadow Branch, bk 12, pg 216.
    1786 - deed from Paulser Ness for 5 acres on the north side of Rocky River, bk 12, pg 582.
    1790 - 236 00 - twp 12
    1793 - Account ledger of John Melchor's store.
    1800 - Cabarrus County

Hagler, John & Barbara
    1772 - Loose estate papers
    Children: John (a cripple- club foot), Jacob

Hagler, John (the cripple) & Catherine
    Wife: Catherine Sides
    Children: Peter, Henry, Leonard, Jacob, Charles, John

Hahn/Hoan/Honer, Henry
    1790 - 105 00 - twp 12
    1792 - Account ledger of John Melchor's store.
    1800 - Cabarrus County

Hall, Halbert
    1782 - Halbert's will was probated in Mecklenburg Co.
    Children: Samuel, William

Hall, James
    1776 - in Capt. Charles Polk's Light Horse Company.
    1778 - trustee of Liberty Hall
    1790 - 123 00 - twp 14

Hall, John & Jane
    1779 - deed to Joseph Galbreath for 13 acres on Goose Creek, Test: Joseph Robb, bk 10, pg 328.

1779 - deed from Thomas Polk, attorney for David
Oliphant, on Goose Creek, Test: Will Lusk, and James
Johnston, bk 10, pg 547.
1790 - 2233 00 - twp 14
1800 - Cabarrus County
Hall, Morgan
1790 - 113 00 - twp 9
1800 - Cabarrus County
Hall, Thomas
1766 - listed in the militia company of Capt. Adam
Alexander of Clear Creek.
1775 -Thomas was a signer of the petition to pardon the
Cabarrus Black Boys.
Hall, Thomas
1790 - 134 00 - twp 14
Hall, William
1754 - named as land owner of 240 acres at the head of
Rockey River on the north side of the Cataba River, bk
10, pg 365.
Hall, William
1784 - named as an adjoining land owner to Walter Bell,
George Davies, and Samuel Ziklegg on Caudle Creek, bk
12, pg 351.
Hambright, Frederick
1767 - Militia, Mecklenburgh Regiment (Lieutenant)
Hames, Thomas
1784 - named as an adjoining land owner to John Ramsey,
and William Smith on Four Mile Creek, bk 12, pg 385.
Hamilton, Hugh
1772 - Loose estate papers
Hamilton/Hambelton, Hugh
1784 - named as an adjoining land owner to Ephraim Pharr
on Rocky River, bk 12, pg 178.
1790 - 112 00 - twp 8
1800 - Cabarrus County
Hamilton, John
1784 - witnessed a deed from Thomas Polk to Paul
Barringer on Dutch Buffalo Creek, bk 12, pg 398.
1785 - deed to John and William Hamilton from Ephraim
Pharr on the east side of Rockey River joining Mitchel's
barony line, bk 12, pg 531.
Hamilton, William
1779 - deed to William Ferril for 100 acres on the north
side of Waxhaw Creek, Test: John McClanahan, and Robert
Crocket, bk 11, pg 67.
1785 - east side of Rockey River joining Mitchel's
barony line (see John Hamilton)
Hamilton, William
1790 - 000 10 - twp 7
1800 - Mecklenburg County
Hammond, Mathias
1790 - 114 00 - twp 6

Hampton, Patrick
    1790 - 314 09 - twp 7
Hanks, Thomas
    1790 - 111 00 - twp 1
Hann, Margret
    1790 - 000 20 - twp 1
Hanna, John & Sarah
    1769 - Loose estate papers for John
    1774 - witnessed a deed along with James Boyas, from
    Abraham & Jannet Miller to Robert Bell on McCalpin's
    Creek, bk 10, pg 18.
    1784 - witnessed a deed from John Sloan to Jesse Clark
    on a branch of Sugar Creek, bk 12, pg 466.
    Children: Andrew, John
Hansill, John
    1790 - 132 00 - twp 7
Hanson, Charles, Sr.
    1793 - Account ledger of John Melchor's store.
Hanson, Daniel
    1793 - Account ledger of John Melchor's store.
Hanston, William
    1779 - witnessed a deed, with Archibald Crockett, from
    Nathaniel Johnson to Hugh Crye on the middle fork of
    Twelve Mile Creek, bk 10, pg 309.
Harbison, William
    1790 - 111 00 - twp 14
Hardis, Robert
    1783 - Loose estate papers
Harding, Ambrose
    1763 - original grantee of 12,500 acres, later conveyed
    to John & Elizabeth Mitchell of Rowan County, bk 10, pg
    180.
    1769 - named as the original grantee of a tract that was
    later conveyed to John & Elizabeth Mitchell under the
    hand of the sheriff in 1768.
    Ambrose, counselor at law, was living in Dublin at the
    time of these grants.
Harding, Joseph
    1778 - named as an adjoining land owner to James and
    Patrick Scott, and William McCleary on Long Creek, bk
    10, pg 363.
Hardision, Benjamin
    1767 - Militia, Mecklenburgh Regiment (Captain)
Hardman, George
    1790 - 101 00 - twp 12
Hardwick/Hardway, Cunrod/Conrad
    1780 - witnessed a deed, with George Keiser, from Henry
    & Mary Powell to Frederick Ciser on Rocky River, bk 11,
    pg 27.
    1782 - deed from George & Mary Kizer for 25 acres in the
    fork of Meadow Creek and Canada's branch, witnessed by
    Frederick Kizer and John Rite, bk 12, pg 482.

1785 - witnessed a deed from Frederick & Rebhel Kiser to
John Rette on Medor Creek, bk 12, pg 511.
1790 - 102 00 - twp 15
1792 - Account ledger of John Melchor's store.
Hardwick, George
1790 - 103 00 - twp 12
Hargey, Martin
1790 - 133 00 - twp 12
1800 - Cabarrus County
Hargitt, Henry & Nanna
1775 - witnessed a deed, with Joshua Hightower, from
John & Sarah Ashley to Reese Shelby on Richardson's
Creek, bk 10, pg 177.
1782 - grant for 150 acres on Richardson's Creek, bk 12,
pg 8.
1790 - 112 00 - twp 16
1800 - Mecklenburg County
Children: Elizabeth (? Chaney), Rachel (? Pellum),
Rebecca (? Broom), Mary (? Craig), Sarah (?
Helms), Agness (? Laney), Henry, Peter, Joseph,
Daniel
Hargitt, Henry, Jr.
1790 - 162 00 - twp 16
1800 - Mecklenburg County
Son of Henry & Nanna Hargett
Hargitt, James
1790 - 111 00 - twp 16
Hargrove, John
1790 - 213 00 - twp 1
Hargrove, Thompson
1790 - 125 00 - twp 1
1800 - Mecklenburg County
Harkey, John, Sr.
1790 - 212 00 - 15
Children: David ? (Catherine Eudy)
Harkey/Harchie, Martin, Sr.
1792 - Account ledger of John Melchor's store.
Harkey/Harchie, Martin, Jr.
1792 - Account ledger of John Melchor's store.
Harkness, George & Mary
1790 - 136 00 - twp 19
Harlan, Isaac
1778 - Loose estate papers
Harper, William & Mary
1790 - 123 03 - twp 7
Harrington, Willmill
1793 - Account ledger of John Melchor's store.
Harris, Charles, Dr.
Children: William Shakespeare, Charles J.
Brothers: Robert, James, Richard, Thomas
Charles died Sept 21, 1825.
Harris, Charles

1779 - Rockey River, Beaverdam Creek, Brown's Creek of
Broad River in SC in 1777.
1778 - mentioned as an ajoining land owner and dec'd in
a May 1778 deed from George Alexander to Samuel Linton
for a tract on Rocky River, bk 10, pg 314.

Harris, Charles & Elizabeth
1776 - Charles' will was probated in Meckelburg Co.
1777 - Loose estate papers
Children: Martha (married a Harris), Robert, Thomas,
Margaret Alexander, Jane Ruse , Samuel, James, Charles.

Harris, Elinor(2)
Elinor died Aug 22, 1789 at the age of 63.

Harris, Ephraim "Drake"
1790 - 216 00 - twp 11
1793 - Account ledger of John Melchor's store.
1800 - Cabarrus County
Children: Ann Barbra (Henry Miller)
Ephraim D. Harris bought lot 17 in Asheville, Buncombe
Co., NC in 1795.
Ephraim was born 1753, died 1816, buried in the Harris
Family Cemetery in Cabarrus County on Hwy 49.

Harris, George
1766 - listed in the militia company of Capt. Adam
Alexander of Clear Creek.
1783 - deed to William Reed for 68 acres on Crooked
Creek, witnessed by Edward Koulp(Culp), and John Reed,
bk 12, pg 522.

Harris, Grace
1803 - Loose estate papers

Harris, Hugh & Martha(2)
1780 - named as an adjoining land owner to John
Johnston, and Samuel & Deborah McCleary, bk 11, pg 173.
1782 - witnessed a deed, with Robert McCleary, from
William Elliott to James Witherspoon for lot 115 and 123
in Charlotte, bk 11, pg 143.
1782 - Big Sugar Creek.
1790 - 123 00 - twp 2
Children: James
Hugh died Aug 11, 1825 at the age of 72.
Martha died Jan 25, 1834 at the age of 83.

Harris, James
1767 - Militia, Mecklenburgh Regiment (Ensign)

Harris, James
1790 - 214 01 - twp 8
1797 - Loose estate papers

Harris James, Capt(2)   Steel Creek   born-1722
1777 - named as an adjoining land owner to James
Stafford, William Adams, and James Carruth on Reedy
Creek, bk 10, pg 254.
1779 - named as an adjoining land owner to James
Alexander on Mallard Creek, bk 10, pg 530.

1781 - deed to James Orr for 294 acres lying on a
branch, Test: Abraham Alexander, bk 11, pg 300.
1790 -604 06 - twp 13
James died Sept 7, 1811 at age 89.
Harris, James & Margaret
1773 - deed to Robert Stewart for 300 acres, Test:
Thomas Harris, and Robert Lewis, bk 10, pg 105.
James was one of the signers of the Mecklenburg
Declaration of Independence on May 20, 1775.
He was also a signer of the petition to pardon the
Cabarrus Black Boys in 1775.
1775 - witnessed a deed of gift from Moses Shelby to his
granddaughter, Mary Carruthers, bk 11, pg 61.
1779 - deed from Thomas Polk, attorney for David
Oliphant, for 30 acres, and another tract on Clear
Creek, bk 11, pg 265 & 267.
1790 - 404 013 - twp 14
Wife - Margaret Davidson, daughter of John Davidson.
Children: Robert, Samuel, Jennett, John, James,
Elizabeth, William, Mary.
Margaret Harris died 1791.
1791 - Loose estate papers for Margaret
Harris, James, Sr. & Mary
1766 - listed in the militia company of Capt. Adam
Alexander of Clear Creek.
1775 - James was a signer of the petition to pardon the
Cabarrus Black Boys.
1778 - deed to James Benson for 153 acres lying on a
tract known as the Welch Tract, Test: James Neal, and
Thomas Benson, bk 10, pg 289.
1778 - Signer of 1778 Petition.
1780 - A James Harris was a trustee for the congregation
of Rocky Sping.
Harris, James & Agnes Hunter
Wife - Agness Hunter, daughter of John & Mary Hunter.
Harris, James, Sr.
1779 - Loose estate papers
Harris, James(2)   Steel Creek born 1767
Died Dec 12, 1833 at the age of 66.
Harris, James
1778 - James' will was probated in Mecklenburg Co.
Children: Robert, Samuel, John
Harris, Jeremiah
1766 - listed in the militia company of Capt. Adam
Alexander of Clear Creek.
Harris, Jesse & Agnes
1779 - deed to George Harris for 68 acres, witnessed by
William and Thomas Irvin, bk 12, pg 552.
1783 - named as an adjoining land owner to Samuel
Buchanan, and James Holland on Crooked Creek and
McCalpin's Creek, bk 12, pg 104.
Harris, John(2)

1766 - listed in the militia company of Capt. Adam
Alexander of Clear Creek.
Died June 8, 1808 at the age of 81. Born 1727.
Harris, John, Capt.(2) & Rachel Gingles
    1777 - witnessed a deed, with Josham Irvin, from William
& Agness Henderson to Robert Galbreath on Crooked Creek,
bk 10, pg 291.
    1779 - witnessed a deed from Thomas & Sarah Greble to
William Irwin on McCason's Creek (near McCalpin's
Creek), bk 11, pg 40.
    1790 - 112 01 - twp 13
    Wife: Rachel Gingles, daughter of Samuel & Margaret
McAllister Gingles.
John died Sept 26, 1821 at the age of 61. Born 1760.
Harris, John & Martha Hunter
    1790 - 105 00 - twp 16
    1800 - Mecklenburg County
Harris, Joseph
    1773 - witnessed a deed, with John Rabinett, from
William & Elizabeth Morris to Richard Stillwell on the
north side of White Oak Branch known as the No. 2 tract,
bk 10, pg 115.
Harris, Joseph, Jr. & Jane
    1766 - listed in the militia company of Capt. Adam
Alexander of Clear Creek.
    1777 - witnessed a deed, with Joseph Harris, Jr., from
James Bradley to Benjamin Bryan, Jr., on Crooked Creek,
bk 10, pg 228.
    1785 - witnessed a deed from William Love to Manuel
Stevens on Crooked Creek, bk 12, pg 529.
    1786 - deed to Jonathan Query for 77 acres on both sides
of Crooked Creek, witnessed by John Query, and John
Donaldson, bk 12, pg 591.
Harris, Laird & Mary
    1779 - witnessed a deed, with Matthew Harris, from
Thomas Harris, sheriff, to Samuel Harris, Sr. on Neel's
Creek, a branch of Reedy Creek, by a judgement against
the estate of John Wylie, bk 10, pg 426.
Harris, Margaret
    Margaret died in 1789.
    Children: Robert, William, Mary, Margaret (?
Ferguson)
Harris, Mathew
    1779 - witnessed a deed, with Laird Harris, from Thomas
Harris, sheriff, to Samuel Harris, Sr. for which a
judgement was obtained against the administrators of
John Wylie, deceased, on Neel's branch of Reedy Creek,
bk 10, pg 426.
Harris, Oliver
    1790 - 102 01 - twp 8
    Son of Robert & Margaret Harris.
Harris, Richard

Residents of Mecklenburg County, North Carolina   1762-1790

1775 - Richard was one of the signers of the Mecklenburg Declaration of Independence on May 20, 1775.
Brothers: Dr. Charles, Robert, James, Thomas

Harris, Robert, Capt. & Frances
1790 - 116 01 - twp 8
1800 - Cabarrus County
A Robert Harris owned land on Coddle Creek which was the home of the meeting house and school house.
A member of Poplar Tent Presbyterian Church.

Harris, Robert, Esqr. & Margaret
1778 - deed from Joseph & Rebekah Patterson for 312 acres on Rocky River, adjoining Samuel Pickens, and Thomas Shields, Test: John Hamilton, Robert Allison, and Robert Hope, bk 11, pg 287.
1781 - witnessed a deed, with John Smith, from Nathaniel & Jane Gilmore to Zacheus Wilson, bk 12, pg 317.
1783 - witnessed a deed, with Andrew Alexander, from Robert & Catherine Hope to Zacheus & Keziah Wilson, bk 12, pg 303.
1790 - 214 011 - twp 8
Children: Margaret, Mary, Hannah (? Wiley), Samuel, Oliver, James.
1794 - Robert's will was probated in Mecklenburg Co.

Harris, Robert S. & Martha
1766 - listed in the militia company of Capt. Adam Alexander of Clear Creek.
1767 - Militia, Mecklenburgh Regiment (Lieut. Colonel)
1777 - deed to Robert Martin for 140 acres on Caldwell Creek, Test: Martha Harris, and Robert Harris, Jr., bk 10, pg 3. This Robert Harris is identified as being of Mount Harris in Mecklenburg County.
1779 - Robert was one of the administrators of John Wiley, bk 10, pg 426.
1780 - named as an adjoining land owner to John Driskell, James Carrothers, and Andrew Greer on Caldwell Creek, bk 11, pg 54.
1782 - grant on the east side of Cane Run, a branch of Footy (Fuda) Creek adjoining Robert Cochran, Sr., bk 12, pg 163.
1782 - grant on both sides of Footy (Fuda) Creek near William Harris
1782 - grant on both sides of Footy Creek near William Harris, bk 10, pg 521.
1782 - named as an adjoining land owner to George Davis on Reedy Creek, bk 12, pg 87.
1783 - grant for 145 acres on Goose Creek, bk 12, pg 152
1790 - 121 00 - twp 13
1800 - Cabarrus County

Harris, Robert
1762 - grant for 185 acres on Dutch Buffalo Creek, mentioned in bk 10, pg 409.

1768 - witnessed a deed, with Robert Harris, from Hugh
Edgar to James Bradshaw on Rocky River, bk 10, pg 118.
1774 - deed to Jacob Myer for 135 acres on Dutch Buffalo
Creek, Test: Jacob Richey, and William Harris, bk 10, pg
149.
1780 - witnessed a deed, with John Davidson, and Thomas
Mitchel, from James Barr and Margaret Wallace to John
Levison for 200 acres on Rocky River near Dutch Buffalo
Creek, bk 11, pg 79.
1790 - 101 08 - twp 13

Harris, Robert
1765 - witnessed a deed, with Moses Ferguson, from James
Armour to Andrew Armour on the Catawba River between
Croder's Creek and Allison Creek, Vol 1, pg 573.

Harris, Samuel & Elizabeth Harris
1766 - listed in the militia company of Capt. Adam
Alexander of Clear Creek.
Wife - Elizabeth Harris, daughter of Robert Harris.
1798 - Samuel died in 1798 and is buried in Rock
Springs.

Harris, Samuel, Sr. & Margaret, Jane
1766 - listed in the militia company of Capt. Adam
Alexander of Clear Creek.
Samuel was a signer of the petition to pardon the
Cabarrus Black Boys in 1775.
1779 - deed for 414 acres on Neel's branch of Rockey
River, another 141 acres, another 70 acres, and another
55 acres from a judgement obtained against the
administrators of John Wylie, deceased, bk 10, pg 426.
1790 - 216 011 - twp 13

Harris, Samuel H. & Martha(5)
1790 - 102 01 - twp 13
1800 - Cabarrus County
Martha died Aug 2, 1797 at the age of 29.

Harris, Thomas & Rachel
1767 - Militia, Mecklenburgh Regiment (Captain)
1776 - Thomas' will was probated in Mecklenburg Co.
1776 - Loose estate papers
Children: James Wallace, Agness, Jeremiah, Rachel,
Thomas, William

Harris, Thomas
1777 - Lacolet(Pacolet) River, South Carolina in 1776.
1778 - named as an ajoining land owner to Robert Arthur,
James Way, and Henry Downs on Four Mile Creek, bk. 10,
pg 73.
1779 - witnessed a deed, with Will Polk, from Thomas
Polk, attorney for David Oliphant, to James Harris on
Clear Creek, bk 11, pg 265 & 267.
1779 - deed from James Ramsey for 138 acres on the south
side of Four Mile Creek, bk 10, pg 450.

1779 - witnessed a deed, with Esther Ramsey, from James
& Rachell Ramsey to Henry McWherter on Four Mile Creek,
bk 10, pg 552.
1779 - witnessed a deed, with John Flennigan, from John
Smith to Andrew Neel on Twelve Mile Creek, bk 11, pg 52.
1785 - deed from James Williamson for 52 acres,
witnessed by Robert Potts, bk 12, pg 584.
Harris, Thomas, Majr. & Mary
1783 - deed to William Means for 428 acres joining James
Ways, witnessed by Adam Meek and William Caule, bk 12,
pg 255.
1785 - witnessed a deed, with Thomas Donnall, from David
Wilson to John Alison, adjoining Ephraim Farr's old line
and Nathaniel Ervin's old line, bk 12, pg 520.
1790 - 205 07 - twp 7
Harris, Virginia(2)
Virginia died Oct 6, 1830 at the age of 69.
Harris, William H., Jr. & Martha(5)
1774 - witnessed a deed, with Jacob Richey, from Robert
& Frances Harris to Jacob Myer on Dutch Buffalo Creek,
bk 10, pg 149.
1790 - 141 00 - twp 13
1800 - Cabarrus County
Martha died Jan 25, 1818 at the age of 44.
Harris, William, Sr.
1766 - listed in the militia company of Capt. Adam
Alexander of Clear Creek.
1778 - witnessed a deed, with Robert Harris, from
William Adams to George Davis on Reedy Creek, bk 10, pg
256.
1782 - named as an adjoining land owner to Robert Harris
on Footy (Fuda) Creek, bk 12, pg 168 and pg 548.
1790 - 135 02 - twp 13
1800 - Cabarrus County
Harrison, Davis
1785 - witnessed a deed, with Samuel Harris, from
William & Martha Willie to Nehemiah Harrison, on McKee's
Creek, bk 12, pg 548.
Harrison, Isaiah
1790 - 133 02 - twp 19
Harrison, Josiah
1785 -deed from John & Jean Baxter on Sugar Creek, bk
12, pg 544.
Harrisson, Nehemiah
1785 - deed from William & Martha Willie for 150 acres
on the north side of McKee's Creek, adjoining Samuel
Harris, witnessed by David Harrison and Samuel Harris,
bk 12, pg 548.
1790 - 135 02 - twp 15
1800 - Mecklenburg County
Harrison, Robert

1769 - witnessed a deed, with Adam Alexander, from John
& Elizabeth Mitchell to James Wallace, bk 10, pg 128.
Hartt, Andrew(2)
Andrew died Sept 1788 at the age of 17.
Hart, David/Daniel & Dinah(2)
1790 - 100 00 - twp 2
Children: William, Mary, Tibath Adeline, David Milton
Brother-Joseph Hartt.
A daughter died in 1802(9)
Hartt, Elizabeth(2)
Elizabeth died July 1775 at the age of 42.
Hartt/Hert, Jacob, Sr.
1794 - Account ledger of John Melchor's store.
Hartt/Hert, Jacob, Jr.
1794 - Account ledger of John Melchor's store.
Hartt/Hurt, James & Sarah Hamilton(2)
1790 - 102 00 - twp 2
1800 - Mecklenburg County
James & Sarah were married in 1788.
James died Aug 10, 1822 at age 61.
Hart, James & Hannah
James and Hannah's son is buried in Steel Creek
Cemetery, 1799.
Hart, Joseph
1778 - Loose estate papers
Hart, Joseph & Mary
1790 - 111 00 - twp 2
Hart/Hert, Martin
1793 - Account ledger of John Melchor's store.
Hart, Samuel
1780 - deed from Alexander/Moses Hutchison for lots 340,
341, and 342 in Charlotte, Test: William Hutchison, and
Joseph Dickson, bk 11, pg 23.
Hartt, William & Jane
William died before 1802
Children: James, Matthew
Hartis, Elizabeth
Elizabeth died in 1822.
Hartis, John
1790 - 224 00 - twp 12
Hartis/Hastin, Lewis
1790 - 124 00 - twp 15
1800 - Mecklenburg County
Hartman, George
1790 - 116 00 - twp 10
1800 - Cabarrus County
Hartsal, Rosena
Rosena was born Oct 31, 1764, died Aug 31, 1845, buried
in St John's Evangelical Lutheran Church Cemetery.
Hartsell, George
George was born Oct 20, 1755, died June 11, 1833, buried
in St John's Evangelical Lutheran Church Cemetery.

Hartsell, Andrew & Catherine Reed, Sallie Love
    Wife - Catherine Reed, daughter of John & Sarah Kiser
    Reed; Sallie Love, daughter of Jonah Love.
    Children: Millie T.
    Son of Leonard Hartsell
Hartsell, Leonard
    1774 - Mentioned in the estate papers of Nicholson Ross.
    Children: Andrew
    Leonard was born about 1763, died Jan 3, 1822, buried in
    St Martin's Lutheran Church Cemetery.
    1793 - Account ledger of John Melchor's store.
Hartsel, John
    1790 - 224 00 - twp 12
Hartwick, Conrad
    1790 - 102 00 - twp 15
Hartwick, Conrad
    1782 - Meadow Creek and Canada's Branch.
    1790 - 132 00 - twp 12
Harwood, Absolum
    1795 - Account ledger of John Melchor's store.
Haynes, Bartholomew & Sarah(2)
    Children: David
    Bartholomew died June 20, 1815 at age 50.
    Sarah died April 18, 1839 age 69.
Haynes, David
    1780 - witnessed a deed, with Moses Swann, from James
    Sawyer to John Farris on Sugar Creek, bk 11, pg 122.
    1790 - 323 02 - twp 1
    Children: Margaret ? (John Greene)
    Son of Bartholomew & Sarah Haynes.
Hayns/Hayone, William
    1767 - Militia, Mecklenburgh Regiment (Captain)
    1779 - deed from Thomas Polk for 326 acres on Muddy
    Creek, Test: Michael Garmon, and William Polk, bk 10, pg
    311.
    1779 - witnessed a deed, with John Nicholson, from John
    Carroll to Joseph Carroll on Sugar Creek, bk 10, pg 324.
    1780 - witnessed a deed, with Jacob Self, from Linard &
    Ann Green to Samuel Bonds on Rocky River, bk 11, pg 9.
    1781 - deed to Jacob Self for 70 acres, Test: William
    Mitchel, and John Allison, bk 11, pg 93.
    1781 - deed to William Mitchel for 144 acres on both
    sides of Muddy Creek, and 28 acres on Muddy Creek, Test:
    John Allison, and Joseph Selfe, bk 11, pg 95.
    1782 - deed to Susana Daniel for 140 acres on Muddy
    Creek, bk 11, pg 189.
Hays, Adam
    1778 - Signer of 1778 Petition.
Hayes, David & Jane(2)
    1778 - David died April 7, 1778 at age 57, his will was
    probated in Mecklenburg Co.

Children: Moses, Robert, Margaret, Elizabeth, Phebe, Mary, John, Hugh Barnett Hays.

Hays, David, Sr.
1780 - witnessed a deed, with William Hays, from Samuel & Elizabeth Hemphill to William Hemphill on a large branch of Stony fork of Mallard Creek, bk 11, pg 57.
1784 - named as an adjoining land owner to Isaac & Eleanor Williams, George Hutchison, Adam Caruthers, James Taggert, and Thomas Polk, bk 12, pg 437.

Hays, Hugh
1785 - witnessed a deed, with George Reed, from William & Frances Hays for to Patrick Hays on Wolf Meadow Branch of Coddle Creek, bk 12, pg 464.

Hays, Patrick C. & Rachel Russell
1785 -deed from William & Frances Hays for 101 acres on both sides of Wolf Meadow Branch of Coddle Creek, adjoining John Wallace, Samuel Patten, and Adam Ross, Test: George Reed, and Hugh Hayes, bk 12, pg 464.
1785 - witnessed a deed, with William Russel, from Robert Russel, Sr. to James Russel for 306 acres on the west side of Buffalo Creek, adjoining David Purviance, and Alexander Ferguson, bk 12, pg 445.
1790 - 125 01 - twp 13
Wife - Rachel Russell, daughter of James and Jane Carson Russell.
Patrick and Rachel moved to GA, TN, then AL where they both died.
Son of William & Frances Hays.

Hays, Robert
1779 - deed from Robert Graham for 116 acres on Sugar Creek, adjoining William Wilson, James Wilson, and John McClure, Test: William Reed, and Joseph Douglas, bk 10, pg 340.
1781 - named as an adjoining land owner to Nathaniel & Jane Gilmore, and Zacheus Wilson, bk 12, pg 317.
1790 - 214 00 - twp 20
1795 Sugar Creek

Hays, William & Prudence
1779 - deed to Prudence from Francis Johnston and Agnes Henderson, executor's of William Henderson, for 32 acres on McCalpin's Creek, and another tract containing 65 acres, bk 11, pg 64.
Prudence was named as adminstrator and wife of William Hays in the above deed.

Hays, William & Frances
1780 - witnessed a deed, with David Hays, from Samuel & Elizabeth Hemphill to William Hemphill on a large branch of Stony fork of Mallard Creek, bk 11, pg 57.
1782
1783 - named as an adjoining land owner to William & Jane Ross, Seth Rodgers, and William White, bk 11, pg 290.

Residents of Mecklenburg County, North Carolina   153
1762-1790

   1784 - grant for 101 acres on Wolf Meadow Branch, bk 12,
   pg 125.
   1785 - deed to Patrick Hays for 101 acres on Wolf Meadow
   Branch of Coddle Creek, adjoining Adam Ross, John
   Wallace, and Samuel Patten, Test: George Reed, Hugh
   Hayes, bk 12, pg 464.
   Children: Patrick (Rachel Russell), and possibly Hugh.
Hazelhart, Henry
   1770 - Loose estate papers
Headright, John
   1784 - named as an adjoining land owner to John
   Patterson, Caleb and Martin Phifer, Joseph Rogers, and
   Robert Patterson on Longreen Branch of Coldwater Creek,
   bk 12, pg 181.
Hearne, George
   1782 - George's will was probated in Mecklenburg Co.
   Children: Jesse
Heaslet, William
   1776 - witnessed a deed, with Charles Alexander, from
   William & Margaret Alexander to Samuel Hemphill on a
   large branch of Stony fork of Mallard Creek, bk 11, pg
   49.
Hellums/Heloms, George, Jr.
   1782 - grant for 150 acres on Richardson's Creek, bk 12,
   pg 97.
   Stuart's fork of Richardson's Creek.
   1790 - 133 00 - 16
   1800 - Mecklenburg County
Hellums/Helms, George, Sr.
   1782 - grant for 100 acres on both sides of Richardson
   Creek, beginning on the west side of the wagon road that
   goes from Col. Alexander's to Camden, running with the
   road and Gilbert Dunlap's line, bk 12, pg 159.
   1783 - deed from James & Mary Cochran for 200 acres on
   Stuart's fork of Richardson Creek, Test: William and
   Amelia Madelph, bk 12, pg 505.
   1790 - 101 01 - twp 16
   1800 - Mecklenburg County
Hellums, Isaac
   1790 - 102 00 - twp 16
   1800 - Mecklenburg County
Hellums, John
   1790 - 124 00 - twp 16
   1800 - Mecklenburg County
Helms/Holmes, Jacob
   1790 - 114 00 - twp 16
Helms, Tilmon
   1790 - 122 00 - twp 16
   1800 - Mecklenburg County
Hemphill, Samuel & Elizabeth
   1776 - deed from William & Margaret Alexander for 300
   acres on a large branch of Stoney fork of Mallard Creek,

Test: Charles Alexander, and William Heaslet, bk 11, pg 49.
Signer of 1778 Petition
1779 - named as an adjoining land owner to Charles Alexander on the middle fork of Stone Creek, grant No. 53, no book and page number given.
1780 - deed to William Hemphill for 300 acres on a large branch of Stoney fork of Mallard Creek adjoining William Alexander, Test: David and William Hays, bk 11, pg 57.
1779 - deed from John Garrison for lots 201, 204, 330, 331, 335, 336 in Charlotte, bk 11, pg 16.
1780 - deed from Ezekiel Polk for lot 65 in Charlotte, bk 11, pg 22.
1782 - deed to Samuel McCombs for lot 65 in Charlotte, bk 11, pg 194.

Hemphill, William
1779 - grant for 196 acres on Mallard Creek adjoining Benjamin Alexander, bk 10, pg 535.
1780 - named as an adjoining land owner to Alexander Wallace, John Cook, Michael Henderson, Mathew Robinson, and Thomas Frohock on Mallard Creek, bk 12, pg 120.
1783 - deed to Joseph Martin for 300 acres on a large branch of Stoney Fork of Mallard Creek, Test: William and Charles Alexander, bk 11, pg 236.

Henderson, Andrew
1782 - witnessed a deed, with Edward Maloney, from Hugh & Elizabeth Rondles to David Crocket for 50 acres on a branch of Sugar Creek adjoining James Reed, and Alexander Mitchell, bk 11, pg 98.
1790 - 113 00 - twp 4
1800 - Mecklenburg County
Pension denied June 7, 1832 - did not serve 6 months.

Henderson, Archibald
1777 - witnessed a deed, with John and William Henderson, from Robert & Isabell Henderson to Robert Bell on the Catauba River adjoining Richard Barry, bk 10, pg 40.
1778 - Archibald's will was probated in Mecklenburg Co. Children: James, Rebecca

Henderson, Archibald & Sarah
1779 - deed to William Henderson for 59 acres adjoining John Henderson beginning on the east bank of the Cataba River, Test: Benjamin Wilson, Richard Barry, and John Henderson, bk 12, pg 427.
1783 - grant for 224 acres joining Patrick Knox and William Henderson, bk 12, pg 122.
Wife - Sarah Alexander, daughter of William Lee & Elizabeth Alexander
Children: Archibald, female (Nathaniel Boyden)
Archibald died Oct 21, 1822.

Henderson, Cairns/Cerns

1783 - grant for 24 acres on Sugar Creek, adjoining
Robert Crocket, bk 12, pg 111.
1790 - 301 01 - twp 4
1800 - Mecklenburg County
Henderson, John
1790 - 111 03 - twp 7
1800 - Mecklenburg County
Henderson, John
1790 - 202 00 - twp 8
Henderson, John, Jr.
1777 - deed from Robert Harris for 164 acres in the
Welsh Tract on Rocky River, and another tract for 74
acres, Test: Abraham and John McKnitt Alexander, bk 10,
pg 199.
1783 - witnessed a deed, with John McCain, from George
McWhirter to John Ramsey on Waxhaw Creek, bk 12, pg 247.
Henderson, John, Jr.
1790 - 116 00 - twp 7
1800 - Mecklenburg County
Henderson, Michael
1780 - named as an adjoining land owner to John Cook,
and Alexander Wallace on Mallard Creek, bk 12, pg 138.
1790 - 024 00 - twp 6 (Widow Henderson)
Henderson, Robert & Isabell
1788 - Robert's will was probated in Mecklenburg Co.
Children: John, James
Henderson, Thomas, Dr.
1779 - witnessed a deed, with Robert Barlned, Jr., from
George Greer to Mary Baldwin for lot 92 in Charlotte, bk
10, pg 344.
1783 - witnessed a deed, with Samuel McCombs, and James
Tagert, from Joseph Nicholson to William Hutchison for
158 acres on the head waters of Sugar Creek adjoining
Robert and William Elliot, bk 11, pg 209.
1790 - 116 02 - twp 3
1800 - Mecklenburg County
Henderson, William, Jr.
1790 - 244 06 - twp 7
1800 - Mecklenburg County
Henderson, William, Sr. & Mary Giles
1790 - 222 03 - twp 7
Wife - Mary Giles, daughter of John Giles.
Henderson, William
1779 - Crooked Creek
Henderson, William & Agnes
1777 - deed to Robert Galbreath for 70 acres on Crooked
Creek, Test: John Harris, and Josham Irvin, bk 10, pg
291.
1779 - deed from Agnes and Francis Johnston to Prudence
Hays for 32 acres on McCalpins Creek, and another 65
acres, Test: James Boys, John Morris, and William Kerr,
bk 11, pg 64.

Children: John, Joseph, William, Alexander, Jean, one unborn.
1777 - William's will was probated in Mecklenburg Co. Agnes was executor of William's estate with Francis Johnston.
1778 - Loose estate papers

Hennager/Hannager, Michael & Rabeckah
    1790 - 133 00 - twp 12
    1800 - Cabarrus County (widow)

Henninger, Dennis
    1790 - 236 00 - 16

Henry, Henry, Capt
    1784 - named as an adjoining land owner to George and Mitchell Fleming, David Houston, Thomas McQuown, and Hugh & Margaret Parks, on Coddle Creek, bk 12, pg 344.
    1790 - 246 00 - twp 7
    1800 - Mecklenburg County

Henry, James
    1767 - Militia, Mecklenburgh Regiment (Lieutenant)

Henry, James
    1790 - 143 00 - twp 6
    1800 - Mecklenburg County

Henry/Hendry, John
    1775 - named as an adjoining land owner to Samuel Knox, Thomas Ferguson, William Barnett, and George Cahoon on Steel Creek, bk 10, pg 251.
    1776 - Loose estate papers

Henry, Thomas
    1781 - deed to James Simson from Thomas Henry of Lincoln County for 150 acres on Clemmes branch in New Providence, adjoining Alexander McGinty, Test: James Sharp, and William McCleary, bk 10, pg 500.

Henson, William
    1794 - Account ledger of John Melchor's store.

Hepworth, John
    1790 - 105 00 - twp 1

Herchie, Jacob
    1793 - Account ledger of John Melchor's store.

Herrel, Alexander
    1778 - named as an adjoining land owner to John & Jane Wear, John Provane, Ebenezer Newton, Andrew Trot, William Wilson, and John McEwell on Abraham Alexander's Mill Creek, bk 10, pg 283.

Herod, Joseph
    1794 - Account ledger of John Melchor's store.

Heron, Absolam
    1793 - Account ledger of John Melchor's store.

Herren, Allen
    1790 - 123 00 - twp 2
    1800 - Mecklenburg County

Herron, Andw & Margaret Irwin(2)
    1790 - 202 00 - twp 2

1800 - Mecklenburg County
Andrew died April 14, 1805 at the age of 77.
Margaret died June 7, 1793 at the age of 69.
Herron, Elijah
   1790 - 233 01 - twp 11
Herron, Francis(2)
   1780 - witnessed a deed, with Joseph Wishard, from Peter Mathews to John Herron for lot 68 in Charlotte, bk 11, pg 244.
   Francis died Oct 30, 1780 at the age of 38.
Herron, Francis
   1782 - named as an adjoining land owner to Hector & Margaret McLane, William Cooper, William McDowell, John Bigham, James Sprott, and Thomas Barnett on King's Branch of Sugar Creek, Test: Isaak Herron, John Humter, and Robert Hunter, bk 12, pg 234.
Herron, Hugh & Elizabeth B. McGill(2)
   1790 - 124 05 - twp 2
   1800 - Mecklenburg County
   Hugh died June 14, 1805 at the age of 76.
Herron, James
   1779 - James' will was probated in Mecklenburg Co.
Herron/Hern, Jesse
   1790 - 136 03 - twp 11
   1800 - Cabarrus County
Herron, John
   1780 - deed from Peter Mathews for lot 68 in Charlotte, Test: Francis Herron, bk 11, pg 244.
Harrin/Herron, Paul
   1784 Coldwater Creek
Herron, Samuel
   1790 - 000 10 - twp 2
Herron, William(2)
   William died Sept 29, 1785 at age 45.
Hertough, Frederick
   1784 - named as an adjoining land owner to Jacob Teem, and John Eagle on Hamby's Run, bk 12, pg 145.
Herzel, John
   1793 - Account ledger of John Melchor's store.
Hese/Hise, Conrad
   1790 - 135 00 - twp 11
   1800 - Cabarrus County
Hewit, James & Elizabeth
   1783 - deed to Joseph Shinn for 300 acres on Three Mile Branch, adjoining Samuel Patton, Test: John Rodes, and John Weigler, bk 12, pg 335.
Hightower, Joshua
   1775 - witnessed a deed, with Henry Harget, from John & Sarah Ashley to Reese Shelby on Richardson's Creek, bk 10, pg 177.
Hill, John(2)
   John died Jan 15, 1780 at age 23.

Hill, Robert
   1786 - Robert's will was probated in Mecklenburg Co.
   Children: John
Hill, Walter, Sr.
   1796 - Loose estate papers
Hill, William
   1790 - 146 00 - twp 7
   1800 - Mecklenburg County
Hineman, William
   1790 - 111 00 - twp 12
Hipp, Andrew W. & Mabel(8)
   Son of Stephen Hipp.
   Andrew died Oct 22, 1843.
   Mabel was born Feb 20, 1779, died Aug 15, 1844.
Hipp, Stephen & Ann Walkin
   1790 - 213 00 - twp 6
   Son of Stephen Hipp.
Hipp, Stephen
   1782 - Stephen's will was probated in Mecklenburg Co.
   Children: Andrew W., Stephen, John, George, Joseph,
   Jacob, Valentine.
Hipp, Valentine & Margaret Allison
   1790 - 121 00 - twp 6
   1800 - Mecklenburg County
   Son of Stephen Hipp.
Hise, George
   1790 - 125 00 - twp 12
   1793 - Account ledger of John Melchor's store.
   1800 - Cabarrus County
Hise, Leonard
   1790 - 133 00 - twp 16
   1793 - Account ledger of John Melchor's store.
Hobbs, Joseph & Sarah
   1769 - mentioned as the original grantee of a tract
   later conveyed to John Jackson Moore, bk 10, pg 90.
   1777 - deed to Thomas Givens for 150 acres on McDowell's
   Creek, Test: Lewis Jetton, and Samuel Givens, bk 10, pg
   269.
   1777 - deed to Lewis Jetton for 150 acres on McDowell's
   Creek, Test: Thomas and Samuel Givens, adjoining John
   Jetton, bk 10, pg 24.
Hobley/Holly, John & Elizabeth
   1790 - 132 00 - 10
   1800 - Cabarrus County
Hodge, John & Katy McKee
   1790 - 112 00 - twp 19
   1800 - Mecklenburg County
Hodgins/Hagans, John
   1779 - deed from John Hodgins/Haggans to Robert Newton
   and James Osmond/Ormond for 180 acres on a fork of
   Twelve Mile Creek above Robert Ramsey, Test: William
   Haggans, bk 11, pg 106.

Residents of Mecklenburg County, North Carolina 1762-1790

Hogden/Hogan, Nehemiah
   1790 - 102 00 - twp 1
   1800 - Mecklenburg County
Hoge, Francis
   1790 - 204 00 - twp 19
   1800 - Mecklenburg County
Hogland, Tunas
   1782 - deed from George Buckalow for 36 acres on McCalpin's Creek, adjoining James McClure, Test: James Walker, and Robert Donalson, bk 12, pg 508.
   1784 - deed to Tunas Shafer for 36 acres on McCalpin's Creek, Test: Tunas Hood, and Frederick Shafer, bk 12, pg 496.
Hogshead, Samuel
   1778 - named as an adjoining land owner to Andrew & Margaret Robinson, and Hugh Neely on Mallard Creek, bk 10, pg 1.
Hogshead, Walter
   1766/1768 - Walter's will was probated in Mecklenburg County.
   Children: Samuel, William, Walter
Hogton, William
   1778 - Singer of 1778 Petition
Hoiy, Catherine
   1774 - named as an heir of Eloner McDowel, deed for 640 acres to Mathew Lock on Buffalo Creek, Test: Alexander Martin, and Griffith Rutherford, bk 10, pg 144.
Holbrook, Caleb & Druscilla Baker
   1778 - Signer of 1778 Petition
   1790 - 125 00 - twp 9
   Moved to GA before 1800.
Holbrook, John
   1782 - English Buffalow Creek
   1790 - 204 00 - twp 9
   Children: Vachel (Charlotte ?), Caleb (Drucilla Baker), Jacob, William, Sarah (Elias Baker), John, Elizabeth (Benjamin Baker)
   Moved to GA before 1800.
Holbrook, Vaitch (Vachel)& Charlotte
   1790 - 123 00 - twp 9
   1800 - Cabarrus County
   Children: John, Samuel (Elizabeth Russell)
Holbrook, William
   1790 - 131 00 - twp 9
   Moved to GA before 1800.
Holland, Lyon
   1793 - Account ledger of John Melchor's store.
Holland, James
   1783 - named as an adjoining land owner to Samuel Buchanan, and Jesse Harris on McCalpin's Creek and Crooked Creek, bk 12, pg 104.
Holland, William

1778 - deed to Andrew Stinson for 86 acres on McCalpin's Creek, Test: Abraham Miller, and Thomas Mann, bk 10, pg 378.
1779 - grant for 138 acres on Campbell's Creek, a branch of McCalpin's Creek adjoining James Osburn, bk 10, pg 539.

Holt, William
1790 - 001 00 - twp 3

Holton, Thomas
Revolutionary Soldier - died Nov 18, 1837 in Eatonville, GA, age 78 according to The Charlotte Journal dated Dec 1, 1837. Thomas' son was the editor of the Journal at the time.

Holtzclaw/Holsklaw, William
1793 - Account ledger of John Melchor's store.

Hood, James
1785 - deed from Thomas Grible for 12 acres on McCalpin's Creek adjoining Tunas Hood, Test: John Foard, bk 12, pg 434.

Hood, John
1783 - deed from Joseph Galbreath to John and Tunas Hood for 53 acres on Goose Creek, a branch of Rockey River, Test: Benjamin McKenzey, bk 12, pg 206.

Hood, Reuben
1790 - 123 00 - twp 15
1800 - Mecklenburg County
Son of Tunis & Jane Hood.

Hood, Tunis, Capt
1784 - witnessed a deed, with Frederick Shafer, from Tunas Hogland to Tunas Shafer on McCalpin's Creek, bk 12, pg 496.
1790 - 144 04 - twp 15
1800 - Mecklenburg County
Son of Tunis & Jane Hood.

Hood, Tunis, Senr. & Jane
1783 - deed from Joseph Galbreath to John and Tunas Hood for 53 acres on Goose Creek, a branch of Rockey River, Test: Benjamin McKenzey, bk 12, pg 206.
1790 - 100 07 - twp 15
Tunis died in 1797
Children: John, Tunas, Solomon, Reuben, Elizabeth(living near Fort Natches), Rachel (? Shaffer, Lydia (? McGinty), Phebe (? Harrison), Mary (? Neal)

Hope, Peter
1784 - named as an adjoining land owner to Jacob Fagot, Michael Fogleman, and Martin Phifer on Adam's Creek, bk 12, pg 146.

Hope, Robert & Catherine
1778 - witnessed a deed, with John Hamilton, and Robert Allson, from Joseph & Rebekah Patterson to Robert Harris

for 312 acres on Rockey River adjoining Samuel Pickens and Thomas Shields, bk 11, pg 287.
1779 - deed from Jonathan Newman for 380 acres on Rockey River and 29 acres on Clark's Creek, Test: John Alison, and Seth Collins, bk 11, pg 46.
1779 - witnessed a deed, with William Polk, from Thomas Polk, attorney for David Oliphant, to John Lemonds for 20 acres on Caldwell Creek, adjoining John Luckey, and James Marrison, bk 11, pg 36.
1783 - deed to Zacheus Wilson for 15 ¼ acres, Test: Robert Harris, and Andrew Alexander, bk 12, pg 303.
Wife - Catherine Allison
Catherine was born 1750, died 1837, buried in Poplar Tent Presbyterian Cemetery

Hosey, Jonathan
1790 - 102 00 - twp 9

Hough, Jacob
1783 - named as an adjoining land owner to John Meisenheimer, William Leopard, Jacob Richey, John Charles, and Michael Cline on Dutch Buffalow Creek, bk 12, pg 147.

Houghup, James
1767 - Militia, Mecklenburgh Regiment (Lieutenant)

House, Elias
1790 - 202 00 - twp 12
1800 - Cabarrus County

House, John
1790 - 221 00 - twp 12
1793 - Account ledger of John Melchor's store.

House, Mark & Mary ?
1789 - Loose estate papers
1790 - 006 00 - twp 12
1800 - Cabarrus County (widow)

Houston, Aaron
1776 - Aaron's will was probated in Mecklenburg Co.
Children: David, James, John

Housten, David
1784 - named as adjoining land owner to George and Mitchell Fleming on Coddle Creek, bk 12, pg 344.
1790 - 112 00 - twp 9

Houstin, Archabeld
1776 - witnessed a deed, with James Humphrey, from John McLiley to David Wilson on Tinker Branch of Coddle Creek, bk 10, pg 35.
1777 - witnessed a deed, with Caleb Phipher, and Jason Frizell, from Martin & Catherine Phipher to Robert Morton on Coddle Creek, adjoining Archibald Templeton, and John Frohock, bk 10, pg 69.
1784 - witnessed a deed, with Richard Trotter, and William Fraser, from Martin, Sr. and Ephraim Farr on Caudle (Coddle) Creek, bk 12, pg 366.

1785 - deed from Ephraim Farr for 75 acres, Test: David Wilson, bk 12, pg 481.
1790 - 201 03 - twp 8
1800 - Cabarrus County
Archibald died in 1843 after a long and severe illness. (Charlotte Journal- Oct 24, 1843)

Houstin, David
1783 - named as an adjoining land owner to Andrew Snoddy, George Fleming, and David Templeton on Coddle Creek, bk 12, pg 348.
1790 - 102 02 - twp 8

Houston, George & Margaret
Wife - Margaret McClure?
Children: Hugh, Matthew M.
1776 - George's will was probated in Mecklenburg Co.

Houston, James
1777 - witnessed a deed, with Robert Carruth, to Andrew Baxter for lots 146 and 154 in Charlotte, bk 11, pg 7.
1779 - deed from Robert Scott for 150 acres on Six Mile Creek, adjoining Thomas Davis, Test: William Elliott, and Robert Abernathy, bk 10, pg 317.
1779 - deed from Robert Scott for 123 acres on Twelve Mile Creek, Test: Robert Abernathy, and William Ellis, bk 10, pg 333.
1783 - deed from William Haggins and James Houston to William Potts for 200 acres between Back Creek and Six Mile Creek, Test: Charles Alexander, Hugh Philips, and John Potts, bk 12, pg 290.

Houston, John & Ann Howey
1778 - witnessed a deed, with John and Hugh Park, Jr., from Samuel Templeton to William Penny Coddle Creek, bk 11, pg 278.
1780 - witnessed a deed, with Alexander McEwen, and John Grimes, from William Penny to William Ross on Coddle Creek, bk 11, pg 111.
1780 - witnessed a deed, with James Humphreys, from Richard Martin to John McCulough, Jr. on Muddy Branch of Coddle Creek, bk 12, pg 432.
1781 - deed to Archibald Gilmore for 140 acres on a branch of Coddle Creek called Hugh Park's Creek, adjoining James Templeton, Test: John Tanner, and Hugh Rodgers, bk 10, pg 444.
1783 - witnessed a deed, with George Knox, and James Kirkpatrick, from Andrew Snoddy to George Fleming, bk 12, pg 348.
1790 - 134 01 - twp 8
1800 - Cabarrus County
Children: J. Thompson, Allen, Stephen, Peggy, Jane

Houston, David
1784 - east side of Coddle Creek.
1790 - 101 01 - twp 19

Houston, Henry

Residents of Mecklenburg County, North Carolina 163
1762-1790

    1790 - 102 01 - twp 4
    1800 - Mecklenburg County
Houston, Hugh
    1790 - 301 04 - twp 16
    1800 - Mecklenburg County
Houston/Huston, James
    1781 - deed from Robert Dunn for 112 acres adjoining James Alexander, James Dunn, and Robert Dunn, Test: John Robinson, and Thomas and Henry Downs, bk 11, pg 248.
    1790 - 315 05 - twp 16
    1800 - Mecklenburg County
    Wife - Grizzy
    James died in 1802 at the age of 73, buried at Providence Church.
Houston, Lewis
    1783- named as adjoining land owner to Robert Robison, Jr., and Sr. on Reedy Creek, bk 11, pg 296.
Houston, Lisanis
    1783 - grant for 100 acres on the north fork of Back Creek adjoining Ezekiel Alexander, bk 12, pg 631.
Houston, Richard
    1784 - witnessed a deed, with David Allison, from Abraham & Mary Barnett to Joseph Graham, bk 12, pg 499.
Houston, William, Capt.
    1790 - 223 04 - twp 9
Houston, William, Dr.
    1790 - 101 02 - twp 16
Houston, William, Junr.
    1780 - grant for 20 acres on Soder Branch of Twelve Mile Creek adjoining James Way, bk 12, pg 162.
    1790 - 103 01 - twp 16
    1800 - Mecklenburg County
Houston, William, Sr.
    1774 - deed from Francis & Mary McCall for 200 acres on the Cedar fork of Twelve Mile Creek, Test: Thomas McCall, John McCall, and John Osburn, bk 10, pg 226.
    1780 - grant for 80 acres on Newton branch of Twelve Mile Creek, bk 12, pg 22.
    1790 - 103 01 - twp 16
Hovis, John, Sr.
    Wife - Elizabeth Hoyle, daughter of Peter Hoyle
    Children: Frederick, George, Margaret, Susanna, John, Andrew, Peter, Michael, Sarah
Hovis, John, Jr. (Rev)
    Wife - Sarah Catherine Rhyne, daughter of Jacob & Elizabeth Wiltz Rhyne
Howard, William
    1790 - 113 00 - twp 16
    Revolutionary Soldier - died March 14, 1842 in Union Co., NC, age 79 according to The Charlotte Journal dated April 27, 1842.
Howell, Burdock/Burdick

1766 - listed in the militia company of Capt. Adam
Alexander of Clear Creek.
1780 south bank of Rockey River.
Howell, John
    1790 - 102 00 - 13
    1800 - Cabarrus County
Howell, Joseph
    1766 - listed in the militia company of Capt. Adam
    Alexander of Clear Creek.
    1784 - named as an adjoining land owner to George
    Tucker, Henry Smith, and Widow Ciser on Rockey River, bk
    12, pg 174.
    1790 - 332 03 - twp 13
    1800 - Cabarrus County
Howey, George
    1790 - 122 00 - twp 16
    1800 - Mecklenburg County
    Son of John & Frances Howey.
Howey, James
    1745 - mentioned in a deed as follows: ". . . lying on
    Rockey River, known by the name of the Great Tract, and
    granted by the King of Great Britain to Arthur Dobbs as
    one of the abstracts of Murey Crimble and James Howey in
    eight patents on the 3rd March 1745, being the same land
    purchased by Abner Nash of Arthur Dobbs." bk 10, pg 259.
Howey, John & Frances
    1790 - 103 05 - twp 16
    1800 - Mecklenburg Co.
    Children: George, Elizabeth (William Howey), Jane
    (William Stewart), Ann (John Houston), Mary (Robert
    Howey)
Howey/Huey, Samuel & Jane Morrison
    Children: John G.L. (Mary Russell), Josiah (Eliza ?),
    Silas, Pleasant M., Robert C. (Mary C. ?)
    Wife - Jane Morrison, daughter of James & Jeanette Hall
    Morrison.
    Samuel's will was probated in Mecklenburg Co. in 1817.
Howey, William & Elizabeth Howey
    1790 - 211 01 - twp 16
    Wife - Elizabeth Howey, daughter of John & Frances
    Howey.
Hoyle, Andrew
    Wife - Catherine ?
    Children: Catherine, Absolom, Caleb W., Eli, Cynthia
    Andrew was born Jan 13, 1771, died Feb 19, 1857 in
    Gaston County
Hoyle/Hoile, Jacob
    1763 - Loose estate papers
Huber, Jacob
    1790 - 134 00 - twp 12
Hucheson, George
    1790 - 211 01 - twp 1

Residents of Mecklenburg County, North Carolina 1762-1790

Hutchison, John
    1800 - Mecklenburg County
Hucheson, John
    1777 - Loose estate papers
Hud, John
    1790 - 101 00 - twp 1
    1783 - named as an adjoining land owner to Robert Harris, and Hugh Carringer on Goose Creek, bk 12, pg 152.
Hudson, Richard
    1790 - Richard's will was probated in Mecklenburg Co. Children: Joseph, Richard, Thomas, Edward
Hugans, William
    1780 - deed to William Merchant for 170 acres on Meekels' Creek, adjoining William McMurrey, and William Brown, Test: William Kerr, and William Brown, bk 11, pg 148.
Huggins, John
    1780 - deed from John McKnitt Alexander for 145 acres on Garr Creek, bk 12, pg 424.
Hughey, John & Jean Russell
    1790 - 106 00 - twp 18
    Wife - Jean Russell, daughter of James & Jane Carson Russell
Hughes, Samuel
    1776 - in Capt. Charles Polk's Light Horse Company.
    1779 - grant for 128 acres on Coddle Creek, adjoining John McAbley, no book or page number given.(March 3, 1779, should be book 10, pg 495-497)
    1783 - named as an adjoining land owner to Francis and Matthew Lock, and Samuel Patton on Buffalow Creek, bk 12, pg 115.
Hughs, John
    1779 - named as an adjoining land owner to Ephraim Farr, John Farr, and Archibald Houston on Coddle Creek, bk 10, pg 517.
    1779 - grant for 85 acres on Coddle Creek, adjoining Ephraim Farr, David Wilson, and John McAbley, bk 10, pg 493.
    1785 - named as an adjoining land owner to Ephraim Farr, and Archibald Houston, bk 12, pg 481.
Humphrey, James
    1776 - witnessed a deed, with Archibald Houston, from John McLiley to David Wilson on both sides of the Tinker Branch of Coddle Creek, bk 10, pg 35.
    1779 - witnessed a deed, with Arthur McCree, from John McAliley to Richard Martin on Muddy Branch and Stony Run of Coddle Creek, bk 12, pg 439.
    1780 - witnessed a deed, with John Houston, from Richard Martin to John McCulough, Jr. on Muddy Branch of Coddle Creek, bk 12, pg 432.
Hunneycut/Honnicut, Droury

1793 - Account ledger of John Melchor's store.
Hunneycut, Elijah
   1793 - Account ledger of John Melchor's store.
Hunneycut, Howell
   1790 - 111 00 - twp 7
Hunneycut, John
   1793 - Account ledger of John Melchor's store.
Hunneycut/Honeycut/Honnicut, Richard
   1793 - Account ledger of John Melchor's store.
Hunneycut/Honeycut, Thomas
   1790 - 212 00 - twp 12
Hunt, Thomas
   1774 - Mentioned in the estate papers of Nicholson Ross.
Hunt, Turner
   1790 - 116 015 - twp 7
Hunter, Charles & Eus Rosanah
   1803 - will probated in Mecklenburg Co.
Hunter, Edward
   1782 - witnessed a deed, with Henry Searing, from John
   Moore to Samuel Martin for lot 93 in Charlotte, bk 11,
   pg 185.
   1782 - witnessed a deed from Duncan Ochiltree, Samuel
   Martin, Adlai Osburn, and William Polk to John Moore on
   Sugar Creek, bk 11, pg 204.
Hunter, Henry & Martha Sloan(2)
   1778 - Signer of 1778 Petition
   1790 - 273 02 - twp 5
   1800 - Mecklenburg County
   Henry died in 1836 at age 85.
   Children: Humphrey, John, Andrew, Jane, Henry, Betsy,
   Thomas, Robert, James, Joseph, Silas, Abner.
   Brothers: James, Humphrey, Thomas, John
Hunter, Humphrey, Rev.
   1776 - in Capt. Charles Polk's Light Horse Company.
   Brothers: James, Henry, Thomas, John
   Moved to Lincoln Co., NC
Hunter, James
   1774 - witnessed a deed, with Adam Meek, from Nathaniel
   & Sarah Johnston to Peter Steel on the head branches of
   Mallard Creek, bk 10, pg 113.
   1785 - named as an adjoining land owner to William &
   Margaret Alexander, and John McCaughey on the north fork
   of Stoney Creek, bk 12, pg 485.
   Brothers: Henry, Humphrey, Thomas, John
Hunter, John(2)
   John died March 7, 1800 at the age of 34.
   Brother: Robert
   Sisters-Mary Beaty, Rachel McNeely, Agnes Harris, Martha
   Harris
Hunter, John, Sr. & Mary(2)

1782 - witnessed a deed, with Robert Hunter, and Isack
Herron, from Hector & Margaret McLane to William Cooper
in King's Branch of Sugar Creek, bk 12, pg 234.
1790 - 212 06 - twp 1
Children: John, Robert, Mary (James Beaty), Rachel
(Andrew McNeely), Agness (James Harris), Martha (John
Harris)
Brothers: James, Thomas, Humphrey, Henry
John died June 12, 1794 at the age of 74.
Mary died Nov 9, 1810 at the age of 87.
Hunter, John
   1790 - 103 01 - twp 5
   1800 - Mecklenburg County
Hunter, Michael
   1799 - Loose estate papers
Hunter, Robert
   1779 - witnessed a deed, with Samuel Bigham, and
   Alexander Porter, from Samuel Bigham, Sr. to John Porter
   on the north fork of Steel Creek, bk 10, pg 439.
   1782 - witnessed a deed, with John Hunter, and Isack
   Herron, from Hector & Margaret McLane to William Cooper
   in King's Branch of Sugar Creek, bk 12, pg 234.
   1790
   Son of Henry & Martha Sloan Hunter.
Hurlaugher/Horlacher, Christian
   1793 - Account ledger of John Melchor's store.
Hurlaugher/Horlacher, Christor & Ann Mary
   1790 - 303 00 - twp 12
   Children: Elizabeth (John Melchor), Mary (Conrad
   Lidaker), Christian, Rosena (John Hartsel), Barbara
   (John Lippard), Catherine (John Plaster)
   1794 - Account ledger of John Melchor's store.
   Christopher's will was probated in July 1800.
Hurt/Hart, James
   1779 - witnessed a deed, with Jason Frizell, from Mannie
   Justice to Owen Forrister on the Long Branch of Coddle
   Creek, bk 10, pg 385.
Hurst, Henry
   1778 - witnessed a deed, with Joseph Douglas, and
   William Givens, from William Haggins to Abraham Cook on
   Waxhaw Creek and Twelve Mile Creek, bk 10, pg 394.
   1782 - deed to John Galaspy of Guilford Co., for 202
   acres, Test: Andrew Walker, and William Cry, bk 12, pg
   220.
Hutchison, Alexander   see Moses Hutchison
Hutchison, David
   1790 - 112 00 - twp 7
Hutchison, George
   1784 - deed from Isaac & Elenor Williams for 100 acres
   on a branch of Sugar Creek, about a mile from the path
   that leads from Charlotte to John Tatt's, formerly from
   the Widow Pickens to the Cataba Nation, bk12, pg 430.

1784 - deed from Isaac & Elenor Williams for 100 acres on Little Sugar Creek adjoining Adam Carruthers, James Taggert, Thomas Polk, and David Hays, Sr., Test: William McCafferty, James Tagert, and William Berryhill, bk 12, pg 437.
1790 - 211 01 - twp 1
1800 - Mecklenburg County

Hutchison, John
1777 - John's will was probated in Mecklenburg Co. Children: Alexander, James

Hutchison, Moses/Alexander
1779 - deed from Patrick McDonel for lots 390, 391, and 392 in Charlotte, Test: William Reed, and William Hutchison, bk 11, pg 42.
1780 - deed to Samuel Hart for lots 340, 341, 342 in Charlotte, Test: William Hutchison, and Joseph Dickson, bk 11, pg 23. (Moses in deed, Alexander in the signature.)

Hutchison, William
1773 - deed for lots 41, 43, and 48 on the north side of Tryon Street, bk 12, pg 468.
1779 - witnessed a deed, with William Reed, from Patrick McDonel to Alexander Hutchison for lots 390, 391, and 392 in Charlotte, bk 11, pg 42.
1780 - witnessed a deed, with Daniel Ford, from Patrick McDonnel to Alexander Sterroh for lots 204, 335, and 336 in Charlotte, bk 11, pg 130.
1783 - deed from Joseph Nicholsonfor 158 acres on Sugar Creek, adjoining Robert & William Elliot, bk 11, pg 209. 1790 Sugar Creek beginning at a corner of the town land.
1790 - 242 03 - twp 3
1800 - Mecklenburg County

Idglie, William
1779 - witnessed a deed, with Joseph Wilson, from Gilbert McNarr to Francis Nixon on the head branches of Rockey River, joining Zebulon Brevard, Robert Potts, bk 12, pg 490.

Irest, Joseph
1773 - named as an adjoining land owner to John Nicholson , John Newman, and John Carson on Sugar Creek, bk 10, pg 46.

Irvin, Josham
1777 - witnessed a deed, with John Harris, from William & Agness Henderson on Crooked Creek, bk 10, pg 291.

Irwin, Christopher & Jeanette
1790 - 106 00 - twp 20
1796 - Christopher's will was probated in Mecklenburg.

Irwin, Hugh
1770 - Loose estate papers

Irwin, Nathaniel

1774 - named as an adjoining land owner to William
Starret, Nathaniel Cook, Andrew Sprotts on Sugar Creek,
bk 10, pg 370.
1784 - witnessed a deed, with John Nichelson, Thomas
Henderson, from Joseph Nickelson to Samuel McCombs for
lot 6 in Charlotte, bk 12, pg 239.
Irwin, Robert
   1777 - witnessed a deed, with Robert S. Harris, from
   James Stafford and William Adams to James Carruth on
   Reedy Creek, bk 10, pg 254.
   1790 - 122 01 - twp 5
   1800 - Cabarrus County
Irwin/Irvin, Robert & Hannah
   1775 - Robert was one of the signers of the Mecklenburg
   Declaration of Independence on May 20, 1775.
   1777 - deed to John Wier for 315 acres adjoining John
   Price, Alexander Cathey, James Armour on the upper edge
   of Mill Creek, Test: William Graham, Samuel Blyth,
   William Bowen, bk 10, pf 230.
   1780 - named as the previous land owner of 185 acres
   originally granted to James Armour, then conveyed to
   John Miller, then from Miller to Alexander Lewis, then
   to the wife of Miller, then to John Wear from Robert
   Irwin, bk 10, pg 456.
   1784 - witnessed a deed, with John Hana, John Carruth,
   from John & Jane Sloan to Jesse Clark on a branch of
   Sugar Creek joining Isaac Williams, Robert Walker, James
   Taggert, David Hays, Alexander McKee, bk 12, pg 466.
   1786 McCalpin's Creek
   1790 - 226 03 - twp 2
   Robert died Dec 23, 1800, buried in Steel Creek
   Cemetery.
Irwin, Samuel
   1790 - 111 01 - twp 7
Irwin, Thomas
   1790 - 124 00 - twp 8
   1800 - Cabarrus County
Irwin, Thomas
   1779 - witnessed a deed, with William Irvin, from Jesse
   & Agnes Harris to George Harris, bk 12, pg 552.
   1786 - McCalpin's Creek (twp 15)
   1790 - 112 00 - twp 15
   Son of William and Sarah.
Irwin, William, Jur.
   1790 - 111 00 - twp 15
Irwin, William & Sarah
   1779 - witnessed a deed, with Thomas Irvin, from Jesse &
   Agnes Harris to George Harris, bk 12, pg 552.
   1785 - deed to Thomas Irwin for 126 acres on McCalpin's
   Creek, Test: John & Samuel Black, bk 12, pg 453.
   1790 - 303 00 - twp 15
   Children: Thomas

Irwin, William & Mary
  1766 - listed in the militia company of Capt. Adam
  Alexander of Clear Creek.
  1783 - William's will was probated in Mecklenburg Co.
  Children: Samuel
Isenhaker, Nicholas
  1790 - 000 10 - twp 11
Isham, John
  1790 - 103 00 - twp 3
Isler, Nicholas
  1790 - 212 00 - twp 1
Izel, Fredrick
  1790 - 213 00 - twp 16
  1800 - Mecklenburg County
Jack, Charity
  1774 - witnessed a deed with Will Reed, from John Rillah
  to John Davis between McMichael's Creek and McCalpin's
  Creek, adjoining John Frohock, bk 10, pg 135.
Jack, James, Capt.
  1773 - Commissioner for the town of Charlotte.
  1775 - deed for lots 196,144,166,168,390,399,and 167 in
  the town of Charlotte, bk 11, pg 220.
  1777 - deed to Robert Scott for lot 27 in Charlotte, bk
  10, pg 281.
  1778 - witnessed a deed from the trustees to Adlai
  Osbourne of Rowan Co. for lots 451,455,466,and 457 in
  Charlotte, bk 10, pg 235, lots 472,479,490,and 491, bk
  10, pg 237.
  1778 - Commissioner for the town of Charlotte.
  1779 - Commissioner for the town of Charlotte.
  1779 - deed from Joel Brevard for lot 165 in Charlotte,
  bk 10, pg 300.
  1780 - deed from Robert Elliott for 100 acres on the
  west side of Sugar Creek, Test: Edward Elliott, Dun
  Ochiltree, bk 11, pg 59.
  1780 - witnessed a deed, with Samuel Elliott, from
  William Elliott to Joseph Nicholson on the head waters
  of Sugar Creek, bk 11, pg 73.
  1780 - witnessed a deed, with Peter Johnston, from
  Thomas Polk to John Davies on the Catawba River about a
  mile above the mouth of the 8th fork, bk 11, pg 33.
  1783 - deed to James Orr for lot 25 in the town of
  Charlotte, bk 11, pg 269.
  1783 - deed to Phineas Alexander for 100 acres on Sugar
  Creek, originally granted to Robert Elliott, then Samuel
  Elliott, then James Jack, Test: Robert Irwin, Thomas
  Elliott, bk 11, pg 274.
  1783 - deed to lot 25 in the town of Charlotte, bk 11,
  pg 294.
  Children: Cynthia (A.S. Cosby), Patrick, William
  Houston, Archibald, James

Residents of Mecklenburg County, North Carolina 1762-1790

James and his family moved to Augusta, GA, then Elbert Co., GA
Son of Patrick & Lillis Jack.
Jack, John
   1777 - witnessed a deed, with David Weeks, from John Phillip Weeks to John McGivert on Rockey River, bk 10, pg 243.
   Son of Patrick & Lillis Jack.
Jack, Joseph
   1777 - witnessed a deed, with James McMahon, J. McDowell, from George & Margaret Cathey to Hugh Lucas, bk 10, pg 242.
Jack, Margaret
   1779 - witnessed a deed, with John Allen, from John Ford to Ochilltree Martin and Company for lots 85, 93 in Charlotte, bk 10, pg 350.
Jack, Patrick & Lillis
   1774 - witnessed a deed, James Simson, from Andrew Baxter to John Baxter, bk 10, pg 153.
   Patrick died in 1780.
   Wife - Lillis McAdoo
   Children: Mary (Robert Alexander), Margaret (Samuel Wilson), Charity (Cornelius Dysart), Jane (William Barnett), Lylly (Joseph Nicholson), James, John, Samuel, Robert
Jack, Patrick
   Patrick died between May 1790-Jan 1791.
   Son of James Jack.
Jack, Samuel
   1774 - witnessed a deed, with James Easter, to William Davison for lot 52 in Charlotte, bk 10, pg 163.
   1776 - named as an adjoining land owner to Augustine Culp, John Wilson on McMichal's Creek, bk 11, pg 222.
   1778 - witnessed a deed, with James Foster, to Joseph Nicholson for lot 6 in Charlotte, bk 10, pg 54.
   Wife - ? Knight, Margaret Stewart
   Children: Eliza D. (? Hodge), James, Samuel S. (Elizabeth Meredith), John McCormick, William D., Mary E., Amanda M.
   Son of Patrick & Lillis Jack.
Jackson, Benjamin
   1779 - grant for 250 acres on Twelve Mile Creek beginning near the Indian Path, bk 10, pg 496.
   The Widow Jackson was on Twelve Mile Creek in 1780.
Jackson, James
   1784 - witnessed a deed with James Latta, from Peter Johnston to Hardwick Davies on McCalpin's Creek, bk 12, pg 404.
Jackson, John
   1779 - witnessed a deed, with David Moore, Andrew Moore, Joseph Robbs, from William & Mary Watson to James Dickson on Clear Creek, bk 11, pg 191.

Jackson, Shadrick
    1790 - 271 00 - twp 1
Jacob, Jeremiah
    1781 - named in a deed, no book or page number given.
Jadeson, Shadrack & Chloe
    1795 - Shadrack's will was probated in Mecklenburg Co.
    Children: Martha, Richard
Jarret, Daniel
    1790 - 325 00 - twp 12
    1795 - Account ledger of John Melchor's store.
Jeem, Jacob
    1782 - deed from Matthias Beaver to Jacob Jeem and Susan
    Beaver for 146 acres on both sides of Dutch Buffelow
    Creek, Test: John Barringer, George McKee, bk 11, pg
    162.
    1782 - executor of Matthias Beaver's estate, with Susan
    Beaver.
Jegler, Johanes
    1786 - witnessed a deed, with Samuel Black, from Paulser
    & Franney Ness to Paul Furrow on Dutch Buffalo Creek, bk
    12, pg 580.
Jemison/Jamison, Arthur
    1785 - witnessed a deed with John Buchannon, from Andrew
    Dun to John Dun on Long Creek, bk 12, pg 519.
    1785 - witnessed a deed with John Buchannon, from Andrew
    Dune to Robert Dune on Long Creek, bk 12, pg 541.
    1790 - 144 00 - twp 6
    1800 - Mecklenburg County
Jemison, Thomas
    1790 - 102 00 - twp 6
    1800 - Mecklenburg County
    Wife: Mary Sullivan
Jemison/Jamison, William & Polly(8)
    Children: Isabella, Andrew M., William J.
    William was born in 1782, died Nov 6, 1846.
Jenkins, Elener
    1785 - Loose estate papers
Jenkins, Jonathan
    1785 - Loose estate papers
Jennings, Robert
    1775 - named as an adjoining land owner to John & Elinor
    McDowel, Joseph Wallace, John Brevard, John Burnett, bk
    10, pg 286.
Jetton, Abram/Abraham
    1777 - named as an adjoining land owner to John &
    Elizabeth Jetton, Isaac Jetton, Zebulon Brevard, John
    Jetton, Jr., Hugh Lawrin and Lewis Jetton, bk 12, pg
    494.
    1790 - 111 02 - twp 7
    1800 - Abram's will was probated in Mecklenburg Co.
    Children: Isaac, John, Ephraim
    1800 - Loose estate papers

Residents of Mecklenburg County, North Carolina 1762-1790

Jetton, Isaac
   1770 - witnessed a deed, with Robert Bourns, to John Davies for lot 74 on the south side of Tryon St in Charlotte, bk 11, pg 18.
   1777 - deed from John & Elizabeth Jetton for 188 acres, bk 12, pg 494.
   1785 - witnessed a deed, with Robert Potts, from John & Elizabeth Jetton to Lewis Jetton, bk 12, pg 555.
   1786 - Loose estate papers
   Son of Abraham Jetton.
Jetton, Joel
   1784 - court records of Lincoln Co.
Jetton, John & Elizabeth
   1777 - deed to Isaac Jetton for 188 acres, Test: Zebulon Brevard, John Jetton, Jr., Lewis Jetton, bk 12, pg 494.
   1785 - deed to Lewis Jetton for 200 acres conveyed to John on Aug 12, 1766, Test: Isaac Jetton, Robert Potts, bk 12, pg 555.
   Land that John owned was on or near McDowell's Creek.
   John was a blacksmith.
Jetton, John
   1754 - grant for a tract later conveyed to Isaac Jetton, bk 12, pg 494.
Jetton, John , Jr.
   1777 -
Jetton, Lewis
   1777 - deed from Joseph & Sarah Hobbs for 150 acres on McDowell's Creek, adjoining John Jetton, Test: Thomas and Samuel Givens, bk 10, pg 24.
   1777 - witnessed a deed, with Samuel Givens, from Joseph & Sarah Hobbs to Thomas Givens on McDowell's Creek, bk 10, pg 269.
   1777 - witnessed a deed, with Zebulon Brevard, John Jetton, Jr., from John & Elizabeth Jetton to Isaac Jetton, bk 12, pg 494.
   1785 - deed from John & Elizabeth Jetton for 200 acres, Test: Isaac Jetton, Robert Potts, bk 12, pg 555.
   1790 -
Jimeson, Robert
   1790 - 112 00 - twp 6
Jinkins, John
   1790 - 323 00 - twp 20
John/Johns, Daniel
   1790 - 113 01 - twp 19
   1800 - Mecklenburg County
John, Mary
   1777 - mentioned in a deed, no book or page number given.
   Children: Zephaniah, Benjamin, Daniel, Roger
John, Robert
   1783 - deed from Susana Daniel for 140 acres on Muddy Creek adjoining Thomas Mary, William Michel, Test:

Thomas Morrow, Rees Shelby, Daniel Metheny, bk 12, pg 287. (names also appears in the deed as **Roger John**)

John/Johns, William
    1764 - Loose estate papers

John, Zeph
    1779 - named as an adjoining land owner on Six Mile Creek near Stillhouse Branch, bk 12, pg 272.

Johnston, Alexander
    1770 - witnessed a deed, with Thomas and Hugh Neely, from Moses & Martha Ferguson, Samuel & Mary Knox, to Francis and Joseph Johnston, Vol 5, pg 198.
    1777 - witnessed a deed, with Thomas Neely, from Abraham & Jannet Miller to John Johnston on the north side of McCalpin's Creek, bk 10, pg 231.
    1781 - deed from Francis & Margaret Johnston for 158 acres adjoining Mathew Knox, John Whitfield, Thomas Nealy, then down a branch to Hugh Herron's line, Test: Joseph Swann, Hugh Rodgers, bk 12, pg 228.

Johnson, Bartholomew
    1778 - witnessed a deed, with John Maxwell, from Andrew & Anne Downs to John Morrow joining Zebulon Brevard, bk 10, pg 39.

Johnston, David
    1790 - 113 00 - twp 4
    1800 - Mecklenburg County

Johnston, Francis & Margaret
    1770 - deed from Moses & Martha Ferguson, Samuel & Mary Knox for 400 acres on east side of Catawba and SE side of path leading from Jean Armour's to the Catawba Nations, Test: Thomas and Hugh Neely, Alexander Johnston, Vol 5, pg 198.
    1779 - deed from Francis Johnston and Anges Henderson, executors of William Henderson, to Prudence Hays on McCalpin's Creek for 32 acres, another for 65 acres, Test: James Boys, John Morris, William Kerr, bk 11, pg 64.
    1781 - deed to Alexander Johnston for 158 acres adjoining Mathew Knox, John Whitfield, Thomas Nealy, then down a branch to Hugh Herron's line, Test: Joseph Swann, Hugh Rodgers, bk 12, pg 228.
    Executor of estate of William Henderson.

Johnson, Isaac
    1770 - Loose estate papers

Johnston, Isaac
    1790 - 141 01 - twp 6

Johnston/Johnson, James
    1775 - deed to William Gardner for 73 acres on Sugar Creek, Test: Robert Campbell, Ebenezer Newton, bk 10, pg 191.
    1779 - witnessed a deed, with Will Lusk, from Thomas Polk, attorney for David Oliphant, to John Hall on Goose Creek, bk 10, pg 547.

Residents of Mecklenburg County, North Carolina
1762-1790

1782 - named as an adjoining land owner to George Dods, Joseph Davis on Sugar Creek, bk 11, pg 154.
Johnston, John
 1777 - deed from Abraham & Jannet Miller for 100 acres on the north side of McCalpin's Creek, Test: Thomas Neely, Alexander Johnston, bk 10, pg 231.
 1780 - J. Johnston witnessed a deed, with Mary Clark, from Robert & Hannah Craighead to Joseph Mitchell on Rockey River adjoining Adam Meek, John Mitchell's wagon road bk 11, pg 197.
 1780 - deed to Samuel McCleary for 11 ½ acres adjoining Hugh Harris, Test: Ezekiel Polk, Will Polk, bk 11, pg 173.
 1783 - witnessed a deed, with William Ramsey, from David McCord to John Buchanon on Long Creek about half a mile west of Toole's Road, bk 11, pg 196.
 1784 - named as an adjoining land owner to John & Prudence Smith, John King on McCalpin's Creek at the wagon road, bk 12, pg 280.
 1784 - deed to Edward Stockes for 200 acres on the barren ridge between Long Creek and Thomason's Branch, beginning on the north edge of the wagon road, Test: William Ramsey, Justice Beech, bk 12, pg 267.
 1790 - 124 01 - twp 6
 1800 - Mecklenburg County
Johnston, John & Ann
 1779 - deed to John Smith for 81 acres known as Lofton's Bottom on McCalpin's Creek, Test: William Black, George Montgomery, bk 10, pg 390.
 1790 - 341 00 - twp 7
Johnston, Nathaniel & Sarah
 1774 - deed to Peter Steel for 200 acres on Mallard Creek which was originally granted to John W. Alexander in 1768, Test: James Hunter, Adam Meek, bk 10, pg 113.
 1780 - grant for 180 acres on Long Creek beginning near the Mill Race adjoining Ezekiel Alexander, bk 12, pg 41.
 1790 - 135 00 - twp 6
Johnston/Johnson, Nathaniel
 1779 - deed to Hugh Crye for 220 acres on the middle fork of Twelve Mile Creek which was originally granted to Natheniel Alexander in 1753, Test: William Hanston, Archibald Crockett, bk 10, pg 309.
Johnston, Peter
 1769 - deed from Thomas Dearmond for the tract below, but no book or page number given.
 1777 - deed to Isaiah Fitten for 160 acres on Sugar Creek, adjoining Zebulon Alexander, Thomas Alexander, James Yandel, William Yandel, Charles Alexander, Test: Will Reed, Dan Ocheltree, Adam Stuart, bk 10, pg 94.
 1779 - named as an adjoining land owner to Andrew Yandel, William Manson, Thomas Polk on McMichal's Creek, bk 10, pg 513.

1780 - P. Johnston named as adjoining land owner to
Robert McIntire on Sugar Creek, bk 12, pg 53.
1780 - witnessed a deed, with James Jack, from Thomas
Polk to John Davies on the Cataba River near the 8th
fork, bk 11, pg 33.
1781 - deed to Andrew McKee for 200 acres joining Gideon
Thompson, William Lawing, John Anderson, Test: Mat Troy,
Hugh Colloden Boyd, bk 12, pg 444.
1784 - deed to Hadawick Davies for 182 acres on
McMichal's Creek adjoining William Flanagan, Test: James
Latta, James Jackson, bk 12, pg 404.

Johnston, Widow
1790 - 123 00 - twp 14

Johnston, William
1781 - deed from Mathew McClure for 110 acres on the
head branch of McDowel's Creek near One Mile Creek,
Test: Jane Alexander, John McKnitt Alexander, Hezekiah
Alexander, bk 12, pg 451.

Johnston, William
1790 - 122 00 - twp 14

Johnston, William
1779 - named as an adjoining land owner to David Smith,
Andrew Burns on Rockey River close to the meeting house
land, bk 10, pg 541.
1779 - witnessed a deed, with John Carson, from John
Garrison to Samuel Hemphill for lots 201, 204, 330, 331,
335, 336 in the town of Charlotte, bk 11, pg 16.
1780 - grant for 60 acres on Mallard Creek adjoining
James Clark, William McLure, bk 12, pg 91.
1784 - deed from James Wiley for 414 acres on both sides
of Neel's Branch and the south side of Reed's Creek, the
waters of Rockey River, Test: Abraham Alexander,
Hezekiah Alexander, bk 12, pg 619.
1790 - 335 02 - twp 4

Johnston, William
1790 - 122 00 - twp 14
1800 - Cabarrus County

Jones, Adam C.
1767 - Loose estate papers

Jordon, Phillip
1793 - Account ledger of John Melchor's store.

Jordon, William
1794 - Account ledger of John Melchor's store.

Joy, Jeremiah
1768 - sold 29 acres, part of a grant to Jeremiah for
12,500 acres, to John Mitchell on the south side of
Clark's Creek, no book or page number given, bk 10, pg
169.
In Feb 1769 he was mentioned as "late of London".
1780 - named as an adjoining land owner to John McKnitt
Alexander, John Huggins, Richard Stephenson, John
Buchanon on Garr Creek, bk 12, pg 424.

Residents of Mecklenburg County, North Carolina 1762-1790

Juke, John
   1790 - 135 00 - twp 11
Julian, Jacob
   1777 - Jacob's will was probated in Mecklenburg Co.
   Children: George, Graham, James, Decatur
Jung, John
   Wife - Elizabeth Diderich
   John was born 1766, died Feb 13, 1799, buried in Old
   Coldwater Church Cemetery.
Justice, Hance & Mary
   1780 - deed to Samuel Sensill (Hemphill ?) for 250 acres
   on the east side of Cuflon's Creek, adjoining John
   Baker, John Armstrong, James McDowel, William Houston,
   Test: Henry Sensill, Jason Frissell, bk 11, pg 4.
   1782 Cuflon's Creek, English Buffalow Creek.
Justice, Mannie
   1779 - deed to Owen Forrister for 200 acres on Long
   Branch of Coldwater Creek, Test: James Hurt, Jason
   Frizell, bk 10, pg 385.
Justice, Mounce/Hance ?
   1772 - grant on Long Creek of Coldwater Creek, no book
   or page number given, bk 10, pg 431.
   1779 - deed to Andrew McClenhan for 440 acres on Long
   Branch of Coldwater Creek, Test: John March, Jason
   Frizell, bk 10, pg 431.
   Moved to Iredell County before 1790 ?
Karrel, Alexander
   1777 - witnessed a deed, with Nathaniel From, Jonathan
   Coates, from Capt. James PettigAndrew to George Greer
   for lots in the town of Charlotte, bk 10, pg 275.
Karriker/Carriger, George & Susan
   1778 - Signer of 1778 Petition.
   1785 - deed to John George William for 100 acres on a
   branch of Rockey River joining James Beaty/Beatchey,
   Test: Lewis Wilham, Qudray Wilonlee, Paul Farrow, bk 12,
   pg 592.
   1790 - 134 00 - twp 12
   1800 - Cabarrus County
Kearh, Samuel
   1779 - named as an adjoining land owner to David Reed,
   Nicholas Gibbony, Henry Varner, John Carson on Sugar
   Creek, bk 10, pg 412.
Kefer, John
   1778 - Signer of 1778 Petition.
Kelly, Thomas
   1790 - 000 10 - twp 7
Kelugh, Samuel
   1790 - 234 03 - twp 5
   1800 - Cabarrus County
Kendel/Kindal, William, Jr.
   1792 - Account ledger of John Melchor's store.
Kendel/Kindal, William, Sr.

1792 - Account ledger of John Melchor's store.
Kenedy, Joseph, Dr. & Esthesth
   1773 - deed from Hannah McKee for 60 acres on Six Mile Creek and the Great Waggon Road, adjoining James Lynn, John Haggins, Test: Richard and Sussah Springsteen, bk 10, pg 122.
   1777 - deed to John McCullough for 60 acres on Six Mile Creek and the Great Waggon Road, adjoining John McKee, deceased, Test: Robert and Adam Motherall, bk 10, pg 423.
   1779 - named as an adjoining land owner to Thomas Ozburn, Noble Oxburn on McCalpin's Creek, bk 10, pg 511.

Kennady, David
   1786 - deed from Robert Barnet, Jr. for 7 acres on Sugar Creek, Test: William Reed, bk 12, pg 586.
   1790 - 222 00 - twp 4

Kennaday, Esther
   1790 - 301 01 - twp 3

Kennedy, James
   1798 - Loose estate papers

Kennaday, James
   1780 - deed from Robert & Sarah Arthur for 227 acres on Four Mile Creek adjoining Henry Downs, Thomas Harris, Test: John Stewart, John Flenniken, bk 11, pg 2.
   1790 - 214 00 - twp 3
   1800 - Mecklenburg County
Mentioned in the estate settlement of William Sample.

Kennedy, Joseph
   1769 - witnessed a deed, with William Orr, from Thomas Polk to John White of Rowan Co., for a tract between the "widder" Armour and the Catawba Indians District, bk 4, pg 542.
   1777 - Joseph's will was probated in Mecklenburg Co. Children: Joseph, David, Samuel
   1778 Six Mile Creek on both sides of the Great Waggon Road.

Kennedy, Samuel
   1797 - Loose estate papers

Kennaday, Samuel
   1790 - 000 10 - twp 3
   1800 - Mecklenburg County

Kennaday, William
   1783 - deed from Robert McGinty (late of Meckelburg Co.) for 122 acres on McCalpin's Creek, Test: William Miller, James Finney, bk 12, pg 491.
   1790 - 132 00 - twp 15

Kennon, William
   1775 - William was one of the signers of the Mecklenburg Declaration of Independence on May 20, 1775.
   William moved to GA after the Revolutionary War.

Kent, Henry

Residents of Mecklenburg County, North Carolina   179
1762-1790

    1778 - deed from Adam & Anney Garrison for a tract on
    Rockey River, Test: Robert Sholty, George Green, no book
    or page number given, but it should be bk 11, page 31,
    32, or 33.
Kerlock/Carlock, Fredrick & Clary
    1784 - deed to John George William for 91 acres on
    English Buffalo Creek, adjoining Martin Phifer, Test:
    Seth Rodgers, William White, bk 12, pg 564.
    1785 - Bill of sale to Rachel Williams, bk 12, pg 557.
    1790 - 101 00 - twp 10
    Wife - Clarey
    Children: Rachel (? Williams)
Kerlock/Carlock, Fredrick
    1790 - 201 00 - twp 12
Kerlock/Carlock, George
    1790 - 114 00 - twp 12
    1800 - Cabarrus County
Kerr, Andrew
    1790 - 123 03 - twp 6
Kerr/Carr, James
    1778 - witnessed a deed, with James Bayly, from Mathew
    Tate to Adam Tate, both of Donegal Township, Lancaster,
    PA, bk 12, pg 414. (Their father was Joseph Tate)
    1778 - Loose estate papers
Kerr, James
    1790 - Loose estate papers
Kerr/Carr, John
    1784 - deed from Mathew Miller for 500 acres on south
    side of Meadow Branch on the south side of Clear Creek,
    Test: Oliver Wiley, Adam Alexander, bk 12, pg 371.
    1784 - Loose estate papers
Kerr/Carr, John
    1789 - John's will was probated in Mecklenburg Co.
    1789 - Loose estate papers
    Children: William
Kerr/Carr, Joseph, Sr. & Elizabeth
    1771 - Joseph's will was probated in Mecklenburg Co.
    1772 - Loose estate papers
    Children: Joseph, Rachel (? Crockett), Elizabeth (?
    Parker), William
Kerr/Carr, Joseph, Jr.
    1778 - witnessed a deed, with Hugh Eadger, from John &
    Sarah Allen to William Eadger on a branch of Long Creek,
    bk 10, pg 88.
    1780 - witnessed a deed, with John Todd, from James
    Brown to William Blackwood in Gum Branch of Long Creek,
    bk 11, pg 103.
    1790 - 126 00 - twp 6
    1800 - Mecklenburg County
Kerr/Carr, Mary(2)
    Mary died March 15, 1806 at age 60.
Kerr/Carr, Robert

1784 - Robert's will was probated in Mecklenburg Co.
1789 - Loose estate papers
Children: John, Robert, Samuel, Richard
Kerr/Carr, Robert
1773 - deed to Benjamin Wallace for 125 acres on Long
Creek, Test: Robert Carr, Joseph Kerr, bk 10, pg 124.
1789 Long Creek branch of the Cataba River.
1790 - 134 00 - twp 6
1800 - Mecklenburg County
Revolutionary Soldier - died May 10, 1843, age 93
according to The Charlotte Journal dated May 16, 1843.
Kerr/Carr, Walter
1779 - witnessed a deed, with James Russel, from William
& Elizabeth McWhorter to John Means, on English Buffalo
Creek and Coddle Creek, bk 12, pg 238.
Kerr/Carr, William
1777 - witnessed a deed, with Samuel Chambers, Joseph
McKinley, from John & Catherine Bigger to William Tenant
on the Cataba River opposite the mouth of Crowder's
Creek, bk 10, pg 84.
Kerr/Carr, William & Anna McKnight
1779 - witnessed a deed, with James Boys, John Morris,
from Francis Johnston and Agnes Henderson to Prudence
Hays on McCalpin's Creek, bk 11, pg 64.
1780 - witnessed a deed, with William Brown, from
William Hugans to William Merchant on Meekel's Creek, bk
11, pg 148.
Wife - Anna McKnight, daughter of Robert & Margaret
McKnight.
1790 - 013 01 - twp 1 (Widow - was this Anna?)
Kess, Adam
1784 - named as an adjoining land owner to William &
Frances Hayes, John Wallace on Wolf Meadow Branch, bk
12, pg 125.
Kewer/Keever, Henry
1790 - 122 00 - twp 4
1800 - Mecklenburg County
Kidwell, William
1790 - 125 00 - twp 15
Kile, James
1774 - witnessed a deed, with Hugh Carothers, from Isaac
& Rebecah Sellers, on Rocky River, bk 10, pg 188.
1782 - grant for 200 acres on English Buffalow Creek
adjoining Martin Phifer, William McReasner, bk 12, pg
36.
Killough, Samuel
1783 - witnessed a deed, with James Stephenson, from
Thomas Finley to Hugh Patterson on Rockey River, bk 12,
pg 393.
1784 - deed from David & Mary Smith for 126 acres on
Rocky River, adjoining William Gardner, Test: James
Stevenson, Richard Smith, bk 12, pg 327.

Kimmins, Alexander
    1790 - 000 10 - twp 13
Kimmins, Hugh
    1782 - named as an adjoining land owner to George Davis
    on Reedy Creek, bk 12, pg 80.
    1790 - 125 00 - twp 13
    1800 - Cabarrus County
Kendrack/Kindrack, John
    1790 - 131 02 - twp 2
Kendrick, Philand
    1790 -
Kendrack, William & Winny
    1790 - 102 01 - twp 2
    1800 - Mecklenburg County
King, John
    1779 - named as an adjoining land owner to James and
    John Potts, William Betts, William Courtney on Six Mile
    Creek, bk 12, pg 248.
    1779 - named as an adjoining land owner to James and
    William Potts, Hugh McLile, Archibald Crocket, Zeph John
    on Six Mile Creek near the mouth of Stillhouse Branch,
    bk 12, pg 272.
    1784 - deed from John & Prudence Smith on McCalpin's
    Creek adjoining John Johnston, Thomas Frohock, Test:
    Robert and William Smith, bk 12, pg 280.
    1784 - deed from John & Prudence Smith for 100 acres on
    McCalpin's Creek, Test: William and Robert Smith, bk 12,
    pg 297.
    1790 - 234 00 - twp 20
King, Robert
    1790 - 132 00 - twp 16
King, William
    1777 - named as an adjoining land owner to Daniel
    Cairns, Archibald Cowsert of Craven Co., SC, on Waxaw
    Creek, bk 10, pg 207.
    1783 - named as an adjoining land owner to William
    Haggins, James Houston, William Potts, James Potts,
    Jacob Scroft on Back Creek, otherwise the Six Mile
    Branch of Twelve Mile Creek, bk 12, pg 290.
    1791 Six Mile Branch of Twelve Mile Creek.
Kirkes, Thomas
    1790 - 121 00 - twp 1
Killpatrick/Kirkpatrick, James
    1773 - witnessed a deed, with Michael Goodnight, from
    Jacob Swink to Peter Bogar, on Shenawolf Creek of Rocky
    River, bk 10, pg 106.
    1777 - named as a previous owner on the ridge between
    Buffelow and Coddle Creek adjoining Griffith Rutherford,
    bk 12, pg 252.
    1783 - witnessed a deed, with George Knox, John Houston,
    from Andrew Snoddy to George Fleming on Coddle Creek, bk
    12, pg 348.

Kirkpatrick, John
   1784 - witnessed a deed, with James Bays, from John,
   Samuel, David, James Flennikin to John Smith on
   McCalpin's Creek, bk 12, pg 587.
   1790 - 303 03 - twp 20
   1800 - Mecklenburg County
Kirkpatrick, Valentine
   1790 - 133 00 - twp 13
   1800 - Cabarrus County
Kithcart, John
   1790 - 121 00 - twp 1
   1800 - Mecklenburg County
Kizer/Kiser, Frederick & Rebhel
   1773 - deed from Thomas Polk, attorney for David
   Oliphant, for 56 acres on Rockey River, Test: George
   Kizer, Peter Kizer, bk 10, pg 548.
   1782 - witnessed a deed, with John Rite, from George &
   Mary Kizer to Coonrad Hardwick on Meadoe Creek, bk 12,
   pg 482.
   1785 - deed to John Rette for 30 acres on both sides of
   Medor (Meadow ?) Creek, Test: Cunrod Hardwick, bk 12, pg
   511.
   1790 - 133 00 - twp 14
   1800 - Cabarrus County
Kizer/Kiser, George & Mary
   1773 - witnessed a deed, with George Kizer, from David
   Oliphant to Frederick Kizer, bk 10, pa 548.
   1779, 1782 tract lying in the fork of Meadow Creek and
   Canada's branch
   1780 - witnessed a deed, with Conrad Hardway, from Henry
   & Mary Powell to Frederick Ciser on Rockey River, bk 11,
   pg 27.
   1782 - deed to Coonrad Hardwick for 25 acres in the fork
   of Meadoe Creek and Canada's Branch, Test: Frederick
   Kizer, John Rite, bk 12, pg 482.
   1785 - deed from George Garmon on both sides of Rockey
   River adjoining John Letsinger, John Finney, Peter Reap,
   John Biger, Test: Michael Garmon, Adam Alexander, bk 12,
   pg 484.
   1790 - 143 00 - twp 14
   1800 - Cabarrus County
Kiser, Laurence
   Laurence died 1786, buried in Kiser Cemetery, Gaston
   County. His will was probated in 1786 in Lincoln Co.
   Children: George, Adam
Kiser/Ciser, Peter, Sr.
   1773 - witnessed a deed, with George Kizer, from David
   Oliphant to Frederick Kizer, bk 10, pa 548.
   1780 - Peter's will was probated in Mecklenburg Co.
   1784 - the widow Ciser is named as an adjoining land
   owner to George Tucker, Henry Smith, Joseph Howel on
   Rocky River, bk 12, pg 174.

1785 - deed from George Garmon, executor of Peter's
estate, to George Kizer on both sides of Rockey River,
adjoining John Letsinger, John Finney, Peter Reap, John
Biger, Test: Michael Garmon, Adam Alexander, bk 12, pg
484.
Children: Peter

Kline/Cline, John
   1792 - Loose estate papers

Kline/Cline, Michael
   1784 - Michael's will was probated in Mecklenburg Co.
   Children: George, Daniel, John

Kline/Cline, Michael
   1790 - 105 00 - twp 12

Kneese, Bolser/Paulser
   1790 - 222 00 - twp 12

Knighton, Thomas
   1776 - Thomas' will was probated in Mecklenburg Co.
   Children: John, Thomas, William

Knox, Allison
   1790 - 206 00 - twp 7
   1800 - Mecklenburg County

Knox, Ann(2)
   Ann died Nov 30, 1813 at age 86.

Knox, Benjamin & Jemimah
   1781 - deed from James & Lidiah Knox tor 206 acres on
the south fork of McDowell's Creek, Test: William Berry,
John McNitt Alexander, bk 11, pg 82.
   1783 - witnessed a deed, with David Cance, from George
Cathey to William Moore on McDowell's Creek, bk 11, pg
276.
   1784 - deed to John Davidson for 206 acres on the south
fork of McDowell's Creek, part of a tract granted to
James Knox in 1778, another tract containing 90 acres,
Test: Samuel Davidson, Joseph Fraser, bk 12, pg 353.

Knox, Daniel
   1790 - 000 10 - twp 20

Knox, George
   1783 - witnessed a deed, with James Kirkpatrick, John
Houston, from Andrew Snoddy to George Fleming on Coddle
Creek, bk 12, pg 348.

Knox, James, Capt. & Lidiah
   1778 - deed from George Cathey for 607 acres on the
south fork of McDowel's Creek joining John McDowel,
William Moore, Test: Thomas Gilespy, Isaac Gilespy, bk
11, pg 211. (James was from Rowan County)
   1781 - deed to Benjamin Knox tor 206 acres on the south
fork of McDowell's Creek, Test: William Berry, John
McNitt Alexander, bk 11, pg 82.
   1785 - witnessed a deed, with Margaret Alexander, from
James Moor of Hampshire Co., VA, to John McKnitt
Alexander on McDowell Creek, bk 12, pg 563.

Knox, James

Residents of Mecklenburg County, North Carolina
1762-1790

1790 - 201 00 - twp 2
Knox, John, Sr.
   1772 - John's will was probated in Mecklenburg Co.
   Children: James, Samuel, Matthew, Joseph
Knox, John(2)
   John died June 27, 1777 at age 55.
Knox, John
   1790 - 102 00 - twp 2
   1792 - John's will was probated in Mecklenburg Co.
   Children: Robert
Knox, Mathew
   1762 - deed from Reese & Sarah Price (all of Anson Co.,
   NC), for a tract near land formerly granted to James
   Armour and near an old Indian path, Test: Thomas Price,
   Richard & Ann Barry, Vol 1, pg 80.
   1781 - named as an adjoining land owner to Francis &
   Margaret Johnston, Alexander Johnston, John Whitfield,
   Thomas Nealy, Hugh Herron, bk 12, pg 228.
   1790 - 202 05 - twp 2
   1800 - Mecklenburg County
   Son of John Knox
Knox, Patrick
   1783 - named as an adjoining land owner to Archibald and
   William Henderson, bk 12, pg 122.
Knox, Samuel, Jur.(2)
   1790 - 101 02 - twp 2
   1800 - Mecklenburg County
   Samuel died March 10, 1833 at age 70.
Knox, Samuel & Mary(2)
   1768 - grant for a tract on Steel Creek, being the one
   he sold to Thomas Ferguson in 1775, no book or page
   number given.
   1770 - deed from Moses & Martha Ferguson (of Tryon Co.,
   NC), Samuel & Mary Knox (of Meck. Co., NC), to Francis
   and Joseph Johnston, for 400 acres on east side of
   Catawba and SE side of path leading from Jean ARmour's
   to the Catawba Nations, Test: Thomas Neely, Hugh Neely,
   Alexander Johnston, Vol 5, pg 198.
   1772 - named as an adjoining land owner to Thomas Polk,
   James Moore, John Henry, Samuel Davis, bk 10, pg 137.
   1774 - named as an adjoining land owner to Samuel
   Bigham, John Whiteside, Dinnes McCormick, Moses Ferguson
   on Stell (Steel) Creek, bk 10, pg 411.
   1775 - deed to Thomas Ferguson for a tract on Steel
   Creek, adjoining William Barnett, George Cahoon, John
   Henry, Edward Williams, Test: James Tate, Robert
   Maxwell, John Bigham, bk 10, pg 251.
   1779 - witnessed a deed, with Hugh Barnet, from George
   Nicklson to Margaret Wilson for lots 129, 137 in the
   town of Charlotte, bk 11, pg 28.
   1790 - 303 09 - twp 2
   1800 - Mecklenburg County (widow)

Residents of Mecklenburg County, North Carolina

1762-1790

Samuel died in 1800 at the age of 70.
Knox, Sarah(2)
　　Sarah died Nov 8, 1763 at the age of 66.
Koch, Jacob
　　Jacob was born 1722, died Dec 10, 1799, buried in Old Coldwater Church Cemetery.
Kobb, John
　　1783 - witnessed a deed, with Adalyh Nussman, from John/George Barringer to Matthias Barringer, his son, on Dutch Buffalo Creek, bk 12, pg 332.
Koon/Kuhn, Lewis
　　1794 - Account ledger of John Melchor's store.
Lacey, Samuel
　　1767 - Militia, Mecklenburgh Regiment (Ensign)
Lackey, Robert
　　1790 - 102 00 - twp 18
Lackey, Thomas
　　1786 - deed from John & Catherine Nutt to Thomas Lackey and Robert Orr for 300 acres on Waxhaw Creek, adjoining William Davis, Rebeckah Moor, Alexander Carnes, Robert Crockett, James Lashley, Test: Archibald Cowait, Alexander Carns, John Lithem, bk 12, pg 609.
　　1786 - witnessed a deed, with James Epelman, Samuel Farr, from Dennis & Mary Fittes to Alexander Carns on Waxhaw Creek, bk 12, pg 612.
　　1790 - 133 01 - twp 18
Laigh, Jacob
　　1790 - 114 00 - twp 15
Lamble, Joseph
　　1793 - Account ledger of John Melchor's store.
Lance, John
　　1783 - named as an adjoining land owner to Christian Overshine on Coldwater Creek, bk 12, pg 167.
Landers, Daniel
　　1783 - witnessed a deed, with John McKnitt Alexander, from William Lawing to Justice Beach, bk 12, pg 208.
Landis, Christopher/Christian Ruth
　　1764 - deed from James & Ruth McClain to Christopher Landis and Michael Goodnight for 190 acres on Three Mile Creek, Test: Martin Phifer, Moses Shiddel, bk 10, pg 155.
Laney, Titus
　　1784 - deed to George Laney for 150 acres on a branch of Richardson's Creek adjoining the property of Willis Smith, Test: John Belk, Mary Ann Laney, bk 12, pg 540.
Lanley/Laney, George
　　1784 - deed from Titus Laney for 150 acres on a branch of Richardson's Creek adjoining the property of Willis Smith, Test: John Belk, Mary Ann Laney, bk 12, pg 540.
　　1790 - 124 01 - twp 18
　　1800 - Mecklenburg County
Larking, Samuel

1785 - witnessed a deed, with George Garman, from Dunnon
& Mary Corion to Henry Colledge on Cane Branch, bk 12,
pg 536.

Larver/Carver ?, James
1779 - named as adjoining land owner on Starret's Creek
and Sugar Creek, joining William Wilson, bk 10, pg 491.

Lasley, James
1786 - named as an adjoining land owner to John &
Catherine Nutt, Robert Orr, Thomas Lackey, Alexander
Carnes, Rebeckah Moor, William Davis, Robert Crockett on
Waxhaw Creek, bk 12, pg 609.
1790 - 123 01 - twp 18
Children: John ?

Lathlin, John
1790 - 103 00 - twp 18

Lathlin, Samuel
1790 - 102 00 - twp 18

Lata/Tate, Adam (deed is signed as Adam Lata, though the
name in the body of the deed is Adam Tate. There are
several other deeds for an Adam Tate in the same
area of the county.)
1779 - deed to Joseph Lata for 600 acres in Anson Co.,
NC beginning below Davidson Logg's, running on both
sides of the south fork of Rocky River, Test: Ruth
Bayly, Alexander Lawrey, bk 12, pg 407. (Adam is of
Donegal Township, Lancaster Co., PA)

Latta, James
1784 - witnessed a deed, with James Jackson, from Peter
Johnston to Hadawick Davies on McCalpin's Creek, bk 12,
pg 404.

Latta, Joseph
1778 - Signer of 1778 Petition
1779 - deed from Adam Tate/Lata of Donegal Township,
Lancaster Co., PA, for 600 acres in Anson Co., NC
beginning below Davidson Logg's, running on both sides
of the south fork of Rocky River, Test: Ruth Bayly,
Alexander Lawrey, bk 12, pg 407.
1790 - 115 00 - twp 7
1800 - Mecklenburg County

Latto, David
1778 - Signer of 1778 Petition.

Laughland, William
1777 - deed from John & Jean Criswell for a tract
granted to Joseph Hobbs in 1769, Test: William Graham,
Abel Mankens, bk 10, pg 303.

Laurance/Lawrin, Hugh
1777 - named as an adjoining land owner to John &
Elizabeth Jetton, Isaac Jetton, Abram Jetton, bk 12, pg
494.
1779 - deed from John and Joseph McDowell for a tract on
McDowell's Creek beginning on the boundary line of

McCulloch's Great Tract, Test: William Stephenson, James Dawson, bk 10, pg 305.

Lawing, Andrew
   1784 - witnessed a deed, with Robert Dunn, from Thomas Polk to Andrew Dune on Long Creek, bk 12, pg 283.

Lawing, William
   1781 - named as an adjoining land owner to Peter Johnston, Andrew McKee, Gideon Thomson, John Anderson, bk 12, pg 444.
   1783 - witnessed a deed from James & Sarah Thorn to John Johnston near Long Creek of the Catawba River, beginning on the north edge of the Wagon Road, bk 10, pg 58.
   1783 - deed to Justice Beach for 125 acres on the Catawba River about ten or twelve poles above Thomas Thompson's line, Test: Daniel Landers, John McKnitt Alexander, bk 12, pg 208.
   1784 - named as an adjoining land owner to Thomas Polk, Andrew Dune, Gideon Thompson, Thomas Clark on Long Creek, bk 12, pg 283.

Lawrey, Alexander
   1779 - witnessed a deed, with Ruth Bayly, from Adam Tate/Lata, of Lancaster Co., PA, to Joseph Lata, in Anson Co., NC, bk 12, pg 407.
   1779 - witnessed a deed, with Ruth Bayly, from Adam Tate, of Donegal Township, Lancaster Co., PA, to Joseph Lata, in Anson Co., NC, bk 12, pg 408.

Lawson, John
   1790 - 102 00 - twp 16

Lawson, Moses
   1790 - 101 00 - twp 16

Lawson, Thomas
   1790 - 202 00 - twp 16

Layden, Francis
   1761 - Loose estate papers

Leys/Lee, Andrew, Sr.
   1794 - Account ledger of John Melchor's store.

Leys/Lee, Christopher
   1794 - Account ledger of John Melchor's store.

Leagh/Lee, Henry
   1790 - 106 00 - twp 15
   Buried in St John's Evangelical Lutheran Church Cemetery, but dates and location have been lost.

Lee, James
   1792 - Account ledger of John Melchor's store.

Lefeever, Joseph & Elizabeth
   1790 - 202 00 - twp 3
   1800 - Mecklenburg County
   Wife - Elizabeth

Lemmonds, John & Martha
   1776 - 2nd Lieutenant in Capt. Charles Polk's Light Horse Company.

Residents of Mecklenburg County, North Carolina
1762-1790

    1779 - deed from Thomas Polk, attorney for David
    Oliphant, for 20 acres on Caldwell's Creek, adjoining
    John Luckey, James Morrison, Test: William Polk, Robert
    Hope, bk 11, pg 36.
    1790 - 223 00 - twp 15
    1800 - Mecklenburg County
Lemmond, William
    1776 - Clerk in Capt. Charles Polk's Light Horse Company
    and surgeon to the same.
Lemons, Robert
    1790 - 132 00 - twp 4
    1800 - Mecklenburg County
Lentz, Peter J. & Anna
    Wife - Anna M. Geren
    Children: John C. (Mary Barbara Klutz)
Leopard/Lippard, John & Catherine
    1782 - witnessed a deed, with Samuel Suther, from John
    Buzzard to John Barriger on the east side of Dutch
    Buffalow Creek adjoining Fight Gorright, bk 11, pg 125.
    1783 - witnessed a deed, with George Soatman, from John
    Michael & Margaret Clonts to Christian Goodman on Dutch
    Buffalo Creek, bk 12, pg 293.
    1790 - 345 05 - twp 11
    1793 - Account ledger of John Melchor's store.
    1800 - Cabarrus County
    Childern: Elizabeth (Daniel Sossaman)
Leopard/Lippard, William
    1783 - named as an adjoining land owner to John
    Mesenhimer, Jacob Richey, Jacob Hough, John Charles,
    Michael Cline on the south side of Dutch Buffalow Creek,
    bk 12, pg 147.
    1781 - William's will was probated in Mecklenburg Co.
    Children: John
Leopard/Lippard, William
    1790 - 122 00 - twp 11
Lepper, James
    1766 - named in a deed, no book or page number given.
Lepper/Leeper, Robert
    1764 - witnessed a deed, with Samuel Bigham, Moses
    Ferguson, from Andrew Armour to James Armour on the
    Catawba River between Croders Creek and Allison Creek,
    Vol 1, pg 550.
Lesley, Robert
    1791 - Loose estate papers
Lesley, Widow
    1790 - 211 00 - twp 18
Letsinger, John
    1786 - judgement against John Letsinger and Andrew
    Crocket for 106 pounds, ten shillings, by George Kizer.
    To satisfy judgement, 270 acre tract on Coldwater and
    Buffalow Creek adjoining John Wilie, George Corzine,
    Jr., Alexander Ferguson, James Morison was sold at

Residents of Mecklenburg County, North Carolina 1762-1790

public auction to Robert Harris, Test: David Alison, Waitstill Avery, bk 12, pg 616.
Levingston, Abraham
 1784 - witnessed a deed, with Henry Levingston, from Bruce Levingston to Robert Campbell on King's Branch and Sugar Creek, bk 12, pg 289.
Levingston, Bruce
 1784 - deed to Robert Campbell for 130 acres on King's Branch and Sugar Creek, adjoining Tobe Campbell, Test: Abraham and Henry Levingston, bk 12, pg 289.
Levingston/Leviston, Henry
 1784 - witnessed a deed, with Abraham Levingston, from Bruce Levingston to Robert Campbell on King's Branch and Sugar Creek, bk 12, pg 289.
 1784 - witnessed a deed of gift, with George Davidson, and John Linn, from John Crocket, of Craven Co., SC to his two sons, Robert and Elijah Crocket on Waxhaw Creek, bk 12, pg 419.
Levison, John
 1781 - deed from James Barr and Margaret Wallace on Rockey River beginning on the Baroney line and adjoining James Dysart, Test: Robert Harris, John Davidson, Thomas Mitchel, bk 11, pg 79.
Leviston, Robert
 1782 - grant for 200 acres on the east side of Coddle Creek adjoining William Young, James Means, bk 12, pg 72.
Lewing/Lawing, Andrew
 1790 - 104 00 - twp 6
 1800 - Mecklenburg County
Lewing/Lawing, William
 1790 - 315 00 - twp 6
 1800 - Mecklenburg County
Lewis, Alexander & Ann Miller
 1777 - deed from Thomas Davis for 45 acres on Reedy Creek, Test: Thomas Fadon (McFadden), William Newel, bk 10, pg 401.
 1779 - mentioned as the 1753 grantee of a tract transferred from Gilbert & Margaret McNair to George Duckworth, bk 11, pg 153.
 1782 - named as an adjoining land owner to Robert McMurray on John Cromwell's branch of Reedy Creek, bk 12, pg 14.
 1782 - grant for 98 acres on the south side of Reedy Creek, bk 12, pg 32.
 1780 - named as the owner of a tract conveyed to James Armour in 1752, the to to John Miller, then to Alexander, then from Alexander to the wife of John Miller, then to John Wear, by Robert Irwin, bk 10, pg 456.
 1784 - Alexander's will was probated in Mecklenburg Co. Children: Benjamin

Lewis, Benjamin
    1784 - witnessed a deed, with John Davis, from Joseph &
    Margaret Fraser to Samuel Davis, Jr. on Clark's Creek,
    bk 12, pg 470.
    1790 - 121 04 - twp 8
    1791 - Loose estate papers
Lewis, Christor & Catherine
    1790 - 201 00 - twp 10
    Wife - Catherine Yost/Jost, daughter of Phillip
    Yost/Jost
    Catherine was born Feb 13, 1772, Aug 6, 1799, buried in
    Old Coldwater Church Cemetery.
Lewis, Henry
    1783 - named as an adjoining land owner to James Belk,
    David & Cathron Griffith on Leintraces (Lynches) Creek,
    bk 11, pg 224.
Lewis, Jacob
    1790 - 125 00 - twp 10
    1800 - Cabarris County
Lewis, James
    1790 - 153 00 - twp 16
    1800 - Mecklenburg County
Lewis, Lewis
    1788 - Loose estate papers
Lewis, Martha
    1790 - 101 01 - twp 16
Lewis, Michael
    1778 - Signer of 1778 Petition.
    1789 - Loose estate papers
Lewis, Robert
    1773 - witnessed a deed, with Thomas Harris, from James
    & Margaret Harris to Robert Stewart, bk 10, pg 105.
    1784 - Loose estate papers
Lewis, Widow
    1790 - 116 00 - twp 10
Lewis, William
    1790 - 124 00 - twp 16
    1800 - Mecklenburg County
Libley, John
    1783 - witnessed a deed, with John Belk, Sr., from John
    & Anne Thompson to Charles Cook on Big Ritcheson Creek
    bk 11, pg 292.
Lidaker, Conrad & Mary
    1790 - 102 00 - twp 12
    1794 - Account ledger of John Melchor's store.
    1800 - Cabarrus County
    Wife - Mary Horlacher, daughter of Christopher Horlacher
    Children: Catherine (Charles Barnhart), Sophia (George
    Barnhart), John (Elizabeth Faggart), Matthias (Mary ?)
    Conrad was born Jan 29, 1766, died Nov 15, 1825, buried
    in St John's Evangelical Lutheran Church Cemetery.
Lidaker/Littigar/Lietecker/Leidiker, John Phillip

1784 - witnessed a deed, with Adolph Niesmann, from James & Mary White, Jr. to Paul Barringer on Dutch Buffalow Creek, bk 12, pg 395.
1790 - 225 01 - twp 12
1793 - Account ledger of John Melchor's store.
1800 - Cabarrus County
Children: Conrad (Mary Horlacher)
Phillip was born March 28, 1736, died May 10, 1801, buried in St John's Evangelical Lutheran Church Cemetery.

Lierly/Lively, Christopher
1790 - 123 00 - twp 12
1793 - Account ledger of John Melchor's store.

Lierly/Lively, Zamah/Zenoah
1790 - 131 00 - twp 12

Leggit, Esther
1790 - 234 02 - twp 16
1800 - Mecklenburg County

Liggett, Jackson/Jack
1784 - deed from Benjamin Cook for 250 acres on the head of the Mile Branch of Two Mile Creek, adjoining Robert McClure, Test: Joshua Yarbrough, Sylvanus Philips, bk 12, pg 443.
1788 - Loose estate papers

Liggett, John
1778 - Loose estate papers

Liggett, Michael, Jr.
1778 - witnessed a deed, with R. Smith, to Adlai Osborn for lots in Charlotte, bk 10, pg 212.
1779 - grant for 124 acres adjoining William Haggin, bk 10, pg 498.
1781 - Loose estate papers

Liggett/Siggett, Michael, Sr.
1764 - grant for 103 acres on Clear Creek, no book or page number given.
1779 - deed to Jacob Taft for 103 acres on Clear Creek, Test: Adam Alexander, Sam Martin, bk 10, pg 321.
1779 - deed to Jacob Self for 108 acres on Clear Creek, Test: Samuel Martin, Adam Alexander, bk 10, pg 341.
1779 - deed to Grace Harrison for one negro woman named Levinia, Test: Alexander Finley, Margaret McCurdy, bk 11, pg 31.
1780 - named as an adjoining land owner to Joseph Douglas, John Wilson, Robert Crocket on Twelve Mile Creek, bk 12, pg 95.
1780 - Michael's will was probated in Mecklenburg Co.
Children: Michael, Grace (? Harris), Jackson

Liggett, William
1769 - Loose estate papers

Liggett, William
1767 - Militia, Mecklenburgh Regiment (Lieutenants)

1779 - named as an adjoining land owner to Thomas
McCall, John Ray, William Appleton on Findley's Creek of
Twelve Mile Creek, bk 10, pg 488.
1790 - 222 01 - twp 16
Limbach, Peter
1793 - Account ledger of John Melchor's store.
Lindsay, Hugh(2)
1776 - Drummer in Capt. Charles Polk's Light Horse
Company.
Probably lived in the Clear Creek area.
Hugh died Sept 6, 1791 at the age of 64.
Lindsey, Walter
1790 - 103 00 - twp 20
1800 - Mecklenburg County
Lingle, Anthony
1794 - Account ledger of John Melchor's store.
Lingle, Casper
1790 - 123 00 - twp 11
Lingle, Conrad
1790 - 104 00 - twp 11
1793 - Account ledger of John Melchor's store.
Lingle, Jacob
1790 - 104 00 - twp 11
1800 - Cabarrus County
Lingle, Lorentz & Eva Catherina
1775 - Loose estate papers
Lingo, Daniel
1790 - 114 00 - twp 9
1792 - Loose estate papers
Linker, Henry & Barbara
1790 - 122 00 - twp 12
1800 - Cabarrus County
Wife - Barbara Efrid
Children: John (Martha Whitley)
Linton, Edward
1776 - Edward's will was probated in Mecklenburg Co.
Children: Samuel
Linton, John
1781 - witnessed a deed, with Arthur Elliott, from
Andrew & Esther Elliott, of Wake Co., GA, to Samuel
Linton on Mallard Creek, bk 11, pg 29.
Linton, Samuel
1776 - in Capt. Charles Polk's Light Horse Company.
1778 - deed from George Alexander for 40 acres on Rockey
River adjoining James Brown, Charles Harris, deceased,
Test: Robert Cowdon, Alexander Brown, bk 10, pg 314.
1779 - named as an adjoining land owner to Alexander
McClellan, James Flanigan, Robert Barns, Archibald
McNeal, bk 10, pg 502.
1781 - deed from Andrew & Esther Elliott, of Wake Co.,
GA, for 200 acres on Mallard Creek, bk 11, pg 29.

1782 - grant for 73 acres on both sides of King's Branch
adjoining Alexander McClellan, James Flenigin, John
Bigham, bk 12, pg 108.
1783 - deed to David Meade for a tract joining James
Brown, Charles Haris, deceased, George Alexander, Test:
Aaron Alexander, Adam Meek, bk 12, pg 377.
1784 - Bill of sale from John and William Gardner for a
negro fellow, bk 12, pg 380.
Samuel was a tanner.
Libe/Lipe, Gotfort/Godreid, Sr.
   1778 - Signer of 1778 Petition.
   Godfrey died before 1800.
   1790 - 000 10 - twp 12
   1800 - Cabarrus County (Barbary)
Lipe/Lype, Godfrey, Jr. & Barbara
   Barbara was born Feb 11, 1768, died Nov 29, 1844, buried
   in St John's Evangelical Lutheran Church Cemetery.
   Godfrey was born 1773, died Aug 22, 1849, buried in St
   John's Evangelical Lutheran Church Cemetery.
   1790 - 111 00 - twp 12
   1800 - Cabarrus County
Lipe/Lype, John
   1795 - Account ledger of John Melchor's store.
Lipe/Lype, Jonas
   1790 - 105 00 - twp 12
   1793 - Account ledger of John Melchor's store.
   1800 - Cabarrus County
Lipper, Leonard
   1790 - 112 00 - twp 15
Lippard, William
   1784 - Loose estate papers
Litham, David
   1779 - grant for 140 acres on Waxhaw Creek adjoining
   John Barnett, William Davies, bk 10, pg 507.
Lithem, John
   1786 - witnessed a deed, with Archibald Cowait,
   Alexander Carns, from John & Catherine Nutt to Robert
   Orr and Thomas Lackey on Waxhaw Creek, bk 12, pg 609.
Little, Daniel
   1773 - witnessed a deed, with James Brandon, Thomas
   Polk, from Henry Eustace McCulloch to John Nicholson, bk
   10, pg 46.
   1790 - 124 00 - twp 12
   1793 - Account ledger of John Melchor's store.
   1800 - Cabarrus County
Little, James
   1790 - 111 00 - twp 12
   1800 - Cabarrus County
Little, William
   1773 - witnessed a deed, with John Brown Skeringshire,
   to George Nicholson for lots in Charlotte, bk 10, pg 54.

In 1800, Richard Mason's will names John Little as his stepson, his wife as Elizabeth. He lived in twp 3 in 1790.
1776 - Loose estate papers
Lock, Blench
1777 - deed from Griffith Rutherford for 190 acres on the ridge between Buffalow and Coddle Creek adjoining Caleb Phifer, James Kilpatrick, Test: James Rutherford, Will Alexander, William Sharpe, bk 12, pg 252.
Lock, Francis
1777 - deed from Mathew Lock for 144 acres on Buffelow Creek, joining James McDowel, Test: Griffith Rutherford, Will Alexander, James Rutherford, bk 12, pg 250.
1782 - grant for 360 acres joining Archibald Templeton, bk 12, pg 64.
1783 - grant for 199 acres on Buffalow Creek joining Mathew Lock, Samuel Patton, Samuel Hughs, bk 12, pg 115.
1790 - 124 05 - twp 9
Children: Francis (never married)
Francis is buried in Thiatyria Presbyterian Church Cemetery.
Lock, Matthew
1774 - deed from Mary Conway and Catharine Hoiy for 640 acres on Buffalo Creek adjoining Michael Patton, Test: Alexander Martin, Griffith Rutherford, bk 10, pg 144.
(Deed states he is of Roan Co., NC)
1777 - deed to Francis Lock for 144 acres on Buffelow Creek, joining James McDowel, Test: Griffith Rutherford, Will Alexander, James Rutherford, bk 12, pg 250.
(Deed states he is of Roan Co., NC)
Children: Francis,
Mathew was born about 1730
Lock, William
1783 - witnessed a deed, with Richard Smith, from Nathaniel Alexander to Moses Meek, Jr., on Stony Creek, adjoining Joseph Mitchel, bk 12, pg 305.
Lockamoir, Jacob
1789 - Loose estate papers
Lockhart, John
1773 - deed from Benjamin Brown for 170 acres, Test: Robert Smith, bk 10, pg 276.
Lofton, Isaac
1784 - named as an adjoining land owner to Frederick Cerlock/Carlock/Kerlock, William Waggoner on a branch of Coldwater Creek, bk 12, pg 196.
Lofton, Samuel
Sameul was a signer of the petition to pardon the Cabarrus Black Boys in 1775.
1778 - west side of Twelve Mile Creek
Long, Agnes
1801 - Loose estate paper
Long, Alexander

1777 - witnessed a deed, with Ephraim Brevard, from
George Cusick to John Davison on the north side of the
Catawba River, bk 11, pg 93A.
Long, Henry & Catherine
 1790 - 324 00 - twp 11
 1800 - Mecklenburg County
 Wife - Catherine
 Children: Catey (? Clance),), Jason, Henry, John,
 Peggy, Mary (? Hegler)
 Catherine's will was probated Feb 1824.
Long, James
 1790 - 102 00 - twp 14
 1793 - Account ledger of John Melchor's store.
 1800 - Cabarrus County
 Children: George, William, Peter
 Brother of Samuel Long.
Long, John
 1790 - 115 00 - twp 10
 1800 - Cabarrus County
 Brother of Samuel Long
Long, John, Capt
 1778 - deed from Robert & Hannah Craighead for 225 acres
 on Long Creek, Test: William Shields, Samuel Crawford,
 bk 10, pg 252.
 1782 - witnessed a deed, with Jean Graham, from Thomas
 Beaty to William and James Beaty on the Catawba River
 joining Beaty Ford, bk 12, pg 489.
 1790 - 323 01 - twp 6
 1799 - Loose estate papers
 1800 - Mecklenburg County (widow)
Long, Nancy
 1803 - Loose estate papers
Long, Peter
 1793 - Account ledger of John Melchor's store.
 Son of James Long.
Lossinger, John
 1778 - Signer of 1778 Petition.
Lotter, Tobias
 1793 - Account ledger of John Melchor's store.
Love, James & Elizabeth
 1778 - Signer of 1778 Petition.
 1782 - grant for 180 acres on the west side of Rockey
 River adjoining William McMullen, bk 12, pg 33.
 1782 - named as an adjoining land owner to William
 Wadlington on the south side of Rockey River, bk 12, pg
 49.
 1784 - named as an adjoining land owner to David
 Purviance on the north side of Rockey River, bk 12, pg
 182.
 1785 - deed to Archibald McCordy/McCurdy for 180 acres
 on the west side of Rockey River joining William

McAnulty, Test: William McAnulty, John and Archibald
White, bk 12, pg 560.
Children: Jonah, Charles (Fereby Osburn)
Love, John & Sarah
    1778 - Signer of 1778 Petition.
    1790 - 212 00 - twp 1
    1791 - John's will was probated in Mecklenburg Co.
    Children: David, Christopher, Jane (? Ramey), Mary (
    ? Adamson), William, John, Thomas, Samuel, Joseph,
    Sarah, Elizabeth (Stewart Banks)
Love, Samuel
    1790 - 101 00 - twp 1
    Son of John & Sarah Love.
Love, William & Sarah
    1779 - deed from Thomas Polk, attorney for David
    Oliphant, for 17 acres on Crooked Creek, Test: John
    Polk, William Lusk, bk 10, pg 554.
    1779 - deed from Thomas Polk, attorney for David
    Oliphant, for 30 acres on Crooked Creek, Test: John
    Polk, William Lusk, bk 10, pg 546.
    1784 - deed to Emanuel Stephens for 78 acres on the
    south side of Crooked Creek, Test: Rob Donaldson, George
    McWhirter, bk 12, pg 285.
    1785 - deed to Manuel Stevens for 17 acres on Crooked
    Creek, Test: Joseph Harris, John Donnelson, bk 12, pg
    529.
    1785 - governor
Lowrance, John & Anne
    1781 - mentioned in a deed, no book or page number
    given.
Lowrance, Joseph & Margaret
    1779 - mentioned in a deed, no book or page number
    given.
Lowrance, Michael
    1790 - 112 00 - twp 7
    1800 - Mecklenburg County
Lowrance, Peter & Mary
    1767 - mentioned in a deed, no book or page number
    given.
Lucas, Hugh
    1777 - deed from George & Margaret Cathey for 200 acres
    on the north side of the Catawba River, Test: Joseph
    Jack, James McMahan, J. McDowell, bk 10, pg 242.
    1780 - witnessed a deed, with William Graham, from John
    & Jean Wear to Thomas Walker, bk 10, pg 456.
    1790 - 135 00 - twp 7
Luckey, John
    1779 - named as an adjoining land owner to John Lemonds,
    James Morrison on Caldwell's Creek, bk 11, pg 36.
Luckey, Robert
    1790 - 133 00 - twp 4
Luckey, William

Residents of Mecklenburg County, North Carolina
1762-1790

1790 - 133 01 - twp 3
1800 - Mecklenburg County
Ludwick, Henry & Elizabeth
   Wife - Elizabeth Fisher
   Children: Catherine (Daniel Cress), Charles (Catherine
   Bost), Martin A.(Adeline L. House), Jacob (Sophia House)
   Elizabeth was born March 20, 1779, died March 15, 1855,
   buried in St John's Evangelical Lutheran Church
   Cemetery.
   Henry was born June 12, 1777, died Oct 24, 1853, buried
   in St John's Evangelical Lutheran Church Cemetery.
Ludwick, Nicholas
   1781 - Nicholas' will was probated in Mecklenburg Co.
   Children: Henry
Ludwick/Lodwick, Nicholas
   1784 - named as an adjoining land owner to Henry
   Seaceman/Sossamon on Dutch Buffalow Creek, bk 12, pg
   128.
Ludwick, Nicholas
   1782 - Loose estate papers
Lusk, John
   1777 - John's will was probated in Mecklenburg Co.
   Children: John, Samuel
Lusk, Samuel & Elizabeth
   1777 - witnessed a deed from James Tate to Hugh
   McClelland on Four Mile Creek, bk 10, pg 262, bk 10, pg
   265.
   1777 - named in John Lusk's will.
   Son of John Lusk.
Lusk, William
   1779 - witnessed a deed, with John Polk, from Thomas
   Polk, attorney for David Oliphant, to William Love on
   Crooked Creek, bk 10, pg 546.
   1779 - witnessed a deed, with Charles Polk, from Thomas
   Polk, attorney for David Oliphant, to Archibald McCurdy
   on Long Run, a branch of Clear Creek, bk 10, pg 543.
   1779 - witnessed a deed, with Ephraim Barker, from
   Thomas Polk, attorney for David Oliphant, to William
   Barker, bk 10, pg 433.
Luther, Daniel
   1785 - witnessed a deed, with Samuel Luther, Joseph
   Shinn, from John & Anna Bargar to Frederick Beck on
   Buffalow Creek, bk 12, pg 501.
Luther, John (See John Suther)
Luther/Lather, Robert
   1790 - 000 10 - twp 6
Luther, Samuel
   1785 - witnessed a deed, with Daniel Luther, Joseph
   Shinn, from John & Anna Bargar to Frederick Beck on
   Buffalow Creek, bk 12, pg 501.
Lynn/Linn, James & Sarah

1773 - named as an adjoining land owner to John & Hannah McKee, Joseph Kennedy, John Haggin on Six Mile Creek, bk 10, pg 122.
1777 - deed to John Osborn for 144 acres, Test: William Osburn, John Foster, bk 10, pg 214.
1779 - James' will was probated in Mecklenburg Co.
1790 - 213 00 - twp 16 (widow)
Children: William

Lynn/Linn, John
1784 - witnessed a deed of gift, with George Davidson, and Henry Leviston, from John Crocket, of Craven Co., SC to his two sons, Robert and Elijah Crocket on Waxhaw Creek, bk 12, pg 419.

Lype, Godfryt, Jr.
1790 - 111 00 - twp 12
1800 - Cabarrus County

Lype, Godfryt, Sr. & Barbara
1790 - 000 10 - twp 12
1800 - Cabarrus County (widow)

Lype, Jonas
1790 - 105 00 - twp 12

Macloveny, Samuel
1780 - named as an adjoining land owner to George & Elizabeth McWhirter, Samuel Wylie, Robert Caldwell on Waxhaw Creek, bk 12, pg 447.

Madelph, William & Amelia
1783 - witnessed a deed from James Cochran to George Helms on Stuart's Fork of Richardson's Creek, bk 12, pg 505.

Maffit (See Moffitt)

Magill, James
James died Oct 12, 1810, age 25, buried in Blackstock Cemetery.

Magill, Thomas
Thomas died Feb 9, 1805, age 52, buried in Blackstock Cemetery.

Malony, Edward
1782 - witnessed a deed, with Andrew Henderson, from Hugh & Elizabeth Rondles to David Crocket on a branch of Sugar Creek joining James Reed, Alexander Mitchell, bk 11, pg 98.
1782 - witnessed a deed, with Moses Robison, from David & Elizabeth Crocket to Joseph Galbreath on a branch of Sugar Creek joining James Reed, Alexander Mitchell, bk 11, pg 91.

Mankens, Abel
1777 - witnessed a deed, with William Graham, from John & Jean Criswell to William Laughland, bk 10, pg 303.

Mann, John
1780 - named as adjoining land owner to Robert Archibald, and James & Susannah Russell on the Half Meadow Branch, a branch of Coddle Creek, bk 12, pg 11.

Mann, Thomas
   1775 - witnessed a deed, with Samuel Patton, John
   Phifer, from Joseph Rodgers and David Russell to Michael
   Shaver for 144 acres, bk 10, pg 185.
   1778 - witnessed a deed, with Abraham Miller, from
   William Holland to Andrew Stinson on McCalpin's Creek,
   adjoining Joseph Sample, William Black, bk 10, pg 378.
Manson, William
   1774 - witnessed a deed, with Thomas Polk, from William
   Starret to Nathaniel Cook on Sugar Creek, adjoining
   Nathaniel Irwin, Andrew Sprotts, bk 10, pg 370 and pg
   379.
   1779 - named as an adjoining land owner to Andrew
   Yandell, Thomas Polk, Peter Johnston on McMichal's
   Creek, bk 10, pg 513.
March, John
   1779 - witnessed a deed, with Jason Frizell, from Mounce
   Justice to Andrew McClenhan on the Long branches of
   Coldwater Creek, bk 10, pg 431.
Mariner, John
   1790 - 101 00 - twp 1
Martin, Alexander
   1774 - witnessed a deed, with Griffith Rutherford, from
   Mary Conway and Catharine Hoiy to Mathew Lock on Buffalo
   Creek, bk 10, pg 144.
   1782-1783 - Governor
Martin, Charles & Deborah
   1771 - Charles' will was probated in Mecklenburg Co.
Martin, Widow
   1790 - 102 00 - twp 9
Martin, Daniel
   1766 - listed in the militia company of Capt. Adam
   Alexander of Clear Creek as deceased.
Martin, Daniel
   Mentioned in the estate papers of Nicholson Ross 1774.
Martin, Ephraim
   1790 - 112 00 - twp 3
Martin, James & Peggy
   1787 - James' will was probated in Mecklenburg Co.
   Children: James, Robert, William, John
Martin, Joseph
   1783 - deed from William Hemphill for 300 acres on a
   large branch of the Stoney fork of Mallard Creek, Test:
   William and Charles Alexander, bk 11, pg 236.
   1799 - Loose estate papers
Martin, Ochillice
   1779 - deed from Ochillice Martin and Company to William
   McCulloh for lot 17 in Charlotte, Test: William
   Patterson, Ephraim Brevard, bk 10, pg 326.
   1779 - deed from John Foard to Ochilltree Martin and
   Company for lots 85 & 93 in Charlotte, Test: John Allen,
   Margaret Jack, bk 10, pg 350.

Martin, Richard
   1778 - Signer of 1778 Petition
   1779 - deed from John McAliley for 150 acres on both sides of the Muddy Branch and a Stony Run of Coddle Creek, Test: Arthur McCree, James Humphreys, bk 12, pg 439.
   1780 - deed to John McCulogh, Jr. for 150 acres on both sides of the Muddy Branch of Coddle Creek, Test: John Houston, James Humphreys, bk 12, pg 432.
   1790 - 145 00 - twp 9
Martin, Robert
   1780 - grant for 41 acres on Coddle Creek joining James Martin, bk 12, pg 25.
   1790 - 213 00 - twp 8
   Son of James & Peggy Martin.
Martin, Robert
   1778 -deed to John Driskell for 140 acres on Caldwell Creek beginning on the north side of a branch, Test: William Driskel, Robert Harris, Jr., bk 10, pg 5.
   1784 - deed from John Davidson for 200 acres on Rockey River, adjoining James Dysard, Test: William Waddle, Sam Davidson, John Wier, bk 12, pg 308.
   1790 - 232 00 - twp 9
   1800 - Cabarrus County
Martin, Samuel
   1777 thru 1783 - clerk of court
   1777 - deed from Alexander Martin of Guiford Co., NC, for 209 acres on McCalpin's Creek, Test: John and William Patterson, bk 10, pg 263.
   1779 - Sam Martin witnessed a deed, with Adam Alexander from Michael Liggett to Jacob Taft on Clear Creek, bk 10, pg 321.
   1779 - witnessed a deed, with James McGinty, from Francis & Elizabeth Miller to William Simmonds on the south branch of Caldwell's Creek, adjoining James Morrison, bk 10, pg 351.
   1782 - deed from Thomas Polk for lots 86 & 94 in Charlotte, bk 11, pg 188.
   1782 - deed from Samuel, Duncan Ochiltree, Adlai Osburn, William Polk to John Moore for 150 acres on Sugar Creek, another tract on Sugar Creek containing 85 acres, Test: Edward Hunter, Henry Searing, bk 11, pg 204.
   1782 - deed from Samuel, Duncan Ochiltree, Adlai Osburn, William Polk to John Moore for lots 15 & 17 in Charlotte, bk 11, pg 214.
   1782 - deed from Samuel, Duncan Ochiltree, Adlai Osburn, William Polk to John Moore for lots 145 & 153 in Charlotte, bk 11, pg 217.
   1783 - deed from James Orr for lot 25 in Charlotte, bk 12, pg 572.
   1790 - Loose estate papers
Martin, Samuel

Residents of Mecklenburg County, North Carolina
1762-1790

1790 - 401 00 - twp 8
1800 - Cabarrus County
Martin, Thomas
   1796 - Loose estate papers
Martin, Thomas
   1790 - 121 00 - twp 3
   1800 - Mecklenburg County
Martin, Thomas & Ann Blythe
   1790 - 112 00 - twp 7
   Wife - Ann Blythe, dau of Samuel & Elizabeth Blythe.
Martin, Widow
   1790 - 102 00 - twp 9
Martin, William
   1790 - 122 00 - twp 9
Mary, Thomas
   1783 - named as an adjoining land owner to Susana
   Daniel, Robert John, William Michel on Muddy Creek, bk
   12, pg 287.
Mash, Ebenezer
   1790 - 202 00 - twp 13
Mason, Charles
   1774 - Charles' will was probated in Mecklenburg Co.
   1774 - Loose estate papers
   Children: Richard, Gideon, Joseph
Mason, David
   1784 - witnessed a deed, with Robert Scott, George Rice,
   from Arthur Garrison to Richard Mason on Middle Branch,
   a branch of Sugar Creek beginning on top of ridge 35
   rods from the town of Charlotte, bk 12, pg 313.
   1808 - Loose estate papers
Mason, Richard & Elizabeth
   1772 - witnessed a deed, with William Patterson, from
   Henry Eustace McCulloh to William Clark, on Sugar Creek
   joining John McClure, bk 10, pg 238.
   1778 - deed from William and James McCafferty for lot 11
   in Charlotte, bk 10, pg 77.
   1779 - deed to Ochiltree, Martin, Company for lots 145 &
   153 in Charlotte, Test: Ezekiel Polk, James Jack, bk 11,
   pg 304.
   1783 - deed from Thomas Polk for lot 12 in Charlotte, bk
   12, pg 301.
   1784 - deed from Arthur Garrison for 186 acres on Middle
   Branch, a branch of Sugar Creek beginning on top of
   ridge 35 rods from the town of Charlotte, Test: Robert
   Scott, George Rice, David Mason, bk 12, pg 313.
   1790 - 242 05 - twp 3
   1800 - Mecklenburg County
   Wife - Elizabeth (Little, widow of William Little ?)
   Children: Henry, Winfield, Richard, Isaac, Charles
   Stepson: John Little
   Grandson: Richard Huson
   Richard's will was written in 1800.

Residents of Mecklenburg County, North Carolina
1762-1790

1800 - Loose estate papers
Masser/Masson, George
　1790 - 111 00 - twp 14
Masters, George
　1782 - named as an adjoining land owner to James Russle,
　James White, Michael Winecoff, William Erwin on Coddle
　Creek, bk 12, pg 86.
　1790 - 230 01 - twp 10
Mathews, Andrew
　1790 - 143 00 - twp 12
Mathews, Peter
　1780 - deed to John Herron for lot 68 in Charlotte,
　Test: Francis Herron, Joseph Wishard, bk 11, pg 244.
Mathews, William, Esqr.
　1783 - named as an adjoining land owner to Moses Crague
　on Twelve Mile Creek on the south side of Glady Fork, bk
　12, pg 136.
　1790 - 131 01 - twp 19
　1800 - Mecklenburg County
Mattinger, Henry
　1768 - Loose estate papers
Maudint, John
　1782 - named as an adjoining land owner to Thomas Meek,
　Martin Phifer on English Buffalow Creek, bk 12, pg 103.
Maxwell, Ann
　1790 - 104 00 - twp 6
　1800 - Mecklenburg County
　Son-in-law: Allen Curry
Maxwell, Benjamin
　1790 - 213 00 - twp 7
　1800 - Mecklenburg County
Maxwell, James & Jean McChung
　1790 - 142 00 - twp 7
Maxwell, James & Elizabeth
　1766 - listed in the militia company of Capt. Adam
　Alexander of Clear Creek.
　1774 - witnessed a deed, from John, Jane, Robert,
　Benjamin Brevard of Rowan Co., NC to Andrew Downes on
　the branches of Rockey River, bk 10, pg 183.
　1776 - in Capt. Charles Polk's Light Horse Company.
　1780 - deed to George Caughon for 115 acres on Rockey
　River, Test: John Hagler, Joyauurn Goylorw (Dutch), bk
　12, pg 226.
　1784 - deed to Robert Morison for 170 acres on Rockey
　River, Test: James Stafford, James Finney, bk12, pg 364.
　1784 - grant for 31 acres on the north side of his own
　land, adjoining James Stafford, bk 12, pg 179.
　No date - bill of sale from James Harris for a wagon and
　four bay horses and their geer, Test: John Cochran,
　James Finley, bk 10, pg 318.
　1790 - 241 00 - twp 13
Maxwell, John

1776 - in Capt. Charles Polk's Light Horse Company.
1778 - witnessed a deed, with Bartholomew Johnson, from Andrew & Anne Downs to John Morrow, bk 10, pg 39.

Maxwell, Joseph
1784 - named as an adjoining land owner to Joseph & Margaret Fraser, David Smith, Samuel Davis, Jr., on Clark's Creek, Test: Benjamin Lewis, John Davis, bk 12, pg 470.

Maxwell, Robert(2) & Mary
1775 - witnessed a deed, with James Tate, John Bigham, from Samuel Knox to Thomas Ferguson on Steel Creek, bk 10, pg 251.
1779 - named as an adjoining land owner to Samuel Bigham, John Porter, Robert Bigham on Steel Creek, bk 10, pg 439.
1785 - Robert died Oct 1, 1785 at the age of 44, his will was probated in Mecklenburg Co.
1785 - Loose estate papers

Maxwell, Widow
1790 - 244 01 - twp 2

McAbley/ McAliley, John
1779 - named as an adjoining land owner to John Hughs, David Wilson on Coddle Creek, bk 10, pg 493.
1779 - named as an adjoining land owner to Samuel Hughs on Coddle Creek, bk 10, pg 496 or 497.
1779 - deed to Richard Martin for 150 acres on both sides of the Muddy Branch and a Stony Run of Coddle Creek, Test: Arthur McCree, James Humphreys, bk 12, pg 439.

McAllister/McLister, John
1793 - Account ledger of John Melchor's store.

McAnulty, William
1782 - grant for 156 acres on Reedy Creek beginning on the old Indian path, adjoining Charles McKinley, David McKinley, bk 12, pg 127.
1785 - witnessed a deed, wht John and Archilbald White, from James & Elizabeth Love to Archibald McCurdy on the west side of Rockey River, bk 12, pg 560.

McBoyd, Patrick
1790 - 123 00 - twp 19

McEachin/McCachron, Robert
1782 - Anderson Creek

McAhron/McCachron, John & Mary
1778 - Signer of 1778 Petition
1790 - 106 00 - twp 13(widow)
John died in 1790 of before, Mary remarried to Peter Huie before 1800.

McCafferty, James
1776 - witnessed a deed, with Thomas Allison, Joseph Moore, William Todd, from James & Martha Todd to John Todd on Sugar Creek, bk 10, pg 21.

1777 - witnessed a deed, with Hugh Pollock, from James
Jack to Robert Scott for lot 27 in Charlotte, bk 10, pg
281.
1778 - deed from James and William McCafferty to Richard
Mason for lot 11 on Traid Street in Charlotte, Test:
Joseph Moore, Charles Purveance, bk 10, pg 77.
1778 - deed from James and William McCafferty to Thomas
Polk for lot 9 on Traid Street in Charlotte, Test: John
Foard, Ezekiel Polk, bk 10, pg 66.
1778 - deed from Moses Steel to James and William
McCafferty for 100 acres on Sugar Creek, joining William
Wilson, Alexander Starret, Test: Duncan Ocheltree,
William Reed, bk 10, pg 20.
Son of Jeremiah McCafferty.

McCafferty, Jeremiah
1773 - Commissioner/Trustee of the town of Charlotte
1774 - Commissioner/Trustee of the town of Charlotte, bk
10, pg 109.
1777 - Commissioner/Trustee of the town of Charlotte
1778 - (January)Commissioner/Trustee of the town of
Charlotte, bk 10, pg 211 & 235.
Jeremiah died before July 1778, executors of his estate
were James and William McCafferty, bk 10, pg 77.

McCafferty, Jeremiah (Jeremy)
1779 - named as an adjoining land owner to William
Wilson, James McCord on a branch of McCulloch Creek, bk
10, pg 505.
1785 - Loose estate papers

McCafferty, William
1778 - deed from James and William McCafferty to Richard
Mason for lot 11 on Traid Street in Charlotte, Test:
Joseph Moore, Charles Purveance, bk 10, pg 77.
1778 - deed from Moses Steel to James and William
McCafferty for 100 acres on Sugar Creek, joining William
Wilson, Alexander Starret, Test: Duncan Ocheltree,
William Reed, bk 10, pg 20.
1778 - deed from James and William McCafferty to Thomas
Polk for lot 9 on Traid Street in Charlotte, Test: John
Foard, Ezekiel Polk, bk 10, pg 66.
1784 - witnessed a deed, with James Tagert, William
Berryhill, from Isaac & Elenor Williams to George
Hutchison on Little Sugar Creek, bk 12, pg 437.
1784 - witnessed a deed, with James Tagert, from Isaac &
Elenor Williams to George Hutchison on a branch of Sugar
Creek about a mile from the path that leads from
Charlotte to John Tatt's, bk 12, pg 430.
1785 - judgement obtained against William by John
Thompson on Tryon Creek. Highest bidder was Samuel
Martin, Test: William Polk, John Nelson, Daniel Brown,
bk 12, pg 567.
1799 - Loose estate papers
Son of Jeremiah McCafferty.

McCabb/MaCabb/McCaleb, James
    1790 - 133 01 - twp 8
    1800 - Cabarrus County
McCabben/MaCabben, Mightry
    1790 - 115 00 - twp 16
McCain, Andrew
    1790 - 111 00 - twp 18
McCain, Hance & Agness Givens/Gibbons
    1790 - 102 00 - twp 16
    1800 - Mecklenburg County
    Agnes was the daughter of William & Jannett Givens.
McCain, Hugh & Jane
    1790 - 310 03 - twp 18
    1800 - Mecklenburg County
    Children: James, Joseph, Hugh
McCain, John
    1790 - 000 10 - twp 16
McCain, John
    1783 - deed from Ambrose & Magdalen Walker for 330 acres on both sides of Cane Creek, Test: John Ramsey, John Shelby, bk 12, pg 230.
    1783 - witnessed a deed, with John Henderson, from George McWhirter to John Ramsey on Waxhaw Creek, bk 12, pg 247.
    1790 - 114 00 - twp 18
    1800 - Mecklenburg County
    John was about 81 years old in 1835 according to pension records.
McCain, John
    1798 - Loose estate papers
McCain, Joseph
    1797 - Loose estate papers
McCain, Thomas, Junr.
    1790 - 131 00 - twp 18
    1800 - Cabarrus County
McCain, William
    1790 - 114 - twp 17
    1800 - Mecklenburg County
McCall, Francis & Mary
    1774 - deed to William Houston for 200 acres on both sides of the Cedar fork of Twelve Mile Creek, Test: Thomas McCall, John McCall, John Osburn, bk 10, pg 226.
    1779 - grant for 50 acres on Twelve Mile Creek, bk 10, pg 510.
    1790 - 103 00 - twp 16
    Children: Jane (? Porter), Thomas, Joseph, Francis, Elizabeth (Thomas Walker), Mary (John Gibbens), Libby (Michael Secrist)
    Francis died Nov 25, 1793, his will was probated in April 1794.
    Mary died before 1793.
McCaull/McCall, Harris

1778 - deed from the commissioners of Charlotte to the trustees of Liberty Hall for lots 69,70,77, & 78 on the south side of Tryon Street in Charlotte, Test: Hezekiah Alexander, James Tagert, bk 10, pg 211.

McCall, James
 1766 - listed in the militia company of Capt. Adam Alexander of Clear Creek.
 1774 - James' will was probated in Mecklenburg Co. Children: William

McCall/McCawl, James
 1766 - listed in the militia company of Capt. Adam Alexander of Clear Creek.
 1782 - named as an adjoining land owner to Joseph & Elizabeth McKinley, John Carruthers, Daniel Williams, bk 11, pg 149.
 1784 - grant for 110 acres adjoining Phebe Williams, John Carothers, bk 12, pg 177.
 1784 - named as an adjoining land owner to James Wiley, William Johnston, John Neel, John Parks on Reedy Creek, bk 12, pg 619.
 1790 - 224 00 - twp 4
 1800 - Mecklenburg County

McCall, John & Gennet/Jane
 1774 - witnessed a deed, with Thomas McCall, John Osburn, from Francis & Mary McCall to William Houston on both sides of the Cedar Fork of Twelve Mile Creek, bk 10, pg 226.
 1778 - deed to James Dickson for 93 acres on Clear Creek, Test: Samuel Montgomery, John Wylie, bk 11, pg 56.

McCall, Joseph
 1779 - grant for 100 acres on the south branch of Cane Creek beginning on a stoney hill on the south side of the branch, bk 10, pg 531.

McCall, Thomas
 1774 - witnessed a deed, with John McCall, John Osburn, from Francis & Mary McCall to William Houston on both sides of the Cedar Fork of Twelve Mile Creek, bk 10, pg 226.
 1774 - grant for 224 acres on Findley's Creek, a branch of Twelve Mile Creek, joining William Ligget, John Ray, William Appleton, bk 10, pg 488 or 489.
 1779 - grant for 200 acres on the watery branch, beginning on the west side of the Waggon Road by the side of Ligget's path, bk 10, pg 499.
 1784 - named as the previous owner of a tract belonging to James McCawl on Reedy Creek, bk 12, pg 619.
 1798 - Loose estate papers

McCall, William & Elizabeth
 1790 - 132 00 - twp 15
 Pension denied July 7, 1838 - no proof of marriage or service.

Residents of Mecklenburg County, North Carolina   207
1762-1790

McCallister, John
    1790 - 124 00 - twp 5
McCalmonnt, Charles
    1778 - Signer of 1778 Petition.
McCallum, John
    1790 - 101 00 - twp 16
McCallum, Thomas
    1790 - 112 00 - twp 16
McCamey, George
    1779 - named as an adjoining land owner to Daniel Cairn,
    William Hamilton on Waxhaw Creek @ the SC state line, bk
    10, pg 537.
    Great-uncle of Andrew Jackson.
McCammon, Charles
    1782, 1790 south side of Rockey River.
McCammon/McCannon/McKimene, John
    1766 - listed in the militia company of Capt. Adam
    Alexander of Clear Creek.
    1780 - grant for 91 acres on McKee's Creek joining
    Daniel McKeeman, bk 12, pg 42.
    1780 - witnessed a deed, with Alexander McGinty, from
    Samuel Montgomery to Adam Alexander, James Harris,
    Mathew Stuart, John Ford, John Quirry, bk 11, pg 71.
    1782 - grant for 195 acres on Rockey River joining
    Thomas Wilson and the Indian path, bk 12, pg 96.
    1784 - witnessed a deed, with William Meyer, Green
    Rives, from John Curry to John Foster on Waxhaw Creek,
    bk 12, pg 579.
    1790 - 335 00 - twp 17
    1795 - Loose estate papers
McCandeless, John
    1776 - in Capt. Charles Polk's Light Horse Company.
    1779 - deed from Henry & Ann Sadler for three tracts on
    Mallard Creek, the first containing 150 acres, the
    second containing 110 acres, the third containing 34
    acres, adjoining Andrew Elliott, John Disart, Test: John
    Alexander, bk 12, pg 614.
    1790 - 112 03 - twp 5
McCandrack, Patrick
    1764 - Loose estate papers
McCanter, Moses
    1783 - named as an adjoining land owner to Daniel
    Carrins, Benjamin Ford on the dividing ridge between
    Twelve Mile Creek and Waxhaw Creek, bk 12, pg 112.
McCaragan, Andrew
    1777 - mentioned in a deed on the south side of Rocky
    River, no book or page number given.
McCachron,McCutchen,McEachern,McAhron, Hector & Elizabeth
    Wife - Elizabeth Huie, daughter of Peter Huie, married
    July 26, 1791, Peter Huie bondsman.
    Children: Peter Roland
    1800 - Cabarrus County

McCachron, McCutchen, McEachern, McAhron, John & Mary
    1782 - grant for 150 acres on both sides of Bake(Back
    Creek) joining James White, bk 12, pg 37.
    1790 - 106 00 - twp 13
    John died in 1789 and Robert Harris of Fuda Creek was
    the administrator of his estate.
    1791 - Loose estate papers
    Children: Susannah (Armsted Brown), Hanah (Ira Vallace),
    Polly (William Allison Russell), Ann (Isaac R. Shinn),
    Hector (Elizabeth Huie), Elizabeth (Alexander Huie),
    Nancy (Benjamin Shinn), Ruth (? Robinson), Catherine
    (John Farr), Thomas ? (Jeane Caldwell McKinley), William
    ? (Martha Brown), James ? (Martha McKinley)
    Mary remarried to Peter Huie, father of her daughter-in-
    law Elizabeth Huie.
    1800 - Cabarrus County (widow)
McCachron, McCutchen, McEachern, McAhron, Robert
    1782 - named as an adjoining land owner on Anderson
    Creek joining Thomas McFadan, bk 12, pg 46.
McCauley, Daniel & Martha
    1790 - 103 00 - twp 19
    1800 - Mecklenburg County
    Wife: Martha Black, daughter of John & Mary Black
McCaughey, John
    1785 - deed from William & Margaret Alexander for 100
    acres on the north fork of Stoney Creek adjoining James
    Hunter, Test: Charles and Andrew Alexander, J.M.
    Garrison, bk 12, pg 485.
    1785 - deed from Benjamin & Susana Alexander for 400
    acres on Back Creek adjoining Even Shelby, Henry
    Mitchel, Test: Andrew and William Alexander, J.W.
    Garrison, bk 12, pg 487.
McCauslin, James
    1790 - 103 00 - twp 16
McCay, Arthur
    1764 - deed from Arthur & Justina Dobbs to Arthur McCay
    of Brunswick Co., NC, surveyor, for 79 acres on both
    sides of Three Mile Branch of Rockey River, bk 10, pg
    435.
McClain, Allen
    Mentioned in the estate papers of Nicholson Ross 1774.
    1790 - 224 00 - twp 13
    1800 - Cabarrus County (widow)
McClain/McLane, Hector & Margaret
    1782 - deed to William Cooper for a tract lying on both
    sides of King's Branch of Sugar Creek bounded by Francis
    Herron, William McDowel, John Bigham, James Sprott,
    Test: Isack Herron, John & Robert Hunter, bk 12, pg 234.
McClain, James & Ruth
    1764 - deed to Christopher Landis and Michael Goodnight
    for 190 acres joining Joseph Rodgers on Three Mile

Creek, Test: Martin Phifer, Moses Shiddel, bk 10, pg 155.
McClain, Joseph
  1790 - 202 00 - twp 5
  1797 - Joseph's will was probated in April 1797.
  Children: Sarah (? Crawford)
  Granddaughter: Jane McCain Crawford
McClanahan, John
  1779 - witnessed a deed, with Robert Crocket, from William Hambilton to William Ferril on Waxhaw Creek, bk 11, pg 67.
McClanachan, Robert
  1767 - Militia, Mecklenburgh Regiment (Major)
McClarey, Michael
  1790 - 221 03 - twp 1
  1800 - Mecklenburg County
McCarter, Alexr & Mary Gingles
  Wife: Mary Gingles, daughter of Samuel & Margaret McAllister Gingles.
McClartey, Alexander & Jennie Morrison
  1790 - 214 00 - twp 9
  1800 - Cabarrus County
  Children: James (Sarah Ellen Shelby, Deborah Freeman), Archibald (Elizabeth Hasty, Ellen Beckman Collins), Nancy (Isaac Helms), Polly (William Weddington), Sallie (Archibald Brown), Katie (Thomas Jerome), Jean (Johnston N. Bigger)
  Alexander's will was written in 1824 and filed in Mecklenburg County. Jennie moved to Arkansas with her son James after Alexander's death.
McClartey, Archabeld
  1790 - 104 00 - twp 9
  1800 - Cabarrus County
  Children: Alexander (Jennie Morrison)
McCleary, Jean(2)
  Jean was born 1731, died Aug 28, 1791 at the age of 60.
McCleary/McClary, Michael
  1790 - 221 03 - twp 1
McCleary, Robert & Abigail McDowell(2)
  1778 -
  1790 - 225 02 - twp 2
  1791 - Loose estate papers
  Brother of Samuel McCleary.
  Robert was born 1736, died March 23, 1791 at age 55.
  Abigail died Oct 5, 1805.
  1806 - Loose estate papers
McCleary, Robert & Elizabeth
  1783 - deed to David Russel for 200 acres on the head branch of Mallard Creek and Long Creek, conveyed to Robert in 1771, Test: Robert Morris, John McKnitt Alexander, William Goth, Joseph Rodgers, bk 12, pg 257.

Children: Andrew, James, Samuel, Martha? (Richard Robison).

McCleary, Samuel & Deborah(3)
   1778 - witnessed a deed to Martha Davis for lots 79 & 712 in Charlotte, bk 11, pg 133.
   1782 - grant for 50 acres on Sugar Creek on both sides of the wagon road to Charlotte town, joining Robert McKee, bk 12, pg 40.
   1784 - deed from Robert McCree for 5 ½ acres beginning on the Indian line, Test: Elisha Smith, Ezekiel Polk, bk 12, pg 435.
   1785 - deed to Moses Bigham for 56 acres on Big Sugar Creek adjoining Robert McCrees, Hugh Harris and the Catawba Indian lands, Test: Ezekiel Polk, John Pelly, bk 12, pg 447.
   Samuel was born 1732, died Dec 11, 1798 at age 66. His will only names nephews and sister Hannah Beard. Brother of Robert McCleary.

McCleary/McClary, Widow
   1790 - 112 00 - twp 3

McCleary, William
   1770 - witnessed a deed, with James Sharp, from Thomas Henry to James Simson on Clemmes branch in New Providence adjoining Alexander McGinty, Thomas Henry, bk 10, pg 500.
   1778 - deed from James and Patrick Scott of Tryon Co., NC, for 200 acres at the mouth of Long Creek adjoining Joseph Harding, John Smith Test: William Richey, bk 10, pg 363 & pg 381.
   1781 - witnessed a deed, with William Ritchey, from Abraham and Samuel Barnet to Robert Crocket on Long Creek, bk 12, pg 476.
   1790 - 200 00 - twp 1
   1795 - Loose estate papers

McClellan, Alexander(2)
   1779 - grant for 242 acres joining James Flanigan, Robert Barns, Archibald McNeal, Samuel Linton, bk 10, pg 502 or 503.
   1781 - King's branch of Sugar Creek.
   Alexander died May 13, 1781 at the age of 40.

McClelland, Hugh
   1777 - deed from James Tate for 120 acres on Four Mile Creek joining Andrew Rea, Test: Samuel & Elizabeth Lusk, bk 10, pg 262 & 265.
   Six Mile Creek. Of Craven Co. SC in 1777.

McClelland, James
   1754 - mentioned as the previous owner of a tract joining John Bravard, Robert Jennings, John & Elinor McDowel, bk 10, pg 286.

McClelland, John
   1790 - 133 00 - twp 13

McClelland, Margaret(2)

Margaret died Sept 28, 1831 at the age of 94.

McClelland, Mary(2)
Mary died Oct 1841 at the age of 73.

McClelland, Robert & Rebecca
1767 - deed to Charles McCommon for 77 acres on Poplar Ridge between English Buffaloe and Coddle Creek and the waters of Rockey River, Test: J. White and L. White, bk 10, pg 375.
1775 - Robert was a signer of the petition to pardon the Cabarrus Black Boys.
1790 - 113 00 - twp 13

McClenhan, Andrew
1779 - deed from Mounce Justice dor 440 on the long branches of Coldwater Creek, Test: John March, Jason Frizell, bk 10, pg 431.

McClanahan, John
1779 - witnessed a deed, with Robert Crockett, from William Hambilton to William Ferril on the north side of Waxhaw Creek, adjoining John Rogers, bk 11, pg 67.
Son of Robert McClenahan.

McClennahan, Reuben
1790 - 122 00 - twp 6

McClenahan, Robert
1767 - Robert's will was probated in Mecklenburg Co. Children: John, Elizabeth, Janet
1767 - Loose estate papers

McClure, James
1798 - Loose estate papers

McClure, James(2)
1782 - named as an adjoining land owner to George Buckalow, Tunas Hogland, James Clark on McCalpin's Creek, bk 12, pg 508.
James died July 20, 1785 at the age of 44.

McClure, James & Peggy
1779 - deed to Aron McWherter for 153 acres on the Middle Fork of Twelve Mile Creek, Test: Andrew Neely, Hugh Barnet, bk 12, pg 329.
1772 - deed to James Potts for 550 acres on the Flat Branch of Twelve Mile Creek, Test: Henry Downs, James Tate, bk 10, pg 257.

McClure, John(2)
1778 - John died Jan 27, 1778, his will was probated in Mecklenburg Co.
1778 - Loose estate papers
Children: Joseph

McClure, John, Junr. & Ann
1778 - deed from Robert and John Allison for 200 acres on Long Creek joining Jeremiah Joy, test: Thomas Allison, William Allen, bk 10, pg 92.
1790 - 124 00 - twp 6
1800 - Mecklenburg County

McClure, John, Jur

1779 - named as an adjoining land owner to Robert
Graham, Robert Hays, William Wilson, James Wilson,
Thomas Polk on Sugar Creek, bk 10, pg 340.
1783 - deed from Robert & Rachel Crocket for 44 acres on
the head branches of Sugar Creek, Test: Thomas McClure,
William Ramsey, bk 11, pg 271.
1783 - deed from Thomas Polk for 112 acres on Sugar
Creek, Test: William Polk, Thomas McLure, bk 11, pg 251.
1790 - 412 00 - twp 1

McClure, Mathew, Capt.
1775 - Matthew was one of the signers of the Mecklenburg
Declaration of Independence on May 20, 1775.
1779 - witnessed a deed, with Robert Brownfield, to John
Foard for lots 85 & 93 in Charlotte, bk 10, pg 368.
1781 - deed to William Johnston for 110 acres on the
head branch of McDowel's Creek and One Mile Creek, Test:
Jane Alexander, John McKnitt Alexander, Hezekiah
Alexander, bk 12, pg 451.
1781 - named as an adjoining land owner to John McKnitt
Alexander, John Neil on the head branches of the Reedy
Branch of Long Creek, bk 11, pg 78.
1784 - named as an adjoining land owner to Benjamin &
Jemimah Knox, John Davidson on the south fork of
McDowell's Creek, bk 12, pg 353.
Reedy branch of Long Creek, head branch of McDowel's
Creek.
Mentioned in the estate settlement of William Sample.
1790 - 302 06 - twp 6
1800 - Mecklenburg County
1812 - Loose estate papers
Children: female (George Houston)

McClure, Moses
1790 - 123 00 - twp 6
Son of Thomas McClure.

McClure, Moses, Jr.
1790 - 000 10 - twp 1

McClure, Robert
1784 - named as an adjoining land owner to Benjamin
Cook, Jack Liget on the Mile Branch, a branch of Two
Mile Creek, bk 12, pg 443.

McClure, Thomas, Jur.
1783 - witnessed a deed, with William Polk, from Thomas
Polk to John McLure/McClure on Sugar Creek, bk 11, pg
251.
1790 - 101 00 - twp 1

McClure, Thos, Senr.
1783 - named as an adjoining land owner to Robert &
Elizabeth McCleary, David Russel, John Boal on the head
branch of Mallard Creek and Long Creek, bk 12, pg 257.
1783 - witnessed a deed, with William Ramsey, from
Robert & Rachel Crockett to John McClure on the head
branches of Sugar Creek, bk 11, pg 271.

Residents of Mecklenburg County, North Carolina   1762-1790

1790 - 211 00 - twp 4
McClure, Widow
    1790 - 112 00 - twp 1
McClure, William
    1777 - witnessed a deed, with James Roberson, from James
    & Mary Meek to David Daugherty on Rockey River, bk 10,
    pg 219.
    1780 - named as an adjoining land owner to William
    Johnston, James Clark on Mallard Creek, bk 12, pg 91.
    1790 - 323 00 - twp 6
    1800 - Mecklenburg County
McCollum, Malcom
    1790 - 132 00 - twp 15
    1796 - Loose estate papers
    1800 - Mecklenburg County (widow)
McCombs, Andrew
    1779 - witnessed a deed, with John Queen, from Thomas
    Harris, sherrif, to Robert Graham, the highest bidder,
    on Sugar Creek, in a judgement against the estate of
    William Walker, bk 10, pg 356.
McCombs, James & Mary(2)
    1778 - deed from William Simmond for 210 acres known as
    the No. Two Tract, Test: Samuel McComb, William Wylie,
    bk 10, pg 335.
    Children: female (Ezekiel Black), Robert, Jane, Mary,
    Rachel
    1790 - 205 05 - twp 15
    James died Oct 19, 1813 at age 74, his will was probated
    in Feb 1814.
    Mary died March 2, 1821.
McCombs, Samuel & Mary(4)
    1776 - named as the previous owner of lots 34 & 92 in
    Charlotte, bk 10, pg 275.
    1778 - witnessed a deed, with William Wylie, from
    William Simmond to James McComb, bk 10, pg 335.
    1782 - deed from Samuel Hemphill for lot 65 in
    Charlotte, Test: Ezekiel Polk, Samuel Wilson, bk 11, pg
    194.
    1783 - witnessed a deed, with James Tagert, Thomas
    Henderson, from Joseph Nicholson to William Hutchison on
    the head waters of Sugar Creek, bk 11, pg 209.
    1784 - deed from Joseph Nicholson of Wilks Co., GA for
    lot 6 in Charlotte, Test: John Nickelson, Nathaniel
    Irwin, Thomas Henderson, bk 12, pg 239.
    1790 - 111 03 - twp 3
    1800 - Mecklenburg County
    Samuel died March 28, 1798.
McCommon, Charles & Sarah
    1766 - listed in the militia company of Capt. Adam
    Alexander of Clear Creek.

1767 - deed from Robert & Rebeckah McClelland for 77 acres on Poplar Ridge between English Buffalo and Coddle Creek, bk 10, 375.
1771 - deed to John White for 77 acres on Poplar Ridge between English Buffalo and Coddle Creek and on the waters of Rockey River, Test: William White, bk 10, pg 224.

McConnaughey, Joseph & Martha
1785 - named in a deed, no book or page number given.
1839 - Loose estate papers

McConnell, Alexander
1763 - Loose estate papers

McConey, John
1773 - deed to James Kergin for 50 acres, Test: Witt Carragin, John Tanner, bk 10, pg 182.

McCong, Thomas
1790 - 001 00 - twp 7

McCord, David
1781 - named as an adjoining land owner to Abraham and Samuel Barnet, Robert Crocket, Samuel Sprott, David Miller on Long Creek, bk 12, pg 476.
1783 - deed to John Buchanan for 200 acres on both sides of Long Creek about half a mile west of Toole's road, Test: John Johnston, William Ramsey, bk 11, pg 196.

McCord, James(2)
1774 - named as an adjoining land owner of William Starret, Nathaniel Cook, Thomas Polk, James Moore, Andrew Sprott, bk 10, pg 379.
1779 - named as an adjoining land owner to William Wilson, Jeremy McCafferty on a branch of McCulloch Creek, bk 10, pg 505.
James died Nov 12, 1781.

McCord, John
1790 - 414 01 - twp 1
1800 - Mecklenburg County

McCord, Robert(2)
1790 - 214 00 - twp 1
1800 - Mecklenburg County
Robert died July 19, 1801 at the age of 62.

McCord, James
1785 - Loose estate papers

McCord, John, Sr.
1787 - Loose estate papers

McCorkle, Andrew
1781 - deed to John Wilson for 202 acres on Pickens Creek, a branch of Twelve Mile Creek, Test: John Nutt, William McMurry, bk 12, pg 274.

McCorkle, Archabeld & Joanna
1790 - 101 00 - twp 17
Wife - Joanna White
Son of John & Margaret McCorkle.

McCorkle, James & Hannah

Residents of Mecklenburg County, North Carolina 1762-1790

    1790 - 142 00 - twp 18
    1795 - James' will was probated in Mecklenburg County.
McCorkle, James
    1784 - mentioned in a deed as a deceased adjoining land owner to William Hagens and Robert Crocket on Twelve Mile Creek near the wagon road, bk 12, pg 382.
McCorkle, John & Margaret, Susannah
    1779 - witnessed a deed, with John Foster, from Hugh & Elizabeth Cry to Jacob Seeres, bk 11, pg 96.
    1780 - grant for 200 acres on Twelve Mile Creek joining the Widow Jackson, bk 12, pg 18.
    1790 - 113 00 - twp 16
    1800 - Mecklenburg County
    Wife - Margaret Evans, Susannah Gordon
    Children: Matthew, Owen, Archibald, James, Robert, John, Mary (Hugh Forbes), Margaret (John Williams), Elizabeth (Samuel Gordon), Milly (Jonathan Gordon)
    John's will was probated Jan 1811.
McCorkle, John
    1812 - Seventh Company detached from the First Mecklenburg Regiment.
McCorkel, Matthew
    1778 - named as an adjoining land owner to William & Sarah Givens, John Thompson, bk 10, pg 285.
McCorkle, Owen
    1790 - 102 00 - twp 18
McCorkle, Samuel E. & Margaret
    1778 - trustee of Liberty Hall.
    Wife - Margaret Gillespie
McCorlis, William
    1782 north fork of Waxhaw Creek.
McCortle, Stephen
    1774 - deed from Samuel & Rachel McCrume for 100 acres on Jean Armour's Creek, previously owned by Samuel Moses, Test: Robert Gawin, Justin Forbes, bk 10, pg 133.
McCorkle, Thomas
    1790 - 202 06 - twp 7
    1800 - Mecklenburg County
McCormack, William & Elizabeth
    1790 - 112 00 - twp 1
    Wife: Elizabeth
    Children: William, Daniel
    1794 - William's will was probated in April 1794.
McCormick, Darius
    1782 - Darius' will was probated in Mecklenburg Co.
    Children: Robert, John
McCormick, Dennis/Dinnes(2)
    1774 - named as an adjoining land owner to Samuel Bigham, John Whiteside, Samuel Knox, Moses Ferguson on Steel Creek, bk 10, pg 411.
    1782 Dennis died March 9, 1782 at the age of 55.
McCormick, Robert

1790 - 204 00 - twp 2
1800 - Mecklenburg County
McCown, Margt
    1790 - 013 01 - twp 8
McCoy, Beaty
    1790 - 453 05 - twp 6
McCoy, Daniel
    1766 - Loose estate papers
McCoy, John & Catherine
    1777 - deed to Martain Phifer, Sr. for 255 acres on the
    north side of Buffalo Creek, Test: Zaccheus Wilson,
    Martin Fifer, bk 11, pg 34.
    1780 - deed to Jacob Croner for 79 acres on Three Mile
    Creek on both sides of a branch, Test: Richard Trotter,
    Martin Orr, bk 11, pg 66.
    1783 - named as an adjoining land owner to William &
    Elizabeth Ross, Christian Barbrick on Coldwater Creek,
    bk 12, pg 360.
McCoy/McKoy, John
    1780 - deed from John Province for 257 acres on the east
    fork of Sugar Creek adjoining Robert Phillips, Andrew
    Sprott, Alexander Starrett, William Wilson, John
    McElwes, bk 12, pg 245.
    1782 - deed to John Springs for 257 acres on the east
    fork of Sugar Creek adjoining Robert Phillips, Andrew
    Sprott, Alexander Starrett, William Wilson, John McEwus,
    bk 12, pg 244.
McCracken, James
    1790 - 227 00 - twp 6
    1800 - Mecklenburg County
    1802 - Loose estate papers
    Children: Samuel ? (Sinthe Russell)
McCracken, John
    1766 - listed in the militia company of Capt. Adam
    Alexander of Clear Creek.
    1779 - deed from Thomas Polk, attorney for David
    Oliphant, for 66 acres on Clear Creek joining Col. Adam
    Alexander, Moses Shelby, Test: John Adam Miller, William
    Pickens, bk 12, pg 265.
    1790 - 334 00 - twp 14
McCracken, Samuel
    1776 - Loose estate papers
McCraven, John, Sr.
    1783 - named as an adjoining land owner to Samuel
    Buchannan on Beard's Branch of McCalpin's Creek, bk 12,
    pg 101.
    1783 - named as an adjoining land owner to John Buchanan
    on the dividing ridge between Four Mile Creek and
    McCalpin's Creek, joining Mathew Stephenson, bk 12, pg
    98.
    1790 - 123 00 - twp 15
    1800 - Mecklenburg County

McCraven, John, Jr.
   1790 - 103 00 - twp 15
   1800 - Mecklenburg County
McCraw, James
   1784 - named as an adjoining land owner to John
   Chamberlain, James and William Voyls, Philip Wise on
   Coldwater Creek, bk 12, pg 187.
McCrery, Isabel(2)
   Isabel died July 1775.
McCrorey, Hugh & Jean Rogers
   1790 - 112 00 - twp 16
McCrume, Samuel & Rachel(2)
   1774 - deed to Stephen McCortle for 100 acres on Jean
   Armour's Creek, purchased from Samuel Moses, Test:
   Robert Gawin, Justin Forbes, bk 10, pg 133.
   Samuel died Oct 10, 1778 at the age of 49.
   Rachel died Sept 4, 1822
   1778 - Loose estate papers
McCulloch, Elizabeth
   Elizabeth died March 4, 1797
McCulloch, Henry Eustace
   1765, 1770, 1773 Sugar Creek, McCalpin's Creek
   1775 - deed by his attorney, Thomas Frohock, to
   Alexander McKee for 160 acres on both sides of Rockey
   River and the waters of McCalpin's Creek, Test: Thomas
   Polk, Dan Ockeltree, bk 10, pg 272.
   1779 - named as an adjoining land owner to John Wilson
   and Charles Caldwell on Coddle Creek, bk 12, pg 68.
   Henry E. McCulloch of Halifax Co., NC in 1765 when he
   bought land on Rocky River.
   Mentioned in the estate settlement of William Sample.
McCulloch, James
   1785 - named as an adjoining land owner to William
   McCree, John Brevard, John Dickey, William Sharp on
   Davidson and Back Creek in Rowan Co., NC, bk 12, pg 574.
McCulloch, John & Katherine
   1790 - 524 03 - twp 20
   John is buried at Providence Church.
McCulloch, John
   1780 - deed from Richard Martin for 150 acres on the
   Muddy Branch of Coddle Creek, Test: John Houston and
   James Humphreys, bk 12, pg 432.
   1790 - 126 00 - twp 8
McCulloch, John
   1777 - deed from Joseph & Esthesth Kenedy for 60 acres
   on Six Mile Creek on both sides of the Great Waggon
   Road, Test: Robert and Adam Motherall, bk 10, pg 423.
   1779 - deed from William Haggins for 87 acres on Twelve
   Mile Creek, Test: Duncan Ochiltree, bk 10, pg 425.
   1779 - witnessed a deed, with Archibald Crockett, John
   Wilson, from William & Rachel Robison to John Gibbins on

Four Mile Creek near Providence, a tar Kiln branch, bk 11, pg 298.
1782 - witnessed a deed, with William Cry, from James Cook to Andrew Walker for 200 acres on the north fork of Waxhaw Creek, bk 11, pg 126.

McCulloch, William
1783 - deed to John Wilson for 190 acres on McCalpin's Creek joining Robert Parks, Test: William Polk, John M. Powel, bk 11, pg 241.
1790 - 200 01 - twp 3

McCulloch, William
1779 - deed from Ochillice Martin and Company for lot 17 in Charlotte, Test: William Patterson, Ephraim Braivard, bk 10, pg 326.
1789 - Loose estate papers
1790 - 012 00 - twp 4 (widow)

McCummons, John
1790 - 234 01 - twp 14

McCurdy, Archabeld & Maggie Sellers(5)
1779 - deed from Thomas Polk, attorney for David Oliphant, for 50 acres on the head of the Long Run, a branch of Clear Creek, Test: Charles Polk, Will Lusk, bk 10, pg 543.
1779 - Margaret McCurdy witnessed a deed, with Alexander Finley, from Michael Ligget to his daughter Grace Harrison, bk 11, pg 31.
1780 - Margaret McCurdy witnessed a deed, with Alexander Finley, from Adam Alexander to Samuel Montgomery on Clear Creek, bk 11, pg 70.
1785 - deed from James & Elizabeth Love for 180 acres on the west side of Rockey River adjoining William McAnulty, Test: William McAnulty, John and Archibald White, bk 12, pg 560.
1790 - 145 06 twp 13
1800 - Cabarrus
Children: Archibald, Sophia
Revolutionary Soldier - died Nov 11, 1843 in Cabarrus Co, NC, age 92 according to the Charlotte Journal dated Nov 17, 1843.

McCurdy, Henry
1769 - Mentioned as original land owner in a deed, no book or page number given.

McCurdy, Margaret
1780 - witnessed a deed, with Alexander Finney, from Adam Alexander to Samuel Montgomery on Clear Creek, bk 11, pg 70.

McDanny, James
1793 - Account ledger of John Melchor's store.

McDonald, Arthur
1790 - Loose estate papers

McDonald, David & Elizabeth Hays(2)
1790 - 000 10 - twp 1

David died May 14, 1838 at age 72.
Elizabeth died Oct 24, 1849 age 83.
McDonald, Patrick
  1778 - deed from the commissioners of Charlotte for lots 345, 346, & 347 in Charlotte, Test: Joseph Nicholson, Hugh Pollock, bk 10, pg 64.
  1778 - deed from the commissioners of Charlotte for lots 340, 341, 342 in Charlotte, Test: Joseph Nicholson, Hugh Pollock, Jr., bk 10, pg 71.
  1780 - deed to James Moore for lots 46, & 47 in Charlotte, Test: Joseph Moore, James Orr, bk 10, pg 437.
  1780 - deed to Alexander Sterroh for lots 204, 335, & 336 in Charlotte, Test: William Hutchison, Daniel Ford, bk 11, pg 130.
  1779 - deed to Alexander Hutchison for lots 390, 391, 392 in Charlotte, Test: William Reed, William Hutchison, bk 11, pg 42.
McDough, Robert
  1783 - Loose estate papers
McDowell, Archabeld
  1790 - 000 10 - twp 4
McDowell, Esther
  Esther died Feb 5, 1804
  1806 - Loose estate papers
McDowell, James
  1777 - named as an adjoining land owner to Mathew and Francis Lock on Buffelow Creek, bk 12, pg 250.
McDowell, John & Jane Parks(2)
  1773 - deed from James & Margaret Boyer for 150 acres on Sugar Creek adjoining Thomas Polk, Alexander McKee, Test: James and Joseph Tagert, bk 10, pg 319.
  1778 - deed from Mary McDowel for 320 acres on the south side of Sugar Creek, granted to Mary McDowel on April 20, 1754, Test: Aaron Wilson, bk 10, pg 29.
  1779 - witnessed a deed, with Aaron Wilson, from Robert Wilson to Joseph Wilson on Sugar Creek, bk 10, pg 366.
  1790 - 134 05 - twp 1
  John died July 29, 1795 at age 52.
  Jane died Oct 8, 1824 age 77.
  1795 - Loose estate papers
  Children: John, James, Hugh, Margaret, Mary, Jane.
  Brother-in-law: Samuel Watson
McDowel, John & Elinor
  1774 - Mary Conway and Catherine Hoiy heirs of Eloner's estate, bk 10, pg 144.
  1775 - deed to Joseph Wallace for 200 acres, Test: Benjamin Walace, Robert Dowel, bk 10, pg 286.
  1777 - J. McDowell witnessed a deed, with Joseph Jack, James McMahan from George & Margaret Cathey to Hugh Lucas, bk 10, pg 242.

1777 - named as an adjoining land owner to Joseph & Sarah Hobbs, Thomas Givens, Charles Moses, John Miller on McDowel's Creek, bk 10, pg 269.

McDowel, Joseph
1779 - deed from John and Joseph McDowel to Hugh Laurance on McDowel Creek, Test:William Stephenson, James Dawson, bk 10, pg 305.

McDowel, Luther
1790 - 103 00 - twp 1

McDowel, Mary(2)
1778 - deed from Mary McDowel for 320 acres on the south side of Sugar Creek, granted to Mary McDowel on April 20, 1754, Test: Aaron Wilson, bk 10, pg 29.
Died Oct 6, 1789 at age 80.
Mother of John McDowell.

McDowell, Robert
1770 - Robert's will was probated in Mecklenburg Co.
Children: Thomas

McDowell, Robert
1781 - Loose estate papers

McDowell, Thomas
1782 - deed from Thomas McDowell and William Berryhill to James Clark for 120 acres on Sugar Creek joining William Clark, Test: Thomas Allison, Will Reed, bk 11, pg 183.

McDowell, William & Esther(2)
1782 - named as an adjoining land owner to Hector & Margaret McLane, Francis Herron, John Bigham, James Sprott, Thomas Barnet on King's Branch of Sugar Creek, bk 12, pg 234.
William died Dec 14, 1781 at age 70.
1784 - Loose estate papers

McDowell, William & Dorothy
1780 - William's will was probated in Mecklenburg Co.

McElroy, James
1790 - 133 01 - twp 18
1800 - Mecklenburg County

McElroy, John
1790 - 422 00 - twp 18

McElwee, James
1766 - listed in the militia company of Capt. Adam Alexander of Clear Creek.

McElwes/McEwus, John
1780 - named as an adjoining land owner to John Province, John McKoy, Robert Phillips, Andrew Sprott, Alexander Starrett, William Wilson on the east side of Sugar Creek, bk 12, pg 245.
1782 - named as an adjoining land owner to John McKoy, John Springs, Robert Phillips, Andrew Sprott, Alexander Starret, William Wilson on the east fork of Sugar Creek, bk 12, pg 244.

McElwrath, Robert

1779 - deed for lot 5 in Charlotte, Test: Ephraim
Brevard, Isaac Alexander, bk 11, pg 145.
1779 - deed for lot 1 in Charlotte, Test: Ephraim
Brevard, John Alexander, bk 11, pg 127.

McEuken, James
   1803 - Loose estate papers

McEwell, John
   1778 - named as an adjoining land owner to John & Jean
Wear, John Provane, Ebenezer Newton, Andrew Trot,
Alexander Herrel, William Wilson on Abraham Alexander's
Mill Creek, bk 10, pg 283.

McEwen, Alexander
   1780 - witnessed a deed, with John Houston, John Grimes,
from William Penny to William Ross on Coddle Creek, bk
11, pg 111.
   1783 - witnessed a deed, with Hugh Rodgers, John
Fleming, from William & Jane Ross to Seth Rogers, bk 11,
pg 290.

McEwen, Hugh & ? Watson
   Hugh died Feb 2, 1792
   1792 - Loose estate papers
   Children: Samuel, Mary, Eleanor, Sarah, Abigail (William
Morrison), Elizabeth.

McEwen, James
   Wife: ? Davies

McEwen, Mary
   1807 - Loose estate papers

McEwen/McQuown, Thomas
   1781 - Loose estate papers

McEwus/McElwes, John
   1782 - named as adjoining land owner to John McKoy, John
Springs, Robert Phillips, Andrew Sprott, Alexander
Starret, and William Wilson, bk 12, pgs 244 & 245.
   1782 - named as adjoining land owner to John McKoy, John
Springs, Robert Phillips, Alexander Starret, William
Wilson, and Andrew Spratt on Sugar Creek, bk 12, pg 244.
   1782 - deed from John McKoy for 257 acres on the east
fork of Sugar Creek joining Robert Phillips, Andrew
Sprott, Alexander Starret, William Wilson, and John &
Sarah Springs, Test: Adam and Isac Alexander, bk 12, pg
244.

McFadian, Thomas & Hannah(5)
   1778 - Signer of 1778 Petition.
   1779 - witnessed a deed, with Henry Rock, from Thomas
Polk, attorney for David Oliphant, to Robert Carothers
on the ridge between Henderson and Caldwell's Creeks, bk
10, pg 432.
   1782 - grant for 133 acres on Anderson Creek adjoining
William Newell, bk 12, pg 140.
   1782 - named as an adjoining land owner to Francis
Newell, Robert McEachin/McCachron on Anderson Creek, bk
12, pg 46.

1790 - 111 00 - twp 13
Thomas died May 24, 1799.
Mentioned in the estate papers of Nicholson Ross 1774.
McFall, Dennis & Mary
    1783 - deed to Joseph Wilson for 260 acres on a branch
    of McDowell's Creek, Test: William Waddle and John Belk,
    bk 12, pg 497.
McFalls, John
    1790 - 000 10 - twp 1
McFarlin, John & Letice
    1783 - deed to Robert Mitchel for 100 acres (near Waxhaw
    Creek?), Test: William Beard and John Bigham, bk 12, pg
    362.
McFersion, John
    1790 - 000 10 - twp 15
McFee, Robert
    Mentioned in the estate papers of Nicholson Ross 1774.
McGee, Hall
    1803 - Loose estate papers
McGee, John
    1790 - 221 00 - twp 4
McGee, Thomas(2)
    1774 - witnessed a deed, with William Reed, from Samuel
    Bigham to John Whiteside on Steel Creek, bk 10, pg 411.
    1778
    Thomas died Dec 30, 1777 at age 47.
    1778 - Loose estate papers
McGehey, Amos
    1790 - 101 00 - twp 14
McGill, Thomas
    1790 - 000 10 - twp 2
McGinn, James
    1771 - Loose estate papers
McGinnis, Charles
    1790 - 303 00 - twp 13
    1800 - Cabarrus County
McGinnis, Peter
    1790 - 313 00 - twp 15
McGintey, Alexander
    1776 - witnessed a deed, with William Miller, John
    Miller, from David & Martha Miller to David Park on
    Reedy Creek, bk 11, pg 239.
    1780 - witnessed a deed, with John McKiman/McCommon?,
    from Samuel Montgomery to Adam Alexander, James Harris,
    Mathew Stuart, John Ford, and John Quirry (trustees for
    the congregation of Rocky Spring), for 3 acres, bk 11,
    pg 71.
    Clemmes branch in New Providence, McKee's Creek.
    1790 - 101 02 - twp 4
McGintey, James

Residents of Mecklenburg County, North Carolina   223
1762-1790

1779 - witnessed a deed, with Samuel Martin, from Francis & Elizabeth Miller to William Simmonds on the south branch of Caldwell's Creek, bk 10, pg 351.
1790
McGinty, John
   1780 - named as an adjoining land owner to Daniel McKeeman, William Miller, Alexander McGinty, on the head branches of McKee Creek, bk 12, pg 48.
   1782 - witnessed a deed, with Joseph Galbreath, from William & Margaret Query to David Whipple on the Middle Fork of Goose Creek joining Robert Glass, bk 11, pg 151.
   1782 - Loose estate papers
McGinty, Mary Ann
   1808 - Loose estate papers
McGinty, Robert
   1783 - deed to William Kenedy from Robert McGinty, late of Mecklenburg Co., for 122 acres on McCalpin's Creek adjoining William Miller, Thomas Gribble, Test: William Miller, James Finney, bk 12, pg 491.
McGivert, John
   1777 - deed from John Phillip Weeks for 48 acres on the south bank of Rockey River, Test: David Weeks, John Jack, bk 10, pg 243.
McGoin, John
   1774 - witnessed a deed, with Brace Miller, James Tate, from Archibald & Mary Crockett to John Willson on Six Mile Creek, bk 10, pg 130.
McGough, Robert
   1778 - Robert's will was probated in Mecklenburg Co. Children: John, Robert
McGoughen, James
   1790 - 000 10 - twp 19
McGraw, James
   1778 - Signer of 1778 Petition.
   1790 - 341 00 - twp 12
   1800 - Cabarrus County
McGraw, William
   1790 - 111 00 - twp 10
   1800 - Cabarrus County
McGuire, James
   1770 - James' will was probated in Mecklenburg Co. Children: Eliza, Thomas, John
McGuist, John
   1790 - 243 00 - twp 14
McHarris, James
   1778 - Loose estate papers
McHarritt, John
   1778 - deed from the commissioners of Charlotte to the trustees of Liberty Hall for lots 69,70,77, & 78 on the south side of Tryon Street in Charlotte, Test: Hezekiah Alexander, James Tagert, bk 10, pg 211.
McHarry, James

McIntire, James
1774 - James' will was probated in Mecklenburg Co.
1790 - 102 01 - twp 6
brother: John
sister: Sarah McIntire.

McIntire, Robert
1780 - grant for 34 acres on Sugar Creek near the Waggon Road, and P. Johnston, bk 12, pg 53.

McIntire, William
1790 - 104 00 - twp 15

McKay/McCay, Arthur
1764 - deed from Arthur & Justina Dobbs for 187 acres on Connerford Branch and both sides of Great Coldwater Creek, Test: Martain Fifer, Richard Berrey, bk 10, pg 404.

McKay/McCay, McKinney & Martha Robinson
1788 -

McKay/McCay, Michael
1790 - 103 00 - twp 5

McKee, Alexander
1763
1773 - deed to William Berryhill for 150 acres on Sugar Creek joining Robert Walker, Test: Joseph Montgomery, Robert Barnet, bk 11, pg 129.
1773 - named as an adjoining land owner to James & Margaret Boyer, John McDowel, Thomas Polk, on Sugar Creek, bk 10, pg 319.
1775 - deed from Henry Eustace McCulloch for 160 acres on both sides of Rockey River and McCalpin's Creek, Test: Thomas Polk, Dan Ockeltree, bk 10, pg 272.
1782 - deed to William Berryhill for 200 acres on Sugar Creek joining William Clark, Test: John Bigham, James Clark, bk 11, pg 157.
1784 - named as an adjoining land owner to John & Jane Sloan, Jesse Clark, Isaac Williams, Robert Walker, James Tagart, David Hayes on a branch of Sugar Creek, bk 12, pg 466.
1790 - 134 00 - twp 19
Children: John, Alexander, William, Thomas, Sarah (William Hall), Katy (John Hodge), Mary (William Graham), Kilsey, Elizabeth, Ruth
1798 - Loose estate papers
Alexander's will was probated April 1798.

McKee, Ambrose
1779 - Ambrose's will was probated in Mecklenburg Co.
1785 - Loose estate papers
Children: Thomas, John, William, Ambrose

McKee, Ambrose
1783 - deed to Alexander Robison for 164 acres on Steel Creek joining John Bigham, William Bigham, Test: David Robison, William Patterson, bk 11, pg 262.

Residents of Mecklenburg County, North Carolina

1783 - deed from Richard and David Robison for 200 acres joining John Davis, Andrew Cathey, Test: Andrew Cathey, William Patterson, bk 11, pg 301.
Son of Ambrose McKee.
McKee, Andrew
    1781 - deed from Peter Johnston for 200 acres joining Gideon Thomson, William Lawing, John Anderson, Test: Mat Troy and Hugh Colloden Boyd, bk 12, pg 444.
McKee, David
    1774 - witnessed a deed, with Jeremiah Alexander, from the commissioners of Charlotte to John Patterson and William Patterson, Jr. for lots 195, & 198 on the north side of Tryon Street in Charlotte, bk 10, pg 109.
    1774 - witnessed a deed, with David Byars, from the commissioners of Charlotte to John Work for lot 156 in Charlotte, bk 10, pg 217.
    1779 - witnessed a deed, with Will Lusk, from Thomas Polk, attorney for David Oliphant, to Christopher Osburn, bk 10, pg 542.
    1790 - 253 03 - twp 3
McKee, George
    1782 - witnessed a deed, with John Barringer, from Matthias & Susan Beaver to Jacob Jeem on Dutch Buffalo Creek, bk 11, pg 162.
McKee, James
    1778 - deed from Samuel & Patience Allen for 400 acres on Beaver Dam Creek joining John Davis, Test: William Berryhill, Robert Irwin, Thomas Greer, bk 11, pg 110.
    1780 - witnessed a deed, with William Bigham, from Samuel Bigham to Thomas Spencer on Steel Creek, bk 11, pg 1.
    1781 - deed from Samuel Bigham for 83 acres on Steel Creek, Test: Samuel Bigham, John Shannon, bk 11, pg 252.
    1782 - witnessed a deed, with Robert Irwin, from Thomas Spencer to John Taylor on the North Fork of Steel Creek joining John Bigham, Robert Wilson, Robert Irwin, bk 11, pg 177.
Half brother of William Chronicle.
McKee, John & Hannah
    1773 - deed from Hannah to Joseph Kennedy (doctor) for 60 acres on Six Mile Creek on both sides of the Great Waggon Road, adjoining James Lynn, John Haggin, Test: Richard & Sussah Sprinsteen, bk 10, pg 122.
    1777 - named as a land owner (deceased) on Six Mile Creek, bk 10, pg 423.
John died May 17, 1764 and is buried in Providence Presbyterian Church Cemetery.
    1764 - Loose estate papers
McKee, John
    1785 - named as an adjoining land owner to Alexander Mitchel, Robert Alison on a branch of Sugar Creek, bk 12, pg 462.

McKee, Robert
    1782 - named as an adjoining land owner to Samuel
    McCleary on Sugar Creek, bk 12, pg 40.
McKee, William
    1790 - 132 06 - twp 19
    1800 - Mecklenburg County
McKee, Widow
    1790 - 147 00 - twp 2
McKee, William, Junr.
    1790 - 132 06 - twp 19
    1800 - Mecklenburg County
McKelvey, James
    1780 - Loose estate papers
McKentire, William
    1790 - 104 00 - twp 15
McKenzie/McKenzey, Benjamin
    1783 - witnessed a deed from Joseph Galbreath to John
    and Tunas Hood on Goose Creek, bk 12, pg 206.
McKibben, James
    1798 - Loose estate papers
McKibben, James
    1807 - Loose estate papers
McKibben, John
    1799 - Loose estate papers
McKibben, John
    1809 - Loose estate papers
McKibben, Thomas
    1804 - Loose estate papers
McKillipe, William
    1766 - listed in the militia company of Capt. Adam
    Alexander of Clear Creek.
McKimmon/McKeeman, Daniel
    1780 - named as an adoining land owner to John McKeeman
    on McKee's Creek, bk 12, pg 42.
    1780 - grant for 50 acres on McKee's Creek joining
    Alexander McGinty, John McGinty, William Miller, bk 12,
    pg 48.
    1786 head branches of McKee's Creek.
McKiman, John (see McCammon)
    1780 - grant for 91 acres on McKee's Creek joining
    Daniel McKeeman, bk 12, pg 42.
    1780 - witnessed a deed, with Alexander McGinty, from
    Samuel Montgomery to Adam Alexander, James Harris,
    Mathew Stuart, John Ford, John Quirry, bk 11, pg 71.
    1786 - Loose estate papers
McKinley/McCinley, Charles
    1782 - named as an adjoining land owner to William
    McAnulty and David McKinley on Reedy Creek, bk 12, pg
    127.
    1790 - 132 00 - twp 13
    1800 - Cabarrus County
McKinley/McCinley, David

1782 - named as an adjoining land owner to William
McAnulty and Charles McKinley on Reedy Creek, bk 12, pg
127.
1783 - grant for 228 acres on Anderson Creek joining
Hugh Campbell, William Phillips, bk 12, pg 109.
1790 - 107 00 - twp 13
McKinley, John
1790 - 212 00 - twp 9
1800 - Cabarrus County
McKinley, Joseph & Elizabeth
1777 - witnessed a deed, with Samuel Chambers, William
Kerr, from John & Catherine Biggar to Rev. William
Tenant on the Catawba River opposite the mouth of
Crowder's Creek, bk 10, pg 84 & 97.
1782 - deed to John Carruthers for 100 acres joining
Daniel Williams, James McCall, Test: William McKinley,
James Miller, Adam Calhoon, bk 11, pg 149.
1782 - deed to James R. Alexander for 115 acres on the
Catawba River above the mouth of Crowder's Creek, Test:
Isaac Price, John Carothers, bk 11, pg 280.
McKinley, Robert
1765 - references a grant for 100 acres on Paw Creek, no
book or page number, bk 10, pg 322.
1774 - Robert's will was probated in Mecklenburg Co.
Children: James, Elizabeth, Martha, William
McKinley/McCendley, William & Margaret(2)
1779 - grant for 100 acres on both sides of Paw Creek,
bk 10, pg 486.
1782 - witnessed a deed, with James Miller and Adam
Calhoon, from Joseph & Elizabeth McKinley, bk 11, pg
149.
1790 - 147 00 - twp 1
William died May 29, 1815 at age 72.
Heir of Robert McKinley.
Margaret died June 15, 1826 age 66.
McKinnie, Daniel
1786 - Daniel's will was probated in Mecklenburg Co.
Children: Daniel
McKnight, Catherine(2)
Catherine died Nov 4, 1805 at age 88.
McKnight, James(3)
1762 owned land on the creek where Armour Road crosses.
Children: Robert (Margaret Brownfield ?)
Died Oct 23, 1764 at age 60.
McKnight/McRight, James & Ann
1785 - deed from James & Elizabeth Barr for 293 acres on
Rocky River beginning on the Barony line on the north
side of Lewis Branch, Test: Joseph Graham, George Ross,
bk 12, pg 574-B.
1785 - deed from James & Elizabeth Barr to James
McKnight of Rowan Co., NC for 53 acres on the south side

of Rocky River, Test: George Ross, Joseph Graham, bk 12, pg 559.
1790 - 111 00 - twp 1
1800 - Mecklenburg County
Son of Robert & Margaret McKnight.
McKnight, Robert(3)
Robert died Oct 19, 1778 at age 60.
McKnight, Robert & Margaret
1778 - deed to James McKnight for 1 dollar for 350 acres on the creek where Armour Road crosses, previously owned by Thomas Sprott, then James McKnight, deceased, Test: William Motherall, John Brownfield, Thomas Burnet, bk 10, pg 42.
1790 - 128 00 - twp 1
1800 - Mecklenburg County
Wife - Margaret (Brownfield ?)
Children: James, Robert, Jane, Margaret, Agness, Susannah, Catherine (Joseph Nicholson), Mary (James Craig), Anna (William Kerr)
Son of James McKnight.
McKnighton, Thomas
1776 - Thomas' will was probated in Mecklenburg Co.
Children: John, Thomas, William
McLarty (see McClarty)
McLile, Hugh
1779 - named as an adjoining land owner to James & Margaret Potts, William Potts, Archibald Crocket, Zeph John, John Potts on the north side of Six Mile Creek near Stillhouse Branch, bk 12, pg 272.
McLiley, John
1771 - deed to John McKnitt Alexander for 200 acres on the eastern branches of Mallard Creek joining Moses Alexander, Test: Alexander Wallace, John Farr, bk 11, pg 192.
1776 - deed to David Wilson for 50 acres on both sides of the Tinker Branch (of Coddle Creek ?), Test: Archibald Houston, James Humphrey, bk 10, pg 35.
MacLoveny, Samuel
1780 - named as adjoining land owner to George & Elizabeth McWhirter, and Dennis Titus on Waxhaw Creek, bk 10, pg 447.
McMahan, James & Susanna
1777 - witnessed a deed, with Joseph Jack, J. McDowell, from George & Margaret Cathey to Hugh Lucas, bk 10, pg 242.
McMahan, James
1790 - 134 00 - twp 11
1800 - Cabarrus County
McMahan, John
1776 - mentioned in a deed, no book or page number given.
McMason, David

Mentioned in the will of Samuel Knox.
McMicken, David
    1777 - named as an adjoining land owner to John &
    Catherine Bigger, John Turner of Craven Co., SC, Adam
    Calhoon, bk 11, pg 141.
    1777 - Loose estate papers
McMullin, William
    1782 - named as an adjoining land owner to James Love on
    Rockey River, bk 12, pg 33.
McMurray, Edward
    1775 - Loose estate papers
McMuray, Francis
    1790 - 102 00 - twp 13
McMurray, James
    1790 - 145 01 - twp 14
    1800 - Cabarrus County
McMurray, Robert
    1774 - Mentioned in the estate papers of Nicholson Ross.
    1775 - Signer of the petition to pardon the Cabarrus
    Black Boys.
    1782 - grant for 116 acres on both sides of John
    Cromwell's Spring branch, a branch of Reedy Creek,
    joining Alexander Lewis, bk 12, pg 14.
    1790 - 101 03 - twp 13
McMurray, Robert
    1800 - Cabarrus County
McMurray, Sarah
    1782 - Sarah's will was probated in Mecklenburg Co.
    naming James W. McCracken.
McMurray, William
    1780 - Meekels' Creek
    1781 - witnessed a deed from Andrew McCorkle to John
    Wilson on Pickens Creek, a branch of Twelve Mile Creek,
    bk 12, pg 274.
McNabb, Duncan
    1790 - 113 00 - twp 3
    Duncan was a loyalist who lost property.
McNair, Gilbert & Margaret
    1779 - deed to George Duckworth for 150 acres, being the
    same tract granted to Alexander Lewis in 1753, Test:
    Simon and Abel Hankines Duckworth, bk 11, pg 153.
    1779 - deed to Francis Nixon for 150 acres on one of the
    head branches of Rockey River bounded by Zebulon Brevard
    and Robert Potts, Test: Joseph Wilson, William Idglie,
    bk 12, pg 490.
    1783 - named as an adjoining land owner to Joseph
    Wilson, Adam Terrence on Dowel's Creek near the wagon
    road that goes from Adam Terrence to Charlotte, bk 12,
    pg 166.
McNair, James
    1790 - 122 00 - twp 7
McNeal, Archibald

1779 - named as an adjoining land owner to Alexander
McClellan, James Flanigan, Samuel Linton, bk 10, pg 502
or 503.
McNeal, Martha
   1775 - Loose estate papers
   1779 - named as an adjoining land owner to John Barnet,
   Francis Ross on Sugar Creek, bk 10, pg 526.
McNeely, Andrew & Rachel
   1790 - 101 00 - twp 1
   1800 - Mecklenburg County
   Wife: Rachel Hunter, daughter of John & Mary Hunter
   Andrew died in 1828 at the age of 71.
McNeely, Grissel Robinson(2)
   Grissel died June 6, 1793 at the age of 30.
McNeely, James
   1790 - 143 00 - twp 1
McNeely, John
   1790 - 200 01 - twp 16
McQuirk, John
   1793 - Account ledger of John Melchor's store.
McQuistion, Joseph
   1790 - 104 00 - twp 16
McQuown, Alexander
   1777 - deed from Thomas & Elizabeth McQuown for 132
   acres on both sides of Coddle Creek joining James Neel,
   Test: Robert Cochran, Henry Fleming, bk 10, pg 234.
   Son of Thomas and Elizabeth McQuown.
McQuonn, Hugh
   1779 - grant for 120 acres on Reedy Creek joining Thomas
   Neel and David Parke, bk 10, pg 540.
   1780 - named as an adjoining land owner to David Parks,
   Thomas Neely on Reedy Creek, bk 12, pg 89.
McQuown, Thomas & Elizabeth
   1752 - grant on Coddle Creek referenced, no bk or page
   number, bk 10, pg 234.
   1777 - deed from Thomas & Elizabeth to their son,
   Alexander, for 132 acres on both sides of Coddle Creek,
   adjoining James Neel, Test: Robert Cochran, Henry
   Fleming, bk 10, pg 234.
   1784 - named as an adjoining land owner to George
   Fleming, Mitchell Fleming, David Templeton, David
   Houston, Henry Henry on the east side of Coddle Creek,
   bk 12, pg 344.
   Children: Alexander
McReasner, William
   1782 - named as an adjoining land owner to James Kile,
   and Col. Martin Phifer on English Buffalo Creek, bk 12,
   pg 36.
McCree/McRee, Hugh
   1780 - named as an adjoining land owner to James & David
   Reese, Martin McCree on Coddle Creek, bk 12, pg 194.
McCree/McRee, Martin

1780 - named as an adjoining land owner to James & David Reese, Hugh McCree on Coddle Creek, bk 12, pg 194.

McRee, Andrew & Martha Eliott(2)
Married in Mecklenburg County May 28, 1791, John B. Elliot, bondsman.
1790 - 102 06 - twp 1
1800 - Mecklenburg County
Andrew died Jan 13, 1801 at the age of 45.
Sons: William, Richard, James

McRea/McCree, Arthur
1779 - witnessed a deed, with James Humphreys, from John McAliley to Richard Martin on Muddy Branch and Stony Run of Coddle Creek, bk 12, pg 439.
1783 - witnessed a deed, with Joseph Graham, Archibald Trotter, from William Penny to Martin Phifer (near Muddy Branch of Coddle Creek), bk 12, pg 320.
1790 - 103 00 - twp 9
1800 - Cabarrus County

McRee, David
David died before 1800.

McRee, David, Sr.
1779 - guardian bond between Daid McCree and Ezekiel Polk whereas Ezekiel Polk is appointed guardian of Samuel Polk and Samuel Wilson, providing for them out of the estate of Samuel Wilson, bk 10, pg 455.
David died before 1805

McRee, Dinah(2)
Dinah died March 28, 1798 at age 81.

McRee/McCree, Hugh
1778 - witnessed a deed, with Martin Phifer, Archibald White, from Caleb & Barbara Phifer to Andrew Carothers, bk 10, pg 462.

McRea/McRee, James
1790 - 132 08 - twp 2

McRee, Jean(2)
Jean died Sept 14, 1793 at age 26.

McRee, John & Ruth Alexander(2)
1767 - Militia, Mecklenburgh Regiment (Ensign)
1790 - 125 00 - twp 1
1795 - John died Oct 11, 1795 at age 54.
1795 - Loose estate papers
Wife - Ruth Alexander, dau of Zebulon & Jane Alexander.
Children: James, William Elliott, John, Hannah, Mary, Sarah Alexander, Ruth.

McRee, Robert
1775 - Robert's will was probated in Mecklenburg Co.
Children: Alexander, William

McCree/McRee, Robert
1784 - deed to Samuel McCleary for 5 ½ acres beginning on the Indian line near Big Sugar Creek, Test: Elisha Smith, Ezekiel Polk, bk 12, pg 435.

1785 - named as an adjoining land owner to Samuel &
Deborah McCleary, Hugh Harris, Moses Bigham on Big Sugar
Creek, bk 12, pg 447.
1790 - 336 01 - twp 2
1800 - Mecklenburg County
1802 - Loose estate papers
McRee, William(2)
1785 - deed to John Brevard, John Dickey and William
Sharp for 435 acres in Rowan Co., NC, being a tract
conveyed to McCree by Andrew & Margaret Allison in 1760,
Test: Ad Osborn, Jacob Brown, bk 12, pg 574.
1789 - William died Oct 30, 1789 at age 75.
McRee, William, Jr.
1790 - 101 01 - twp 4
McSparren, James
1790 - 101 00 - twp 19
1800 - Mecklenburg County
McVey, John
1795 - Loose estate papers
McWhorter, Aaron & Fannie
1778 - deed to John Smith for 160 acres on the west side
of Twelve Mile Creek, Test: John Wilson, Peter Roland,
William Smith, bk 10, pg 16.
1779 - deed from James & Peggy McClure for 153 acres on
the Middle Fork of Twelve Mile Creek, Test: Andrew
Neely, Hugh Barnet, bk 12, pg 329.
1790 - 214 00 - twp 16
Children: Moses, Henry Marlin McWhorter, Fanny, Kezia,
Elizabeth (Aaron Thompson)
Aaron's will was probated in Mecklenburg Co. in July
1799.
McWhorter, George
1806 - Loose estate papers
McWhorter, George & Elizabeth
1779 - named as an adjoining land owner to Alexander
Cairns, James Waugh on Waxhaw Creek, bk 10, pg 524.
1780 - deed to Dennis Titus of Camden Dist., SC, for 517
acres on Warshaw Creek, Test: Alexander Cairns, Henry
Foster, bk 10, pg 447 & bk 11, pg 307.
1783 - deed to John Ramsey for 150 acres on Waxhaw
Creek, Test: John Henderson, John McCain, bk 12, pg 247.
1784 - witnessed a deed, with Rob Donaldson, from
William & Sarah Love to Emanuel Stephens on Crooked
Creek, bk 12, pg 285.
1790 - 302 00 - twp 18
1800 - Mecklenburg County
McWhorter, George M.
1786 - witnessed a deed, with Thomas Allison, from John
& Mary Sconnel to Rachel Sconnel, bk 12, pg 606.
McWhorter, Henry

Residents of Mecklenburg County, North Carolina   233
1762-1790

1779 - witnessed a deed, with Esther Ramsey, from James
Ramsey to Thomas Harris on the south side of Four Mile
Creek, bk 10, pg 450.
1779 - deed from James & Rachell Ramsey for 169 acres on
the south side of Four Mile Creek joining Thomas Harris,
Test: Thomas Harris, Esther Ramsey, bk 10, pg 552.
McWhorter, James
1780 - named as an adjoining land owner to George &
Elizabeth McWhorter, and James Waugh on Waxhaw Creek, bk
11, pg 307.
1790 - 112 00 - twp 17
McWhorter, John
1790 - 101 00 - twp 18
1800 - Mecklenburg County
McWhorter, Moses & Agnes Jones
1778 - Signer of 1778 Petition.
1790 - 125 00 - twp 18
1800 - Mecklenburg County
Son of Aaron & Fannie McWhorter.
McWhorter, William & Elizabeth
1779 - deed to John Means for 17 acres between English
Buffelow Creek and Coddle Creek, Test: James Russel,
Walter Karr, bk 12, pg 238.
1779 - deed from Rev. Robert Archibald for a tract
conveyed to Arthur Dobbs, then John Fleming, then
William, bk 11, pg 37.
1780 - named as an adjoining land owner to John Means,
Phifer, James White, Walter Farr, James Baker on Wolf
Meador Branch of Coddle Creek, bk 12, pg 77.
McWilliams, Lewis
1796 - Loose estate papers
Meade, David
1783 - deed from Samuel Linton adjoining Charles Harris,
deceased, George Alexander, Samuel Linton, Test: Aaron
Alexander, Adam Meek, bk 12, pg 377.
Meanor, John
1793 - Account ledger of John Melchor's store.
Meanor, William
1793 - Account ledger of John Melchor's store.
Means, James
1782 - named as an adjoining land owner to Robert
Leviston and William Young on Coddle Creek, bk 12, pg
72.
1783 - grant for 230 acres on Coddle Creek beginning on
Black's branch to the banks of Wolf Meadow Branch then
to the mouth, adjoining Lodwick Wallace, John Means,
William Means, bk 12, pg 117.
1792 - Loose estate papers
Means, John
1778 - Signer of 1778 Petition.

1779 - deed from William & Elizabeth McWhorter for 17 acres between Coddle Creek and English Buffalow Creek, Test: James Russel, Walter Karr, bk 12, pg 238.
1780 - grant for 400 acres on Wolf Meadow Branch of Coddle Creek joining James White, Phifer, Walter Farr, James Baker and William McWhirter, bk 12, pg 77.
1782 - grant for 89 acres on Coddle Creek joining Walter Farris and William Means, bk 12, pg 75.
1783 - named as an adjoining land owner to James Means, Lodwick Wallace, William Means on Coddle Creek at Black's branch to the banks of Wolf Meadow branch, then to the mouth, bk 12, pg 117.

Means, William & Sarah
1778 - Signer of 1778 Petition.
1780 - deed to Moses Meek for 173 acres on the head branches of Rocky River in the Welch tract, Test: William Scott, James Meek, bk 11, pg 72.
1790 - 135 01 - twp 19

Means, William
1774 - deed from Robert & Elizabeth Campbell for 61 acres on Coddle Creek and Rocky River, Test: William McWhorter, John Means, Thomas Barns, bk 12, pg 237.
1782 - named as an adjoining land owner to John Means and Walter Farris on Coddle Creek, bk 12, pg 75.
1783 - grant for 337 acres on Coddle Creek adjoining John Means and David Purviance, bk 12, pg 141.
1783 - named as an adjoining land owner to Peter Burns, Hugh Caruthers on Coddle Creek at Wolf Meadow Branch, bk 12, pg 151.
1783 - deed from Thomas & Mary Harris for 428 acres joining James Way, Test: Adam Meek, William Caule, bk 12, pg 255.

Meek, Adam, Sr. & Elizabeth Miller
1774 - witnessed a deed, with James Hunter, from Nathaniel & Sarah Johnston to Peter Steel on Mallard Creek, bk 10, pg 113.
1774 - deed from David & Marry Garrison for 70 acres on Mallard Creek joining Moses Alexander, Test: John and David Garrison, Jr., bk 10 pg 194.
1782 - grant for 50 acres on Mallard Creek joining David Garrison, James Gardner, bk 12, pg 5.
1783 - witnessed a deed, with Aaron Alexander, from Samuel Linton to David Meade, bk 12, pg 377.
1783 - witnessed a deed, with William Caule, from Thomas & Mary Harris to William Means, bk 12, pg 255.
1790 - 202 03 - twp 5

Meek, James, Esq. & Mary
1777 - deed to David Daugherty for 115 acres on Rockey River joining or near Robert Harris, Test: James Roberson, William McClure, bk 10, pg 219.

1780 - witnessed a deed, with William Scott, from
William & Sarah Means to Moses Meek on the head branches
of Rockey River, bk 11, pg 72.
1790 - 103 00 - twp 7
1800 - Mecklemburg County
Son of Adam & Elizabeth Miller Meek.
Meek, James, Jur.
1790 - 112 00 - twp 7
Meek, Lewis
1787 - Magistrate of Mecklenburg County
According to pension papers of James Sloan, Lewis
performed James Sloan's marriage ceremony in the spring
of 1787.
Meek, Moses, Jr. & Margaret
1778 - Signer of 1778 Petition.
1780 - deed from William & Sarah Means for 173 acres on
the head branches of Rockey River in the Welch Tract,
Test: William Scott, James Meek, bk 11, pg 72.
1780 - deed to William Pickens for 173 acres on the head
branches of Rockey River in the Welch tract, Test: John
Neil, bk 11, pg 119.
1783 - deed from Nathaniel Alexander for 110 acres on
Stony Creek, adjoining Joseph Mitchel, Test: William
Lock, Richard Smith, bk 12, pg 305.
1790 - 125 00 - twp 5
1793 - Loose estate papers
Meek, Phillip
1779 - named as an adjoining land owner to John Deasmond
on McMichle's Creek, bk 10, pg 495.
Meek, Reuben
1783 - deed from Nathaniel Alexander for 100 acres on
Rocky River adjoining Adam Meek and on both sides of the
wagon road, Test: William Black, Richard Smith, bk 12,
pg 307.
Meek, Robert
1790 - 111 00 - twp 5
Meek, Samuel
1803 - Loose estate papers
Meek, Thomas
1782 - grant for 173 acres on English Buffalow Creek
joining John Maudint and Martin Phifer, bk 12, pg 103.
Meeken, Samuel
1777 - Loose estate papers
Melchor, Christopher & Elizabeth
Wife - Elizabeth Miller, daughter of George Jacob Miller
Melcher, Henry
1797 - Account ledger of John Melchor's store.
Melcher, John & Elizabeth
1778 - Signer of 1778 Petition.
1790 - 316 00 - twp 12
1800 - Cabarrus County

Wife - Elizabeth Hurlacker, daughter of Christopher
Horlacher
Children: Christopher (Elizabeth Miller)
John was born Jan 1, 1750, died Aug 20, 1824, buried in
St John's Evangelical Lutheran Church Cemetery.
Elizabeth was born Nov 10, 1757, died Feb 3, 1830,
buried in St John's Evangelical Lutheran Church
Cemetery.
Meller/Miller, Buie/Brice
1790 - 134 00 - twp 18
Meloney, Edward
1779 - grant for 100 acres on Sugar Creek joining
William Houston, Hugh Barnet, David Crockett, bk 10, pg
487.
Menander, Adam
1774 - Mentioned in the estate papers of Nicholson Ross.
Mendenhall, Robert
Robert died Jan 20, 1779, age 80.
He's buried in Olney Presbyterian Church Cemetery,
Gaston County.
Mensinger, William
1796 - Account ledger of John Melchor's store.
Children: Christina
Menson, William
1790 - 103 00 - twp 20
Merchant, William & Jane
1780 - deed from William Hugans for 170 acres on
Meekel's Creek joining William McMurray and William
Brown, Test: William Kerr, William Brown, bk 11, pg 148.
1790 - 127 00 - twp 20
Children: William Smith Merchant, Archibald, Margaret,
Jane, Elizabeth, Ann, Linsey.
Meredith, Lewis
1784 - deed to Lewis, of Hertford Co., NC, from William
& Elizabeth Penny for 150 acres on both sides of Coddle
Creek, bounded by Samuel Templeton, John
Purner(Turner?), Test: Caleb Phifer, John Barkley, bk
12, pg 421.
Messer/Mercer, Nicholas
1767 - Loose estate papers
Methine/Metheny, Daniel
1782 - witnessed a deed, with Thomas Morrow, Rees
Shelby, from Susana Daniel to Robert Smith for 140 acres
on Muddy Creek, bk 12, pg 287.
1782 - witnessed a deed, with John Nelson, from William
Hayns to Susana Daniel on Muddy Creek, bk 11, pg 189.
Mewionunk, Anthony
1784 - grant for 200 acres on Dutch Buffalow Creek, bk
12, pg 160.
Michel, Joseph
1779 - named as an adjoining land owner to George Reed,
Benjamin Alexander, bk 10, pg 532.

1779 - named as an adjoining land owner to William
Shields, George Reed, Benjamin & Susannah Alexander,
Andrew Robison on Mallard Creek, bk 10, pg 501.
Miller, Abraham & Jannet
1774 - deed to Robert Bell for 155 acres on McCalpin's
Creek, first granted to Abraham in 1767, Test: James
Boyas, John Hanna, bk 10, pg 18.
1777 - deed to John Johnston for 100 acres on McAlpin's
Creek, Test: Thomas Neely, Alexander Johnston, bk 10, pg
231.
1778 - witnessed a deed, with Thomas Mann, from William
Holland to Andrew Stinson on McCalpin's Creek, bk 10, pg
378.
1779 - named as an adjoining land owner to Noble Ozburn
on McCalpin's Creek, bk 10, pg 488.
1782 - deed from John Black for 122 acres on Beard's
branch of McCalpin's Creek including the forks, Test:
William Query, Thomas Black, bk 11, pg 105.
1790 - 311 00 - twp 15
Children: William, Abraham, Elizabeth Reed, Jannet
McCraven, Catherine Smith (deceased before 1806)
Abraham's will was probated in 1806.
Miller, Adam
1779 - deed from John and Adam Miller to William Bean
for 96 acres on Campbell's Creek, and another tract of
75 acres on Clear Creek, Test: James Morrison, William
Caldwell, bk 11, pg 68.
Miller, Andrew
1776 - Andrew's will was probated in Mecklenburg Co.
Children: William, Andrew, Matthew
In a 1784 deed Andrew was named as the previous owner of
a tract on Clear Creek, bk 12, pg 357.
Miller, Brice/Britt/Brace
1774 - named as the previous owner of a tract on Sugar
Creek, bk 12, pg 544.
1774 - witnessed a deed, with James Tate, John McGoin,
from Archibald & Mary Crockett to John Willson on Six
Mile Creek, bk 10, pg 130.
1790 - 134 00 - twp 18
1795 - Loose estate papers
Miller, Charles, Jr.
1775 - witnessed a deed, with Nathan Barr, Thomas
Crawford, from Robert Crawford to Hugh White on Warsaw
Creek, bk 10, pg 33.
Miller, David & Martha
1776 - deed to David Park for 40 acres on Reedy Creek
joining David Park and Walter Kerr, Test: Alexander
McGinty, William Miller, John Miller, bk 11, pg 239.
1781 - named as the previous owner of a tract on Long
Creek, bk 12, pg 476.
Of Fincastle Co., VA; sold to David Park 1776.
Miller, Francis & Elizabeth

1779 - deed to William Simmonds for 120 acres on the
south branch of Caldwell's Creek joining James Morrison,
Test: Samuel Martin, James McGinty, bk 10, pg 351.
Miller, George & Lese
1784 Linches Creek. George of Camden, SC in 1784.
Miller, George & Lese
1784 - deed from George & Lese Miller of Camden
district, SC, to Tobias Ramsey for 200 acres on Linches
Creek, Test: John and James Belk, bk 12, pg 379.
Miller, George
1790 - 102 00 - twp 19
1800 - Cabarrus County
Miller, George Jacob
1790 - 123 00 - twp 12
1800 - Cabarrus County
George was born Oct 18, 1748 in Germany, died Aug 10,
1840, buried in St John's Evangelical Lutheran Church
Cemetery.
Miller, Jacob
1790 - 133 00 - twp 12
1800 - Cabarrus County
Miller, James
1782 - witnessed a deed, with William McKinley, and Adam
Calhoon, from Joseph & Elizabeth McKinley to John
Carruthers adjoining Daniel Williams, James McCall and
John Bigger, bk 11, pg 149.
Miller, John Adam
1776 - in Capt. Charles Polk's Light Horse Company.
1776 - witnessed a deed, with Alexander McGinty, and
William Miller, from David & Martha Miller to David Park
on Reedy Creek, bk 11, pg 239.
1779 - witnessed a deed, with William Pickens, from
Thomas Polk, attorney for David Oliphant, to John
McCracken for 66 acres on Clear Creek adjoining Col.
Adam Alexander, Moses Shelvie(Shelby), bk 12, pg 265.
1779 - deed from John and Adam Miller to William Bean
for 96 acres on Campbell's Creek, and another tract of
75 acres on Clear Creek, Test: James Morrison, William
Caldwell, bk 11, pg 68.
1779 - witnessed a deed, with John Finly, from Henry &
Mary Shute to Isaac Sellars for 165 acres on the north
side of Rockey River, originally granted to Ambrose
Harding, then to John Mitchel in 1768, then to Thomas
Shields, then to Henry Shute in 1778, bk 11, pg 226.
1782 - deed from Isaac & Rebekah Sellars for 165 acres
on Rocky River, Test: Robert Anderson, Anthony Ross, bk
11, pg 231.
1790 - 122 00 - twp 19
1800 - Mecklenburg County
Miller, John
1777 - named as an adjoining land owner to Joseph &
Sarah Hobbs, Thomas Givens, Charles Moses, John McDowel

on McDowel's Creek, Test: Lewis Jetton, Samuel Givens,
bk 10, pg 269.
1784 - Loose estate papers

Miller, Mathew
1784 - deed to William Ramsey for 131 acres on Clear
Creek, Test: Joseph Graham, Robert Steven, bk 12, pg
357.
1784 - deed to John Karr for three tracts containing 500
acres on the south side of the Meadow Branch on the
south side of Clear Creek, adjoining William Ramsey,
Moses Alexander, Test: Oliver Wiley, Adam Alexander, bk
12, pg 371.
1790 - 123 00 - twp 14
Son of Andrew Miller.
Revolutionary Soldier - died June 6, 1837, age 79
according to The Charlotte Journal dated July 3, 1837.

Miller, Patrick
1766 - listed in the militia company of Capt. Adam
Alexander of Clear Creek.
Mentioned in the estate papers of Nicholson Ross 1774.

Miller, Phillip & Eleanor
1779 - witnessed a deed, with Will Polk, from David
Oliphant, by Thomas Polk, attorney, to John Nelson on
Muddy Creek, bk 10, pgs 343 & 360.
1783 - deed from John Robb for 102 acres on Clear Creek
adjoining Benjamin Cochran, Test: Adam and Evan
Alexander, bk 12, pg 222.
1790 - 201 00 - twp 14
Children: John, James
Sons-in-law: John Nelson, Adam Ormond.
1797 - Phillip's will was probated in Mecklenburg
County.

Miller, Robert & Mary
1765 - Robert's will was probated in Mecklenburg Co.
1765 - Loose estate papers
Children: Nathaniel, John, Robert, Elizabeth (?
Meek), Mary (William Neely), James, Ann (Alexander
Lewis)

Miller, Samuel
1790 - 000 10 - twp 4

Miller, Sara
1784 - Loose estate papers

Miller, Widow
1790 - 106 00 - twp 14

Miller, Widow, Sr.
1790 - 001 01 - twp 14

Miller, Widow
1790 - 101 00 - twp 20

Miller, William
1776 - witnessed a deed, with Alexander McGinty, and
John Miller, from David & Martha Miller to David Park on
Reedy Creek, bk 11, pg 239.

1780 - grant for 45 acres on the head branches of McKee's Creek joining John McGinty and Daniel McKeeman, bk 12, pg 102.
1780 - named as an adjoining land owner to Daniel McKeeman, and Alexander and John McGinty on the head branches of McKee Creek, bk 12, pg 48.
1783 - Loose estate papers

Miller, William
1783 - named as an adjoining land owner to Robert McGinty, William Kenedy, Thomas Gribble on McCalpin's Creek, Test: William Miller, James Finney, bk 12, pg 491.
1790 - 214 00 - twp 10

Millican, William
1797 - Loose estate papers

Miney, Martin
1790 - 132 00 - twp 14

Minsinger, William
1790 - 113 00 - twp 11
1800 - Cabarrus County

Minster, Frederick & Dorothy
1790 - 223 00 - twp 10
1800 - Cabarrus County

Misenhimer, Abraham
1790 - 215 00 - twp 11
1792 - Account ledger of John Melchor's store.
1800 - Cabarrus County

Misenhimer, George
1790 - 123 00 - twp 12
1793 - Account ledger of John Melchor's store.
1800 - Cabarrus County

Misenheimer, Jacob & Elizabeth
1777 - deed from Peter & Eve Delph for 150 acres on the Lick Branch of Buffalow Creek, Test: John Nichler, Joseph Shenn, bk 10, pg 240.
1782 - deed to Abraham Plater for 150 acres on Bafilour(Buffalo) Creek, Test: Joseph Shinn, Margaret ?, bk 11, pg 146.
1783 - deed from Abraham & Susannah Pleeter for 200 acres on both sides of Umberford's Branch adjoining Jacob Croner, Joseph Shinn, Test: Joseph Shinn, M. Messenhimer, bk 12, pg 341.
1784 - named as an adjoining land owner to Kenhatt Overshine, Adam Moyar, Christian Overshine, bk 12, pg 143.
1784 - named as an adjoining land owner to Michael Cline and Martin Stought on a branch of Coldwater Creek, bk 12, pg 192.
Lick branch of Buffalow Creek, both sides of Umberford's Branch.
1790 - 134 00 - twp 10
1800 - Cabarrus County

Misenhimer, Jacob & Anna
  Wife - Anna Margaretha Reiter
  Children: John, George, Jacob, Peter, Abraham, Anna,
  Margaret, Katherine, Maria, Elizabeth, Barbara
  Margaretha was born circa 1728, died circa 1790
  Jacob was born 1718, died circa 1800
  Both are buried in St John's Evangelical Lutheran Church
  Cemetery.
Misenhimer, Jacob & Christena
  Wife - Christina Dry
  Children: Paul, Rufus W.(Catherine Agnes Beaver), John
  H. (Sophia E. Barringer)
Misenhimer, John
  1783 - grant for 200 acres on the south side of Dutch
  Buffalow Creek adjoining William Leopard, Jacob Richey,
  Jacob Hough, Michael Cline, John Charles, bk 12, pg 147.
  1784 - named as an adjoining land owner to Mathias
  Moyer, Cabel Blackwater on Adam's Creek, bk 12, pg 188.
  1790 - 115 00 - twp 11
  1800 - Cabarrus County
Misenhimer, Peter
  1790 - 126 00 - twp 12
  1800 - Cabarrus County
Mitchell, Alexander & Sarah
  1777 - deed to John Garrison for 50 acres on a branch of
  Sugar Creek joining James Reed, Test: Richard Robinson,
  A. McKee, bk 10, pg 23.
  1779 - named as an adjoining land owner to John
  Garrison, Hugh Rondles, and James Reed on a branch of
  Sugar Creek beginning by the mill dam on the west side
  of the creek, bk 11, pg 94.
  1782 - named as an adjoining land owner to David &
  Elizabeth Crocket, Joseph Galbreath, and James Reed, bk
  11, pg 91.
  1785 - deed to Robert Allison for 418 acres on both
  sides of a branch of Sugar Creek beginning on the barony
  line and bounded by John McKee, Test: George Graham,
  James Robison, bk 12, pg 462.
Mitchell, Elijah
  1779 - witnessed a deed, with Robert Robison, from John
  Garrison to Hugh Rondles on a branch of Sugar Creek
  beginning by the mill dam on the west side of the creek,
  bk 11, pg 94.
Mitchell, George
  1779 - Loose estate papers
Mitchell, Harry
  1740 - Harry's will was probated in Mecklenburg Co.
  Children: Robert, Nathan, Jane
Mitchell, Henry
  1785 - named as an adjoining land owner to Benjamin &
  Susana Alexander, John McCaughey, Even Shelby, Edmond
  Bordon, on Back Creek, bk 12, pg 487.

1790 - Loose estate papers
Mitchell, Jacob
    1790 - 101 00 - twp 10
    1800 - Cabarrus County
Mitchell/Michael, John & Elizabeth
    1768 - named as the previous land owner of a tract on Rocky River that he acquired from James Wylie in 1768, then sold to Thomas Shields in 1769, no bk or page number given.
    1768 - named as the previous land owner of a tract (Clark's Creek) bounded by Robert & Catherine Hope, Zacheus & Keziah Wilson, Jonathan Newman, Test: Robert Harris, Andrew Alexander, bk 12, pg 303.
    1769 - deed to Moses Andrews for 130 acres, part of a tract originally granted to Ambrose Harding in 1763, bk 10, pg 180. (Coddle Creek)
    1769 - deed to James Wallace for 184 acres beginning on the barony line corner to James Carruth, acquired by Mitchell under the hand of the sheriff in 1768, Test: Adam Alexander, Robert Harrison, bk 10, pg 128.
    1769 - deed to Jonathan Newman from John & Elizabeth Mitchell of Salisbury in Roan county, 29 acres on the south side of Clark's Creek, Test: Samuel Wilson, Patrick Carr, bk 10, pg 169.
    1769 - named as the previous land owner of a 214 acre tract on a branch of Coddle Creek joining John Findley, Zebulon Brevard, and Archibald & Jean Ramsey, bk 11, pg 85.
    1780 - John Mitchel's wagon road is mentioned in a deed from Robert & Hannah Craighead to Joseph Mitchel on Rockey River joining Adam Meek, bk 11, pg 197.
    1785 - Loose estate papers
Mitchell, John
    1790 - 101 00 - twp 4
    1804 - Loose estate papers
Mitchell/Michael, Joseph & Rachel
    1779 - deed to Samuel Beaty for 115 acres on Rockwide Creek, being a tract granted to Elizabeth Mitchell in 1767, Test: William Shields, bk 10, pg 449.
    1780 - deed from Robert & Hannah Craighead for 100 acres on Rockey River joining Adam Meek and John Mitchell's wagon road, Test: Mary Clark, J. Johnston, bk 11, pg 197.
    1783 Rockwide Creek, Rockey River, Stoney Creek, Mallard Creek
Mitchell, Joseph
    1780 - Joseph's will was probated in Mecklenburg Co., he mentions Alex Mitchell's children.
    1781 - Loose estate papers
Mitchell, Mathias, Sr.
    1782 - grant for 100 acres on Little Coldwater Creek, bounded by James Ross, Jacob Frank, bk 12, pg 144.

1783 - grant for 125 ½ acres on Coldwater Creek, bounded
by Paul Walten, Nicholas Walten, bk 12, pg 124.
1790 - 222 00 - twp 10
1800 - Cabarrus County
Mitchell, Mathias, Jr. & Isabella
1790 - 112 00 - twp 10
1800 - Cabarrus County
Wife - Isabella Franks, daughter of Jacob & Susannah
Roan Franks.
Mitchell, Robert
1783 - deed from John & Letice McFarlin for 100 acres,
bk 12, pg 362.
1790 - 303 02 - twp 4
1800 - Mecklenburg County
1805 - Loose estate papers
Mitchell, Thomas
1781 - witnessed a deed, with Robert Harris, and John
Davidson, from James Barr and Margaret Wallace,
executors of the estate of Joseph Wallace, to John
Levison for 200 acres on Rockey River joining James
Dysart, bk 11, pg 79.
Mitchell/Michel, William & Rebecca
1781 - witnessed a deed, with John Allison, from William
Hayns to Jacob Self, bk 11, pg 93.
1781 - deed from William Hayns for 144 acres on Muddy
Creek, and 28 acres on both sides of Muddy Creek, Test:
John Allison, Joseph Selfe, bk 11, pg 95.
1783 - named as an adjoining land owner to Susana
Daniel, Robert John, Thomas Mary on Muddy Creek, bk 12,
pg 287.
1790 - 102 00 - twp 14
Wife - Rebecca (Baker ?), dau of George Baker.
Mock, Thomas
1778 - Signer of 1778 Petition.
1790 - 223 00 - twp 10
1800 - Cabarrus County
Moffit, Charles
1782 - Charles' will was probated in Mecklenburg Co.
1784 - Loose estate papers
Children: John
Moffit, David
1778 - David's will was probated in Mecklenburg Co.
1778 - Loose estate papers
Children: David, Elizabeth
Moffit/Maffett, John
1775 - John's will was probated in Mecklenburg Co.
1775 - Loose estate papers
Children: William, John, Robert
Son of Charles Moffit.
Moffit, Martha
1785 - deed from James Wilson for 93 acres on the south
side of Coddle Creek at the Barony line, bounded by

Moses Andrews, Hezekiah Alexander, Stephen Alexander,
Test: Anthony Ross, Henry Short, bk 12, pg 558.
1790 - 303 02 - twp 8

Moffitt/Marfoot, Robert & Martha
1778 - Robert's will was probated in Mecklenburg Co.
1778 - Loose estate papers

Moffit/Maffett, William
1790 - 101 00 - twp 6
1800 - William's will was probated in Mecklenburg
County.
Son of John Moffit, brother of John & Robert Moffett.

Molincun, John
Mentioned in the estate papers of Nicholson Ross 1774.

Montgomery, David
1790 - 133 00 - twp 5

Montgomery, George
1779 - witnessed a deed, with William Black, from John &
Ann Johnston on McCalpin's Creek known as Lofton's
bottom, bk 10, pg 390.
1790 - 141 00 - twp 19

Montgomery, Hugh
1774 - deed to John Richey from Hugh Montgomery of Rowan
county for 111 acres joining John Campbell, Test: James
Williams, bk 10, pg 120.

Montgomery, James & Ann
1790 - 143 00 - twp 1
1792 - Loose estate papers for James
1793 - Loose estate papers for Ann

Montgomery, John
1777 - John's will was probated in Mecklenburg Co.
1779 - Loose estate papers
Children: John, Joseph

Montgomery, John
1776 - 1st Sergeant in Capt. Charles Polk's Light Horse
Company.
1790 - 101 00 - twp 4
Children: Samuel, James, John, Robert, Elizabeth (?
Johnston), Isabella, Ruth.
1795 - John's will was probated in Mecklenburg County.
Son of John Montgomery.
1795 - Loose estate papers

Montgomery, John
1790 - 133 00 - twp 15

Montgomery, Joseph
1773 - witnessed a deed, with Robert Barnet, from
Alexander McKee to William Berryhill for 150 acres on
Sugar Creek joining Robert Walker and Thomas Pattin, bk
11, pg 129.
Son of John Montgomery who died 1777.

Montgomery, Robert
1790 - 135 00 - twp 4
Son of John Montgomery who died 1795.

Pension denied June 7, 1832 - did not serve 6 months.
Montgomery, Samuel
    1778 - witnessed a deed, with John Wylie, from John & Jane McCall to James Dickson on Clear Creek, bk 11, pg 56.
    1780 - deed from Adam Alexander for 145 acres on Clear Creek, Test: Margaret McCurdy, Alexander Finney, bk 11, pg 70.
    sold tract of land for Rocky Spring meeting house & burial ground.
    Son of John Montgomery.
Montieth, Alexander, Sr.
    1777 - Loose estate papers
Montieth, Henry
    1790 - 202 00 - twp
Montieth, Jane
    1790 - 304 02 - twp 6
    1800 - Mecklenburg County
Montieth, Nathaniel
    1790 - 100 00 - twp 6
    Nathaniel died before 1805.
Montieth, Samuel
    1790 - 114 00 - twp
    1800 - Mecklenburg County
Moore, Alexander & Sarah(2)
    died April 19, 1797 at age 44. Sarah died Dec 29, 1822 age 68.
Moore, David
    1778 - David's will was probated in Mecklenburg Co.
    Children: Joseph, Hugh
Moore, David, Senr. & Agnes
    1790 - 446 01 - twp 19
    Children: Agnes, Hanna (? Brown), Margaret (? Brown, who had sons William & David), Elizabeth (? Stanfield), Joseph, Jacob, Andrew, David, James
    1793 - David's will was probated in Mecklenburg Co.
Moore, Hugh
    1794 - Loose estate papers
Moore, James
    1765 - granted 204 acres on McDowell Creek from John McDowell, no book or page number given.
    1780 - witnessed a deed, with Archer Baldyoung, from John McKnitt Alexander to John Huggins on Garr Creek, bk 12, pg 424.
    1785 - power of attorney given to John McKnitt Alexander to sell 204 acres on McDowell Creek, bk 12, pg 563.
    Living in Hampshire Co., VA in 1785.
    1790 - 136 00 - twp 6
Moore, James
    James died before 1814. Lots 46 & 47 in Charlotte,
    1772 - deed from Thomas Polk for 600 acres on the head waters of the south branch of Steel Creek near John

Henry and joining Samuel Knox, Samuel Davis, Test: John
Barnet, James Fowler, bk 10, pg 137.
1774 - named as an adjoining land owner to William
Starret, Nathaniel Cook, Thomas Polk, James McCord,
Andrew Sprott, bk 10, pg 379.
1780 - deed from Patrick McDonald for lots 46 & 47 in
Charlotte, Test: Joseph Moore, James Orr, bk 10, pg 437.

Moore, John
1782 - deed for lots 15 & 17 in Charlotte, Test: Edward
Hunter, Henry Searing, bk 11, pg 214.
1782 - deed to Adlai Osborn for lots 17 & 18 in
Charlotte, Test: Edward Hunter, Henry Searing, bk 11, pg
200.
1782 - deed to Duncan Ochiltree for lots 145 & 153 in
Charlotte, Test: Edward Hunter, Henry Searing, bk 11, pg
202.
1782 - deed from Duncan Ochiltree, Samuel Martin, Adlai
Osburn and William Polk for 150 acres on Sugar Creek,
and 85 acres on Sugar Creek joining Thomas Polk, Test:
Edward Hunter, Henry Searing, bk 11, pg 204.
1782 - deed to William Polk for 150 acres and 85 acres
on Sugar Creek joining Mary McKee, Test: Edward Hunter,
Henry Searing, bk 11, pg 207.

Moore, John Jackson & Mary
1768 - named as the previous owner of a tract on the
branches of McDowell's Creek joining John Jetton and
conveyed to Joseph & Sarah Hobbs in 1772, bk 10, pg 24.
1773 - deed to John Criswell for 165 and 3/4 acres
joining Joseph & Sarah Hobbs, Test: Robert Waddle,
William Graham, Abel Duckworth, bk 10, pg 90.

Moore, Joseph
1802 - Loose estate papers

Moore, Joseph, Ser. & Mary
1776 - witnessed a deed, with Thomas Allison, William
Todd, James McCafferty, from James & Martha Todd to John
Todd on the head branches of Sugar Creek, bk 10, pg 21.
1778 - witnessed a deed, with Charles Purveance, from
William and James McCafferty, executors of Jeremiah
McCafferty, to Richard Mason for lot 11 in Charlotte, bk
10, pg 77.
1780 - witnessed a deed, with James Orr, from Patrick
McDonald to James Moore for lot 46 & 47 in Charlotte, bk
10, pg 437.
1790 - 315 00 - twp 1
1798 - Joseph's will was probated in April in
Mecklenburg Co.
1798 - Loose estate papers
Children: Minty, Joseph, James, Lucinda, Narcissa,
Ephraim, John, Mary (? Tanner), Margaret (?
Nelson), George, Jane (? Hill), Sarah (? Dickson),
Esther (? Dickson)

Moore, Joseph

1769 - Joseph's will was probated in Mecklenburg Co.
Children: Josiah, Mary
Moore, Moses
   1767 - Militia, Mecklenburgh Regiment (Captain)
   1785 - Moses' will was probated in Mecklenburg Co.
   1785 - Loose estate papers
   Children: James, William, Abigail
Moore, Phillip
   1790 - 214 00 - twp 19
   1800 - Mecklenburg County
   1808 - Loose estate papers
Moore, Rebecca
   1786 - named as an adjoining land owner to John & Catherine Nutt, Thomas Lackey, Alexander Carnes, William Davis, Robert Crockett on Waxhaw Creek, bk 12, pg 609.
Moore, William
   1775 - witnessed a deed, with George Cathey, Robert Cain, from James Black to George Cathey, bk 10, pg 51.
   1778 - named as an adjoining land owner to George Cathey, James Knox, and John McDowel on the south fork of McDowel's Creek, bk 11, pg 211.
   1780 - grant for 93 acres on Cane Creek joining John Barnet, bk 12, pg 26.
   1783 - deed from George Cathey for 50 acres on a branch of McDowell's Creek, Test: David Cance, Benjamin Knox, bk 11, pg 276.
Moore, William
   1766 - listed in the militia company of Capt. Adam Alexander of Clear Creek.
Moose, Andrew
   1779 - witnessed a deed, with John Jackson, David Moore, Joseph Robb, from William & Mary Watson to James Dickson on Clear Creek, bk 11, pg 191.
   1790 - 123 00 - twp 15
Moose, David, Jur.
   1766 - listed in the militia company of Capt. Adam Alexander of Clear Creek.
   1779 - witnessed a deed, with John Jackson, Andrew Moore, Joseph Robb, from William & Mary Watson to James Dickson on Clear Creek, bk 11, pg 191.
   1790 - 114 00 - twp 15
Moose, Hugh
   1790 - 244 00 - twp 15
Moose, Jacob & Barbara
   Wife - Barbara Barnhart
   Children: Isaac (Elizabeth   ?), Jacob W. (Rebecca E. Cress), Levi
Moose, James
   1790 - 136 00 - twp 6
Moose, Joseph
   1790 - 235 02 - twp 6
Moose, Widow

1790 - 203 03 - twp 6
Morgan, Enoch(5)
   1790 - 121 00 - twp 13
   1800 - Cabarrus County
Morgan, Reese
   1776 - Reese's will was probated in Mecklenburg Co.
   1777 - Loose estate papers
   Children: William, Ramsey
Morgan, Robert
   1790 - 101 00 - twp 13
Morris, Griffin
   1790 - 145 00 - twp 13
   1800 - Cabarrus County
Morris, John
   1779 - witnessed a deed, with James Boys, and William
   Kerr, from Francis Johnston and Agnes Henderson to
   Prudence Hays, wife of William Hays, for 32 acres, and
   another 65 acres on McCalpin's Creek, bk 11, pg 64.
Morris, William & Elizabeth(2)
   1773 - deed to Richard Stillwell for No. 2 tract on the
   north side of White Oak Branch, Test: Joseph Harris,
   John Rabinett/Robinett, bk 10, pg 115.
   1790 -
   Children: John, Philemon, William, Zebulon, James,
   Catherine Stillwell, Elizabeth Young, Mary
   William died April 20, 1804 at the age 69.
   Elizabeth died May 22, 1821 age 71.
Morrison, Alexander
   1790 - 202 01 - twp 19
   Children: Louise
   Son of Annabelle Morrison
Morrison, Andrew & Margaret
   1782 - deed to John Davidson for 170 acres on Rockey
   River on Johnston's River, Test: James & Isaac Davison,
   bk 12, pg 368.
Morrison, Elias Denison & Jennie Kimmons
   Children: Jane (Dr. William Russell), Margaret (Andrew
   Russell), Dorothy, Cynthia (John Pickard), John Cooper,
   David Bradshaw, Robert Kimmons, James Wesly, Elias
   Kirkpatrick, Thomas Brown, Joel Porter
   Elias died March 30, 1852 in Beaver Dam Creek, TN.
   Jennie died June 30, 1893. (The Morrison Family)
   Son of John and Jane Bradshaw Morrison
Morrison, James, Capt. & Jennet Hall(7)
   1766 - listed in the militia company of Capt. Adam
   Alexander of Clear Creek.
   1775 - James was a signer of the petition to pardon the
   Cabarrus Black Boys.
   1779 - witnessed a deed, with William Caldwell, from
   John and Adam Miller to William Bean on Campbell's Creek
   and Clear Creek, bk 11, pg 68.

1779 - named as an adjoining land owner to Francis &
Elizabeth Miller, William Simmonds on the south branch
of Caldwell's Creek, bk 10, pg 351.
1779 - named as as adjoining land owner to John Lemonds,
John Luckey on Caldwell's Creek, bk 11, pg 36.
1783 - named as an adjoining land ower to John
Setsinger, John Weyle, Alexander Ferguson, George
Corzine, John Shaver on Coldwater and Buffalo Creek, bk
12, pg 150.
1783 - named as an adjoining land owner to Joshua
Hadley, and Walter Smiley on Buffalo Creek, bk 12, pg 94
1786 - named as an adjoining land owner to Alexander
Ferguson, John Wilie, George Corzine, Robert Smith on
Coldwater and Buffalo Creek, bk 12, pg 616.
1790 - 322 02 - twp 13
1800 - Cabarrus County
James died Oct 30, 1804 and is buried in Rocky River
Presbyterian Church Cemetery.
Jennet died Feb 4, 1810, is buried in Rocky River
Presbyterian Church Cemetery.
1805 - Loose estate papers
Brother of Robert and John.

Morrison, James M. & Margaret Johnson(5)
James was born in 1777, died Sept 16, 1824 at the age of
47. Margaret died Sept 6, 1844 at the age of 67.
Son of James & Jennett Hall Morrison.

Morrison, James & Margaret Pharr(5), Mary Johnston
Wife - Margaret Pharr, Mary Johnston
Children: John (born & died 1790), Malinda Sarah (Robert
Brice Cochran), Mary (Robert Russell), Samuel F. (Rachel
Gingles), Penelope (Alexander W. Harris), Jenny (Joshua
Teeter), James Cunningham, Dorcas (Eli John McGinnis,
John Gingles), Margaret Clementine (Jeremiah G. Stegall)
Son of John & Mary Morrison.
James was born 1768, died Sept 4, 1846.
Margaret died Nov 24, 1817 at the age of 47.

Morrison, John & Mary
1775 - signer of the petition to pardon the Cabarrus
Black Boys.
1778 - John's will was probated in Mecklenburg Co.
Children: James (Margaret Pharr, Mary Johnston), John
Margaret Pickens), Elias (Mary Stewart), Robert, female
(William Driskell), Sarah (? Ross), Jane (Samuel
Huie), Elizabeth, Mary
John died from Rev. War wounds in 1777.
Mary died before 1781.
1777 - Loose estate papers for John
1781 - Loose estate papers for Mary
Brother of James and Robert.

Morrison, John & Jane Bradshaw, Dolly Rogers
Children: Cynthia (Joel B. Alexander), Silas H., Elias
Denison (Jennie Kimmons), Levi Rogers

Son of Robert C. and Sarah Morrison
Morrison, John & Mary McCurdy
    Wife - Mary McCurdy, daughter of Archibald & Maggie Sellers McCurdy.
    Children: James (Frances Brown), Archibald, Washington (Mary Ann Dinkins, Sara Rosanna Patton), Margaret Sellers (James H. Burns), John Milton (Harriet Amelia Newell), William Newton (Sarah Varick Cozzens), Mary (Charles Harrison Gingles), Jane Janette (George Cook Marvin), Cynthia Caroline (Samuel McKee), Robert Harvey (Mary Ann Stuart)
    Son of James & Jennett Hall Morrison.
    John was born Jan 2, 1768, died March 13, 1846.
Morrison, Neal & Annabelle ?
    1775 - Neil was one of the signers of the Mecklenburg Declaration of Independence on May 20, 1775.
    1777 - witnessed a deed, with John Province, from Arthur & Hannah Starr to John Johnston on McCalpin's Creek, bk 10, pg 248.
    1779 - grant for 27 acres on McCalpin's Creek joining Nelson's line, James Johnston, bk 10, pg 520.
    1780 - grant for 105 acres on McCalpin's Creek joining Samuel Flanakin, bk 12, pg 99.
    1781 - Neil's will was probated in Mecklenburg Co.
    1784 - Loose estate papers
    Children: William, Alexander, James
    Neal is buried in Providence Presbyterian Church Cemetery.
Morrison, Robert C. & Sarah(5)
    1766 - listed in the militia company of Capt. Adam Alexander of Clear Creek.
    1784 - deed from James & Elizabeth Maxwell for 170 acres on Rocky River, Test: James Stafford, James Finney, bk 12, pg 364.
    Children: William (Abigail McEwen), Elizabeth (William Andrew), Jean (Daniel Caldwell), John (Jane Bradshaw, Dolly Rogers), James (Sarah Carithers), Phobe (Robert Caldwell), Sarah (James Watson Bradshaw), Robert (Susannah Walker), Thomas (never married), Mary, Martha (Samuel R. Garrison)
    1790 - 415 00 - twp 13
    Robert died April 1, 1810.
    Brother of James and John.
Morrison, Robert Hall & Mary Graham
    Children: Isabella Sophia (Gen. D.H. Hill), William Wilberforce (never married), Harriet Abigail (James P. Irwin), Mary Anna (Thomas Jonathan Jackson - Stonewall Jackson), Eugenia Erixene (Gen. Rufus Barringer), Sarah M., Elizabath Lee D., Susan Washington (Alphonso C. Avery), Laura Panthea (John E. Brown), Joseph Graham (Jane E. Davis), Robert Hall (Lucy A. Reid), Alfred James (Portia L. Atkinson)

Son of William & Abigail McEwen Morrison.
Morrison, Robert & Margaret McCombs, Mary Wiley
   Wife - Margaret McCombs, daughter of James McCombs.
   Children: Jennie (Matthew Waugh), James Edward
   (Catherine D. Russell, Nancy Gilmer), John Pinckney
   (Mary Elizabeth Underwood, Martha Ann Kimmons), Harvey
   (Martha Underwood), William Newton (Mary Jane McClaun),
   Wiley, Cynthia (Washington Orr), Mary (Henry Gilmer),
   Elizabeth (John Gilmer), Oliver W.
   Son of James & Jennette Hall Morrison.
   Robert and Mary moved to Lafayette Co., MS
Morrison, Samuel & Sarah Johnston(5), Mary McKee Stafford
   Wife - Sarah Johnston, Mary McKee Stafford
   Children: Tirza (Samuel Harvey Gingles), Cyrus (Mary
   Moore), James Elijah (Mary Letitia Krider, Julia L.
   Coulter St. John)), William Johnston (Mary A. Newell),
   Harvey (Margaret Cochran, Martha Pharr), Sarah (Walter
   Franklin Pharr), Samuel Newton, Pinkney (Elizabeth
   Clementine Russell), Elizabeth Catherine (Alexander
   McKinley), George Leroy (Margaret Pharr), Elam (Mary
   Emily Moreland), John Dwight (Cynthia Elizabeth Wilson),
   Quincy Columbus (Susan Elizabeth Grey)
   Son of James & Jennette Hall Morrison.
   Sarah died Dec 14, 1810 at the age of 26.
Morrison, Thomas(5)
   Never married
   Son of Robert & Sarah Morrison
   Thomas died July 17, 1815 at the age of 31 and is buried
   in Spears Cemetery.
Morrison, William & Abigail McEwen(5)
   1790 - 213 01 - twp 13
   1800 - Cabarrus County
   Children: Sarah (Andrew Walker), James McEwen (Eliza
   Morrison), Margaret (John Kimmons), Hugh Hall, Jean
   Erixene, Erixene (Cyrus A. Alexander, M.D.), Robert Hall
   (Mary Graham), unnamed infant
   William died Nov 10, 1821.
   Abigail died Oct 6, 1825.
   Son of Robert and Sarah Morrison.
Morrison, William, Dr.
   1778 - Signer of 1778 Petition.
   1806 - Loose estate papers
Morrow, James
   1782 - named as an adjoining land owner to Robert
   Turner, William Taylor, William Spears, and John
   Cromwell on Calwell's Creek, bk 12, pg 78.
Morrow, John & Jennet
   1778 - deed from Andrew & Anne Downs for land joining
   Zebulon Brevard, Test: John Maxwell, Bartholomew
   Johnson, bk 10, pg 39.
   1790 - 222 00 - twp 7

Children: Robert, John, Richard (who had a son named John), George.
John's will was probated in 1795.
Morrow, John, Jur.
    1790 - 122 00 - twp 7
Morrow, Robert & Martha
    1790 - 123 00 - twp 7
    1800 - Loose estate papers
    Brother of John Morrow.
    Robert's will was probated in 1800.
Morrow, Thomas
    1783 - witnessed a deed, with Rees Shelby, Daniel Metheny, from Susana Daniel to Robert John on Muddy Creek, bk 12, pg 287.
    1785 - near Clear Creek
Morton/Moarton, John
    1783 - witnessed a bill of sale, with Robert Scott, David Templeton, from Eleanor Barkley to William Penny, bk 12, pg 243.
    1784 - witnessed a deed, with Samuel Moarton, from William Penny to James Ross on the west side of Buffalo Creek, bk 12, pg 339.
Morton, Peter
    1776 - Loose estate papers
Morton, Robert
    1777 - deed from Martin & Catherine Phipher for 300 acres on Coddle Creek joining Archibald Templeton, John Forhock, Test: Caleb Phipher, Archibald Houston, Jason Frizell, bk 10, pg 69.
    1778 - Signer of 1778 Petition.
    1778 - Robert's will was probated in Mecklenburg Co.
    Children: Samuel
Morton, Samuel
    1775 - deed to John Farr for 118 acres on the ridge between Coddle Creek and Alton's Run joining John Frohock, Test: Ephraim Farr, William Gardner, bk 10, pg 173.
    1784 - witnessed a deed, with John Moarton, from William Penny to James Ross on the west side of Buffalo Creek, bk 12, pg 339.
    ridge between Coddle Creek and Alton's Run.
    Son of Robert Morton.
Moses, Charles
    1777 - namded as an adjoining land owner to Joseph & Sarah Hobbs, Thomas Givens, John McDowel, John Miller on McDowell's Creek, bk 10, pg 269.
Moses, Moyer
    1788 - Loose estate papers
Moses, Samuel
    1774 - mentioned as the previous land owner of a tract containing 100 acres on Jean Armour's Creek, which he sold to Samuel & Rachel McCrume, bk 10, pg 133.

Motherall, Adam
   1777 - witnessed a deed, with Robert Motherall, from
   Joseph & Esthesth Kenedy to John McCullough on Six Mile
   Creek, bk 10, pg 423.
Motherall, Robert
   1777 - 1777 - witnessed a deed, with Adam Motherall,
   from Joseph & Esthesth Kenedy to John McCullough on Six
   Mile Creek, bk 10, pg 423.
Motherall, William
   1778 - witnessed a deed, with John Brownfield, Thomas
   Burnett, from Robert & Margaret McKnight to James
   McKnight near Armour's Creek, bk 10, pg 42.
Mottle/Mettle, John
   1793 - Account ledger of John Melchor's store.
Mottle, Thomas
   1793 - Account ledger of John Melchor's store.
Moyar, Adam & Cathey
   1777 - deed to Mathias Boston for 200 acres on Little
   Coldwater Creek that Adam acquired in 1768, Test: Joseph
   Shinn, Jason Frizell, bk 10, pg 421.
   1784 - named as an adjoining land owner to Kenhatt
   Overshine, Jacob Misenhimer, Christian Over shine on the
   head of Adam's Creek, bk 12, pg 143.
   1784 - grant for 300 acres on Dutch Buffalow Creek
   adjoining Mathias Moyar, Rhinehalt Overshine, bk 12, pg
   180.
   1790 - 201 00 - twp 11
Moyer, Elias
   1790 - 124 00 - twp 10
Moyer/Meyer, George Eldan
   1793 - Account ledger of John Melchor's store.
Moyer/Meyer, Herman
   1794 - Account ledger of John Melchor's store.
Moyer, Mathias
   1783 - named as an adjoining land owner to Nicholas
   Redenhour, John Charles on Meeting House Branch, bk 12,
   pg 169.
   1784 - named as an adjoining land owner to Adam Moyar,
   Rhinehalt Overshine on Dutch Buffalow Creek, bk 12, pg
   180.
   1784 - grant for 250 on Adam's Creek joining Cabel
   Blackwater, John Misenhimer, bk 12, pg 188.
   1790 - 102 00 - twp 12
   1800 - Cabarrus County
Moyer/Mayer, Merrimon
   1793 - Account ledger of John Melchor's store.
Mullen, Harris
   1790 - 113 00 - twp 6
Mulligan, Jack
   1778 - witnessed a deed, with Walter Davis and Robert
   Mulligan, from James & Sunah Brown to Charles and Samuel
   Calhoon for 400 acres on the Catawba River opposite the

mouth of Crowder's Creek, and joining John Bigger, bk 11, pg 166.

Mulligan, Robert
    1778 - 1778 - witnessed a deed, with Walter Davis and Jack Mulligan, from James & Sunah Brown to Charles and Samuel Calhoon for 400 acres on the Catawba River opposite the mouth of Crowder's Creek, and joining John Bigger, bk 11, pg 166.

Mulls, John
    1790 - 112 00 - twp 14

Mulwee, John
    1790 - 226 00 - twp 20

Murph, Jacob
    1790 - 123 00 - twp 10
    1800 - Cabarrus County

Murphy, James
    1778 - Signer of 1778 Petition.

Murphey, John
    1778 - Signer of 1778 Petition.
    1790 - 215 00 - twp 9

Murphey, John
    1790 - 211 00 - twp 14
    1793 - Account ledger of John Melchor's store.

Murphy, Zephaniah
    1778 - Signer of 1778 Petition.

Murtland, Robert & Eleanor
    1793 - Robert's will was probated in Mecklenburg Co.

Myears, Mathias
    1778 - Signer of 1778 Petition.

Myear, Michael
    1778 - Signer of 1778 Petition.

Myars, Hermon
    1790 - 111 00 - 18

Myer, Jacob
    1774 - deed from Robert & Frances Harris for 135 acres on Duck Buffalo Creek, Test: Jacob Richey, William Harris, bk 10, pg 149.
    1778 - Signer of 1778 Petition
    1779 - deed to Boltes Neas for 185 acres on Dutch Buffaloe Creek, being a tract granted to Robert Harris, then conveyed to Robert Harris, Jr. in 1762, Test: John Blewer, bk 10, pg 409.

Myer/Meyer, William
    1784 - witnessed a deed, with John McCannon, Green Rives, from John Curry to John Foster for 150 acres on the east side of Waxhaw Creek, bk 12, pg 579.

Nail, John
    1790 - 124 00 - twp 15

Nail, Samuel
    1805 - Loose estate papers

Nash, Abner & Justina

1771 - deed to William Black for 95 acres on the middle fork of Beaver Pond Creek, Test: Clement Nash, bk 10, pg 166.
1771 - deed to John Carruthers for 105 acres, Test: Clement Nash, bk 10, pg 416.
1771 - deed to James Clark for 173 acres on Rockey River, Test: Clement Nash, bk 10, pg 387.
1771 - deed to William Black for 95 acres on middle fork of Beaver Pond Creek, Test: Clement Nash, bk 10, pg 166.
1772, 1777 Crooked Creek, tract known as the Welch Tract on Rockey River, Three Mile Branch of Rockey or Johnston River, Caldwell Creek.

Nash, Abner & Mary
1778 - deed from Abner & Mary of the town of Newbern, to David Oliphant of Charles Town for 17,000 acres on Rockey River, known by the name of the Great Tract (Welsh Tract), bk 10, pg 259.

Nash, Clement
1771 - witnessed a deed from Abner & Justina Nash to William Black for 95 acres on the middle fork of Beaver Pond Creek, bk 10, pg 166.
1771 - witnessed a deed from Abner Nash to James Clark on the head branch of Rockey River, bk 10, pg 387.

Nash, Joseph
1797 - Loose estate papers

Nation, John
1790 - 226 00 - twp 6

Nation, Thomas
1790 - 134 00 - twp 1

Neel, Andrew (see Andrew Null)
1779 - deed from John Smith for 160 acres on Twelve Mile Creek, Test: Thomas Harris, John Flenniken, bk 11, pg 52

Neal, Henry(2)
Henry died Feb 28, 1788 at age 52.
1788 - Loose estate papers

Neal, James(2)
1792 - Loose estate papers

Neal, James
1777 - named as an adjoining land owner to Thomas & Elizabeth McQuown, and Alexander McQuown on Coddle Creek, bk 10, pg 234.
1778 - witnessed a deed, with Thomas Benson, from James & Mary Harris to James Benson in the Welsh Tract, bk 10, pg 289.
James died July 5, 1800 at age 67.

Neil, John (see John Null)
1780 - witnessed a deed from Moses, Jr. & Margaret Meek to William Pickens on the head branch of Rockey River in the Welsh tract, bk 11, pg 119.
1781 - deed from John McKnitt Alexander for 96 acres on the head branches of Reedy branch of Long Creek,

adjoining Mathew McClure, Test: Jane Alexander, and
William Bean Alexander, bk 11, pg 78.
1784 - named as an adjoining land owner to James Wiley,
William Johnston, John Wiley, Thomas McCawl, James
McCaul, and John Parks, on Neel's branch and Reedy
Creek, bk 12, pg 619.

Neal, Thomas
1779 - named as an adjoining land owner to Hugh McQuonn
on Reedy Creek, bk 10, pg 540.

Neal, Thomas
1767 - Militia, Mecklenburgh Regiment (Captain)
1767 - witnessed a deed, with John McCulloch, James
Davis, from James & Jennet Armour to James Alcorn on the
south branch of Beaver Dam Creek of the Catawba River,
bk 4, pg 271-272.

Neil, Thomas
1766 - Thomas' will was probated in Mecklenburg Co.
1769 - Loose estate papers
Children: Joseph, Sarah

Neas/Kneese, Boltes/Paulser
1779 - deed from Jacob Myer for 185 acres on Dutch
Buffaloe Creek, Test: John Blewer, bk 10, pg 409.

Ness, Paulser & Franney
1786 - deed to Paul Furrow for 90 acres on both sides of
Dutch Buffalow Creek, Test: Samuel Black, Johanas
Jegler, bk 12, pg 580.
1786 - deed to John Hagler for 5 acres on the north side
of Rockey River, Test: Samuel Black, Paul Foun, bk 12,
pg 582.

Neely, Andrew
1779 - witnessed a deed, with Hugh Barnet, from James &
Peggy McClure to Aron McWherter on the middle fork of
Twelve Mile Creek, bk 12, pg 329.

Neely, Ann
1798 - Loose estate papers

Neely, Hugh
1778 - deed from Andrew & Margaret Robinson for 98 acres
on Mallard Creek, joining Samuel Hogshead, bk 10, pg 1.
1781 - deed from James & Elizabeth Alexander for 190
acres and another tract for 92 acres on Mallard Creek,
Test: Adlai Alexander, bk 11, pg 113.
1783 - witnessed a deed, with John McNitt Alexander,
from Robert Robison, Sr. to John Robison on Mallard
Creek, bk 11, pg 234.
1790 - 233 00 - twp 4
1800 - Mecklenburg County

Neely, John(2) & Isabella
Children: Thomas (Jean)
1790 - 237 06 - twp 2
John died May 10, 1806 at age 56.
1806 - Loose estate papers

Neely, Moses & Ann Campbell(2)

1790 - 214 03 - twp 2
1800 - Mecklenburg County
Moses died April 12, 1837.
Son of Thomas Neely.
Neely, Samuel
1790 - 202 02 - twp 2
Wife - daughter of Andrew & Sarah Carruthers.
Cataba River near Bigger's Ferry.
Son of William and Mary Miller Neely. Mentioned in the will of Samuel Knox.
Neely, Thomas & Ann(2)
Thomas died Feb 7, 1819 at age 58.
Neely, Thomas
1794 - Loose estate papers
Neely, Thomas
   1779 - named as an adjoining land owner to Thomas Weir, and Nathan Orr on the head branches of Reedy Creek, bk 10, pg 490.
   1779 - grant for 44 acres on the head branches of Reedy Creek, joining William Beaty, bk 10, pg 494 or 495.
   1780 - named as an adjoining land owner to David Parks, and Hugh McQuown on Reedy Creek, bk 12, pg 89.
   1781 - named as an adjoining land owner to Francis & Margaret Johnston, Alexander Johnston, Mathew Knox, John Whitfield, and Hugh Herron, bk 12, pg 228.
   1790 - 000 10 - twp 4
   1793 - Thomas' will was probated in Mecklenburg Co.
Children: John, Samuel, Thomas, Moses
Neely, Thomas, Jur. & Sarah(2)
   1790 - 142 02 - twp 2
Thomas died Nov 15, 1795 at age 38.
Sarah died Oct 23, 1789 age 35.
1796 - Loose estate papers
Neely, William & Mary Miller
1778 - Signer of 1778 Petition.
Nelson, John &   ?   Miller
   1773 - deed for lot 26 in Charlotte, bk 11, pg 179.
   1779 - deed from Thomas Polk, attorney for David Oliphant, for 37 acres on the north side of Muddy Creek joining Hardin Warner, Test: Will Polk, and Phillip Miller, bk 10, pg 343.
   1779 - deed from Thomas Polk, attorney for David Oliphant, for 99 acres on both sides of Muddy Creek, Test: William Potts, and Phillip Miller, bk 10, pg 360.
   1782 - witnessed a deed, with Daniel Methine, from William Hayns to Susana Daniel on Muddy Creek, bk 11, pg 189.
   1785 - witnessed a deed, with William Polk, and Daniel Brown, from Joseph Graham, sheriff, in a judgement against William McCafferty, for 91½ acres on Tryon Creek to Samuel Martin, bk 12, pg 567.
   1790 - 112 00 - twp 14

Wife - daughter of Phillip & Eleanor Miller.
Nelson, Richard
   Mentioned in the estate papers of Nicholson Ross 1774.
Netterhever, Paul
   1790 - 000 10 - twp 11
Neusman, Revd/Revell
   1790 - 124 00 - twp 12
Newill, David
   1790 - 103 00 - twp 13
Newill/Nowel, Francis
   1766 - listed in the militia company of Capt. Adam
   Alexander of Clear Creek.
   1774 - witnessed a deed, with George Davis, from William
   Spears to Thomas Davis on Reedy Creek, bk 10, pg 396.
   1778 - Signer of 1778 Petition.
   1782 - grant for 308 acres on both sides of Anderson
   Creek joining Thomas McFadan, and Robert McEachin, bk
   12, pg 46.
   1790 - 114 00 - twp 13
   1800 - Cabarrus County
   Mentioned in the estate papers of Nicholson Ross 1774.
Newill/Nowol, John
   1766 - listed in the militia company of Capt. Adam
   Alexander of Clear Creek.
Newill/Nowel, William
   1766 - listed in the militia company of Capt. Adam
   Alexander of Clear Creek.
   1777 - witnessed a deed, with Thomas Fadon(McFadon), on
   Reedy Creek, bk 10, pb 401.
   1782 - named as an adjoining land owner to Thomas
   McFadon, and Francis Newell on Anderson Creek, bk 12, pg
   140.
   1790 - 303 00 - twp 13
   1800 - Cabarrus County
   Mentioned in the estate papers of Nicholson Ross 1774.
Newman, John
   1767 - named as the grantee of a tract on Sugar Creek on
   Jan 17, 1767, bk 10, pg 412.
   1773 - named as an adjoining land owner to John
   Nicholson , Joseph Irest, and John Carson on Sugar
   Creek, bk 10, pg 46.
   1790 - 133 00 - twp 5
Newman, Jonathan & Rebecca
   1769 - deed from John & Elizabeth Mitchell for 29 acres
   on the south side of Clark's Creek joining John Gilmore,
   Test: Samuel Wilson, and Patrick Carr, bk 10, pg 169.
   1778 - Signer of 1778 Petition.
   1779 - deed to Robert Hope for 380 acres on Rockey River
   and 29 acres on the south side of Clark's Creek joining
   John Gilmore, Test: John Alison, Seth Collins, bk 11, pg
   46.

1779 - named as an adjoining land owner to Robert & Catherine Hope, and Zaccheus & Kezia Wilson, bk 12, pg 303.
1780 - named as an adjoining land owner to James Gilmore, and Nathaniel Gilmore on Rockey River, bk 12, pg 90.
1780 - named as an adjoining land owner to Nathaniel Gilmore on the south side of Rockey River, bk 12, pg 69.

Newton, Ebenezer
1775 - witnessed a deed, with Robert Campbell, from James Johnson to William Gardner on Sugar Creek, bk 10, pg 191.
1778 - named as an adjoining land owner to John & Jean Weir, Andrew Trot, Alexander Herrel, William Wilson, and John McEwell on Abraham Alexander's Mill Creek, bk 10, pg 283.

Newton, Robert
1779 - deed from John Hodgins/Haggans to Robert Newton and James Osmond/Ormond for 180 acres on a fork of Twelve Mile Creek above Robert Ramsey, Test: William Haggans, bk 11, pg 106.
1790 - 125 00 - twp 16

Nichler, John
1777 - witnessed a deed, with Joseph Shenn, from Peter & Eve Delph to Jacob Missonheimer on the Lick branch of Buffalow Creek, bk 10, pg 240.
1778 - Signer of 1778 Petition.
1790 - 344 00 - twp 10
1800 - Cabarrus County

Nichol, Thomas & Rachel
1781 - witnessed a deed, with James Patton, from John Dysart of Burke Co., NC, heir of James Dysert, and Margaret Dysart, to Samuel Alexander on Rockey River in the Welsh tract, bk 11, pg 137.
1787 - Loose estate papers
1787 - Thomas' will was probated in Mecklenburg Co.

Nichols, William
1804 - Loose estate papers

Nicholas, Benjamin
1804 - Loose estate papers

Nicholson, George
1773 - deed for lots 129 & 137 in Charlotte, bk 10, pg 54.
1779 - deed for lots 129 & 137 in Charlotte, bk 11, pg 28.
1790 - 100 00 - twp 1

Nicholson, John, Jur.
1790 - 000 10 - twp 2

Nicholson, John, Senr
1773 - deed from Thomas Frohock, attorney for Henry E. McCulloh, for 99 acres on Sugar Creek joining Joseph

Irest, John Carson, and John Newman, Test: Daniel
Little, James Brandon, and Thomas Polk, bk 10, pg 46.
1777 - witnessed a deed, with John Foayd, from Thomas
Richey to Joseph Nicholson on Sugar Creek, bk 10, pg 9.
1777 - witnessed a deed, with John Foard, from Thomas
Richey to Joseph Nicholson on Haw Creek(Paw?), bk 10, pg
14.
1779 - witnessed a deed, with William Hayns, from John
Carroll to Joseph Carroll on Sugar Creek, bk 10, pg 324.
1784 - witnessed a deed, with Nathaniel Irwin, and
Thomas Henderson, from Joseph Nickelson of Wilks Co., GA
to Samuel McCombs for lot 6 in Charlotte, bk 12, pg 239.
1790 - 215 02 - twp 1

Nicholson, Joseph & Catherine McKnight
1773 - deed for lot 6 in Charlotte, bk 10, pg 53.
1777 - deed from Thomas Richey for 34 acres on Sugar
Creek joining Cubert Nicholson, Test: John Nicholson,
and John Foayd, bk 10, pg 9.
1777 - deed from Thomas Richey for a tract on Haw
Creek(Paw?), Test: John Nicholson, and John Foard, bk
10, pg 14.
1778 - witnessed a deed, with Hugh Pollock, Jr., for
several lots in Charlotte to Patrick McDonald, bk 10, pg
71.
1778 - deed for lots 345, 346, & 347 in Charlotte, bk
10, pg 64.
1780 - deed from William Elliott for 158 acres on Sugar
Creek, Test: James Jack, Samuel Elliott, bk 11, pg 73.
1783 - deed to William Hutchison for 158 acres on the
head waters of Sugar Creek joining Robert Elliott, and
William Elliott, Test: Samuel McCombs, James Tagert, and
Thomas Henderson, bk 11, pg 209.
1784 - deed from Joseph Nichelson of Wilks Co., GA to
Samuel McCombs for lot 6 in Charlotte, Test: John
Nickelson, Nathaniel Irwin, and Thomas Henderson, bk 12,
pg 239.
Wife - Catherine McKnight, daughter of Robert McKnight.

Nichleson, Colbert & Jennett(2)
1777 - named as an adjoining land owner to Thomas
Richey, Joseph Nicholson on Sugar Creek, bk 10, pg 9.
Colbert died Jan 2, 1789 at age 77.
Jennett died March 3, 1790 age 78.
1790 - Loose estate papers for Culbert

Nighten, John
1790 - 113 00 - twp 6

Nixon, Francis
1779 - deed from Gilbert McNarr for 150 acres on one of
the head branches of Rocky River joining Zebulon
Brevard, and Robert Potts, Test: Joseph Wilson, William
Idglie, bk 12, pg 490.
1787 - Francis' will was probated in Mecklenburg Co.
1788 - Loose estate papers

Residents of Mecklenburg County, North Carolina   261
1762-1790

Children: Joseph, John, Allen, Mary
Norris, James
   1770 - James' will was probated in Mecklenburg Co.
   1771 - Loose estate papers
   Children: James
Null, Andrew (see Andrew Neel/Neal)
   1790 - 102 00 - twp 19
Null, James
   1790 - 243 00 - twp 8
Null, James, Jur.
   1790 - 102 01 - twp 2
Null, James, Ser.
   1790 - 126 00 - twp 1
Null, Jesse
   1790 - 111 01 - twp 19
   1800 - Mecklenburg County
Null, John
   1790 - 111 00 - twp 8
Null, Widow
   1790 - 114 03 - twp 2
Nutt, John & Catherine
   1777 - witnessed a deed, with J. Miller, from Daniel
   Cairns to Archibald Cowsert of Craven Co., SC, on Waxaw
   Creek, bk 10, pg 207.
   1781 - witnessed a deed, with William McMurry, from
   Andrew McCorkle to John Wilson for 202 acres on Pickens
   Creek, a branch of Twelve Mile Creek, bk 12, pg 274.
   1786 - deed to Robert Orr and Thomas Lackey for 300
   acres on Waxhaw Creek, joining Alexander Carnes,
   Rebeckah Moor, William Davis, Robert Crockett, and James
   Lashley, Test: Archibald Cowait, Alexander Carns, and
   John Lithem, bk 12, pg 609.
Nutt, William
   1786 - named as the previous owner of a 300 acre
   plantation on Waxhaw Creek belonging to John & Catherine
   Nutt, bk 12, pg 609.
Nussman/Niesmann, Adolph & Elizabeth
   1783 - witnessed a deed, with John Kobb, from John
   Barringer to Matthias Barringer, his son, for 250 acres
   and another tract for 50 acres on both sides of Dutch
   Buffalo Creek joining George Barringer, bk 12, pg 332.
   (deed signed George Barringer)
   1784 - witnessed a deed, with Philip Littiger, from
   James, Jr. & Mary White to Paul Barringer on Dutch
   Buffalo Creek, bk 12, pg 395.
   1793 - Account ledger of John Melchor's store.
   Wife - Elizabeth Rentleman, Barbara Lyerly
   Children: Paul C. (Hannah Holtzman)
   Adolph was born Aug 1739, died Nov 3, 1794, buried in St
   John's Evangelical Lutheran Church Cemetery.
   1796 - Loose estate papers
Oats, Michael

1790 - 113 00 - twp 18
1800 - Mecklenburg County
Ocheltree, Dan
    1775 - witnessed a deed, with Thomas Polk, from Henry Eustace McCulloch, by Thomas Frohock, to Alexander McKee on both sides of Rockey River and the waters of McCalpin's Creek, bk 10, pg 272.
    1777 - witnessed a deed, with Joseph McKinley, and Samuel Chambers, from John & Catherine Biggar to William Tenant on the Catawba River opposite the mouth of Crowder Creek, bk 10, pg 97.
Ocheltree, Duncan
    1773 - witnessed a deed, with William Patterson, for lots 41, 43, and 48 in Charlotte to William Hutchison, bk 12, pg 468.
    1778 - witnessed a deed, with William Rexd, from Moses Steel to William and James McCafferty on Sugar Creek, bk 10, pg 20.
    1778 - witnessed a deed, with John Barton, from Thomas Polk to Rogert Graham for 145 acres on the dividing ridge between Sugar Creek and McMichael's Creek, beginning on the Spring Branch, bk 10, pg 31.
    1780 - witnessed a deed, with Thomas Spencer, from Zaccheus Wilson to Joseph Wilson on Sugar Creek, bk 11, pg 39.
    1780 - witnessed a deed, with Edward Elliott, from Robert Elliott to James Jack on Sugar Creek, bk 11, pg 59.
    1782 - witnessed a power of attorney from Aron Gillett to Samuel Martin and William Polk, bk 11, pg 187.
    1782 - one of the proprietors of Ochiltree, Martin and Company, bk 11, pg 214.
Odum, May
    1790 - 102 00 - twp 17
Oliphant, David
    1778 - deed from Abner Nash of the town of Newbern for a tract of land containing seventeen thousand acres on Rockey River known as the Great Tract originally granted to Arthur Dobbs as one of the abstracts of Murey Crimble and James Howey in eight patents on the 3rd of March 1745, bk 10, pg 259.
    1778 - of the town of Charlestown.
    1779 - deed to John McCracken for 66 acres on Clear Creek, bk 12, pg 265.
    1783 - mentioned in a deed as the previous owner of 53 acres on Goose Creek which he sold to Joseph Galbreath, bk 12, pg 206.
Oliphant, John
    1785 - Loose estate papers
Oliphant, John & Elizabeth Allison
    Wife - Elizabeth Allison, daughter of Archibald Allison.
    1790 - Iredell County ?

Oliver, Richard
   1778 - Signer of 1778 Petition.
Ormond, Adam &   ?   Miller
   1784 - witnessed a deed from John Ramsey to William
   Smith on Four Mile Creek, joining Thomas Hames, and
   James Way, bk 12, pg 385.
   1790 - 101 01 - twp 19
   1800 - Mecklenburg County
   Adam's wife was the daughter of Phillip and Eleanor
   Miller.
   1812 - Seventh Company detached from the First
   Mecklenburg Regiment.
Ormond/Orman, Jacob
   1778 - witnessed a deed, with Francis Bassett, from
   Michael Sigget(Ligget?) to David Ore, bk 10, pg 37.
   1779 - named as an adjoining land owner to Noble Ozburnm
   on McCalpin's Creek, bk 10, pg 527.
   1785 - deed to Robert Osburn for 200 acres on McCalpin's
   Creek, Test: Thomas Downs, John Osburn, bk 12, pg 512.
   1790 - 124 01 - twp 16
   1800 - Mecklenburg County
Ormond/Osmond, James
   James was born in 1669 and is buried in Providence
   Presbyterian Church Cemetery.
Ormond, James
   1769 - James' will was probated in Mecklenburg Co.
   Children: John, Adam, Benjamin, Jacob
Ormond, James
   1779 - deed from John Hodgins/Hagans to James Osmond and
   Robert Newton for 180 acres on Twelve Mile Creek above
   Robert Ramsey, Test: William Haggans, bk 11, pg 106.
   1790 - 122 00 - twp 16
   1800 - Mecklenburg County
Ormond, John & Ann
   1807 - Loose estate papers
Ormond, John
   1789 - Loose estate papers
Orr, Charles
   1787 - Loose estate papers
Orr, David
   1778 - deed from Michael Sigget(Ligget?) for 250 acres
   on Henley's Fork of Twelve Mile Creek joining Reeve's
   land, Test: Francis Bassett, Jacob Ormond, bk 10, pg 37.
   1790 - 144 00 - twp 16
   1800 - Mecklenburg County
Orr, Eleanor(2)
   1778 Eleanor died Jan 27, 1778 at the age of 55.
Orr, George
   1790 - 115 01 - twp 16
   1792 - George's will was probated in Mecklenburg Co.
   Children: George
Orr, James (jockey)

1781 - deed from James Harris for 294 acres on a branch
(near Mallard Creek), Test: Abraham Alexander, bk 11, pg
300.
1790 - 143 06 - twp 4 (near George Allen, Cairns
Henderson, Robert Robinson)
1800 - Mecklenburg County
A James Orr bought lot 25 in Charlotte from James Jack
in 1783, bk 11, pg 269.

Orr, James & Margaret (whistle)
1790 - 122 00 - twp 4 (near George Allen, Cairns
Henderson, Robert Robinson)
1800 - Mecklenburg County
A James Orr, Revolutionary Soldier, died April 2, 1843,
age 96 according to The Charlotte Journal dated April
13, 1843.

Orr, James (whistling)
1790 - 253 00 - twp 15

Orr, James (white)
1790 - 123 00 - twp 15
A James Orr died before 1813.
A James Orr owned lot 25 in Charlotte in 1783, bk 12, pg
572.

Orr, James
1776 - James' will was probated in Mecklenburg Co.
Children: James

Orr, John
1804 - Loose estate papers

Orr, Nathaniel, Jur.
1782 - grant for 299 acres on Sugar Creek and Mallard
Creek joining Ezekiel Alexander, bk 12, pg 9.
1790 - 131 00 - twp 4
1800 - Mecklenburg County

Orr, Nathan, Senr.
1779 - Reedy Creek
1790 - 316 00 - twp 4
1800 - Mecklenburg County
Nathan died before 1806.

Orr, Nathan
1777 - named as an adjoining land owner to Thomas Weir,
and Thomas Neiley on Reedy Creek, bk 10, pg 490.
1779 - Nathan's will was probated in Mecklenburg Co.
Children: James, Sample

Orr, Martin
1780 - witnessed a deed, with Richard Trotter, from John
& Catherine McCoy to Jacob Croner on Three Mile Creek,
bk 11, pg 66.

Orr, Robert
1786- Waxhaw Creek
1786 - deed from John & Catherine Nutt to Robert Orr and
Thomas Lackey for 300 acres on Waxhaw Creek joining
Alexander Carns, Rebeckah Moor, William Davis, Robert

Crockett, and James Lashley, Test: Archibald Cowait,
Alexander Carns, and John Lithem, bk 12, pg 609.
1790 - Robert's will was probated in Mecklenburg Co.
Children: Alexander, John

Orr, William Tassey
1801 - Loose estate papers

Orr, Wm
1769 - witnessed a deed, with Joseph Kennedy, from
Thomas Polk to John White of Rowan Co., for a tract
between the "wider" Armour and the Catawba Indians
District, bk 4, pg 542.
1778 - witnessed a deed, with Hezekiah Alexander, and
Adam Alexander, from William & Mary Alexander to Robert
Arthur on Sugar Creek, bk 10, pg 267.
1790 - 117 09 - twp 4
William died before 1800.

Osbourne/Osborn/Asburn, Alexander & Agnes
1752 - owner of a 235 acre tract on Rockey River which
was later conveyed to James Harris, deceased before
1780, bk 12, pg 200.
1753 - mentioned in a 1779 deed as the grantee of 600
acres from King George II on March 31, 1753 on both
sides of the south fork of Rocky River in Anson Co.
Alexander sold it to Joseph Tate in 1756.
1790 - 113 00 - twp 19 (may have been a son of the
Alexander in 1753)

Osborne, Adlai
1778 - Trustee of Liberty Hall.
1778 - deed from the Trustees of Liberty Hall for lots
222, 223, and 224 in Charlotte, bk 10, pg 212; lots 231,
234, 228, and 229, bk 10, pg 215; lots 451, 455, 466,
467, bk 10, pg 235; lots 472, 479, 490, 491, bk 10, pg
237.
1782 - deed from John Moor to lots 17 & 18 in Charlotte,
bk 11, pg 200.
1782 - one of the proprietors of Ochiltree, Martin and
Company, bk 11, pg 214.
1785 - witnessed a deed, with Jacob Brown, from William
McCree, of Mecklenburg Co., NC to John Brevard, John
Dickey, and William Sharp, of Rowan Co., NC, for 435
acres on Davidson and Back Creeks in Rowan Co., bk 12,
pg 574.
Children: Margaret (Robert Davidson)

Osburn, Christopher
1779 - deed from Thomas Polk, attorney for David
Oliphant, for 87 acres on Anderson's Creek, Test:
William Barker, E. Brevard, bk 10, pg 458.
1784 - named as an adjoining land owner to Michael
Garmon on Rockey River, bk 12, pg 157.
1788 - Christopher's will probated in Mecklenburg Co
Children: Jonathan, Christopher, Fereby (Charles Love)

Osborn, James

1779 - named as an adjoining land owner to William
Holland on the east side of Campbell's Creek, a branch
of McCalpin's Creek, bk 10, pg 539.
1784 - named as an adjoining land owner to John &
Prudence Smith, John King, John Johnston, and Thomas
Frohock on McCalpin's Creek, bk 12, pg 280.
1790 - 146 00 - twp 20
1800 - Mecklenburg County

Osborn, James, Capt.
1774 - deed from John Allain for 160 acres on Rockey
River and the Catawba River joining John Frohock, bk 10,
pg 111.
1790 - 146 00 - twp 20

Osborn, John
1790 - 104 00 - twp 7
1800 - Mecklenburg County
John died before 1802.

Osborn, John
1774 - witnessed a deed, with Thomas and John McCall,
from Francis McCall to William Houston on the Cedar Fork
of Twelve Mile Creek, bk 10, pg 226.
1777 - deed from James & Sarah Lynn/Linn for 144 acres,
Test: William Osburn, John Foster, bk 10, pg 214.
1790 - 222 00 - twp 20
1794 - Loose estate papers

Ozburn, Noble
1779 - named as an adjoining land owner to Abraham
Miller on McCalpin's Creek, bk 10, pg 488.
1779 - named as an adjoining land owner to Thomas
Ozburn, and Dr. Joseph & Elizabeth Kennedy on McCalpin's
Creek, bk 10, pg 511.
1779 - grant for 40 acres on the Mile Branch of
McCalpin's Creek joining Abraham Miller, bk 10, pg 488.
1779 - grant for 50 acres on McCalpin's Creek joining
Jacob Orman, bk 10, pg 527.

Osborn, Robert
1785 - deed from Jacob Orman for 200 acres on McCalpin's
Creek, Test: Thomas Downs, John Osburn, bk 12, pg 512.
1790 - 122 00 - twp 19
1800 - Mecklenburg County

Ozburn, Thomas
1779 - grant for 60 acres on McCalpin's Creek joining
Dr. Kenedy, and Noble Ozburn, bk 10, pg 511.

Osborne, Thomas
1779 - Loose estate papers

Osborn, William
1777 - witnessed a deed, with John Foster, from James &
Sarah Linn/Lynn for 144 acres, bk 10, pg 214.
1790 - 317 00 - twp 16
1800 - Mecklenburg County

Osborne, William
1769 - Loose estate papers

Residents of Mecklenburg County, North Carolina 1762-1790

Oudy/Udy/Perdy, Conrad
   1790 - 143 00 - twp 12
Ouery/Query, Barenhard
   1790 - 113 00 - twp 12
Ouery/Query/Ury, George
   1781 - deed from Nicholas and George Owery to Martin Owery for 164 acres on a branch of Dutch Buffalow Creek, Test: Joseph Shinn, bk 11, pg 97.
Ouery/Query/Ury, Godfryt
   1790 -
Owery/Query/Ury, Martin
   1781 - deed from Nicholas and George Owery to Martin Owery for 164 acres on a branch of Dutch Buffalow Creek, Test: Joseph Shinn, bk 11, pg 97.
Query, William
   1782 -
Ovenshine, Christian
   1783 - grant for 42 acres on Coldwater Creek joining John Lance, bk 12, pg 167.
   1784 - named as an adjoining land owner to Kenhatt Overshine, Adam Moyar, and Jacob Misenhimer on the head of Adam's Creek, bk 12, pg 143.
   Coldwater Creek.
   1790 - 101 00 - twp 11
Overshine, Kenhatt
   1784 - grant for 192 acres on Adam's Creek joining Adam Moyar, Christian Overshine, and Jacob Misenhimer, bk 12, pg 143.
Ovenshine, Mathias
   1775 - Loose estate papers
Ovenshine, Rinholt
   1784 - named as an adjoining land owner to Adam Moyar, and Mathias Moyar on Dutch Buffalow Creek, bk 12, pg 180.
   1790 - 112 00 - twp 11
   1800 - Mecklenburg County
Owens, James
   1779 - deed from William McKinley and Joseph Scott for 100 acres on Paw Creek, Test: James Reed, John Green, Jr., bk 10, pg 322.
   1790 - 145 00 - twp 1
   1800 - Mecklenburg County
Page, Nicholas
   Wife - Jane Troll, married 1793.
   1790 - 000 10 - twp 20
   1800 - Mecklenburg County
   Sister - Mida Page married Littleberry Smart in 1791.
   Nicholas died before 1808
Palmer, John, Sr.
   1793 - Account ledger of John Melchor's store.
Palmer, Marcus
   1793 - Account ledger of John Melchor's store.

Parker, Isaiah
    1790 - 146 00 - twp 6
    1800 - Mecklenburg County
    Isaiah died before 1806
Parker, Thomas & Eleanor
    1767 - Thomas' will was probated in Mecklenburg Co.
    1768 - Loose estate papers
Parks, David & Rebecca Carnes
    1776 - deed from David & Martha Miller of Fincastle Co., VA for 40 acres on Reedy Creek joining Walter Kerr, Test: Alexander McGinty, William Miller, and John Miller, bk 11, pg 239.
    1779 - named as an adjoining land owner to Hugh McQuonn, and Thomas Neel on Reedy Creek, bk 10, pg 540.
    1780 - grant for 174 acres on Reedy Creek joining Hugh McQuown, and Thomas Neely, bk 12, pg 89.
    1790 - 423 04 - twp 4
    1800 - Mecklenburg County
    David died before 1815.
Parks, Hugh & Margaret
    1754 - grant for a tract on Coddle Creek, no book or page number given.
    1778 - witnessed a deed, with John Park, and John Houston, from Samuel Templeton to William Penny on the east side of Coddle Creek, bk 11, pg 278.
    1781 - Hugh's will was probated in Rowan County.
    Children: John, Hugh, Jane (John McDowell)
Parks, Hugh(2)
    1786 - agreed to a bond by Rachel Sconnell to hold in trust for John & Mary Sconnell who granted Rachel 71 acres, bk 12, pg 606.
    1790 - 124 02 - twp 1
    1800 - Mecklenburg County
    Hugh died Jan 12, 1830 at age 76.
Parks, James
    1772 mentioned in the estate settlement of William Sample.
Park, John
    1778 - witnessed a deed, with with Hugh Park, Jr., and John Houston, from Samuel Templeton to William Penny on the east side of Coddle Creek, bk 11, pg 278.
Parks, John, Junr.
    1790 - 102 03 - twp 4
    1800 - Mecklenburg County
Parks, John, Senr. & Mary
    1790 - 334 03 - twp 4
    1800 - Mecklenburg County
    Children: Thomas, William?(Lucille), Joseph? (Sarah)
    John died Dec 9, 1809, age 70
    Mary died Mar 4, 1808, age 71, both buried in Blackstock Cemetery.
    1810 - Loose estate papers

Residents of Mecklenburg County, North Carolina 1762-1790

Parks, Moses & Mary
    1790 - 333 00 - twp 19
    1800 - Mecklenburg County
    Children: George, Thomas, John, Ollivy, Moses, James, Polly.
    Moses' will was probated in May 1828.
Parks, Robert
    1780 - Loose estate papers
Parks, Robert
    1783 - named as an adjoining land owner to William McCullough, and John Wilson on McCalpin's Creek, bk 11, pg 241.
Parks, Samuel
    1790 - 112 00 - twp 4
Parsons, John
    1762 - Loose estate papers
Pasinger, Thomas
    1790 - 122 01 - twp 9
Pass, George
    1767 - Militia, Mecklenburgh Regiment (Ensign)
Patrick, John
    1767 - Militia, Mecklenburgh Regiment (Ensign)
Patterson, Alexander
    1790 - 204 03 - twp 9
    1800 - Cabarrus County
    Son of John & Elizabeth Patterson, born 1756, died 1829, buried in Barberich Cemetery.
Patterson, Charles
    1775 - Charles' will was probated in Mecklenburg Co.
    1777 - Loose estate papers
    Children: John, James D., Sarah
Patterson, Charles
    1786 - Loose estate papers
Patterson, Hugh
    1783 - deed from Thomas Finley for 189 acres on Rockey River joining James Dysart, Test: Samuel Killough, James Stephenson, bk 12, pg 393.
    Wheelright.
Patterson, John & Elizabeth
    Children: Robert, Alexander
    1779 - witnessed a deed, with Edward Givens, Jr., from Robert & Sarah Beaker of Henry Co., VA to Edward Givens on Davison's Creek, bk 11, pg 44.
    1784 - grant for 630 acres on Longreen Branch of Coldwater Creek joining Joseph Rogers, Col. Caleb and Martin Phifer, John Headright, and Robert Patterson, bk 12, pg 181.
    Children: Alexander, Robert
    1786 - John's will was probated in Mecklenburg Co.
Patterson, John
    1774 - deed to William Patterson, Jr. and John Patterson for lots 195 & 198 in Charlotte, bk 10, pg 109.

1777 - witnessed a deed, with William Patterson, from
Alexander Martin to Samuel Martin on McCalpin's Creek,
bk 10, pg 263.
1777 - witnessed a deed, with Samuel Martin, for lots
105, 235, 236, 327, 328, 329, 330, 331, 332, and 333 to
Waitstill Avery, in Charlotte, bk10, pg 61.
1790 - 000 10 - twp 19
1806 - Loose estate papers
Patterson, Joseph & Rebekah
1769 - witnessed a deed, with Patrick Carr, from John &
Elizabeth Mitchell to Moses Andrews, bk 10, pg 180.
1778 - deed to Robert Harris for 312 acres on Rockey
River joining Samuel Pickens, and Thomas Shields, Test:
John Hamilton, Robert Allison, and Robert Hope, bk 11,
pg 287.
Patterson, Robert
1780 - Loose estate papers
Patterson, Robert
1783 - witnessed a deed, with Joseph Shinn, and James
Ross, from William & Elizabeth Ross to Christian
Barbrick on Coldwater Creek, bk 12, pg 360.
1784 - named as an adjoining land owner on Longreen
Branch of Coldwater Creek joining Joseph Rogers, Col.
Caleb and Martin Phifer, John Headright, and John
Patterson, bk 12, pg 181.
1790 - 101 01 - twp 9
1800 - Cabarrus County
Son of John & Elizabeth Patterson.
Patterson, William & Margaret(2)
1773 - witnessed a deed, with Dun Ochiltree, to William
Hutchison for lots 41, 43, and 48 in Charlotte, bk 12,
pg 468.
1774 - deed to William Patterson, Jr. and John Patterson
for lots 195 & 198 in Charlotte, bk 10, pg 109.
1777 - Commissioner of the town of Charlotte.
1777 - witnessed a deed, with John Patterson, from
Alexander Martin to Samuel Martin on McCalpin's Creek,
bk 10, pg 263.
1782 - witnessed a deed, with Alexander Roberson, from
Matthew Roberson to David Roberson on the branches of
Beaverdam Creek joining Thomas Greer, bk 11, pg 158.
1783 - witnessed a deed, with David Robison, from
Ambrose McKee to Alexander Robison on branches of Steel
Creek joining John & William Bigham, bk 11, pg 262.
1783 - witnessed a deed, with Andrew Cathey, from
Richard & David Robison to Ambrose McKee, bk 11, pg 301.
1790 - 222 00 - twp 2
William died Feb 28, 1818 at the age of 74.
Pattison, William
1790 - 213 05 - twp 3
1800 - Mecklenburg County
Patton, Benjamin

1775 - Benjamin was one of the signers of the
Mecklenburg Declaration of Independence on May 20, 1775.
1782 - named as an adjoining land owner to James
Russell, bk 12, pg 88.
1782 - grant for 82 acres on English Buffalow Creek
joining Col. Polk, bk 12, pg 70.
1783 - grant for 79 acres on Coldwater Creek joining
Jacob Phifer, and Harkles Conkrite, bk 12, pg 119.
1784 - witnessed a deed, with William Young, from John
Alexander, Sr. to James Smith on Coddle Creek, bk 12, pg
457.
1790 - 202 00 - twp 9
1800 - Cabarrus County
Member of Poplar Tent Prebyterian Church.
Patton, Charles
   1790 - 201 01 - twp 6
   1800 - Mecklenburg County
   Children: Margaret Blythe, Prudence, Sarah, Robert
   Charles died Aug 1811.
Patton, James
   1781 - witnessed a deed, with Thomas Nickel, from John &
   Margaret Dysert, of Burke Co., NC to Samuel Alexander on
   Rockey River in the Welsh tract, bk 11, pg 137.
Patton, Joseph
   1790 -
Patton, Michael
   1774 - named as an adjoining land owner to Eloner
   McDowell, deceased, on Buffalo Creek, Test: Alexander
   Martin, Griffith Rutherford, bk 10, pg 144.
Patton, Samuel & Ann
   1767 - Militia, Mecklenburgh Regiment (Ensign)
   1774 - deed to Martin Phifer for 200 acres at the head
   of Armstrong's Branch of Buffalo and Coldwater Creek
   joining John Phifer, Test: David and James Reese, bk 10,
   pg 139.
   1775 - witnessed a deed, with Thomas Mann, and John
   Pifer, from Joseph Rodgers and David Russell to Michael
   Shaver for 144 acres, being the land they convey by
   virtue of a will executed by Margaret White, deceased,
   on the 6th day of July 1773, who was appointed executrix
   of the estate of Moses White, her husband, as may appear
   of his will dated the 10th day of March 1766, bk 10, pg
   185.
   1783 - named as an adjoining land owner to Francis Lock,
   Matthew Lock, and Samuel Hughs, bk 12, pg 115.
   1783 - witnessed a deed, with Thomas Faulkner, from
   Robert & Hannah Craighead to Job Williams on both sides
   of Stoney Creek, beginning near the wagon road, bk 12,
   pg 224.
   1783 - named as an adjoining land owner to James &
   Elizabeth Hewit, and Joseph Shinn on Three Mile Branch,
   bk 12, pg 335.

1784 - grant for 30 acres on both sides of Camp Branch, a branch of Coddle Creek and on both sides of the wagon road, bk 12, pg 173.
1785 - named as an adjoining land owner to William & Frances Hays, Patrick & Rachel Russell Hays, Adam Ross, and John Wallace on Wolf Meadow Branch of Coddle Creek, bk 12, pg 464.
1790 - 203 00 - twp 9
1800 - Cabarrus County

Patton, Simon
1790 - 203 00 - twp 19

Patton, Thomas
1761 - Thomas' will was probated in Mecklenburg Co.
1762 - Loose estate papers
1773 - named as the original grantee of a tract on Sugar Creek, which was later conveyed to Alexander McKee, bk 11, pg 129.
Children: William

Paul, Jacob
1777 - south fork of Crooked Creek.

Paxton, James
1781 - James' will was probated in Mecklenburg Co.
Children: John

Paxton, James, Jr.
1803 - Loose estate papers

Paxton, Moses
1790 - 122 00 - twp 16

Payton, John
1781 - witnessed a deed, with Will Reed, from Samuel Bigham to Hugh Bigham on Sugar Creek, bk 11, pg 155.

Peck, Frederick & Elizabeth
Wife - Elizabeth Bushardt
Children: Catherine (Peter Troutman)

Peck, John & Elizabeth
Wife - Elizabeth Barringer, daughter of John Paul & Christiana Killiam Barringer. (Betsey was his 3rd wife)
Children: Henry, John, Michael, Moses, Peter

Peele, James, Jur.
1790 - 112 00 - twp 7

Peele, James, Ser.
1790 - 211 05 - twp 7

Peeler, Paul
1798 - Loose estate papers

Pegen, John
1779 - named as an adjoining land owner to James & Peggy McClure, and Aron McWherter on the Middle fork of Twelve Mile Creek, bk 12, pg 329.

Pelly, John
1785 - witnessed a deed, with Ezekiel Polk, from Samuel & Deborah McCleary to Moses Bigham on Big Sugar Creek, bk 12, pg 447.

Pence, Jacob

Residents of Mecklenburg County, North Carolina 273
1762-1790

1790 - 126 00 - twp 11
Pendergrass, Darby
1781 - Loose estate papers
Penny, Elizabeth
1776 - Loose estate papers
Penny, George
1790 - 133 00 - twp 12
Penny, Godfryt
1790 - 101 00 - twp 12
Penny, Robert
1783 -
Penney, John
1790 - 212 00 - twp 8
Penney, Robert
   1783 - deed from William Penney for 130 acres on the east side of Coddle Creek, and a another tract of 200 acres on both side of Mills Creek, and another tract of 67 acres on the east side of Coddle Creek, Test: John Houston, David Templeton, and Robert Scott, bk 12, pg 259.
   Son of William & Elizabeth Penney.
Penny, William & Elizabeth
   1778 - deed from Samuel Templeton for 67 acres on Coddle Creek, Test: John Houston, Hugh Park, Jr., and John Park, bk 11, pg 278.
   1780 - deed to William Ross for 327 acres on Coddle Creek, Test: Alexander McEwen, John Houston, and John Grimes, bk 11, pg 111.
   1783 - bill of sale from Eleanor Barkley for three negroes, viz, Moses, a negro boy, Lizzy, a wench, and Lucy, a wench, Test: John Morton, Robert Scott, and David Templeton, bk 12, pg 243.
   1783 - deed to Robert Penney, his son, for 130 acres on the east side of Coddle Creek, and a another tract of 200 acres on both side of Mills Creek, and another tract of 67 acres on the east side of Coddle Creek, Test: John Houston, David Templeton, and Robert Scott, bk 12, pg 259.
   1783 - deed to Martin Phifer for 200 acres beginning and running along Houston's line east, then northeast along Templeton's line, Test: Joseph Graham, Archibald Trotter, and Arthur McCree, bk 12, pg 320.
   1784 - deed to Lewis Meredith of Hertford Co., NC for 150 acres on both sides of Coddle Creek joining Samuel Templeton, and John Purner, Test: Caleb Phifer, and John Barkley, bk 12, pg 421.
   1784 - deed to Martain Phifer for 300 acres on Coddle Creek, Test: David Templeton, and John Thompson, bk 12, pg 311.
   1784 - deed to James Ross for 100 acres on the west side of Buffalow Creek, beginning at a branch then running

with Governor Dobbs' tract, Test: Samuel and John
Moarton, bk 12, pg 339.
1790 - 134 00 - twp 8
Children: Robert
Peoples, John
1790 - 121 00 - twp 6
Perry, Jacob
1790 - 301 00 - twp 11
Person, Henry & Jean Sample
1761 - Jean Sample Person, and John M.L. Alexander were
administrators of the estate of Joseph Sample. In 1761
they sold 200 acres of Joseph Sample's estate on
McCalpin's Creek to John Flenikin, bk 10, pg 392.
Peterson, Robert
1778 - Signer of 1778 Petition.
Petterson, Samuel
1778 - Signer of 1778 Petition.
Pettey, Richard
1778 - Signer of 1778 Petition.
Pettigrew, James, Capt.
1777 - deed to George Greer for lots 34 & 92 in
Charlotte, Test: Nathaniel From, Alexander Karrel, and
Jonathan Coates, bk 10, pg 275.
Phifer, Ann Elizabeth
1771 -
Phifer, Caleb, Col. & Barbara
1777 - named as an adjoining land owner to Blench Lock,
Griffith Rutherford, and James Kilpatrick on the ridge
between Buffelow and Coddle Creek, bk 12, pg 252.
1784 - named as an adjoining land owner to John
Patterson, Martin Phifer, John Headright, and Robert
Patterson on the Longreen Branch of Coldwater Creek, bk
12, pg 181.
1784 - witnessed a deed, with John Barkley, from Martin
Phifer, Sr. to Lewis Meredith of Hertford Co., NC, on
both sides of Mill Creek, bk 12, pg 422.
1790 - 116 019 - twp 9
Son of Martin Phifer.
Phifer, George & Elizabeth
1790 - 112 00 - twp 10
Wife - Elizabeth Frank, daughter of Jacob & Susannah
Roan Frank.
Phifer, Henry
1790 - 102 00 - twp 9
Phifer, Jacob
1782 - grant for 384 acres near a draft of Dutch
Buffalow Creek joining Paul Dupley, and Michael Clause,
bk 12, pg 93.
1783 - named as an adjoining land owner to Benjamin
Patton, and Harkles Conkrite on Coldwater Creek, bk 12,
pg 119.
1790 - 212 00 - twp 10

Residents of Mecklenburg County, North Carolina 1762-1790

1791 - Loose estate papers
Phifer, John & Catherine Barringer
   1771 head waters of Little Coldwater Creek.
   1775 - John's will was probated in Mecklenburg Co.
   Wife - Catherine Barringer, daughter of Paul Barringer.
   Children: Martin, Paul, Margaret, Ann Elizabath (Caleb Blackwelder)
   Paul Phifer was under the age of 21 in 1777.
Phifer, John
   1775 - signer of the Mecklenburg Declaration of Independence on May 20, 1775.
   Member of Poplar Tent Presbyterian Church.
   1778 - Loose estate papers
Phifer, Margaret
   1771 -
Phifer, Martin
   1767 - Militia, Mecklenburgh Regiment (Captain)
   1784 - named as an adjoining land owner to Absalom Baker, John Baker, and Samuel Sewell on Buffelow Creek, bk 12, pg 449.
   1789 - Martin's will was probated in Mecklenburg Co.
   1791 - Loose estate papers
   Children: Paul, Martin, Caleb
Phifer, Martin, Jr.
   1780 - deed from James & Jean Wallace for 62 acres on both sides of Coddle Creek, Test: David Wilson, Zaccheus Wilson, bk 11, pg 142.
   1782 - named as an adjoining land owner to James Kile, and William McReasner on English Buffalo Creek, bk 12, pg 36.
   1783 - deed from William Penny for 200 acres joining Houston's line, and Templeton's line, Test: Joseph Graham, Archibald Trotter, and Arthur McCree, bk 12, pg 320.
   1784 - named as an adjoining land owner to Jacob Fagot, Peter Hope, and Michael Fogelman on Adam's Creek, bk 12, pg 146.
   1784 - deed from William Penney for 300 acres on Coddle Creek, Test: David Templeton, and John Thompson, bk 12, pg 311.
   1790 - 104 016 - twp 9
Phifer/Fifer, Martin, Senr. & Margaret Blackwelder
   1764 - witnessed a deed, with Richard Berrey, from Arthur and Justina Dobbs for Arthur McKay on Connerford branch and Coldwater Creek, bk 10, pg 404.
   1764 - witnessed a deed, with Richard Berry, from Arthur and Justina Dobbs to Arthur McKay on the Three Mile Creek of Rockey River, bk 10, pg 435.
   1777 - named as executor of John Phifer, deceased, in a deed to Robert Morton for 300 acres on Coddle Creek, bk 10, pg 69.

1777 - deed from John McCoy for 255 acres on the north side of Buffalo Creek, adjoining Martin Phifer, Test: Zaccheus Wilson, Martin Phifer, bk 11, pg 34.
1779 - witnessed a deed, with Jason Frissell, from George & Catherine Goodnight to Leonard Barbrick on Coldwater Creek, bk 11, pg 10.
1780 - deed to Peter Sell for 190 acres on Little Coldwater Creek adjoining Jacob Seah, Test: Jason Frissel, Nicholas Coleman, bk 11, pg 74.
1782 - deed from Adam & Elinor Bowers for 5 acres on Coldwater Creek at the Coldwater Meeting House, beginning below the spring, Test: Joseph Shinn, bk 11, pg 135.
1782 - named as an ajoining land owner to Frederick Scartauk on English Buffalo Creek, bk 12, pg 632.
1784 - bill of sale from William Penney for six negroes, Jack, Moses, Nancy, Lissey, Hannah, and Lucy, bk 12, pg 241.
1784 - deed to Ephraim Farr for 300 acres on Caudle Creek joining David Templeton, Test: Archibald Houston, Richard Trotter, and William Fraser, bk 12, pg 366.
1784 - deed to Lewis Meredith for 200 acres on both sides of Mill Creek, Test: Caleb Phifer, John Barkley, bk 12, pg 422.
1790 - 201 014 - twp 10
Wife - Margaret Blackwelder, sister of Caleb Blackwelder.
Children: John (Catherine Barringer)
Great Coldwater Creek near Armstrong's branch, near Longreen Branch of Coldwater Creek.

Phifer, Paul
1783 - deed from James & Margaret Fleming for 100 acres on Rockey River on both sides of Meadow Branch, adjoining Douglas Winchester, Test: Archibald White, John Hagler, bk 12, pg 216.

Phillips, Adam
1790 - 111 00 - twp 15
1800 - Mecklenburg County

Phillips, Robert

Phillips, Hugh
1783 - witnessed a deed, with Charles Alexander, and John Potts, from William Haggins and James Houston to William Potts on Back Creek and the Six Mile Branch of Twelve Mile Creek, joining James Potts, Jacob Scroft, and William King, bk 12, pg 290.

Phillips, James
1791 - James' will was probated in Mecklenburg Co.
Children: John

Phillips, Jean
1799 - Loose estate papers

Phillips, Robert

1780 - named as an adjoining land owner to John
Province, John McKoy, Andrew Sprott, Alexander Starret,
William Wilson, and John McElwes, on the east side of
Sugar Creek, bk 12, pg 245.
1782 - named as an adjoining land owner to John McKoy,
John Springs, Andrew Sprott, Alexander Starret, William
Wilson, and John McEwus on the east fork of Sugar Creek,
bk 12, pg 244.
1790 - 112 03 - twp 20
1797 - Loose estate papers

Phillips, Sylvanus
1784 - witnessed a deed, with Joshua Yarbrough, from
Benjamin Cook to Jack Liget on the Mile Branch of Two
Mile Creek, bk 12, pg 443.

Phillips, William
1782 - named as an adjoining land owner to James Doster
on Richardson Creek, bk 12, pg 110.

Phipps, Isaac
1791 - Loose estate papers

Pickens/Pickence, Samuel, Capt.
1773 - witnessed a deed from Caleb Barr to Samuel
Alexander in the Welch tract, twp 4, bk 11, pg 164.
1783 - witnessed a deed, with William Alexander, from
Hannah Clark to Elinor Clark, bk 12, pg 315.
1790 - 144 05 - twp 8
1800 - Cabarrus County

Pickens, Widow
1784 - named as a neighbor to Isaac & Elenor Williams,
George Hutchison, John Tatt on a branch of Sugar Creek
about a mile from the path that leads from Charlotte to
John Tatt's, bk 12, pg 430.

Pickens, William
1754 - granted a tract of land, with Griffith
Rutherford, on Pickens Creek, a branch of Twelve Mile
Creek, no book of page number given, bk 12, pg 274.
1779 - witnessed a deed, with John Adam Miller, from
David Oliphant, by Thomas Polk, attorney, to John
McCracken, on Clear Creek, bk 12, pg 265.
1780 - witnessed a deed, with John Davis, from Joseph &
Agnes Ewart to Alexander Robison on Rockey River,
adjoining Benjamin Brown, bk 10, pg 440.
1780 - deed from Moses & Margaret Meek for 173 acres on
the head branch of Rockey River in the Welsh tract,
Test: John Neil, bk 11, pg 119.
Pickens Creek, a branch of Twelve Mile Creek
1790 - 123 00 - twp 14
William died before 1826.

Pickens/Bickens, William
1790 - 101 02 - twp 5

Pierson, Henry
1790 - 304 00 - twp 1

Pinman, Rueben

1792 - Account ledger of John Melchor's store.
Pinnix, John
    1793 - John's will was probated in Mecklenburg Co.
    Children: Fanny, Mary
Pitman, John
    1801 - Loose estate papers
Pleeter/Plater, Abraham & Susannah
    1782 - deed from Jacob & Elizabeth Misnhimer for 150
    acres on Bafilour (Buffalo) Creek, Test: Joseph Shinn,
    bk 11, pg 146.
    1782 - grant for 200 acres on Cumberford's Branch,
    joining Jacob Croner, bk 12, pg 105.
    1783 - deed to Jacob Messenhimer for 200 acres on
    Umberford's Branch, joining Jacob Croner and Joseph
    Shinn, Test: Joseph Shinn, M. Messenhimer, bk 12, pg
    341.
Pliler, Daniel
    Daniel died April 1783, buried in St John's Evangelical
    Lutheran Church Cemetery.
Pliler, Elizabeth
    Elizabeth was born 1755, died Jan 4, 1837, buried in St
    John's Evangelical Lutheran Church Cemetery.
Pliler/Philer, Fredrick
    1790 - 122 00 - twp 12
    1800 - Cabarrus County
    Frederick was born July 12, 1753, died May 11, 1806,
    buried in St John's Evangelical Lutheran Church
    Cemetery.
Pliler, Henry
    1790 - 105 00 - twp 12
    1800 - Cabarrus County
Plott, George
    1790 - 333 00 - twp 10
Plott, Joseph
    1778 Signer of 1778 Petition.
Plummer, Thomas
    1790 - 000 10 - twp 1
Plummer, Zephaniah
    1790 - 104 00 - twp 1
    1800 - Mecklenburg County
Plunket, James, Senr. & Fereby
    1782 - grant for 152 acres on Rockey River, bk 12, pg
    61.
    1790 - 101 06 - twp 13
    1800 - Cabarrus County
    James died in 1810.
Plunket, James, Jur. & Agness Houston
    1790 - 141 00 - twp 13
    1800 - Cabarrus County
Polk, Charles, Jr.
    1767 - Militia, Mecklenburgh Regiment (Lieutenant)
    1776 - in Capt. Charles Polk's Light Horse Company.

Residents of Mecklenburg County, North Carolina   1762-1790

1790 - 221 09 - twp 1
Charles died before 1812.
Polk, Charles, Capt. & Mary Alexander
    1776 - Captain of Light Horse Company
    1779 - witnessed a deed, with Will Lusk, from Thomas Polk, attorney for David Oliphant, to Archibald McCurday on Long Run, a branch of Clear Creek, bk 10, pg 543.
    1780 - Clear Creek
    1783 - witnessed a deed, with William Polk, from Thomas Polk to Richard Mason for lot 12 in Charlotte, bk 12, pg 301.
    1790 - 233 04 - twp 14
    1793 - Account ledger of John Melchor's store.
    Wife - Mary Alexander, daughter of Hezekiah & Mary Sample Alexander
    Charles died before 1821.
Polk, Ezekiel & Mary Wilson, Sophia Neely
    1773 - witnessed a deed, with Samuel Martin, for lot 26 in Charlotte to John Nelson, bk 11, pg 179.
    1779 - Appointed guardian of Samuel Polk and Samuel Wilson, to be provided for from the estate of Samuel Wilson, deceased.
    1779 - guardian bond between Daid McCree and Ezekiel Polk whereas Ezekiel Polk is appointed guardian of Samuel Polk and Samuel Wilson, providing for them out of the estate of Samuel Wilson, bk 10, pg 455.
    1780 - deed to Samuel Hemphill for lot 65 in Charlotte, bk 11, pg 22.
    1780 - witnessed a deed, with Will Polk, from John Johnston to Samuel McCleary, bk 11, pg 173.
    1782 - commissioner to the court.
    1782 - witnessed a deed, with Samuel Wilson, from Samuel Hemphill to Samuel McCombs for lot 65 in Charlotte, bk 11, pg 194.
    1782 - grant for 50 acres on Big Sugar Creek joining Robert McCleary, and William Barnett, bk 12, pg 43.
    Wife - Mary Wilson, daughter of Samuel & Mary Winslow Wilson.
    1784 - witnessed a deed, with John Hamilton, from Thomas Polk to Paul Barringer on Dutch Buffalo Creek, bk 12, pg 398.
    1784 - witnessed a deed, with Elisha Smith, from Robert McCree to Samuel McCleary, bk 12, pg 435.
    1785 - witnessed a deed, with John Pelly, from Samuel & Deborah McCleary to Moses Bigham on Big Sugar Creek, bk 12, pg 447.
    Children: Samuel
    Brother: Col. Thomas Polk
Polk, John, Sr. & Elinore
    1766 - listed in the militia company of Capt. Adam Alexander of Clear Creek.
    1776 - in Capt. Charles Polk's Light Horse Company.

1779 - witnessed a deed, with William Lusk, from Thomas Polk, attorney for David Oliphant, to William Love on Crooked Creek, bk 10, pg 546.
1780 - deed to Allein Freeman for several tracts on Clear Creek, Test: William and Charles Polk, bk 10, pg 444.

Polk, John, Junr.
1790 - 113 00 - twp 14
1800 - Cabarrus County

Polk, Joseph
1783 - witnessed a deed, with R. Martin, and John Prior, from James Orr to Samuel Martin for lot 25 in Charlotte, bk 12, pg 572.

Polk, Samuel & Jane
1779 - guardian bond between Daid McCree and Ezekiel Polk whereas Ezekiel Polk is appointed guardian of Samuel Polk and Samuel Wilson, providing for them out of the estate of Samuel Wilson, bk 10, pg 455.
Wife - Jane Knox, daughter of James Knox
Children: James Knox, Pres.

Polk, Thomas, Col. & Susanna Spratt
1767 - Militia, Mecklenburgh Regiment (Captain)
1770 - commissioner of Charlotte
Trustee of Liberty Hall.
1775 - Thomas was one of the signers of the Mecklenburg Declaration of Independence on May 20, 1775.
1773 through 1779 - attorney
1779 - deed to Robert McElwrath for lot no. 1 in Charlotte, Test: Ephraim Brevard, John Alexander, bk 11, pg 127, & lot 5, Test: Ephraim Brevard, Isaac Alexander, bk 11, pg 145.
1780 - deed to John Davies for 500 acres on the Catawba River about two miles above the mouth of the 8th fork, conveyed to Thomas in 1773, Test: Peter Johnston, James Jack, bk 11, pg 33.
1782 - deed to Samuel Martin for lot 86 in Charlotte, Test: David Alison, bk 11, pg 188.
1783 - witnessed a deed, with William Polk, from John Stinson to William Stinson on Sugar Creek, bk 11, pg 199
1783 - deed to John McLure for 112 acres on Sugar Creek, Test: William Polk, Thomas McLure, bk 11, pg 251.
1783 - deed to Richard Mason for lot 12 in Charlotte, bk 12, pg 301.
1784 - deed from Joseph Graham, sheriff, in a judgement against James Foster, for a lot in Charlotte, bk 12, pg 262.
1784 - named as an adjoining land owner to Robert Walker, Jr., and John Green on Sugar Creek, bk 12, pg 337.
1784 - named as an adjoining land owner to Isaac & Eleanor Williams, George Hutchison, Adam Caruthers, James Taggert, and David Hays, Sr., bk 12, pg 437.

Residents of Mecklenburg County, North Carolina   281
1762-1790

1784 - deed to Andrew Dune for 660 acres on Long Creek, and another tract of 150 acres, Test: Robert Dunn, Andrew Lawing, bk 12, pg 283.
1790 - 504 047 - twp 3
Children: William
Brother: Ezekiel
Thomas died in 1793, buried in the Presbyterian Cemetery in Charlotte.
1794 - Loose estate papers

Polk, Thomas, Junr.
1776 - Indian Camp Creek, deed unclear which Thomas Polk bought this land.
1779 - deed to John Lemonds for 20 acres on Caldwell Creek joining John Luckey, and James Morrison, Test: William Polk, Robert Hope, bk 11, pg 36.
1780 - witnessed a deed, with Andrew Sprott, from John Province to John McKoy on the east side of Sugar Creek joining Robert Phillips, Andrew Sprott, Alexander Starrett, William Wilson, and John McElwes, bk 12, pg 245.
1784 - deed from Joseph Graham, sheriff, in a judgement against Jacob Agner, for 262 acres on Dutch Buffalo Creek, bk 12, pg 389.
1784 - deed to Paul Barringer for 262 acres on Dutch Buffalo Creek, Test: Ezekiel Polk, John Hamilton, bk 12, pg 398.
1790 - 112 00 - twp 14

Polk, William, Jr.
1790 - 142 00 - twp 14

Polk, William, Sr.
1765 - witnessed a deed, with Thomas Polk, from James & Margaret Davis to John Davis, on the south side of Sugar Creek, bk 11, pg 20.
1775 - witnessed a deed, with Hezekiah Alexander, to James Jack for lots 144, 166, 167, 168, 196, 390, 399 in Charlotte, bk 11, pg 220.
1779 - witnessed a deed, with Michael Garmon, from Thomas Polk to William Hayns on Muddy Creek, bk 10, pg 311.
1779 - witnessed a deed, with Phillip Miller, from Thomas Polk to John Nelson on Muddy Creek, bk 10, pg 343.
1779 - witnessed a deed, with John Purser, from Thomas Polk, attorney for David Oliphant, to Thomas Smith on Duck Creek, bk 11, pg 6.
1779 - witnessed a deed, with John Purser, from Thomas Polk, attorney for David Oliphant, to Samuel Smith on Duck Creek, bk 11, pg 8 and bk 11, pg 15.
1779 - witnessed a deed, with Thomas Harris, from Thomas Polk, attorney for David Oliphant, to James Harris on Clear Creek, bk 11, pgs 265 & 267.

1779 - witnessed a deed, with Robert Hope, from Thomas Polk, attorney for David Oliphant, to John Lemonds on Caldwell Creek, bk 11, pg 36.
1780 - witnessed a deed, with Ezekiel Polk, from John Johnston to Samuel McLeary, bk 11, pg 173.
1782 - one of the proprietors of Ochiltree, Martin and Company, bk 11, pg 217.
1782 - power of attorney for Aron Gillett of NC, physician, Test: Duncan Ochiltree, bk 11, pg 187.
1783 - witnessed a deed, with John M. Powel, from William McCullough to John Wilson on McCalpin's Creek, bk 11, pg 241.
1783 - witnessed a deed, with Thomas McLure, from Thomas Polk to John McLure on Sugar Creek, bk 11, pg 251.
1790 - 101 02 - twp 14
1800 - Cabarrus County

Pollock, Hugh
1777 - witnessed a deed, with Robert Scott, to Joseph Wishart for lot 67 in Charlotte, bk 11, pg 62.
1777 - witnessed a deed, with James McCafferty from James Jack to Robert Scott for lot 27 in Charlotte, bk 10, pg 281.
1778 - witnessed a deed, with John Davies, from William Givens to Robert Scott on Six Mile Creek, bk 10, pg 279.
1780 - witnessed a deed, with John Stewart, from Ezekiel Polk to Samuel Hemphill for lot 65 in Charlotte, bk 11, pg 22.
1781 - witnessed a deed, with Samuel Martin, and Thomas Harris, from Samuel Ferguson to his daughter Agness Ferguson, bk 11, pg 259.
1782 - witnessed a deed, with William Wilson, from Robert Graham to John Springsteet on Sugar Creek, bk 12, pg 383.

Pollock, Hugh, Jr.
1778 - witnessed a deed to Patrick McDonald for lots 340, 341, and 342 in Charlotte, bk 10, pg 71.
1778 - witnessed a deed to Patrick McDonald for lots 345 346, and 347 in Charlotte, bk 10, pg 64.

Pool, Alexander
1793 - Account ledger of John Melchor's store.

Pool, Sander
1793 - Account ledger of John Melchor's store.

Poplin, John
1793 - Account ledger of John Melchor's store.

Porter, Alexander
1779 - witnessed a deed, with Samuel Bigham and Robert Hunter, from Samuel Bigham, Sr. to John Porter on Steel Creek, bk 10, pg 439.
1790 - 117 00 - twp 2
1800 - Mecklenburg County

Porter, Hugh
1790 - 111 00 - twp 2

1800 - Mecklenburg County
Hugh died before 1813.
Porter, James Alexander & Jane Welch
　　1790 - 124 04 - twp 2
Porter, James & Ruth
　　1790 - 124 04 - twp 2
　　Daughter died and buried in Steel Creek Cemetery in
　　1793.
Porter, John(2)
　　1779 - deed from Samuel Bigham, Sr. for 180 acres on the
　　north fork of Steel Creek joining John & Robert Bigham,
　　and Robert Maxwell, Test: Robert Hunter, Samuel Bigham,
　　and Alexander Porter, bk 10, pg 439.
　　1790 - 134 00 - twp 1
　　1800 - Mecklenburg County
　　John died March 6, 1821 at age 80.
Porter, Joseph
　　1790 - 114 00 - twp 2
Porter, Matthew
　　1792 - Loose estate papers
Porter, Robert, Capt. & Elizabeth McBroom
　　1779 - named as an adjoining land owner to Gilbert
　　McNarr, Francis Nixon, and Zebaland Brevard on one of
　　the head branches of Rockey River, bk 12, pg 490.
　　1790 - 235 00 - twp 16
　　1792 - Loose estate papers
Porter, William & Elizabeth(2)
　　1781 - named as an adjoining land owner to Samuel
　　Bigham, Sr. Hugh Bigham, William Bowman, and John
　　Taylor, bk 11, pg 155 & pg 160.
　　William died Sept 14, 1787 at age 78.
　　Elizabeth died June 5, 1778 age 60.
Porter, William
　　1790 - 145 04 - twp 2
Porter, William
　　1790 - 101 00 - twp 16
　　A William Porter owned land on Sugar Creek 1781.
Potter, Gordon
　　1790 - 334 00 - twp 19
Potts, James & Margaret
　　1772 - deed from James McClure for 550 acres on the Flat
　　Branch of Twelve Mile Creek, Test: Henry Downs, James
　　Tate, bk 10, pg 257.
　　1778 - deed to John and William Potts for 250 acres on
　　the Flat Branch of Twelve Mile Creek, Test: James
　　Bratton, Archibald Crockett, bk 10, pg 203 or 204.
　　1779 - deed to John Potts for 400 acres on Six Mile
　　Creek joining John King, and William Courtney, Test:
　　William Courtney, Michael Dely, bk 12, pg 248.
　　1779 - deed to William Potts for 600 acres on Six Mile
　　Creek joining Hugh McLile, Archibald Crocket, Zeph John,

Residents of Mecklenburg County, North Carolina
1762-1790

John Potts, and John King, Test: William Courtney,
Michael Delo, bk 12, pg 272.
Children: Jean (? Baxter), William, John
Grandson: James Potts Baxter
1781 - James' will was written and probated in
Mecklenburg Co.
Potts, John
    1779 - deed from James & Margaret Potts for 400 acres on
Six Mile Creek joining John King, and William Courtney,
Test: William Courtney, Michael Dely, bk 12, pg 248.
    1790 - 115 03 - twp 16
    1800 - Mecklenburg County
Potts, John
    1778 - deed from James Potts for 250 acres on the Flat
Branch of Twelve Mile Creek, Test: James Bratton,
Archibald Crockett, bk 10, pg 203 or 204.
    Six Mile Creek near Stillhouse Branch.
    Brother of James.
    1783 - John's will was probated in Mecklenburg Co.
    Children: Robert
Potts, Jonathan
    1790 - 217 01 - twp 7
    1800 - Mecklenburg County
Potts, Joshua
    1790 - 111 00 - twp 17
Potts, Robert & Elizabeth
    1785 - witnessed a deed, with Isaac Jetton, from John &
Elizabeth Jetton to Lewis Jetton, bk 12, pg 555.
    1785 - witnessed a deed from James Williamson to Thomas
Harris, bk 12, pg 584.
    1790 - 153 020 - twp 7
    1800 - Mecklenburg County
    Wife - Elizabeth McKeown
Potts, William & Margaret Purviance
    1778 - deed from James Potts for 250 acres on the Flat
Branch of Twelve Mile Creek, Test: James Bratton,
Archibald Crockett, bk 10, pg 203 or 204.
    1779 - witnessed a deed, with Phillip Miller, from
Thomas Polk, attorney for David Oliphant, to John Nelson
on Muddy Creek, bk 10, pg 360.
    1779 - deed from James & Margaret Potts for 600 acres on
Six Mile Creek joining Hugh McLile, Archibald Crocket,
Zeph John, John Potts, and John King, Test: William
Courtney, Michael Delo, bk 12, pg 272.
    1783 - deed from William Haggins and James Houston for
200 acres on Back Creek, otherwise the Six Mile Branch
of Twelve Mile Creek joining James Potts, Jacob Scroft,
and William King, Test: Charles Alexander, Hugh
Phillips, and John Potts, bk 12, pg 290.
    1790 - 113 014 - twp 16
    1800 - Mecklenburg County
    1801 - Loose estate papers (Reel 86)

Potts, William
  1801 - Loose estate papers (Reel 87)
Poulson, William
  1797 - Loose estate papers
Povey, Conrad & Magdalena
  1766 - Conrad's will was probated in Mecklenburg Co.
Powell, Abel
  1790 - 102 00 - twp 14
  1800 - Cabarrus County
Powell, David
  1790 - 122 00 - twp 14
Powell, Henry & Mary
  1776 - in Capt. Charles Polk's Light Horse Company.
  1780 - deed to Frederick Ciser for 30 acres on Rocky River, Test: George Keiser and Conrad Hardway, bk 11, pg 27.
Powell, James
  1779 - Loose estate papers
Powell, John M.
  1779 - deed to William Barker for 70 acres in the Welch Tract beginning on the north side of Muddy Creek, Test: Daniel and Ruth Barker, bk 10, pg 384.
  1783 - witnessed a deed, with William Polk, from William McCullough to John Wilson on McCalpin's Creek, bk 11, pg 241.
  tract called the Welch Tract on north side of Muddy Creek.
  1790 - 302 00 - twp 14
  1800 - Cabarrus County
Powell, Joshua
  1766 - listed in the militia company of Capt. Adam Alexander of Clear Creek.
Poynter, Samuel
  1762 - Loose estate papers
Price, Henry
  1790 - 104 00 - twp 12
Price, Isaac & Esther
  1782 - witnessed a deed, with John Carothers, from Joseph McKinley to James R. Alexander on the Catawba River above the mouth of Crowder's Creek, bk 11, pg 280.
  1790 - 443 07 - twp 2
  1800 - Mecklenburg County
  Wife - Esther Bradley
  Son of John & Mary White Price.
Price, James & Mary D(2)
  1790 - 135 00 - twp 7
  Mary Price died Nov 25, 1804 age 79.
  Son of Rachel Price.
Price, Jesse
  1781 - witnessed a deed, with John Barnett and Robert Armstrong, from William Barnett to William Daviss on the line between North and South Carolina, bk 10, pg 445.

Price, John
   1749 - John's will was probated in Mecklenburg Co.
Price, John
   1787 - Loose estate papers
Price, John & Mary(2)
   1764, 1777
   Wife - Mary White
   Children: Isaac, John, Reese, Martha, Mary, William, Elizabeth, Jonathan
   1790 - 213 013 - twp 2
   1800 - Mecklenburg County
   John died Jan 27, 1802 at age 87.
   1803 - Loose estate papers for John
   1804 - Loose estate papers for Mary
Price, John
   1790 - 104 00 - twp 7
Price, John
   1800 - Loose estate papers
Price, Rachel
   1754 - grant mentioned in bk 12, pg 555, but no bk or pg number given for the grant.
   Children: John Price, Margaret Price, James Price.
   Rachel died 1764 or before.
Price, Reese/Reed(2) & Sarah
   1762 - deed from Rees & Sarah Price of Anson Co., to Matthew Nox (Knox) of same, near land formerly granted to James Armour and near an old Indian path, granted to said Price on Apr 3, 1753, Test: Thomas Price, Richard & Ann Barry, Vol 1, pg 80.
   1767 - Militia, Mecklenburgh Regiment (Ensign)
   1790 - 101 013 - twp 8
   Reese died Nov 22, 1794
   Son of John & Mary White Price.
Price, Robert
   1790 - 101 00 - twp 7
   1800 - Mecklenburg County
Prior, John
   1783 - witnessed a deed, with Joseph Polk and R. Martin, from James Orr to Samuel Martin for lot 25 in Charlotte, bk 12, pg 572.
Pritchart, Daniel & Mary
   1764 - Daniel's will was probated in Mecklenburg Co.
Props, Henry
   1790 - 131 01 - twp 11
   1800 - Cabarrus County
   Children: Henry (Catherine ?)
Provane, John
   1778 - deed from John & Jean Wear for 257 acres on Abraham Alexander's Mill Creek joining Ebenezer Newton, Andrew Trot, Alexander Herrel, William Wilson, and John McEwell, bk 10, pg 283.
Province, John

1777 - witnessed a deed, with Neil Morrison, from Arthur
& Hannah Starr on McCalpin's Creek known by the name of
Lofton's Bottom, bk 10, pg 248.
1780 - deed to John McKoy for 257 acres on Sugar Creek
joining Robert Phillips, Andrew Sprott, Alexander
Starrett, William Wilson, and John McElwes, Test: Thomas
Polk, Jr., and Andrew Sprott, bk 12, pg 245.
Pruie(see Price), Reese
Pulley, James & Agnes
1774 - witnessed a deed, from John Carothers to James
Carothers, bk 10, pg 157.
Purner, John
1784 - named as an adjoining land owner to William &
Elizabeth Penny, Lewis Meredith, and Samuel Templeton on
Coddle Creek, bk 12, pg 421.
Purser, John
1776 - in Capt. Charles Polk's Light Horse Company.
1779 - witnessed a deed, with Will Polk, from Thomas
Polk, attorney for David Oliphant, to Thomas Smith, bk
11, pg 6, and to Samuel Smith, bk 11, pgs 8 & 15.
Purveance, Charles
1778 - witnessed a deed, with Joseph Moore, from William
& James McCafferty, executors of Richard Mason, for lot
11 in Charlotte, bk 10, pg 77.
Purviance, David
1782 - named as an adjoining land owner to William
Scott, ? Phifer, John Rodgers, James Walker, and Hugh
Caruthers, bk 12, pg 71.
1783 - named as an adjoining land owner of William and
Means on Coddle Creek, bk 12, pg 141
1784 - grant for 136 acres on the north side of Rockey
River opposite James Love, bk 12, pg 182.
1785 - named as an adjoining land owner to Robert
Russel, Sr., James Russel, and Alexander Ferguson, bk
12, pg 445.
1790 - 314 01 - twp 13
Purviance, James
1790 - 141 01 - twp 13
1800 - Cabarrus County
James died April 1810.
Purviance, John
1790 - 113 00 - twp 13
Purviance, Joseph
1790 - 112 00 - twp 13
Pyron, Charles
1793 - Account ledger of John Melchor's store.
Pyron, John
1790 - 122 00 - twp 14
Pyron/Pirant, William
1790 - 325 00 - twp 14
Pyron/Pirant, William

1812 - Seventh Company detached from the First
Mecklenburg Regiment.
Queben, John
    1790 - 102 00 - twp 16
Queen, John
    1779 - witnessed a deed, with Andrew McCombs, to Robert
    Graham on Sugar Creek, bk 10, pg 356.
Query, Alexander
    1790 - 324 00 - twp 5
    1800 - Cabarrus County
Query, John
    1772 - named as an adjoining land owner to Hugh & Mary
    Carragan, John Ramsey on Whetstone Branch, bk 10, pg
    103.
    1775 - John was one of the signers of the Mecklenburg
    Declaration of Independence on May 20, 1775.
    1780 - Trustee for the congregation of Rocky Spring.
    1786 - witnessed a deed, with John Donaldson, from
    Joseph & Jane Harris to Jonathan Query on Crooked Creek,
    bk 12, pg 591.
    1790 - 301 00 - twp 15
    1797 - Loose estate papers
Query/Quary, John
    Pension denied July 7, 1832 - no proof of service.
Query, Jonathan
    1786 - deed from Joseph & Jane Harris for 77 acres on
    both sides of Crooked Creek, Test: John Query, John
    Donaldson, bk 12, pg 591.
Query, William, Sr. & Margaret
    1766 - listed in the militia company of Capt. Adam
    Alexander of Clear Creek.
    1790 - 101 00 - twp 15
Query/Quary, William, Jr.
    1790 - 124 00 - twp 15
    Pension denied July 7, 1832 - no proof of service.
Quilman, Peter
    1787 - witnessed the will of Jacob Misenhimer.
    1790 - 122 00 - twp 12
    1800 - Cabarrus County
Quiston, Archibald M.
    Mentioned in the will of John Boyse in 1793.
Quiston, David
    Mentioned in the will of John Boyse in 1793.
    Children: Peggy M., Jenny M.
Rabinett, John (see Robinet)
Raddish, Wallis
    1793 - Account ledger of John Melchor's store.
Rainey, John
    1767 - Loose estate papers
Ramey, Thomas
    1790 - 104 00 - twp 2
    1800 - Mecklenburg County

Residents of Mecklenburg County, North Carolina   289
1762-1790

Ramey, William
    1790 - 102 00 - twp 2
Ramey, William, Senr.
    1790 - 212 00 - twp 2
Ramsay, Alexander
    1790 - 111 00 - twp 16
Ramsey, Archibald & Jean
    1781 - deed to John Tanner for 214 acres on a branch of
    Coddle Creek, joining John Findley, and Zebulon Brevard,
    Test: William Ramsey, Isabel Robison, bk 11, pg 85.
Ramsey, Esther
    1779 - witnessed a deed, with Henry McWherter, from
    James Ramsey to Thomas Harris on Four Mile Creek, bk 10,
    pg 450.
    1779 - witnessed a deed, with Thomas Harris, from James
    & Rachell Ramsey to Henry McWherter on Four Mile Creek,
    bk 10, pg 552.
Ramsey, James & Rachel
    1779 - deed to Henry McWherter for 169 acres on Four
    Mile Creek, joining Thomas Harris, Test: Thomas Harris,
    Esther Ramsey, bk 10, pg 552.
Ramsey, James
    1779 - deed to Thomas Harris for 138 acres on the south
    side of Four Mile Creek, bk 10, pg 450.
    Of South Carolina in 1779.
Ramsay, John
    1783 - witnessed a deed, with John Shelby, from Ambrose
    & Magdalen Walker to John McCain on Cane Creek, bk 12,
    pg 230.
    1783 - deed from George McWhirter for 150 acres on
    Waxhaw Creek, Test: John Henderson, John McCain, bk 12,
    pg 247.
    1784 - deed to William Smith for 150 acres on Four Mile
    Creek, joining Thomas Hames, and James Way, Test: Adam
    Ormand, bk 12, pg 385.
    1790 - 132 00 - twp 17
Ramsey, John
    1767 - named in a 1779 deed as the original grantee of
    169 acres on Four Mile Creek, bk 10, pg 552.
    1772 - deed from Hugh & Mary Carragan for 60 acres on
    Whetstone Branch, Test: William Ramsey, Francis Glass,
    bk 10, pg 103.
    1775 - John's will was probated in Mecklenburg Co.

    1776 - Loose estate papers
    Children: James, William, John
Ramsay, Robert & Sarah Givens/Gibbons
    1790 - 133 00 - twp 16
    Sarah was the daughter of William & Jannett Gibbons.
Ramsay, Tobias

1784 - deed from George & Lese Miller, of Camden Dist, SC, for 200 acres on Linches Creek, Test: John Belk, James Belk, bk 12, pg 379.

Ramsay, William & Nancy Boyd
1772
1777 - Loose estate paper

Ramsay, William
1776 - 1st Lieutenant in Capt. Charles Polk's Light Horse Company.
1781 -
1784 - deed from Mathew Miller for 131 acres on Clear Creek, Test: Joseph Graham, Robert Stevens, bk 12, pg 357.
1784 - named as adjoining land owner to Mathew Miller, and John Karr on the Meadow Branch on the south side of Clear Creek, bk 12, pg 371.
1790 - 136 00 - twp 14

Ramsey, William
1781 - witnessed a deed, with Isabel Robison, from Archibald & Jean Ramsey to John Tanner on a branch of Coddle Creek, bk 11, pg 85.
1783 - witnessed a deed, with John Johnston, from David McCord to John Buchanan on Long Creek, bk 11, pg 196.
1783 - witnessed a deed, with Thomas McClure, from Robert & Rachel Crocket to John McClure on the head branches of Sugar Creek, bk 11, pg 271.
1784 - grant for 50 acres on the Catawba River joining Amos Alexander, bk 12, pg 158.
1784 - witnessed a deed, with Justice Beech, from John Johnston to Edward Stockes on the ridge between Long Creek and Thompson Branch, bk 12, pg 267.
1790 - 234 00 - twp 6
1800 - Mecklenburg County

Ramsour, John
1764 - John's will was probated in Mecklenburg Co.
Children: Jacob, David

Ramsower/Ramsour, Henry
1763 - Henry's will was probated in Mecklenburg Co.
1764 - Loose estate papers
Children: John, Jacob, David

Randal, Jacob
1774 - Mentioned in the estate papers of Nicholson Ross.

Rankin, Richard
1804 - Loose estate papers

Rape, Agustian
1790 - 122 00 - twp 12

Rape, Henry
1790 - 112 00 - twp 16
1800 - Mecklenburg County

Rape, Peter
1787 - Loose estate papers

Rape/Reape, Peter, Sr.

Peter died before 1828.
Rape, Peter
   1790 - 124 00 - twp 16
   1800 - Mecklenburg County
   Peter died before 1832.
Raphil, John
   1790 - 112 00 - twp 6
Ray, Andrew, Senr.
   1790 - 324 00 - twp 19
   1800 - Mecklenburg County
Ray, David
   1790 - 134 00 - twp 19
   1800 - Mecklenburg County
Ray, Isaac
   1790 - 115 00 - twp 15
Ray, John
   1779 - named as an adjoining land owner to Thomas McCall, William Ligget, and William Appleton on Findley's Creek, a branch of Twelve Mile Creek, bk 10, pg 488.
   1790 - 111 00 - twp 19
   1800 - Mecklenburg County
Rea, Andrew
   1777 - named as an adjoining land owner to James Tate and Hugh McClelland on Four Mile Creek, bk 10, pg 262.
   1779 - deed from David Rea to Andrew Rea, Archibald Crocket, and John Flenniken for 5 acres on Four Mile Creek, bk 11, pg 25.
   1801 - Loose estate papers
Rea, David
   1779 - deed to Andrew Rea, Archibald Crocket, and John Flenniken for 5 acres on Four Mile Creek, Test: William Cochran, John Cochran, bk 11, pg 25.
   Revolutionary Soldier - died Oct 1, 1839, age 83 according to The Charlotte Journal dated Oct 17, 1839.
Rea, David(2)
   1779, 1784 Four Mile Creek.
   David died March 5, 1784 at age 43.
Rea, John
   1767 - Loose estate papers
Rea, William
   1776 - in Capt. Charles Polk's Light Horse Company.
   1794 - Loose estate papers
Readling, George Michael
   1794 - Account ledger of John Melchor's store.
Reading, Paul
   1793 - Account ledger of John Melchor's store.
Reamy, John
   1765 - John's will was probated in Mecklenburg Co.
   Children: Samuel, Benjamin
Reamy, William
   1796 - Loose estate papers

Reap, Augustine
    1781 - Loose estate papers
Rederick/Redenick, Shadrick
    1790 - 123 00 - twp 16
Redford, John
    1779 - grant for 38 acres on a branch of Twelve Mile
    Creek, bk 10, pg 525.
    1790 - 424 00 - twp 16
    1800 - Mecklenburg County
Redick, Barnabas
    1790 - 141 00 - twp 18
Redland, George M.
    1790 - 208 00 - twp 12
    1800 - Cabarrus County
Reed, David & Catrin
    1779 - deed to Nicholas Gibbony for 200 acres on Sugar
    Creek joining Henry Varner, Samuel Kearh, and John
    Carson, Test: John Allen, John McDowell, bk 10, pg 412.
    1779 - Loose estate papers
Reed, George
    1775 - witnessed a deed, with William Hemphill, from
    John & Susannah Steward to William Alexander on Stony
    Creek of Mallard Creek, bk 11, pg 51.
    1779 - named as an adjoining land owner to William
    Shields, Joseph Michel, Benjamin Alexander, and Andrew
    Robison on Mallard Creek, bk 10, pg 501.
    1779 - grant for 31 acres on Lockard's Branch, joining
    Benjamin Alexander, bk 10, pg 532.
    1785 - witnessed a deed, with Hugh Hayes, from William &
    Frances Hays to Patrick Hays on Wolf Meadow Branch, bk
    12, pg 464.
    1790 - 142 00 - twp 4
Reed, James
    1777 - named as an adjoining land owner to Alexander &
    Sarah Mitchel, and John Garrison on Sugar Creek, bk 10,
    pg 23.
    1782 - named as adjoining land owner to David &
    Elizabeth Crocket, Joseph Galbreath, and Alexander
    Mitchel on a branch of Sugar Creek, bk 11, pg 91.
    1782 - named as adjoining land owner to Hugh & Elizabeth
    Rondles, David Crocket, and Alexander Mitchell on a
    branch of Sugar Creek, bk 11, pg 98.
    1790 - 333 00 - twp 1
Reed, James (miller)
    1779 - witnessed a deed, with John Green, Jr., from
    William McKinley and Joseph Scott to James Owens on Paw
    Creek, bk 10, pg 322.
    1790 - 144 01 - twp 1
Reed, James, Jur.
    1790 - 112 01 - twp 1
Reed, James, Senr.
    1790 - 124 00 - twp 19

1800 - Mecklenburg County
Wife - Elizabeth
Pension denied July 7, 1832 - no proof of husbands identity with soldier of the same name.
Reed, John
   1790 - 134 00 - twp 5
   1800 - Cabarrus County
Reed, John
   1790 - 133 00 - twp 12
   1800 - Cabarrus County
Reed, John & Sarah Kiser
   1783 - witnessed a deed, with Edward Koulp, from George Harris to William Reed on Crooked Creek, bk 12, pg 522.
   1790 - 132 00 - twp 14
   1800 - Cabarrus County
   Children: Conrad (Martha Love), John, George, Elizabeth (? Motley), Martha (George Barnhardt), Catherine (Andrew Hartsell), Fanny (William Creaton), Polly (? Kisor)
   Owner of Reed Gold Mine on Little Meadow Creek.
Reed, John
   1790 - 144 00 - twp 1
Reed, Joseph
   1790 - 102 00 - twp 2
Reed, Joseph
   1790 - 232 02 - twp 19
Reed, Mary
   1796 - Loose estate papers
Reed, Robert
   1790 - 212 01 - twp 1
Reed, Thomas
   1790 - 102 01 - twp 1
   1796 - Loose estate papers
Reed, William
   1774 - witnessed a deed, with Thomas McGee, from Samuel Bigham to John Whiteside on Stell Creek, bk 10, pg 411.
   1776 - witnessed a deed, with Elijah and Abner Alexander, from Augustine Culp to John Wilson on McMichael's Creek, bk 11, pg 222.
   1779 - witnessed a deed, with Joseph Douglas, from Robert Graham to Robert Hays on Sugar Creek, bk 10, pg 340.
   1778 - witnessed a deed, with Duncan Ocheltree, from Moses Steel to William and James McCafferty on Sugar Creek, bk 10, pg 20.
   1779 - witnessed a deed, with William Hutchison, from Patrick McDonel to Alexander Hutchison for lots 390, 391, and 392 in Charlotte, bk 11, pg 42.
   1781 - witnessed a deed, with David Flaniken, and John Clark, from James Fleniken to John Barnett on McCalpin's Creek, bk 11, pg 81.

1783 - deed from George Harris for 68 acres on Crooked Creek, Test: Edward Koulp, John Reed, bk 12, pg 522.
1786 - witnessed a deed from Robert Barnet, Jr. to David Kenneday on Sugar Creek, bk 12, pg 586.

Reed, Will
1774 - witnessed a deed, with Charity Jack, from John Rilliah to John Davis on the ridge between McMichael's Creek and McCalpin's Creek, bk 10, pg 135.
1776 - witnessed a deed, with James Graham, from Elias & Agness Alexander to Samuel Graham, bk 10, pg 11.
1776 - witnessed a deed, with John Barett, and Charles Alexander, from John Dermond to John Wilson on McMichael Creek, bk 11, pg 246.
1777 - witnessed a deed, with Dan Ocheltree and Adam Stuart, from Peter Johnston to Isaiah Fitten on Sugar Creek, bk 10, pg 94.
1781 - witnessed a deed, with John Payton, from Samuel Bigham, Sr. to Hugh Bigham on Sugar Creek, bk 11, pg 155.
1781 - witnessed a deed, with William Bigham, from Samuel Bigham, Sr. to John Taylor on Sugar Creek, bk 11, pg 160.
1782 - witnessed a deed, with Thomas Allison, from William Berryhill and Thomas McDowel to James Clark on Sugar Creek, bk 11, pg 183.

Reed, William
1789 - Loose estate papers

Reid, Ann(2)
Ann died Aug 14, 1771 at age 27.

Reid, Augustinius & Elizabeth
1781 - Augustinius' will was probated in Mecklenburg Co.

Reid, Hugh
1778 - Hugh's will was probated in Mecklenburg Co.
Children: William, John

Reid, William(2)
William died Aug 17, 1771 at the age of 42.
1771 - Loose estate papers

Reid, William
1772 - Loose estate papers

Reisy, Henry
1785 - Loose estate papers

Reese, Charles
1771 - witnessed a bond, with Jason Frissell, between Catherine Phifer and John Barringer, bk 10, pg 198.

Reese/Rees, David
1769 - deed to James Rees for 150 acres on Caddle Creek, Test: David Rees, Jr. and W. Avery, bk 10, pg 147.
1774 - witnessed a deed, with James Reese, from Samuel & Ann Patton to Martin Phifer on Armstrong's Branch of Buffalo and Coldwater Creek, bk 10, pg 139.
David was a member of Poplar Tent Presbyterian Church.

Reese/Rees, David, Jr.

1767 - Militia, Mecklenburgh Regiment (Lietenant)
1769 - witnessed a deed, with W. Avery, from David Rees to James Rees on Caddle Creek, bk 10, pg 147.
1775 - David was one of the signers of the Mecklenburg Declaration of Independence on May 20, 1775.
1780 - named as an adjoining land owner to James Rees, Martin & Hugh McCree on Coddle Creek, bk 12, gp 194.
1787 - David's will was probated in Mecklenburg Co.
Children: Solomon, George

Reese/Rees, James
1769 - deed from David Rees for 150 acres on Caddle Creek, Test: David Rees, Jr., and W. Avery, bk 10, pg 147.
1774 - witnessed a deed, with David Reese, from Samuel & Ann Patton to Martin Phifer on Armstrong's Branch of Buffalo and Coldwater Creek, bk 10, pg 139.
1780 - grant for 106 acres on Coddle Creek, adjoining David Reese, Martin & Hugh McCree, bk 12, pg 194.

Reese/Reas, Peter
1785 - named as adjoining land owner to George & Susan Karriker, John George William, and James Beatchey on a branch of Rockey River, bk 12, pg 592.

Reese, Solomon
1790 - 104 00 - twp 9
Son of David Reese

Rendricks, William
1790 - 102 01 - twp 19

Renick, George
1766 - Loose estate papers

Rentleman, Martin & Experience
Wife - Experience Harris
Children: Catherine M.(Allison Dry)

Rette, John
1785 - deed from Frederick & Rebhel Kiser for 30 acres on both sides of Medor(Meadow) Creek, Test: Cunrod Hardwick, bk 12, pg 511.

Rhodes/Rodes, James
1783 - witnessed a deed, with John Weigler, from James & Elizabeth Hewit to Joseph Shinn on Three Mile Branch, bk 12, pg 335.

Rice, George
1779 - witnessed a deed to Henry Barnhart for lot 169 and 177 in Charlotte, bk 11, pg 136.
1784 - witnessed a deed, with Robert Scott, and David Mason, from Arthur Garrison to Richard Mason on Middle Branch, a branch of Sugar Creek, bk 12, pg 313.
1790 - 111 00 - twp 3
1807 - Loose estate papers

Rich, James, Senr.
1790 - 235 00 - twp 16

Rich, John, Junr.
1790 - 101 00 - twp 16

Richardson, Edward
    1790 - 323 00 - twp 16
    1797 - Loose estate papers
Richardson, William
    1795 - Loose estate papers
Richey, David
    1790 - 215 00 - twp 4
Richey/Ritshee, George
    George was born Feb 27, 1759, died Nov 17, 1823, buried
    in St John's Evangelical Lutheran Church Cemetery.
Richey, Henry & Margaret
    1790 - 152 00 - twp 11
    Wife - Margaret Fesperman ?, daughter of Henry &
    Christina Fesperman.
Richey, Jacob
    1774 - witnessed a deed, with William Harris, from
    Robert & Frances Harris to Jacob Myer on Duck Buffalo
    Creek, bk 10, pg 149.
    1783 - named as adjoining land owner to John Mesenhimer,
    William Leopard, Jacob Hough, John Charles, and Michael
    Cline on Dutch Buffalow Creek, bk 12, pg 147.
    1790 - 203 00 - twp 11
Richey/Ritchie, John
    1774 - deed from Hugh Montgomery for 111 acres, Test:
    James Williams, bk 10, pg 120.
    1785 - John's will was probated in Mecklenburg Co.
    1790 - Loose estate papers
    Children: William, John, David, Elizabeth, Jane
Richey, John
    1790 - 103 00 - twp 4
    1800 - Mecklenburg County
Richey, Michael
    1793 - Account ledger of John Melchor's store.
Richey, Mitch
    1794 - Account ledger of John Melchor's store.
Richey, Thomas
    1777 - deed to Joseph Nicholson for 34 acres on Sugar
    Creek and a tract on Haw Creek, adjoining Cubert
    Nicholson, Test: John Nicholson, and John Foayd, bk 10,
    pg 9 & 14.
    1789 - Loose estate papers
Richey, William
    1778 - witnessed a deed, from James and Patrick Scott to
    William McCleary on Long Creek, bk 10, pg 363 & 381.
    1781 - witnessed a deed, with William McCleary, from
    Abraham and Samuel Barnet to Robert Crocket on Long
    Creek, bk 12, pg 476.
Ridder, William
    1793 - Account ledger of John Melchor's store.
Riddey, Thomas
    1766 - listed in the militia company of Capt. Adam
    Alexander of Clear Creek.

Residents of Mecklenburg County, North Carolina 1762-1790

Ridenaur/Redenhour, Nicholas
　　1783 - grant for 200 acres on the Meeting House Branch joining Mathias Moyar, and John Charles, bk 12, pg 169.
　　1790 - 137 00 - twp 12
　　1794 - Account ledger of John Melchor's store.
　　1800 - Cabarrus County
　　Children: Jacob ?, John Nicholas ?,
Ridge, Henry
　　1778 Signer of 1778 Petition.
Rigey, George
　　1790 - 202 00 - twp 11
Rigsby, Drury
　　1792 - Account ledger of John Melchor's store.
Rigsbey, Thomas
　　1790 - 133 00 - twp 12
Riley, John
　　1790 - 134 00 - twp 3
Rilliah, John
　　1774 - deed to John Davis for 193 acres on the ridge between McMichael's Creek and McCalpin's Creek, Test: Charity Jack, and Will Reed, bk 10, pg 135.
Rine, Elijah
　　1789 - Loose estate papers
Rine/Rhyne, Jacob
　　Wife - Elizabeth Wiltz
　　Children: Jacob (Maria Elizabeth Best), Thomas (Barbara Wise), Magdalene (Adam Cloninger), Peter (Ann Magdalene Wills), Sarah Catherine (John Hovis), Phillip (Hannah Hoyle), Molly, Michael (Barbara Hoyle)
　　Jacob was born about 1720, died about 1794
　　He's buried in the Hovis Family Cemetery in Gaston County.
Rinehart, Andrew & Barbara ?
　　1785 - Andrew's will was probated in Mecklenburg Co.
　　1785 - Loose estate papers
　　Children: John
Rinehart, Andrew
　　1795 - Account ledger of John Melchor's store.
Rinehart, Barbara
　　1794 - Account ledger of John Melchor's store.
Rinehart/Rhinehardt, John
　　1793 - Account ledger of John Melchor's store.
Rite/Wright, John
　　1782 - witnessed a deed, with Frederick Kizer, from George & Mary Kizer to Coonrad Hardwick on Meadoe Creek and Canada's Branch, bk 12, pg 482.
Rives, Green
　　1784 - witnessed a deed, with William Meyer, and John McCannon from John Curry to John Foster on Waxhaw Creek, bk 12, pg 579.
Roach, Samuel
　　Samuel died 1781 at the age of 44.

1786 - Loose estate papers
Robb, John
    1783 - deed to Philip Miller for 102 acres on Clear
    Creek, joining Benjamin Coughran, Test: Adam Alexander,
    Evan Alexander, bk 12, pg 222.
Robb, Joseph
    1778 - deed from John & Mary Robinet for 97 acres on the
    ridge between McCalpin's Creek and Goose Creek, Test:
    John & Catherine Ford, bk 10, pg 330.
    1779 - witnessed a deed, with John Jackson, David Moore,
    and Andrew Moore, from William & Mary Watson to James
    Dickson on Clear Creek, bk 11, pg 191.
    1779 - witnessed a deed, from John & Jane Hall to Joseph
    Galbreath on Goose Creek, bk 10, pg 328.
    1779 - witnessed a deed, with John Foard, from Robert
    Galbreath to Emanuel Stephens on Crooked Creek, bk 10,
    pg 358.
Robb/Rabb, Robert
    1766 - listed in the militia company of Capt. Adam
    Alexander of Clear Creek.
Robb/Rabb, William, Capt. & Elizabeth
    1779 - named as adjoining land owner to John and Adam
    Miller, and William Bean on Clear Creek, bk 11, pg 68.
    1779 - deed from Thomas Polk, attorney for David
    Oliphant, for 30 acres on Clear Creek, Test: Adam
    Alexander, John Springs, bk 11, pg 229.
    1790 - 243 03 - twp 14
    William is buried in Rock Springs Cemetery.
Roberson, Alexander
    1782 - witnessed a deed, with William Patterson, from
    Matthew Roberson to David Roberson on Beaver Dam Creek
    of the Catawba River, bk 11, pg 158.
Roberson, David
    1782 Beaver Dam Creek, branch of Cataba River.
Roberson, James
    1777 - witnessed a deed, with William McClure, from
    James & Mary Meek to David Daugherty on Rocky River, bk
    10, pg 219.
Roberson, Matthew
    1782 - deed to David Roberson for 305 acres on Beaver
    Dam Creek, a branch of the Cataba River, joining Thomas
    Greer, Test: William Patterson, Alexander Roberson, bk
    11, pg 158.
Roberts, James
    1805 - Loose estate papers
Robinet/Rabinett, John & Mary
    1766 - listed in the militia company of Capt. Adam
    Alexander of Clear Creek.
    1773 - witnessed a deed, with Joseph Harris, from
    William & Elizabeth Morris to Richard Stillwell for a
    tract on the north side of White Oak Branch, bk 10, pg
    115.

1778 - deed to Joseph Robb for 97 acres on the ridge between McCalpin's Creek and Goose Creek, Test: John & Catherine Ford, bk 10, pg 330.
Robinett, Zebulon
   1766 - listed in the militia company of Capt. Adam Alexander of Clear Creek.
   1775 - witnessed a deed, with John Ford, from William & Cathron Smith to Jonathan Buckaloe on McCalpin's Creek, bk 10, pg 174.
Robins, Joseph & Eleanor Nation
   1754
Robinson, Alexander
   1785 - Alexander's will was probated in Mecklenburg Co. Children: Matthew
Robison, Alexander
   1780 -Rockey River.
   1790 - 202 00 - twp 5
Robison, Alexander & Rachel
   1780 - deed from Joseph & Agnes Ewart for 106 acres on the branches of Rockey River, Test: John Davis, William Bickens/Pickens, bk 10, pg 440.
   1783 - deed from Ambrose McKee for 164 acres on Steel Creek joining John and William Bigham, Test: David Robison, William Patterson, bk 11, pg 262.
   1790 - 122 00 - twp 6
   1800 - Mecklenburg County
   Wife - Rachel was named in the will of Benjamin Brown.
Robison, Alexander(2)
   Alexander died July 12, 1786 at age 30.
Robison/Robinson, Andrew & Margaret
   1778 - deed to Hugh Neely fot 98 acres on Mallard Creek, Test: Robert Harris, Jr., bk 10, pg 1.
   1779 - named as an adjoining land owner to William Shields, Benjamin Alexander, and Joseph Michel, bk 10, pg 501.
   1792 - Loose estate papers
Robinson, Charles
   1797 - Loose estate papers
Robison, David
   1783 Cataba River
   1790 - 311 00 - twp 4
   1800 - Mecklenburg County
   David died before 1809
Robison, David
   1783 - witnessed a deed, with William Patterson, from Ambrose McKee to Alexander Robison on Steel Creek, bk 11, pg 262.
   1783 - deed to Ambrose McKee from David and Richard Robison for 200 acres joining John Davis and Andrew Cathey, Test: Andrew Cathey, William Patterson, bk 11, pg 301.
   1790 - 121 00 - twp 2

1800 - Mecklenburg County
Robison, George
    1790 - 112 00 - twp 6
Robinson, Isabel Anderson(2)
    1781 - witnessed a deed, with William Ramsey, from
    Archibald & Jean Ramsey to John Tanner on a branch of
    Coddle Creek, bk 11, pg 85.
    Isabel died May 11, 1781 at age 28.
Robison, James
    1767 - Militia, Mecklenburgh Regiment (Captain)
    1785 - witnessed a deed, with George Graham, from
    Alexander Mitchel to Robert Alison on a branch of Sugar
    Creek, bk 12, pg 462.
    1790 - 116 00 - twp 3
    James died before 1810.
Robison, James, Senr.
    1790 - 101 02 - twp 4
    1800 - Mecklenburg County
    James died before 1821.
Robison, John
    1790 - 116 00 - twp 3
    1797 - Loose estate papers
Robison, John
    1783 - deed from Robert Robison, Sr. for 212 acres on
    Reedy Creek, Test: Hugh Neely, John McNitt Alexander, bk
    11, pg 234
    1790 - 112 01 - twp 4
    1800 - Mecklenburg County
    Son of Robert Robison, Sr.
    Died before 1808.
Robinson, John
    Revolutionary Soldier - died Aug 27, 1839 in Cabarrus
    Co, NC, age 90, a native of Mecklenburg County according
    to The Charlotte Journal dated Sept 5, 1839.
    1790 - 153 02 - twp 19
    1800 - Mecklenburg County
Robison, Joseph
    1779 - witnessed a deed, with George Rice, to Henry
    Barnhart, for lot 169 and 177 in Charlotte, bk 11, pg
    136.
Robinson, Mary(2)
    Mary died March 26, 1806 at the age of 83.
Robison, Mathew
    1790 - 145 00 - twp 2
    1800 - Mecklenburg County
    Son of Alexander Robinson.
Robison, Mathew
    1779 - named as adjoining land owner to James Alexander,
    and James Harris on Mallard Creek, bk 10, pg 530.
    1780 - named as adjoining land owner to Alexander
    Wallace, Michael Henderson, William Hemphill, and Thomas
    Frohock, bk 12, pg 120.

1783 - named as adjoining land owner to William
Alexander, Sr., and James Alexander, bk 12, pg 142.
1790 - 123 00 - twp 6
1800 - Mecklenburg County
Robison, Moses
1782 - witnessed a deed, with Edward Malony, from David
& Elizabeth Crocket to Joseph Galbreath on a branch of
Sugar Creek, bk 11, pg 91.
1790 - 101 00 - twp 4
Moses died before 1823.
Robinson, Richard & Martha
sons: Michael M. born 1802, Wallis born 1804.
Robinson, Richard(2)
1789 Richard died Jan 20, 1789 at age 76.
Robison/Robinson, Richard
1777 - witnessed a deed, with A. McKee, from Alexander &
Sarah Mitchel to John Garrison on Sugar Creek, bk 10, pg
23.
1783 - deed to Ambrose McKee, with David Robison, for
200 acres joining John Davis and Andrew Cathey, Test:
Andrew Cathey, William Patterson, bk 11, pg 301.
1797 - Loose estate papers
Robison, Richard
1790 - 102 01 - twp 2
1800 - Mecklenburg County
Robison/Robinson, Robert, Sr.
1783 - deed to son, John, for 212 acres on Reedy Creek,
Test: Hugh Neely, John McNitt Alexander, bk 11, pg 234.
1783 - deed Robert Robison, Jr. for 250 acres on Reedy
Creek joining Lewis Houston, Test: Hugh Neely, J. McNitt
Alexander, bk 11, pg 296.
1789 - Loose estate papers
Robison/Robinson, Robert, Jr.
1790 - 100 00 - twp 4
1800 - Mecklenburg County
Robert died before 1812.
Robison, Robert, Jr.
1779 - witnessed a deed, with Elijah Mitchell, from John
Garrison to Hugh Rondles on a branch of Sugar Creek, bk
11, pg 94.
1779 - named as one of the executors of James Wylie,
with Robert Harris, bk 10, pg 426.
1783 - deed from Robert Robison, Sr. for 250 acres on
Reedy Creek joining Lewis Houston, Test: Hugh Neely, J.
McNitt Alexander, bk 11, pg 296.
1790 - 127 00 - twp 4
1800 - Mecklenburg County
Robert died before 1804.
Robison, Robert
1804 - Loose estate papers
Robison, Thomas
1790 - 125 00 - twp 19

Robinson, Widow
    1790 - 034 00 - twp 20
Robison, William & Rachel
    1778 - Signer of 1778 Petition.
    1779 - deed to John Gibbins for 200 acres on Four Mile Creek near Providence, Test: Archibald Crockett, John McCulloch, John Wilson, bk 11, pg 298.
Robison, William & Richard
    1778 - Signer of 1778 Petition.
    Revolutionary Soldier - A William Robinson died in Madison Co., TN, formerly of Mecklenburg Co., NC, son of Robert Robinson (Revolutionary Soldier), according to the Charlotte Journal dated Nov 16, 1849.
Rock, Henry
    1779 - witnessed a deed, with Thomas McFaddon, from Thomas Polk, attorney for David Oliphant, to Robert Carothers on Henderson and Caldwell's Creek, bk 10, pg 432.
Rodden, Benjamin
    1798 - Benjamin's will was probated in Mecklenburg Co. Children: Upton, Ben, Gabriel, Judy
Rogers, Benjamin
    1795 - Benjamin's will was probated in Mecklenburg Co. Children: James
Rogers, David
    1779 Deed record
Rogers, George
    1793 - Account ledger of John Melchor's store.
Rogers, Hugh
    1781 - witnessed a deed, with Joseph Swann, from Francis & Margaret Johnston to Alexander Johnston, bk 12, pg 228.
    1790 - 153 00 - twp 17
    1800 - Mecklenburg County
Rogers/Rodgers, Hugh
    1778 - deed from John & Martha Rodgers for 82 acres on English Buffalo Creek, Test: William Balch, James Black, bk 10, pg 337.
    1779 - witnessed a deed, with Joseph Rodgers, from William Balch to John Carothers on Muddy Creek, bk 10, pg 372.
    1781 - witnessed a deed, with John Tanner, from John Houston to Archibald Gilmore, on a branch of Coddle Creek called Hugh Park's Creek, bk 10, pg 444.
    1783 - witnessed a deed, with Alexander McEwin, and John Fleming joining William White, and William Hays, bk 11, pg 290.
    1790 - 113 02 - twp 14
    1800 - Mecklenburg County
Rogers, James
    1790 - 303 05 - twp 14
    1793 - Account ledger of John Melchor's store.

Residents of Mecklenburg County, North Carolina 1762-1790

Rogers, James, Junr.
   1790 - 102 00 - twp 9
Rogers, Jane
   1782 - grant for 200 acres on Twelve Mile Creek joining Jacob Fremond, bk 12, pg 39.
Rogers, John
   1790 - 132 00 - twp 17
Rogers, John
   1790 - 132 00 - twp 20
Rogers, John & Martha
   1764
   1791 - Loose estate papers for John
   1791 - Loose estate papers for Martha
Rogers, John & Rebecca
   Wife - Rebecca
   Pension denied July 4, 1836 - no proof of service or marriage.
Rogers, John
   1785 - John's will was probated in Mecklenburg Co. Children: John N.
Rogers, John, Senr. & Anna
   1779 - named as adjoining land owner to William Hambilton, and William Ferril on the north side of Waxhaw Creek, bk 11, pg 67.
   1790 - 102 00 - twp 16
   John died in 1802.
   Children: William, Jean (? McRory)
Rogers, John & Martha
   John died before 1791.
Rogers, John & Margaret
   1778 - deed to Hugh Rodgers for 82 acres on both sides of English Buffaloe, Test: William Balch, James Black, bk 10, pg 337.
   1790 - 111 00 - twp 9
   1800 - Cabarrus County
   Wife - Margaret Russell, possibly a daughter of David & Jane Russell.
Rodgers, Joseph(2)
   1784 - named as adjoining land owner to John Patterson, Caleb and Martin Phifer, John Headright, and Robert Patterson on Longreen Branch of Coldwater Creek, bk 12, pg 181.
   1790 - 117 00 - twp 14
   Joseph died July 6, 1806 at the age 50.
Rogers, Joseph
   1764 - named as an adjoining land owner to James McClain, Christopher Landis and Michael Goodnight near Three Mile Creek, bk 10, pg 155.
   1775 -deed from Joseph Rodgers and David Russell to Michael Shaver for 144 acres, being the land they convey by virtue of a will executed by Margaret White, deceased, on the 6th day of July 1773, who was appointed

executrix of the estate of Moses White, her husband, as may appear of his will dated the 10th day of March 1766, Test: Thomas Mann, Samuel Patton, and John Pifer, bk 10, pg 185.
1779 - witnessed a deed, with Hugh Rodgers, from William Balch to John Carothers on Muddy Creek, bk 10, pg 372.
1783 - witnessed a deed, with Robert Morris, John McKnitt Alexander, and William Goth, from Robert & Elizabeth McCleary to David Russel on the head branch of Mallard Creek and Long Creek, bk 12, pg 257.
1790 - 134 03 - twp 9
1800 - Cabarrus County
Three Mile Creek.

Rogers, Joth
1778 Signer of 1778 Petition.

Rogers, Mathew
1790 - 134 00 - twp 17
1795 - Loose estate papers

Rogers, Moses
1790 - 113 00 - twp 9
1800 - Cabarrus County

Rogers, Nat
1790 - 103 00 - twp 10

Rogers, Robert
1776 - named as adjoining land owner to Charles Alexander, William S. Alexander, William White, and Isaac Sellers on the south side of Rocky River, bk 11, pg 89.

Rogers, Seth
1783 - deed from William & Jane Ross for 250 acres joining William White, and William Hays, Test: Alexander McEwin, Hugh Rodgers, and John Fleming, bk 11, pg 290.
1784 - witnessed a bill of sale, with William White, from Frederick Kerlock to John George William on English Buffellow Creek, bk 12, pg 564.
1785 - witnessed a bill of sale, with William White, from Frederick Kerlock to Rachel Williams, bk 12, pg 557.
1790 - 131 00 - twp 9
1800 - Cabarrus County

Rodgers, Thomas
1779 - mentioned as the previous land owner of a tract on Muddy Creek which he conveyed to William Balch, bk 10, pg 372.
1779 - witnessed a deed, with John Dickson, from Thomas Polk, attorney, to James Black on Anderson Creek, bk 10, pg 313.

Rogers, William
1790 - 243 00 - twp 17
1800 - Mecklenburg County
1793 - Account ledger of John Melchor's store.

Roland, John

1793 - Loose estate papers
Roland, Peter
   1778 - witnessed a deed, with John Wilson and William Smith, from Aaron & Fannie McWhorter to John Smith on the west side of Twelve Mile Creek, bk 10, pg 6.
Rondles, Hugh & Elizabeth
   1779 - deed from John Garrison for 50 acres on a branch of Sugar Creek joining James Reed, and Alexander Mitchell, Test: Elijah Mitchell, Robert Robison, bk 11, pg 94.
   1782 - deed to David Crocket for 50 acres on a branch of Sugar Creek joining James Reed, and Alexander Mitchell, Test: Andrew Henderson, Edward Maloney
Rosberry, Benjamin
   1790 - 132 00 - twp 11
Ross, Adam
   1785 Wolf Meadow Branch of Coddle Creek.
Ross, Anthony
   1782 - witnessed a deed, with Robert Anderson, from Isaac & Rebekah Sellars on the north side of Rockey River, bk 11, pg 231.
   1785 - witnessed a deed, with Henry Short, from James Wilson to Martha Moffitte on Coddle Creek, bk 12, pg 558.
   1789 - Anthony's will was probated in Mecklenburg Co.
   1790 - Loose estate papers
   Children: John, Jean
Ross, Arthur Brown
   Mentioned in the estate papers of Nicholson Ross 1774.
Ross, Francis
   1779 - named as an adjoining land owner to John Barnet and Martha McNeal on Sugar Creek at the Wagon Road, bk 10, pg 526.
   1780 - witnessed a deed, with William Scott, from John Driskell to James Carrothers on Caldwell Creek, bk 11, pg 54.
   1780 Sugar Creek
   1790 - 252 00 - twp 9
   1800 - Cabarrus County
   Francis died before 1822.
Ross, George
   1783 - witnessed a deed, with William and Ezekiel Alexander, from Isaac Alexander to William Rowan on Mallard Creek, bk 11, pg 284.
   1785 - witnessed a deed, with Joseph Graham, from James & Elizabeth Barr to James McKnight of Rowan Co., on Rockey River, bk 12, pgs 559 & 574-B.
   1790 - 121 00 - twp 8
   1800 - Cabarrus County
Ross, George
   1783, 1785,
   1790 - 203 00 - twp 4

Children: Jane
Ross, Isaac M.(5)
　　Isaac was born March 1, 1708, died Feb 13, 1760.
　　M. Ross, wife of Isaac was born June 30, 1722, died May 20, 1766.
Ross, Isaac
　　Mentioned in the estate papers of Nicholson Ross 1774.
Ross, James
　　1782 - Loose estate papers
Ross, James & Jean
　　1777 - witnessed a deed, with Joseph Shinn, from George & Margaret Cagle on Dutch Buffalo Creek, bk 12, pg 373.
　　1782 - named as adjoining land owner to Mathias Mitchel, and Jacob Frank on Little Coldwater Creek, bk 12, pg 144.
　　1782 - witnessed a deed from Staphel & Catron Goodman to Jacob Goodman on Dutch Buffalo Creek, bk 12, pg 346.
　　1783 - witnessed a deed, with Joseph Shinn, and Robert Patterson, from William & Elizabeth Ross to Christian Barbrick on Coldwater Creek, bk 12, pg 360.
　　1784 - deed from William Penny for 100 acres on the west side of Buffaloe Creek, Test: Samuel Moarton, John Moarton, bk 12, pg 339.
Ross, James
　　1779 - bond between James Ross and James Carruth for 593 acres where James Ross lives on Reedy Creek, to be peaceably turned over by James Ross by Oct 6, 1779, Test: Adam Alexander, bk 11, pg 108.
　　1779 - deed from Evan & Susannah Shelby for 227 acres on Caldwell's Beaver Dam Creek, a branch of Rockey River, Test: James Stafford, James Stafford, Jr., bk 12, pg 211.
　　1783 - witnessed a deed, with Joseph Shinn, and Robert Patterson, from William & Elizabeth Ross to Christian Barbrick on Coldwater Creek, bk 12, pg 360.
　　1790 - 100 01 - twp 13
Ross, John
　　1783 - named as adjoining land owner to Nicholas Walter, Nicholas Coon, Paul Walters, and Mathias Mitchel on a branch of Coldwater Creek, bk 12, pg 126.
Ross, Joseph
　　1779 - deed from Henry Shute for 300 acres on the north side of Rocky River, Test: Robert Harris, Robert Anderson, bk 10, pg 354.
　　1790 - 112 02 - twp 8
　　1800 - Cabarrus County
Ross, Nicholson
　　1766 - listed in the militia company of Capt. Adam Alexander of Clear Creek.
　　1767 - Nicholson's will was probated in Mecklenburg Co.
　　1774 - Loose estate papers
　　Children: Hannah, James, Elizabeth

Ross, Peter
   1784 - named as adjoining land owner to Jacob Dean,
   Jacob Faget, Michael Fogleman, and Charles Barnheart, on
   Hamby's Run, bk 12, pg 137.
Ross, William & Jean/Jane
   1778 - Signer of 1778 Petition
   1783 - deed to Seth Rodgers for 250 acres joining
   William White, and William Hays, Test: Alexander McEwin,
   Hugh Rodgers, and John Fleming, bk 11, pg 290.
   1790 - 143 00 - twp 8
Ross, William & Elizabeth
   1780 - deed from William Penny for 327 acres on Coddle
   Creek, Test: Alexander McEwen, John Houston, John
   Grimes, bk 11, pg 111.
   1782 - grant for 250 acres on the south side of English
   Buffalow Creek joining William Hays, bk 12, pg 51.
   1783 - deed to Christian Barbrick for 300 acres on
   Coldwater Creek joining John McCoy, and John Neichler,
   Test: Joseph Shinn, Robert Patterson, and James Ross, bk
   12, pg 360.
   1784 - deed from Moses & Elizabeth Shelby for 30 acres
   on Clear Creek, Test: Thomas and John Shelby, bk 12, pgs
   276 & 295.
   1790 - 325 03 - twp 13
Routh, Edward
   1790 - 101 00 - twp 15
Row, James
   1778 - witnessed a deed, with James Bayly, from Mathew
   Tate to Adam Tate, both of Donegal township in Lancaster
   Co., PA on Rocky River, bk 12, pg 413.
Rowan, Henry
   1790 - 102 00 - twp 17
Rowan, William
   1783 - deed from Isaac Alexander for 106 acres on
   Mallard Creek, Test: William and Ezekiel Alexander,
   George Ross, bk 11, pg 284.
Rowland, Augustus
   1793 - Account ledger of John Melchor's store.
Rowland, Austin
   1793 - Account ledger of John Melchor's store.
Rowland, James
   1793 - Account ledger of John Melchor's store.
Rowland, Jared
   1793 - Account ledger of John Melchor's store. (widow)
Rowland, Joel
   1793 - Account ledger of John Melchor's store.
Rowland, Robert
   1793 - Account ledger of John Melchor's store.
Rowland, Thomas
   1793 - Account ledger of John Melchor's store.
Ruddy, Thomas
   Mentioned in the estate papers of Nicholson Ross 1774.

Rudisill, Philip
    1764 - Philip's will was probated in Mecklenburg Co.
    Children: Mary, Michael, Elizabeth
Rumage, George
    1793 - Account ledger of John Melchor's store.
Rush, Jesse
    1793 - Account ledger of John Melchor's store.
Russell, David & Jane(6)
    1767
    1775 -deed from Joseph Rodgers and David Russell to
    Michael Shaver for 144 acres, being the land they convey
    by virtue of a will executed by Margaret White,
    deceased, on the 6th day of July 1773, who was appointed
    executrix of the estate of Moses White, her husband, as
    may appear of his will dated the 10th day of March 1766,
    Test: Thomas Mann, Samuel Patton, and John Pifer, bk 10,
    pg 185.
    1783 - deed from Robert & Elizabeth McCleary for 200
    acres on the head branch of Mallard Creek and Long
    Creek, conveyed to Robert in 1771, Test: Robert Morris,
    John McKnitt Alexander, William Goth, Joseph Rodgers, bk
    12, pg 257.
    Bondsman for Margaret Russell and John Rogers in 1789.
    1790 - 126 03 - twp 6
    David died 1802, buried in Hopewell Church Cemetery.
    1802 - Loose estate papers
    Children: Isabel, Mary(George Campbell), Elizabeth,
    Martha, Jinsey/Sinthe(Samuel McCracken), Margaret
    (Zaccheus Wilson), David, Matthew.
Russell, David & Elizabeth Morrison(5)
    south side of Clear Creek and both sides of Goose Creek.
    1790 - 121 01 - twp 9
    1800 - Cabarrus County
    Wife - Elizabeth Morrison, dau of James and Jennett
    Morrison.
    Children: James Semianes (Margaret Gingles), Robert
    (Mary Morrison), Jenny (Noah Corzine), Jane (James
    Tucker), Elizabeth (Samuel Holbrook), Catherine (Samuel
    G. White), David Morrison (Elizabeth Purviance), Mary
    Ann (George Corzine), William G. (Margaret Teresa
    Davis), Rachel (William Lee Gingles)
    David died Jan 29, 1831.
    Son of James & Jane Carson Russell.
Russell, James & Susannah
    1780 - named as adjoining land owner to Robert
    Archibald, and John Mann on the Half Meadow Branch, a
    branch of Coddle Creek, bk 12, pg 11.
    1790 - 113 00 - twp 5
    1800 - Cabarrus County
    Children: Joseph (Hannah Fipps), Levi (Sarah Fipps),
    Ellen (Thomas Littleton), Celia (2 sons, 3 dau)
    1790 - Loose estate papers

One of the James' was a signer of the 1778 Petition.
Russell, James & Jane Carson(5)
    1779 - witnessed a deed, with Walter Karr, from William
& Elizabeth McWhorter to John Means for a tract between
English Buffalo Creek and Coddle Creek, bk 12, pg 238.
    1782 - grant for 199 acres on a draft of the three mill
branches, joining Michael Winecoff, James White, George
Masters, and William Erwin, bk 12, pg 86.
    1782 - named as adjoining land owner to Mitchael
Winecoff, William Irwin, and George Conder on Three Mile
Branch, bk 12, pg 113.
    1782 - grant for 292 acres joining Benjamin Patton, bk
12, pg 88.
    1785 - deed from Robert Russel, Sr. for 306 acres on the
west side of Buffelow Creek, joining David Purviance,
and Alexander Ferguson, Test: William Russel, Patrick
Hays, bk 12, pg 445.
    1790 - 205 07 - twp 10
    1800 - Cabarrus County
    Wife - Jane Carson, dau of Robert and Rachel Carson of
Chester Co., PA.
    Children: Robert (Mary Morrison), John (Mary Ferguson),
Rachel (Patrick C. Hays), Catherine D. (William
Morrison), David M. (Elizabeth Morrison), Jane (John
G.L. Huie), William (Sarah McRee), Eleanor (John
Taggert), Mary (Matthew Russell), Ann (James Miller)
    James was the son of Robert Russell, a signer of the
petition to pardon the Cabarrus Black Boys in 1775.
    James died Feb 25, 1799.
Russell, James
    1790 - 101 03 - twp 13
    Wife - Nancy ?
    1800 - Cabarrus County
    Children: 5 daughters, 1 son
Russell, John & Mary(Ferguson)
    1782 - grant for 64 acres on Coddle Creek joining Hugh
Caruthers, bk 12, pg 85.
    1782 - grant for 90 acres on Coddle Creek joining Hugh
Caruthers, bk 12, pg 83
    1790 - 135 00 - twp 10
    1800 - Cabarrus County
    John died 1819.
    Children: James Edward, Alexander Ferguson, Polly
(Josiah Carlock Shinn), Jane (Morvil Suggs), Zachariah,
others, but names unknown.
    Son of James and Jane Carson Russell.
Russell, John
    1765 -
    1767 - Gilkey's Creek of Thicketty Creek. This land is
in what is present day South Carolina.
    1785 - John's will was recorded in Mecklenburg County.
    Children: James, Margaret, Eleanor, Joseph

John was a signer of the petition to pardon the Cabarrus
Black Boys in 1775.
1790 - Loose estate papers
Russell, Matthew & Jane McIntire
   1771 -
   Wife - Jane McIntire, dau of James McIntire.
   Children:
Russell, Robert & Mary Morrison(5)
   1790 - 133 00 - twp 10
   Robert died Jan 20, 1791.
   1800 - Cabarrus County (widow)
   Son of James and Jane Carson Russell.
   Mary was the daughter of James and Jennett Morrison.
   Children: Jean Townsend, James, Elizabeth Russell,
   William Allison, John(died before 1800), Mary Huie.
   Mary was the mother of two illegitimate children by
   Archibald McCurdy. Zacheus and Stewart McCurdy. (See
   records of the Pleas and Quarter Sessions)
Russell, Robert
   1764
   1776
   1784 - grant for 306 acres on the west side of Buffalow
   Creek, joining James Russell, bk 12, pg 116.
   1785 - deed to James Russell for 306 acres on Buffelow
   Creek, joining David Purviance, and Alexander Ferguson,
   Test: William Russel, Patrick Hays, bk 12, pg 445.
   Robert may have moved to Abbeville Co., SC before 1790.
   Children: James, William, Eleanor, Robert.
Russell, William & Jeanette Roberson
   1764
   1785 - witnessed a deed, with Patrick Hays, from Robert
   Russel, Sr. to James Russel on Buffelow Creek, bk 12, pg
   445.
   William moved to Abbeville Co., SC before 1790.
   Son of Robert Russell
Russell, William & Sarah McRee(5)
   William died Feb 13, 1799 at the age of 27.
   Son of James and Jane Carson Russell.
   One son, William James Russell, who became a doctor,
   educated in Cabarrus Co., and Spartanburg Co., SC. Later
   lived in GA.
   Sarah remarried to John Alexander of SC.
Rutherford, Griffith
   1754 - mentioned as previous land owner in a 1781 deed
   from Andrew McCorkle to John Wilson, bk 12, pg 274.
   1773
   1774 - witnessed a deed, with Alexander Martin, from
   Mary Conway and Catharine Hoiy to Mathew Lock on Buffalo
   Creek, bk 10, pg 144.
   1777 - witnessed a deed, with Will Alexander, and James
   Rutherford, from Mathew Lock to Francis Lock on Buffelow
   Creek, bk 12, pg 250.

1777 - deed to Blench Lock for 190 acres on the ridge between Buffelow and Coddle Creek, joining Caleb Phifer, Test: James Rutherford, Will Alexander, and William Sharpe, bk 12, pg 252.
1778 - named as an adjoining land owner to William Haggins and William Givens on McCorkle's Branch of Twelve Mile Creek, bk 10, pg 49.

Rutherford, James
1777 - witnessed a deed, with Will Alexander, and Griffith Rutherford, from Mathew Lock to Francis Lock on Buffelow Creek, bk 12, pg 250.

Rutledge, George
George died before 1779

Ryan/Reyen, Elijah
Elijah died in 1789. No heirs were named in his will and he died on a trip to SC.

Ryener, William
1775 - named as a previous land owner on Dutch Buffalo Creek, bk 10, pg 26.

Sadler, Henry & Ann
1779 - deed on Mallard Creek to John McCandless, near Andrew Elliott and John Disart, witness: John Alexander, bk 12, pg 614.
1786 - Loose estate papers

Safrit, Leonard
1766 - Loose estate papers

Salf/Self, Jacob
1779 - deed from Michael Ligget for 108 acres on Clear Creek, Test: Samuel Martin, Adam Alexander, bk 10, pg 341.

Sammon, William
1766 - listed in the militia company of Capt. Adam Alexander of Clear Creek.

Sample, John
1779
1782 - grant for 38 acres on Sugar Creek, joining William Elliott, bk 12, pg 189.
1786 - Loose estate papers

Sample, Joseph
1778 - named as as adjoining land owner to William Holland, Andrew Stinson, and William Black on McCalpin's Creek, bk 10, 378.

Sample, Joseph
1761 - named as deceased in a deed from John M.L. Alexander and Henry Person to John Flenikin on McCalpin's Creek, bk 10, pg 392.
Children: Jean (Henry Person)
Joseph died before July 1761.

Sample, Joseph
1773 - Loose estate papers

Sample, Samuel
1790 - 213 00 - twp 4

Sample, William & Esther
　1769 - William's will was probated in Mecklenburg Co.
　1770 - Loose estate papers
　Children: William, John, Joseph, Mary Alexander, Esther
Sample, William
　1790 - Loose estate papers
Sawyer, Hannah (2)
　Hannah died Dec 18, 1785 at age 26.
Sawyers, James W. (2)
　1778 - named as an adjoining land owner to Moses Steel, William and James McCafferty, William Wilson, and Alexander Starret on Sugar Creek, bk 10, pg 20.
　1780 - deed to John Farris for 400 acres on Sugar Creek joining Moses Steel, Test: Moses Swann, David Hayns, bk 11, pg 122.
　Children: David, Benjamin, James, Mary
　James died 1784 at the age of 46.
Sawyer, William
　1774 Sugar Creek. Of Lancaster Co., PA in 1774.
Saxer, Gasper
　1783 - named as adjoining land owner to John Michael & Margaret Clonts, Christian Goodman, and Michael Christman on a branch of Dutch Buffalow Creek, bk 12, pg 293.
Scales, John
　1790 - 000 10 - twp 9
　1800 - Cabarrus County
Scartauk, Frederick
　1782 - grant for 96 acres on English Buffalow Creek, joining Martin Phifer, Sr., bk 12, pg 632.
Scholes, Robert
　1778 - Loose estate papers
Schwar, Gotlieb
　Gotlieb was born Nov 8, 1722, died Sept 26, 1794, buried in St John's Evangelical Lutheran Church Cemetery.
Sconnel/Scannell, John & Mary
　1786 - deed to Rachel Sconnel for 71 acres in consideration of her nursing and care of them during both of their natural lives, bond given to Hugh Parks and Hezekiah Alexander in trust for the wards, Test: Thomas Allison, George M. McWherter, bk 12, pg 606.
　1790 - 101 00 - twp 9
　Children: Rachel
Sconnell, Rachel
　1786 - deed from John & Mary Sconnel for 71 acres adjoining William Wallace, bk 12, pg 606.
Scott, Abraham
　1767 - Militia, Mecklenburgh Regiment (Lieutenant)
Scott, Alexander & Mary
　1790 - 124 00 - twp 13
　1800 - Cabarrus County
　Alexander died Apr 10, 1837, age 70

Mary died Nov 11, 1836, age 64, both buried in Blackstock Cemetery.

Scott, Francis
   1792 - Loose estate papers

Scott, George
   1778 - witnessed a deed, with Will Polk, from Thomas Polk to Ezekiel Polk for Lot No. 1 in Charlotte, bk 10, pg 80.

Scott, James
   1771 - James' will was probated in Mecklenburg Co., his will mentions three nephews.
   1772 - Loose estate papers

Scott, James
   1770
   1772 mentioned in the estate settlement of Wm. Sample.

Scott, James
   1778 - deed from James & Patrick Scott, of Tryon Co., to William McCleary for 200 acres at the mouth of Long Creek joining Joseph Harding, Test: William Richey, bk 10, pg 363.
   1778 - deed from James & Patrick Scott, of Tryon Co., to William McCleary for 80 acres joining John Smith, Test: William Richey, bk 10, pg 381.

Scott, James
   1778 - Signer 1778 Petition.
   1783 - grant for 200 acres on Three Mile Branch joining Hardie Conkrite, bk 12, pg 170.
   1790 - 154 00 - twp 10
   1800 - Cabarrus County

Scott, James
   1779 - deed from Benjamin & Susannah Alexander for 170 acres on Back Creek, Test: John Garrison, Thomas Alexander, bk 10, pg 151.
   1779 - grant for 100 acres on Back Creek, bk 10, pg 533.
   1790 - 202 00 - twp 13
   1800 - Cabarrus County

Scott, James
   1790 - 114 00 - twp 2

Scott, John
   1767 - Loose estate papers

Scott, John
   1767 - Militia, Mecklenburgh Regiment (Ensign)
   1799 - Loose estate papers

Scott, Joseph
   1779 - one of the executors of the estate of Robert McKinley who owned land on Paw Creek, bk 10, pg 322.
   1779 - deed from Joseph Scott & William McKinley to James Owens for 100 acres on Paw Creek, Test James Reed, John Green, Jr., bk 10, pg 322.
   Executor to the estate of Robert McKinley.

Scott, Joseph

1779 - deed to Stephen Alexander for 215 acres on the
south branch of Coddle Creek, Test: John Allison, Robert
Allison, bk 10, pg 407.

Scott, Maryann
Maryann died before 1765

Scott, Patrick
1778 - deed from James & Patrick Scott, of Tryon Co., to
William McCleary for 200 acres at the mouth of Long
Creek joining Joseph Harding, Test: William Richey, bk
10, pg 363.
1778 - deed from James & Patrick Scott, of Tryon Co., to
William McCleary for 80 acres joining John Smith, Test:
William Richey, bk 10, pg 381.

Scott, Robert
1777 - witnessed a deed to Joseph Wishart for lot 67 in
Charlotte, bk 11, pg 62.
1777 - deed from James Jack for lot 27 in Charlotte,
Test: James McCafferty, Hugh Pollock, bk 10, pg 281.
1778 - deed from William Givens for 143 acres on Six
Mile Creek joining James Dunn, Test: Hugh Pollock, John
Davies, bk 10, pg 279.
1779 - deed to James Houston for 150 acres on Six Mile
Creek in New Providence, joining Thomas Davis, Test:
William Elliott, Robert Abernathy, bk 10, pg 317.
1779 - deed to James Houston for 123 acres on Twelve
Mile Creek, Test: Robert Avernathy, William Ellis, bk
10, pg 333.
1779 - named as an adjoining land owner to John & Ruth
Disart, and Robert Craighead on Millard and Stoney
Creeks, bk 10, pg 398.
1783 - witnessed a deed, with John Houston, and David
Templeton, from William Penny to Robert Penny, on Mill's
Creek and Coddle Creek, bk 12, pg 259.
1784 - witnessed a bill of sale, with David Templeton,
from William Penny to Martin Phifer, Sr., bk 12, pg 241.
1784 - witnessed a deed, with George Rice and David
Mason, from Arthur Garrison to Richard Mason on Middle
Branch of Sugar Creek, bk 12, pg 313.

Scott, William, Esqr. & Dorothy
William was a signer of the petition to pardon the
Cabarrus Black Boys in 1775.
1774 - Mentioned in the estate papers of Nicholson Ross.
1776 - witnessed a deed, along with John White, from
Hezekiah James Batch and his wife, Martha, to James
Walker for 88 acres on the ridge between Buffalow Creek
and Caddle's Creek, bk 10, pg 221.
1779 - witnessed a deed, with Zacheus Wilson, from Rev.
Robert Archibald to William & Elizabeth McWhirter, bk
11, pg 37.
1780 - witnessed a deed, with Francis Ross, from John
Driskell to James Carrothers on Caldwell Creek, bk 11,
pg 54.

Residents of Mecklenburg County, North Carolina 1762-1790

1780 - witnessed a deed, with James Meek, from William & Sarah Means to Moses Meek on the head branches of Rockey River in the Welch Tract, bk 11, pg 72.
1782 - grant for 140 acres on Buffalow Creek joining David Purvine, John Rodgers, James Walker, and Hugh Caruthers, bk 12, pg 71.
1790 - 302 01 - twp 13
Scroft, Jacob
    1783 - named as adjoining land owner to William Haggins, James Houston, James Potts, and William King on Back Creek, otherwise the Six Mile Branch of Twelve Mile Creek, bk 12, pg 290.
Seah, Jacob
    1780 Little Coldwater Creek.
Seals, Francis
    1792 - Loose estate papers
Searing, Henry
    1782 - witnessed deeds, with Edward Hunter, from John Moore to Samuel Martin, and to John Moore from the commissioners of Charlotte, for lots in Charlotte, bk 11, pgs 185, 214, and 217.
    1782 - witnessed a deed, with Edward Hunter, from John Moor to Duncan Ochiltree for lots 145 & 153 in Charlotte, bk 11, pg 202.
    1782 - witnessed a deed, with Edward Hunter, from Duncan Ochiltree, Samuel Martin, Adlai Osburn, and William Polk for 2 tracts containing 150 acres and 85 acres on Sugar Creek, bk 11, pg 204.
    1782 - witnessed a deed, with Edward Hunter, from John Moore, of the town of Charlotte, to William Polk, of the same place, on Sugar Creek joining Mary McKee and Thomas Polk, bk 11, pg 207.
Seed, Joseph
    1784 - witnessed a deed, with Robert Allison, from Adam Todd to William Todd on the head waters of Paw Creek, bk 12, pg 503.
Seeres, Jacob
    1779 - deed from Hugh & Elizabeth Cry for 270 acres, Test: John McCorkle, John Foster, bk 11, pg 96.
Secrist, Jacob
    1790 - 242 00 - twp 16
    1800 - Mecklenburg County
Secrist, John
    1790 - 103 00 - twp 16
Secrist, Michael & Libby
    1790 - 123 02 - twp 16
    Wife - Libby McCall, daughter of Francis McCall
    1795 - Loose estate papers
Seed, Joseph
    1784
Seferit, Barnhart
    1790 - 114 00 - twp 11

1800 - Cabarrus County
Seferit, Charles
    1790 - 204 00 - twp 11
    1794 - Account ledger of John Melchor's store.
    1800 - Cabarrus County
Self, David
    1793 - Account ledger of John Melchor's store.
Self, Elijah
    1793 - Account ledger of John Melchor's store.
Self, Isaac
    1793 - Account ledger of John Melchor's store.
Self, Jacob
    1780 - witnessed a deed, with William Haynes, from Linard & Ann Green to Samuel Bonds on Rockey River, bk 11, pg 9.
    1781 - deed from William Hayns for 70 acres, Test: William Mitchel, John Allison, bk 11, pg 93.
    1783 - deed from Oliver Wilie for 12 acres on Clear Creek, Test: Adam Alexander, Evan Alexander, Isack Alexander, bk 12, pg 214.
    1785 - deed to Hendry Foard for 78 acres on Clear Creek, Test: George Black, Thomas Morrow, bk 12, pg 513.
    1790 - 232 00 - twp 14
    1800 - Cabarrus County
Self, Joseph
    1781 - witnessed a deed, with John Allison, from William Hayns to William Mitchell on Muddy Creek, bk 11, pg 95.
Self, Prestley
    1793 - Account ledger of John Melchor's store.
Sell, Peter
    1780 - deed from Martin Fifer/Phifer for 190 acres on Little Coldwater Creek joining Jacob Seah, Test: Jason Frissel, Nicholas Coleman, bk 11, pg 74.
    1790 - 103 00 - twp 12
Sell, Phillip
    1790 - 212 00 - twp 12
    1793 - Account ledger of John Melchor's store.
Sellars, Isaac & Rebecca
    1772 - mentioned in a 1782 deed from Charles Alexander to William S. Alexander as the previous owner of a tract on the south side of Rockey River originally granted to William White, bk 11, pg 89.
    1774 - deed to John Davis for 50 acres on the south side of Rockey River, formerly granted to William White in 1752, Test: Hugh Carothers, James Kile, bk 10, pg 188.
    1779 - deed from Henry & Mary Shute for 165 acres on the north side of Rockey River joining Joseph Ross, Test: John Finly, John Adam Miller, bk 11, pg 226.
    1782 - deed to John Adam Miller for 165 acres on the north side of Rockey River joining Joseph Ross, Test: Robert Anderson, Anthony Ross, bk 11, pg 231.
Selwyn, George Augustus

1767 -
1776 - named as a previous owner of a tract belonging to Elias & Agnes Alexander, bk 10, pg 11.
1777 - named as the previous owner of a tract on McCalpin's Creek known as Lofton's Bottom, bk 10, pg 248.
1778 - named as an adjoining land owner to William & Mary Black, and Thomas Black, bk 10, pg 362.

Selwyn/Selvyn, John
1745 - mentioned in a deed from John & Ann Johnston to John Smith as the previous land owner of a tract on McCalpin's Creek known as Lofton's Bottom, bk 10, pg 390.
1777 - mentioned in a deed from Arthur & Hannah Starr to John Johnston on McCalpin's Creek, bk 10, pg 248.
Children: George Augustus

Semions, John
1790 - 116 00 - twp 11

Sensill, Henry
1780 - witnessed a deed, with Jason Frissell, from Hance & Mary Justice to Samuel Sensill on the east side of Cuflon Creek joining John Phifer, John Baker, John Armstrong, William Houston, and James McDowell, bk 11, pg 4.

Sensill, Samuel
1780 -
1782 - grant for 41 acres on English Buffalow Creek joining John Colebrook/Holdbrook, John Baker, and Hane/Hance & Mary Justice, bk 12, pg 65.

Setsinger, John
1783 - grant for 270 acres on Coldwater and Buffalow Creek, joining John Weyle, George Crozine, Alexander Ferguson, James Morrison, and John Shaver, bk 12, pg 150.

Sewell, Samuel
1784 - named as adjoining land owner to John Willis, Absalom Baker, and Martin Phifer on Buffalow Creek, bk 12, pg 449.

Sexton, James
1783 - mentioned as a previous land owner in a 1783 deed from George Harris to William Reed on Crooked Creek, bk 12, pg 522.

Seyte, Christian
1793 - Account ledger of John Melchor's store.

Shafer, Frederick
1784 - witnessed a deed, with Tunas Hood, from Tunas Hogland to Tunas Shafer on McCalpin Creek, bk 12, pg 496.

Shafer, Tunas
1784 - deed from Tunas Hogland for 36 acres on McCalpin's Creek, Test: Tunas Hood, Frederick Shafer, bk 12, pg 496.

Shandy, Jacob
    1799 - Loose estate papers
Shanepaker, Larence
    1784 - deed from David & Hannah Griffith for 200 acres
    on the head of Polecat Branch of Linchous Creek, Test:
    John Belk, James Doster, bk 12, pg 270.
Shank, Manas
    1790 - 141 00 - twp 10
Shankle, John
    1793 - Account ledger of John Melchor's store.
Shanks, James
    1790 - 116 04 - twp 19
    1800 - Mecklenburg County
Shannon, James
    1790 - 111 00 - twp 17
    1800 - Mecklenburg County
    1807 - Loose estate papers
Shannon, John
    1781 - witnessed a deed, with Samuel Bigham, from Samuel
    Bigham to James McKee on Steel Creek, bk 11, pg 252.
Sharpe, Edward, Junr.
    1790 - 102 00 - twp 20
Sharpe, Edward, Senr.
    1784 between Coddle Creek and Rockey River.
    1790 - 102 00 - twp 20
    1791 - Loose estate papers
Sharpe/Sharpie, Ezekel
    1790 - 207 03 - twp 5
    1800 - Cabarrus County
Sharpe, James
    1779 - named as an adjoining land owner to John Sharpe
    and Robert Arthur on a branch of Sugar Creek, bk 10, pg
    494.
    1790 - 225 00 - twp 20
    1800 - Mecklenburg County
Sharpe, James
    1781 - witnessed a deed, along with William McCleary,
    from Thomas Henry to James Simson on Clemmes branch in
    New Providence, bk 10, pg 500.
    1790 - 111 03 - twp 6
    1800 - Mecklenburg County
    Wife - daughter of Roger Cunningham
Sharpe, John
    1779 - grant for 50 acres on Sugar Creek joining James
    Sharpe and Robert Arthur, bk 10, pg 494.
    1790 - 122 00 - twp 19
    1800 - Mecklenburg County
Sharpe, John
    1790 - 532 01 - twp 6
    Wife - daughter of Roger Cunningham
Sharp, Joseph

1785 - witnessed a deed, with David Wilson, from Ephraim
Farr to John and William Hamilton on Rockey River, bk
12, pg 531.
Sharpe, Thomas
   1792 - Loose estate papers
Sharp, William
   1777 - witnessed a deed, with James Rutherford, and Will
   Alexander, from Griffith Rutherford to Blench Lock on
   Buffelow and Coddle Creek, bk 12, pg 252.
   1785 - deed from William McCree to John Brevard, John
   Dickey, and William Sharp of Rowan Co., executors of
   Brigadier William Davidson, deceased, on the branches of
   Davidson and Back Creek in Rowan Co., bk 12, pg 574.
Sharpley, Moses
   1785 - witnessed a deed, with Robert Walker, and John
   Stinson, from William Stinson to John Welch on Sugar
   Creek, bk 12, pg 455.
   1785 - Loose estate papers
Shaver, Fredrick
   1783 - grant for 21 acres on McCalpin's Creek joining
   the widow Buckalew, bk 12, pg 106.
   1790 - 254 01 - twp 15
   1800 - Mecklenburg County
Shaver, John
   1783 - named as adjoining land owner to John Setsinger,
   John Weyle, George Crozine, Jr., Alexander Ferguson, and
   James Morrison on Coldwater and Buffalow Creeks, bk 12,
   pg 150.
   1784 - grant for 150 acres on Coldwater and Buffalow
   Creek joining Joshua Hadley, bk 12, pg 186.
Shaver, Michael
   1775 - deed from Joseph Rodgers and David Russell for
   144 acres, Test: Thomas Mann, Samuel Patton, John Pifer,
   bk 10, pg 188.
   1778 - Signer of 1778 Petition.
Shelby, Evan & Susannah
   1775 - witnessed deed of gift, with James Harris, Thomas
   Shelby, and Alexander Wiley, from Moses Shelby to his
   granddaughter, Mary Carruthers, bk 11, pg 61.
   1779 - deed to James Ross for 227 acres on Caldwell's
   Beaver Dam branch of Rockey River, Test: James Stafford,
   James Stafford, Jr., bk 12, pg 211.
   1790 - 116 04 twp 5
   1800 - Mecklenburg County
   Son of Moses & Isabel Shelby.
Shelby, John
   1783 - witnessed a deed, with John Ramsey, from Ambrose
   & Magdalen Walker to John McCain, on Cane Creek, bk 12,
   pg 230.
   1784 - witnessed a deed, with Thomas Shelby, from Moses
   & Elizabeth Shelby to William Ross on Clear Creek, bk
   12, pgs 276 & 295.

Son of Moses & Isabel Shelby.
Shelby, Moses & Elizabeth
   1774 - Mentioned in the estate papers of Nicholson Ross.
   1775 - deed of gift to his granddaughter, Mary Carruthers, for one negro wench named Ann, Test: Evan and Thomas Shelby, James Harris, Alexander Wiley, bk 11, pg 61.
   1779 - deed from Thomas Polk, attorney for David Oliphant, for 30 acres on Clear Creek, Test: Samuel Smith, Will Lusk, bk 10, pg 555.
   1784 - deed to William Ross for 30 acres on Clear Creek, Test: Thomas and John Shelby, bk 12, pgs 276 & 295. Moses was a signer of the petition to pardon the Cabarrus Black Boys in 1775.
   Son of Moses & Isabel Shelby
Shelby, Moses & Isabel
   1776 - Moses' will was probated in Mecklenburg Co.
   1776 - Loose estate papers
   Children: Moses, John, Thomas, Evan, William, Eleanor
Shelby, Reese
   1766 - listed in the militia company of Capt. Adam Alexander of Clear Creek.
   1774 - witnessed a deed, with Henry Hargritt from John & Mary Cole to John Ashley on Richardson's Creek, bk 10, pg 178.
   1775 -
   1782 - grant for 127 acres on Richardson's Creek (at NC/SC border) joining John Thompson, bk 12, pg 7.
   1782 - greant for 100 acres on a branch of Richardson's Creek, bk 12, pg 12.
   1783 - witnessed a deed, with Thomas Morrow, and Daniel Metheny, from Susana Daniel to Robert John on Muddy Creek, bk 12, pg 287.
Shelby, Robert
   1790 - 101 00 - twp 7
Shelby/Selby, Thomas, Capt. & Sarah
   1775 - witnessed deed of gift, with Evan Shelby, James Harris, and Alexander Wiley, from Moses Shelby to his granddaughter, Mary Carruthers, bk 11, pg 61.
   1776 - in Capt. Charles Polk's Light Horse Company.
   1784 - witnessed a deed, with John Shelby, from Moses & Elizabeth Shelby to William Ross on Clear Creek, bk 12, pgs 276 & 295.
   1790 - 113 06 twp 14
   Thomas died before 1800.
   Son of Moses & Isabel Shelby
Shelds, Robert (see Shields)
Shelhoas, John
   1790 - 102 00 - twp 10
   1800 - Cabarrus County
Shepperd, Edward
   1790 - 121 00 - twp 16

Residents of Mecklenburg County, North Carolina   321
1762-1790

Shepperd, James
    1790 - 113 00 - twp 16
Shepperd, John
    1775 - witnessed a deed, with George Henry Berger from
    Samuel Suther to Christian Goodman on Dutch Buffalow, bk
    10, pg 26.
    1790 - 112 00 - twp 16
Shephard, William & Jemiah
    1782 - deed to John Belk for 200 acres on Stroud's Fork
    of Lynch's Creek, Test: James and Britian Belk, bk 11,
    pg 131.
    1790 - 000 10 - twp 2
Shiddel, Moses
    1764 - witnessed a deed, with Martin Phifer, from James
    & Ruth McClain to Christopher Landis and Michael
    Goodnight for a tract on Three Mile Creek, bk 10, pg
    155.
Shields, David
    1790 - 000 10 - twp 1
    1800 - Mecklenburg County
Shields, John
    1786 - Loose estate papers
Shields/Shelds, Robert
    1805 - Loose estate papers
Shields, Thomas
    1769 - named in a 1779 deed from Henry Shute to Joseph
    Ross as the owner of a tract on Rockey River, bk 10, pg
    354.
    1779 - witnessed a deed, with John Smith, and Aron
    Alexander, from John Tool to David Alexander on the
    south side of the north branch of the Catawba River
    joining Samuel Coburn, and ? Leeper, bk 11, pg 173.
Shields, William
    1776 - in Capt. Charles Polk's Light Horse Company.
    1778 - witnessed a deed, with Samuel Crawford, from
    Robert & Hannah Craighead to John Long, on Long Creek,
    bk 10, pg 252.
    1779 - witnessed a deed from Joseph & Rachel Mitchell to
    Samuel Beaty on Rockwide Creek, bk 10, pg 449.
    1779 - grant for 114 acres on Mallard Creek joining
    Joseph Mitchell, George Reed, Benjamin Alexander, and
    Andrew Robison, bk 10, pg 501.
    1790 - 103 00 - twp 4
    1800 - Mecklenburg County
Shields, Martha
    1806 - Loose estate papers
Shifter, Charles
    1767 - Militia, Mecklenburgh Regiment (Ensign)
Shinn, Benjamin & Rebecca Carlock
    1790 - 155 01 - twp 10
    1800 - Cabarrus County
    1802 -

Shinn, Isaac
    1776 - Loose estate papers
Shinn/Shenn, Joseph & Jane Ross
    1777 - witnessed a deed, with John Nichler from Peter & Eve Delph to Jacob Missonheimer on the Lick Branch of Buffalow Creek, bk 10, pg 240.
    1777 - witnessed a deed, with Jason Frizell, from Adam & Cathey Moyar to Mathias Boston on Little Coldwater Creek, bk 10, pg 421.
    1777 - witnessed a deed, with James Ross, from George & Margaret Cagle to Michael Goodman on Dutch Buffelow Creek, bk 12, pg 373.
    1781 - witnessed a deed from George Owery and Nicolas Cress to Martin Owery on a branch of Dutch Buffalow Creek, bk 1, pg 97.
    1782 - witnessed a deed from Adam & Elinor Bowers to Martin Phifer, Sr. on Coldwater Creek, bk 11, pg 135.
    1782 - witnessed a deed from Jacob & Elizabeth Misnhimer to Abraham Plater on Bafilour/Buffalow Creek, bk 11, pg 146.
    1783 - deed from James Hewit for 300 acres on Three Mile Branch, joining Samuel Patton, Test: James Rodes, John Weigler, bk 12, pg 335.
    1783 - witnessed a deed, with M. Messenhimer, from Abraham & Susannah Pleeter to Jacob Messenhimer on Umberford's branch, bk 12, pg 341.
    1783 - witnessed a deed, with Robert Patterson, and James Ross, from William & Elizabeth Ross to Christian Barbrick on Coldwater Creek, bk 12, pg 360.
    1784 - grant for 50 acres on Little Coldwater Creek, joining Mathias Mitchel, bk 12, pg 129.
    1784 - witnessed a deed, with Jacob Criden, from John Willis to Absolom Baker on Buffelow Creek, bk 12, pg 449.
    1784 - witnessed a deed, with Jacob Crider, from Mathias & Sarah Bostian to Henry Farr on Coldwater Creek, bk 12, pg 459.
    1785 - witnessed a deed, with Samuel & Daniel Luther(Suther?), from John & Anna Bargar to Frederick Beck on Buffalow Creek, bk 12, pg 501.
    1790 - 335 06 - twp 10
    1800 - Cabarrus County
    Joseph died in April 1806.
Shinn, Samuel & Catherine
    Marriage bond March 25, 1793, Cabarrus County, bondsman Leonard Barberick.
    Wife - Catherine Barberick, daughter of Leonard Barberick.
    Samuel died before 1800.
Shive, Phillip
    1790 - 123 00 - 10
    1800 - Cabarrus County

Shmid, Jacob
   1764 - Loose estate papers
Sholty, Robert
   1778 - witnessed a deed, with George Green, from Adam &
   Anney Garrison to Henry Kent on Rockey River, bk 11, pg
   32.
Short, Abraham
   1781 - Abraham's will was probated in Mecklenburg Co.
   Children: William
Short, Henry
   1785 - witnessed a deed, with Anthony Ross, from James
   Wilson to Martha Moffitte on Coddle Creek, bk 12, pg
   558.
Short, James
   1778 - Signer of 1778 Petition.
Shuford, George & Rhoda
   1762 - George's will was probated in Mecklenburg Co.
Shuffert, George & Gertrude
   Children: Catherine (Michael Cline)
   Wife - Gertrude Hubener
Shute/Shue, Henry & Mary
   1779 - deed to Joseph Ross for 300 acres on Rockey
   River, Test: Robert Harris, Robert Anderson, bk 10, pg
   354.
   1779 - deed to Isaac Sellars for 165 acres on Rockey
   River joining Joseph Ross, Test: John Finly, John Adam
   Miller, bk 11, pg 226.
Shue, Henry & Catherine
   Children: John, Jacob, Isaac, Martin, Betsy, Susan,
   Catharine, Elizabeth (? Sides), Polly
Shue/Shoe, John
   1793 - Account ledger of John Melchor's store.
Sibley, John
   1790 - 123 00 - twp 17
   1800 - Mecklenburg County
Sides, Andrew
   1790 - 404 00 - twp 12
   1800 - Cabarrus County
Sides, Christian/Christopher & Mary
   1790 - 201 00 - twp 12
   Children: Mary (George M. Dry)
Sides, Henry
   1790 - 111 00 - twp 12
Sides, Michael
   1790 - 145 00 - twp 11
   1800 - Cabarrus County
Sigget/Liggett, Michael, Jr.
   1778 - deed to David Ore to 250 acres on Henley's Fork
   of Twelve Mile Creek joining Reeve's land, Test: Francis
   Bassett, Jacob Ormond, bk 10, pg 37.
Siler, Nicholas
   1776 - in Capt. Charles Polk's Light Horse Company.

Simeson, John, Capt.
    1790 - 111 00 - twp 19
    1800 - Mecklenburg County
Siminer, John
    1790 - 101 06 - twp 10
    1800 - Cabarrus County
Simmons, Thomas & Margaret(5)
    1790 - 135 00 - twp 5
    1800 - Mecklenburg County
    Thomas died in 1806 at the age of 61.
    Margaret died in 1826 at the age of 67.
    Children: George ? (5)
Simons, Thomas
    1805 - Loose estate papers
Simmond/Simmons, William
    1778 - deed to James McComb, of Tryon Co., for 210 acres
    known as the No. Two Tract, Test: Samuel McComb, William
    Wylie, bk 10, pg 335.
    1779 - deed from Francis & Elizabeth Miller for 120
    acres on the south branch of Caldwell's Creek, Test:
    Samuel Martin, James McGinty, bk 10, pg 351.
    1790 - 124 00 - twp 5
Simons, John
    1790 - 152 00 - twp 13
Simson, James
    1774 - witnessed a deed, with Patrick Jack, from Andrew
    Baxter to John Baxter for a tract beginning on the
    Indian line, bk 10, pg 153.
    1781 - deed from Thomas Henry for 150 acres on Clemmes
    branch in New Providence, Test: James Sharp, William
    McCleary, bk 10, pg 500.
Simpson, William & Agnes
    1790 - 132 00 - twp 14
    Agnes died Oct 7, 1802, age 46, buried in Blackstock
    Cemetery.
Sivert, William
    1785 - Loose estate papers
Skeringshire, John Brown
    1773 - witnessed a deed, with William Little, to George
    Nicholson for Lots 129 and 137 on the west side of Traid
    Street in Charlotte, bk 10, pg 54.
Skillenton, John
    1785 - Loose estate papers
Slaugh, Jacob
    1790 - 124 00 - twp 11
Slavey/Slaven, Robert
    1786 - deed to David Cuthbertson, Jr. for 252 acres on
    both sides of Crooked Creek, Test: Samuel Smith, John
    Cuthburtson, bk 12, pg 589.
Slitt/Stitt, William
    1790 - 252 00 - twp 19
    1800 - Mecklenburg County

Sloan, David
    1790 - 142 00 - twp 7
    1799 - Loose estate papers
Sloan, James & Jean
    1792 - Loose estate papers
    Children: Joseph, Mary, Rachel, John.
Sloan, James
    1790 - 113 00 - twp 5
    1809 - Loose estate papers
Sloan, James, Junr.
    1783 - witnessed a deed, with John Green, from Walter
    Carruth to Henry Vernor on Paw Creek, bk 12, pg 387.
    1790 - 123 01 - twp 1
    1796 - Loose estate papers
Sloan, James, Senr. & Frances Brown
    1790 - 112 00 - twp 5
    Children: William B., Nancy (Reuben Ervin), Thomas, Jane
    (Silas Ervin), Elizabeth (Aaron Dewest), Mary (James
    Farrell), Benjamin
    Sister: Jane Davis (resident of Ramah Congregation)
    James & Frances were married in the spring of 1787
    according to James' pension papers.
    Son Thomas moved to TN as well as James' parents, Jane
    and Elizabeth moved to Alabama.
    James was a close neighbor of Lewis Meek, the
    Christenberry's, William Brown, William Farrell.
    Pension denied July 7 1838 for proof of marriage, death
    of parties, and names of children.
    James died Feb 20, 1839
    Frances died Aug 15, 1843
Sloan, James
    1772 - James' will was probated in Mecklenburg Co.
    1772 - Loose estate papers
    Children: David, James, Agnes
Sloan, John & Jane
    1764 - named in a 1778 deed from John & Sarah Allen to
    William Eadger, as the previous owner of a tract on a
    branch of Long Creek, bk 10, pg 88.
    1784 - deed to Jesse Clark for 200 acres on a branch of
    Sugar Creek joining Isaac Williams, Robert Walker, James
    Tagart, and David Hayes, Test: Robert Irvin, John Hana,
    John Carruth, bk 12, pg 466.
    1790 - 113 00 - twp 1
    1800 - Mecklenburg County
Sloan, John & Asenath
    1781 - named as the previous owner of a tract on Clemmes
    Branch of Sugar Creek in New Providence, bk 10, pg 500.
    1790 - 113 00 - twp 7
    John died in 1826.
Sloan, John & Margaret Bigham(2)
    1778 - Long Creek
    1790 - 122 00 - twp 5

Signer of 1778 Petition.
John died June 1, 1809 at age 75.
Sloan, John
   1790 - 164 00 - twp 10
Sloan, Margaret(2)
   1769
   Margaret died Nov 22, 1769 at the age of 66.
Sloan, Robert
   1790 - 202 00 - twp 7
   1800 - Mecklenburg County
   Wife - daughter of James Curry
Sloan, Robert
   1781 - Loose estate papers
Sloan, Sarah
   1777 - Loose estate papers
Sloan, Robert
   Robert died before 1781
Sloan, Thomas
   1790 - 122 00 - twp 5
Slough, David
   David was a signer of the petition to pardon the Cabarrus Black Boys in 1775.
Slowgh/Slough, Martin
   1790 - 133 00 - twp 10
   1800 - Cabarrus County
Smart, Elijah/Elisha
   1790 - 212 09 - twp 2
   1796 - Loose estate papers
Smart, Francis
   1790 - 212 09 - twp 2
Smart, George & Susannah Barnett
   1790 - 201 04 - twp 2
   1800 - Mecklenburg County
Smart, Littleberry & Mida
   1790 - 100 02 - twp 2
   1800 - Mecklenburg County
   Wife - Mida Page
Smiley, Walter & Mary
   1783 - named as adjoining land owner to Joshua Hadley, and James Morrison on Buffalo Creek, bk 12, pg 94.
   1783 - grant for 185 acres on Buffalo Creek joining William Boyett, John Chamberlain, and George Townsend, bk 12, pg 118.
   1787 - Walter's will was probated in Mecklenburg Co.
   1788 - Loose estate papers
Smith, Barbara
   1793 - Account ledger of John Melchor's store.
Smith, David & Mary
   1779 - grant for 276 acres on Rockey River joining Andrew Burns, William Gardner, Robert Smith, and William Johnston, bk 10, pg 541.

1784 - deed to Samuel Killough for 126 acres on Rockey
River joining William Gardner, Test: James Stevenson,
Richard Smith, bk 12, pg 327.
1790 - 101 05 - twp 7
1800 - Mecklenburg County
Smith, David
    1784 - named as adjoining land owner to Joseph &
Margaret Fraser, Samuel Davis, Jr., and Joseph Maxwell
on Clark's Creek, bk 12, pg 470.
Smith, Elisha
    1784 - witnessed a deed, with Ezekiel Polk, from Robert
McCree to Samuel McCleary, bk 12, pg 435.
Smith, George
    1790 - 102 00 - twp 12
    1800 - Cabarrus County
Smith, Henry, Maj. & Mary Barbara
    1784 - named as adjoining land owner to George Tucker,
the widow Ciser, and Joseph Howel on Rockey River, bk
12, pg 174.
    1790 - 223 00 - twp 12
    1793 - Account ledger of John Melchor's store.
Children: Elizabeth (Valentine Faggart), Phillipine
Henry was born Dec 25, 1741, died Aug 5, 1855, buried in
St John's Evangelical Lutheran Church Cemetery.
Mary died July 31, 1827, buried in St John's Evangelical
Lutheran Church Cemetery.
Smith, Henry
    1790 - 223 00 - twp 12
    1800 - Cabarrus County
Smith, Jacob
    1763 - Loose estate papers
Smith, James
    1790 - 000 10 - twp 7
Smith, James
    1790 - 133 00 - twp 20
Smith, James
    1784 - grant for 28 acres on Coddle Creek and Rockey
River joining Dr. Nathaniel Alexander, John Alexander,
Jr., and John Alexander, Sr., bk 12, pg 149.
    1785 - witnessed a deed, with William Young, from John
Alexander to Abraham Alexander on Coddle Creek, bk 12,
pg 538.
    1790 - 112 00 - twp 5
    1800 - Cabarrus County
Smith, John
    1774 - John's will was probated in Mecklenburg Co.
    1774 - Loose estate papers
    Children: James, Margaret, Jane
Smith, John
    1782 - Loose estate papers
Smith, John
    1795 - Loose estate papers

Smith, John
    1803 - Loose estate papers
Smith, John
    1803 - Loose estate papers
Smith, John & Prudence
    1776 - in Capt. Charles Polk's Light Horse Company.
    1778 - deed from Aaron & Fannie McWhorter for 160 acres
    on the west side of Twelve Mile Creek, Test: John
    Wilson, Peter Roland, William Smith, bk 10, pg 16.
    1778 - witnessed a deed, with Samuel Fleniken and
    William Pickens, from William & Mary Black to Thomas
    Black, bk 10, pg 362.
    1779 - deed from John & Ann Johnston for 81 acres on
    McCalpin's Creek, known as Lofton's Bottom, Test:
    William Black, George Montgomery, bk 10, pg 390.
    1779 - grant for 48 acres on McCalpin's Creek beginning
    at John Johnston's line, bk 10, pg 528.
    1779 - deed to Andrew Neel for 160 acres on Twelve Mile
    Creek, Test: Thomas Harris, John Flenniken, bk 11, pg
    52.
    1779 - witnessed a deed, with Aron Alexander, Thomas
    Shields, from John Toole to David Alexander on the south
    side of the north branch of the Catawba River, bk 11, pg
    174.
    1784 - deed to John King for 48 acres on McCalpin's
    Creek known as Lofton's Bottom, Test: Robert & William
    Smith, bk 10, pg 280.
    1784 - deed to John King for 48 acres, and 100 acres on
    McCalpin's Creek joining Thomas Frohock, and James
    Osburn, Test: Robert and William Smith, bk 12, pgs 280 &
    297.
    1784 - deed from John, Samuel, David, and James
    Flenniken for 198 acres on the north side of McCalpin's
    Creek, joining Abraham Miller and James Bauy, Test:
    James Bays, John Kirkpatrick, bk 12, pg 587.
    1790 - 122 01 - twp 19
Smith, John
    1781 - witnessed a deed, with Robert Harris from
    Nathaniel & Jane Gilmore to Zacheus Wilson, bk 12, pg
    317.
    1790 - 113 00 - twp 20
    1800 - Mecklenburg County
Smith, John & Martha
    1778 - witnessed a deed from Andrew & Susannah Burns to
    Robert Smith, Jr. on Rockey River, bk 10, pg 82.
    1778 - named as an adjoining land owner to William
    McCleary, Test: William Richey, bk 10, pg 381.
    1790 - 121 01 - twp 10
    1800 - Cabarrus County
Smith, Joseph
    1803 - Loose estate papers
Smith, Peter

Residents of Mecklenburg County, North Carolina   1762-1790

1767
Smith, Richard
   1783 - witnessed a deed, with William Lock, from
   Nathaniel Alexander to Moses Meek, Jr., joining Joseph
   Mitchel on Stoney Creek, bk 12, pg 305.
   1784 - witnessed a deed, with James Stevenson, from
   David & Mary Smith to Samuel Killogh on Rockey River, bk
   12, pg 327.
Smith, Robert
   1775 - deed to Robert Smith, Jr. for 200 acres on the
   north side of Rockey River joining Charles Harris, Test:
   William and James Alexander, bk 12, pg 595.
   1779 - grant for 77 acres on the south side of South
   side of McCalpin's Creek, joining Hezekiah Alexander, bk
   10, pg 508.
   1784 - witnessed a deed, with William Smith, from John &
   Prudence Smith to John King on McCalpin's Creek, bk 12,
   pgs 280 & 297.
   1784 - witnessed a bill of sale, with Mathew Alexander,
   from William & John Gardner to Samuel Linton, bk 12, pg
   380.
Smith, Robert, Capt. & Sarah
   1765 - deed of Mortgage from Robert to Henry Eustace
   McCulloch for 218 acres on Rockey River, Test: Moses
   Alexander, John Frohock, bk 10, pg 160.
   1773 - Henry E. McCulloch acknowledged full satisfaction
   for the 1765 mortgage, Test: Robert Smith, Jr., James
   Brown, bk 10, pg 160.
   1773 - witnessed a deed from Benjamin Brown to John
   Lockhart, bk 10, pg 276.
   1778 - deed from Andrew & Susannah Burns for 172 acres
   on Rockey River joining William Gardner, and James
   Wallace, Test: John & Martha Smith, bk 10, pg 82.
   1779 - deed from Nathaniel Gilmore for 22 acres on
   Rockey River, Test: Edward Giles, bk 10, pg 374.
   1785 - highest bidder for a tract joining Mr.
   McCullough, formerly belonging to Robert Hogsheadd,
   Test: Sam Martin, bk 12, pg 523.
   1785 - witnessed a deed, with Isaac Wilson, from John
   Wilson to Dr. Thomas Donnell on Coddle Creek joining
   Charles Caldwell, and Joseph Campbell, bk 12, pg 533.
   1786 - deed for 270 acres on Buffelo and Coldwater
   Creeks, to satisfy a judgement against John Letsinger,
   bk 12, pg 616.
   1790 - 113 015 - twp 5
   1800 - Cabarrus County
   Children: Robert W.(Margaret   ?   )
   Robert was born 1746, died July 17, 1805, buried in
   Smith Family Cemetery, Cabarrus Co.
   Sarah was born 1733, died Oct 1813, buried in Smith
   Family Cemetery, Cabarrus Co.
Smith, Samuel & Agnes(son of Saml.)

1786 - witnessed a deed, with John Cuthburtson, from
Robert Slaven to David Cuthbertson, Jr. on Crooked
Creek, bk 12, pg 589.
1790 - 101 00 - twp 14
1800 - Mecklenburg County
Wife - Agnes McRaven

Smith, Samuel, Junr.
1779 - deeds from Thomas Polk, attorney for David
Oliphant, for 102 on Duck Creek, Test: Will Polk, John
Purser, bk 11, pgs 8 & 15.
1790 - 101 00 - twp 14
1800 - Mecklenburg County

Smith, Samuel, Senr.
1779 - witnessed a deed, with Will Lusk, from Thomas
Polk, attorney for David Oliphant, to Moses Shelby for
30 acres on Clear Creek, bk 10, pg 555.
1790 - 212 04 - twp 14

Smith, Thomas
Thomas was a signer of the petition to pardon the
Cabarrus Black Boys in 1775.
1779 - deed from Thomas Polk, attorney for David
Oliphant, for 45 acres on Duck Creek, Test: John Purser,
Will Polk, bk 11, pg 6.
1790 - 101 00 - twp 14
Thomas died before 1813

Smith, William
1784 - deed from John Ramsey for 150 acres on Four Mile
Creek joining Thomas Hames, and James Way, Test: Adam
Ormond, bk 12, pg 385.
William died before 1786

Smith, William & Catherine
1778 - witnessed a deed, with John Wilson and Peter
Roland, from Aaron & Fannie McWhorter to John Smith on
Twelve Mile Creek, bk 10, pg 16.
1775 - deed to Jonathan Buckaloe for 58 acres on
McCalpin's Creek, Test: John Ford, Zebulon Robinett, bk
10, pg 174.
1784 - witnessed a deed, with Robert Smith, from John &
Prudence Smith to John King on McCalpin's Creek, bk 12,
pgs 280 & 297.
1790 - 101 00 - twp 14
1795 - Loose estate papers
Mentioned in the estate settlement of Wm. Sample.

Smith, William
1786 - Loose estate papers

Smith, William
1808 - Loose estate papers

Smith, Willis
1784 - named as adjoining land owner to Titus and George
Laney on a branch of Richardson Creek, bk 12, pg 540.

Snell, Francis
1790 - 134 00 - twp 14

1794 - Loose estate papers
Snoddy, Andrew
1783 - deed to George Fleming for 205 acres on the east side of Coddle Creek, joining David Templeton, and David Houston, Test: George Knox, James Kirkpatrick, and John Houston, bk 12, pg 348. Andrew was of Rowan Co., in 1783.
Snoddy, John
1755 - named as the grantee of a tract on Coddle Creek in 1755, bk 12, pg 344.
Soatman, George
1783 - witnessed a deed, with John Leopard, from John Michael & Margaret Clonts to Christian Goodman on Dutch Buffalow Creek, bk 12, pg 293.
Soores, Jacob
1780 - grant for 50 acres on a branch of Twelve Mile Creek, bk 12, pg 15.
Sossaman, Daniel & Elizabeth
1793 - Account ledger of John Melchor's store.
Wife - Elizabeth Lippard, daughter of John & Catherine Lippard.
Sosseman/Seaceman, Henry
1783 - Henry's will was probated in Mecklenburg Co.
1783 - Loose estate papers
Children: Henry, Andrew, David, Jacob
Sosseman/Seaceman, Henry & Elizabeth
1784 - grant for 622 acres on Dutch Buffalow Creek joining Nicholas Lodwick, bk 12, pgs 128 & 131.
Children: Daniel (Elizabeth Lippard), John
Son of Henry Sossaman.
Sossaman, John
1793 - Account ledger of John Melchor's store.
Sower, George
George died before 1786
Spain, Thomas
1804 - Loose estate papers
Sparkman, John
1795 - Loose estate papers
Spearman/Sperman, Michael
Michael died 1791, age 66, buried in St John's Evangelical Lutheran Church Cemetery.
Spears, James
1790 - 136 00 - twp 2
Spears, Joseph
1791 - Loose estate papers
Spears, William & Agness(5)
1766 - listed in the militia company of Capt. Adam Alexander of Clear Creek.
William was a signer of the petition to pardon the Cabarrus Black Boys in 1775.

1774 - deed to Thomas Davis for 45 acres on both sides of Reedy Creek, Test: Francis Newel, George Davis, bk 10, pg 396.
1782 - named as adjoining land owner to Robert Turner, James Morrow, and John Cromwell on Caldwell's Creek, bk 12, pg 78.
1790 - 424 00 - twp 13
William died March 2, 1803 at the age of 72.

Spears, William & Jane
Wife - Jane Gray

Spears, William Wallace & Elizabeth
Wife - Elizabeth Gilmer/Gilmore
Children: Columbus W., Wade Hampton, Sidney W., Harvey, Mary (? Davis), Margaret (? Davis), James G.,

Speck, David   (Theobald, Desbald)
1781 - Loose estate papers

Spencer, Samuel
1783 - judge in the court of Pleas & Quarter Sessions, bk 12, pg 444.

Spencer, Thomas & Mary
1775 - deed from William, Jr. & Sarah Bigham to Thomas Spencer for 15 acres on the north part of Steel Creek, Test: Robert Wilson, James Turner, bk 10, pg 171.
1780 - deed from Samuel Bigham, Sr. for 122 acres on Steel Creek joining Robert Wilson, and William Bigham, Test: William Bigham, James McKee, bk 11, pg 1.
1780 - witnessed a deed, with Dun Ochiltree, from Zaccheus Wilson to Joseph Wilson on Sugar Creek, bk 11, pg 39.
1782 - deed to John Taylor for 332 acres on the north fork of Steel Creek joining John Bigham, Robert Wilfon, and Robert Irwin, Test: Robert Irwin, James McKee, bk 11, pg 177.

Sprott, Andrew & Mary(3)
Andrew died Nov 19, 1772 at age 64.
Mary died June 7, 1771 age 64.

Spratt, Andrew
1774 - named as adjoining land owner to William Starret, Nathaniel Cook, James Moore, and James McCord, bk 10, pgs 370 & 379.
1780 - witnessed a deed, with Thomas Polk, Jr., from John Province to John McKoy on Sugar Creek, bk 12, pg 245.
1782 - named as adjoining land owner to John McKoy, John Springs, Robert Phillips, Alexander Starret, William Wilson, and John McEwus on Sugar Creek, bk 12, pg 244.
1790 - 155 00 - twp 16

Spratt, James & Catherine(2)
1782 - named as adjoining land owner to Hector & Margaret McLane, William Cooper, Francis Herron, William McDowel, and John Bigham on King's Branch, a branch of Sugar Creek, bk 12, pg 234.

Residents of Mecklenburg County, North Carolina 1762-1790

1790 - 214 03 - twp 1
Children: Andrew, Hugh, John, William.
James died Feb 4, 1802 at age 73.
Catherine died Oct 3, 1826 age 84.
1802 - Loose estate papers
Spratt, James & Elizabeth Barnett
son of James Spratt.
Sprot, Martha
   1762 - mentioned in a 1778 deed from Robert & Margaret McKnight to James McKnight as having received land from her father, Thomas Sprott, on the creek where Armour's Road crosses, bk 10, pg 42.
Sprott, Samuel
   1781 - named as adjoining land owner to Abraham and Samuel Barnet, and David McCord on Long Creek, bk 12, pg 476.
Sprot, Thomas
   1753 - named as the original grantee, March 1753, in a 1778 deed from Robert & Margaret McKnight to James McKnight on the creek where Armour's Road crosses, bk 10, pg 42.
   Children: Martha, Ann (John Barnett)
Springs, Adam Alexander
   1800 - Mecklenburg County
   Son of John & Sarah Alexander Springs
   Adam was born Jan 9, 1776, died 1840, buried in Adam Springs Cemetery in McAdenville, Gaston County.
Springs, John & Sarah
   1782 - deed from John McKoy for 257 acres on the east fork of Sugar Creek joining Robert Phillips, Andrew Sprott, Alexander Starret, William Wilson, and John McEwus, Test: Adam and Isac Alexander, bk 12, pg 244.
   1790 - 335 050 - twp 3
   Wife - Sarah
Springs, John, Senr.
   1779 - witnessed a deed, with Adam Alexander, from Thomas Polk, attorney for David Oliphant, for 30 acres on Clear Creek, bk 11, pg 229.
   1790 - 102 02 - twp 19
   1793 - Loose estate papers
   John was born about 1717, died before 1793. It is said that his name was Springsteen and that he dropped the steen after coming from Holland.
Springsteen, Richard & Susanna
   1773 - witnessed a deed from Hannah McKee to Joseph Kennedy on Six Mile Creek and both sides of the Great Wagon Road, bk 10, pg 122.
Springstreet, John
   1782 - deed from Robert Graham for 200 acres on Sugar Creek joining a tract formerly owned by David Garison, Test: William Wilson, Hugh Pollock, bk 12, pg 383.
Stafford, James, Junr.

1779 - witnessed a deed, with James Stafford, from Evan Shelby to James Ross on Caldwell's Beaver Dam Branch of Rockey River, bk 12, pg 211.
1784 - named as adjoining land owner to James Maxwell, bk 12, pg 179.
1784 - witnessed a deed, with James Finney, from James & Elizabeth Maxwell to Robert Morison for 170 acres on Rockey River, bk 12, pg 364.
1790 - 143 00 - twp 13
1800 - Cabarrus County

Stafford, James, Senr.
1777 - deed from James Stafford (original grantee in 1765) & William Adams to James Carruth for 88 acres on Reedy Creek, Test: Robert Irwin, Robert S. Harris, bk 10, pg 254.
1778 - Signer of 1778 Petition
1790 - 200 01 - twp 13
Mentioned in the estate papers of Nicholson Ross 1774.

Stains, James
1790 - 000 10 - twp 15

Stanford, Isaac
1790 - 101 00 - twp 7

Stanford, Samuel
1790 - 214 00 - twp 7
1800 - Mecklenburg County
Samuel died before 1822

Stansill, Jesse
1790 - 104 00 - twp 15
1800 - Mecklenburg County

Stansill, John
Wife - Edith Powell
Children: (9 children)
1790 - 112 00 - twp 15

Stansill, John
1776 - in Capt. Charles Polk's Light Horse Company.
1790 - 123 00 - twp 14

Starling, James
1790 - 000 10 - twp 4

Starns, Charles
1790 - 111 00 - twp 12
1793 - Account ledger of John Melchor's store.
1800 - Cabarrus County

Starns, Conrad
1790 - 135 00 - twp 12
1793 - Account ledger of John Melchor's store.

Starns, David
1790 - 131 00 - twp 17
1800 - Mecklenburg County

Starns, Fredrick & Mary Fisher
1790 - 103 00 - twp 17
1800 - Mecklenburg County
Frederick died before 1816.

Starnes, Jacob
    1793 - Account ledger of John Melchor's store.
Starnes, John
    1781 - Loose estate papers
Starnes, John
    1790 - Loose estate papers
Starnes, Joseph
    1793 - Account ledger of John Melchor's store.
    Blacksmith
Starnes, Katherine
    1793 - Account ledger of John Melchor's store.
Starnes, Lucy
    1793 - Account ledger of John Melchor's store.
Staphel, Michael
    1782
Starr, Arthur & Hannah
    1777 - deed to John Johnston for 81 acres on McCalpin's Creek known as Lofton's Bottom, Test: Neil Morrison, John Province, bk 10, pg 248.
    1779 - deed to William Irwin for 230 acres on McCapion's Creek, Test: Robert Irwin, Martin Fifer, bk 11, pg 12.
    1799 - Loose estate papers for Hannah
    Son of John Starr.
Starr, John
    1776 - Loose estate papers
    1777 - named as the previous owner of a tract deeded from Arthur Starr to John Johnston containing 81 acres on McCalpin's Creek, known as Lofton's Bottom, Test: Neil Morrison, John Province, bk 10, pg 248. (John named as the natural father of Arthur Starr)
    1779 - named as the previous owner of a tract deeded from Arthur Starr to William Irwin containing 230 acres on McCapion's Creek, bk 11, pg 12.
    Children: Arthur
Starret, Alexander
    1778 - named as adjoining land owner to Moses Steel, William & James McCafferty, James W. Sawyer, and William Wilson, bk 10, pg 20.
    1782 - grant for 58 acres on Sugar Creek joining William McCafferty, John Beaty, and William Irwin, bk 12, pg 38.
    1782 - named as adjoining land owner to John Beaty, and Nathaniel Erwin on Sugar Creek, bk 12, pg 175. (possibly on the Reedy Branch of Sugar Creek)
    1782 - named as adjoining land owner to John McKoy, John Springs, Robert Phillips, Andrew Sprott, William Wilson, and John McEwus on Sugar Creek, bk 12, pgs 244 & 245.
Starret, William
    1774 - deeds to Nathaniel Cook for 50 acres and 40 acres on Sugar Creek joining Nathaniel Irwin and Andrew Sprott, James Moore and James McCord, Test: Thomas Polk, William Manson, bk 10, pgs 370 & 379.
Stearns, Adam

1778 - Signer of 1778 Petition.
Stearns, Peter
   1778 - Signer of 1778 Petition.
Steel, Aaron
   1764 - named as the original grantee of a tract of 450 acres on Six Mile Creek which he sold to James Tate on Jan 22, 1765, bk 10, pg 265.
Steele, John
   1790 - 102 02 - twp 8
   Son of Moses Steel.
Steele/Stell, Moses
   1778 - deed to William & James McCafferty for 100 acres on Sugar Creek joining James W. Sawyer, William Wilson, and Alexander Starret, Test: Duncan Ocheltree, William Reed, bk 10, pg 20.
   1780 - named as adjoining land owner to James Sawyer, and John Farris, on Sugar Creek, bk 11, pg 122.
   1784 - named as adjoining land owner to John Beaty on Reedy Branch of Sugar Creek, bk 12, pg 176.
   1787 - Moses' will was probated in Mecklenburg Co.
   1787 - Loose estate papers
   Children: John, Lavinia
Steele, Peter
   1774 - deed from Nathaniel & Sarah Johnston for 200 acres on the head branches of Mallard Creek, Test: James Hunter, Adam Meek, bk 10, pg 113.
   1779 - named as adjoining land owner to William Hemphill, and Benjamin Alexander on Mallard Creek, bk 10, pg 535.
   1790 - 112 00 - twp 6
Steel, William & Jane
   1771 - William's will was probated in Mecklenburg Co.
Steel, William & Elizabeth
   Wife: Elizabeth ? Gillespie, widow of ? Gillespie.
   Children: John
Steel, William
   1795 - Loose estate papers
Stephenson, Andrew
   1779 - Loose estate papers
Stephenson, Mathew
   1783 - named as adjoining land owner to John Buchanan, and John McCraven on the dividing ridge between Four Mile Creek and McCalpin's Creek, bk 12, pg 98.
Stephenson, Richard
   1765
   1779 - Goose Creek
   1790 - 301 00 - twp 6
   Richard died before 1795
Stephenson, Richard
   1784 - Garr Creek
Stephenson, William

1779 - witnessed a deed, with James Dawson, from John &
Joseph McDowel to Hugh Laurance on the branches of
McDowel Creek, bk 10, pg 305.
Sterroh, Alexander
1780 - deed for lots 204, 335, 336 in Charlotte, Test:
William Hutchison, Daniel Ford, bk 11, pg 130.
Stevens, Emanuel & Sarah
1779 - deed from Robert Galbreath for 70 acres on both
sides of Crooked Creek, Test: John Foard, Joseph Robb,
bk 10, pg 358.
1784 - deed from William & Sarah Love for 78 acres on
the south side of Crooked Creek, Test: Rob Donaldson,
George McWherter, bk 12, pg 285.
1785 - grant for 37 acres on both sides of Crooked
Creek, Test: Joseph Harris, John Donaldson, bk 12, pg
515.
1785 - deed from William Love for 30 acres on Crooked
Creek, Test: Joseph Harris, John Donnelson, bk 12, pg
527.
1785 - deed to Jesse Stilwell for 30 acres on Crooked
Creek, Test: John and Elijah Stilwell, bk 12, pg 597.
1790 - 143 00 - twp 15
Stevens, Robert
1784 - witnessed a deed, with Joseph Graham, from Mathew
Miller to William Ramsey on Clear Creek, bk 12, pg 357.
Stevens, William E. & Isabel E.
1764 - deed from Isabel, Andrew Allison, William Lucky
as executors of the estate of William E. Stevens of
Rowan Co., NC to Thomas Price for 300 acres on the south
side of the Catawba River, granted to James Armour in
1750, then to William Alexander in 1753, the to said Wm.
E. Stevens in 1756, Test: Thomas Black, Adam & Elizabeth
Allison, Vol2, pg 361.
Stevenson, David
1790 - 000 10 - twp 19
Stevenson, James
1783 - witnessed a deed, with Samuel Killough, from
Thomas Finley to Hugh Patterson on Rocky River, bk 12,
pg 393.
1784 - witnessed a deed, with Richard Smith, from David
& Mary Smith to Samuel Killough on Rockey River, bk 12,
pg 327.
1790 - 125 00 - twp 8
1800 - Cabarrus County
Stevenson, Jas
1790 - 144 00 - twp 16
1800 - Cabarrus County
Stevenson, John
1790 - 143 01 - twp 17
Stevenson, John
1790 - 000 10 - twp 19
Stevenson, Richard & Hannah

1765 - named as the original grantee, in a 1780 deed, of
a tract on Garr Creek, bk 12, pg 424.
1777 - deed to John McKnitt Alexander and Robert Ewart
for 5 acres on Garr Creek for the congregation of
Hopewell Presbyterian Church, Test: Hezekiah Alexander,
Robert Carr, bk 12, pg 472.
1780 - named as adjoining land owner to John McKnitt
Alexander, John Huggins, Jeremiah Joy, and John Buchanan
on Garr Creek, bk 12, pg 424.
1784 - grant for 100 acres on Garr Creek, bk 12, pg 630.
Steward, John & Susannah
1775 - deed to William Alexadner for a tract on a large
branch of Stoney Fork of Mallard Creek, Test: William
Hemphill, George Reed, bk 11, pg 51.
1780 - named as the previous owner of a tract on Stony
fork of Mallard Creek, bk 11, pg 57.
Stewart, John
1780 - witnessed a deed, with John Flenniken, from
Robert & Sarah Arthur to James Kenedy on Four Mile
Creek, bk 11, pg 2.
Stewart, Robert
1773 - deed from James & Margaret Harris for 300 acres,
Test: Thomas Harris, Robert Lewis, bk 10, pg 105.
1777 - Robert's will was probated in Mecklenburg Co.
1777 - Loose estate papers
Children: Jane, Isabel
Stewart, Thomas
1766 - listed in the militia company of Capt. Adam
Alexander of Clear Creek.
1778 - Signer of 1778 Petition.
Mentioned in the estate papers of Nicholson Ross 1774.
1778 - Thomas' will was probated in Mecklenburg Co.
1779 - Loose estate papers
Children: John
Stickleather/Stricklether, George
1784 - named as adjoining land owner to Henry Soceman,
and George Files on Dutch Buffalow Creek, bk 12, pg 131.
Stickleather, John Gorge & Margaret
1780 - John's will was probated in Mecklenburg Co.
1782 - Loose estate papers
Children: John George
Stierwalt, Adam
1790 - 111 00 - twp 11
Stillwell, Elijah
1785 - witnessed a deed, with Elijah Stilwell, from
Manuel Stevens to Jesse Stilwell, bk 12, pg 597.
Stilwell, Jesse
1785 - deed from Manuel Stevens for 30 acres on Crooked
Creek, Test: John and Elijah Stilwell, bk 12, pg 597.
1790 - 103 00 - twp 15
1800 - Mecklenburg County
Stillwell, John

1785 - witnessed a deed, with Elijah Stilwell, from
Manuel Stevens to Jesse Stilwell, bk 12, pg 597.
Pension denied July 7, 1832, awaiting additional
evidence.
Stillwell, Richard
1766 - listed in the militia company of Capt. Adam
Alexander of Clear Creek.
1773 - deed from William & Elizabeth Morris for 120
acres known as the No. 2 tract on the north side of
White Oak Branch, Test: Joseph Harris, John Rabinett, bk
10, pg 115.
Stinson, Andrew
1778 - deed from William Holland for 86 acres on
McCalpin's Creek joining Joseph Sample, and William
Black, Test: Abraham Miller, Thomas Mann, bk 10, pg 378.
1779 - Andrew's will was probated in Mecklenburg Co.
1779 - Loose estate papers
Children: David, John, Andrew
Stinson, Hugh
1778 - Hugh's will was probated in Mecklenburg Co.
Children: Hugh, Michael, Anna
Stinson, John & Eleanor(2)
1783 - deed to William Stinson for 125 acres on Sugar
Creek, Test: Thomas Polk, William Polk, bk 11, pg 199.
1785 - witnessed a deed, with Moses Sharpley and Robert
Walker, from William Stinson to John Welch on Sugar
Creek, bk 12, pg 455.
1790 - 103 02 - twp 1
1800 - Mecklenburg County
John died Jan 19, 1837 at age 80.
Stinson, John & Edith Powell
Married in 1786.
Stinson, Michael
1790 - 000 10 - twp 1
1800 - Mecklenburg County
Son of Hugh Stinson
Stinson, Michael & Ann(2)
Michael died Oct 15, 1776 at the age of 63.
Ann died Feb 1, 1778 at the age of 55.
Stinson, Richard
1797 - Loose estate papers
Stinson, Samuel (Stephenson?)
1802 - Loose estate papers
Stinson, William
1783 - deed from John Stinson for 125 acres on Sugar
Creek, Test: Thomas Polk, William Polk, bk 11, pg 199.
1785 - deed to John Welch for 10 acres on Sugar Creek,
joining Robert Walker, and William Barnet, Test: Moses
Sharpley, Robert Walker, and John Stinson, bk 12, pg
455.
Stitt, James
1806 - Loose estate papers

Stockes, Edward
  1784 - deed from John Johnston for 200 acres on the
  barren ridge between Long Creek and Thompson's Branch
  beginning on the north edge of the wagon road, Test:
  William Ramsey, Justice Beech, bk 12, pg 267.
Storey, James
  1790 - 413 01 - twp 16
Stough/Stouth, Andrew
  1784 - grant for 150 acres on Buffalow Creek, bk 12, pg
  133.
  1790 - 111 00 - twp 12
  1800 - Cabarrus County
Stought, Martin
  1784 - near Lick Branch of Coldwater Creek.
Strachback, Daniel
  1790 - 101 00 - twp 4
Strain, Doc William
  1790 - 100 00 - twp 5
Stricker, Moses
  1787 - Loose estate papers
Stuart, Adam
  1777 - witnessed a deed, with Will Reed, and Dan
  Ochiltree, from Peter Johnston to Isaiah Fitten, on
  Sugar Creek, bk 10, pg 94.
Stuart, David
  1790 - 134 00 - twp 4
Stuart, John
  1790 - 103 00 - twp 13
Stuart, John
  1778 - witnessed a deed, with Benjamin B. Allet, from
  James Way to Robert Arthur on Four Mile Creek, bk 10, pg
  73.
  1790 - 234 00 - twp 19
  1800 - Mecklenburg County
Stuart, Joseph
  1790 - 112 00 - twp 16
  1800 - Mecklenburg County
Stuart, Mathew
  Matthew was a signer of the petition to pardon the
  Cabarrus Black Boys in 1775.
  1780 - Trustee for the congregation of Rocky Spring,
  deed from Samuel Montgomery for 3 acres, Test: Alexander
  McGinty, John McKiman, bk 11, pg 71.
  1790 - 212 00 - twp 15
  1800 - Mecklenburg County
  Mathew died before 1808.
Stuart, Samuel
  1790 - 135 00 - twp 13
Stuart, William
  1790 - 124 00 - twp 13
Stuart, William
  1790 - 202 00 - twp 19

Stucker, Daniel
Sturgeon, John
   1790 - 222 00 - twp 20
   1800 - Mecklenburg County
Suggs, John Harbard
   1793 - Account ledger of John Melchor's store.
Suggs, Thomas
   1793 - Account ledger of John Melchor's store.
Suggs, William
   1793 - Account ledger of John Melchor's store.
Sullivan, Jeremiah & Zelpah Ramsey
   1790 - 101 00 - twp 6
Sullivan, Patrick & Mary Hannah Roots
   1790 - 113 01 - twp 6
   1800 - Mecklenburg County
   Children: Ezekiel, Daniel, Zelpah, Patrick.
Sumter, John
   1790 - 211 05 - twp 1
Suther, David
   1790 - 102 00 - twp 12
Suther, John
   1790 - 132 00 - twp 12
Suther, Samuel, Rev.
   Samuel was a minister living in Orange Co., NC in 1775.
   1775 - deed to Christian Goodman for 125 acres on Dutch
   Buffelow, joining George Tucker, Test: George Henry
   Berger, John Sheppard, bk 10, pg 26.
   1782 - witnessed a deed, with John Lippard, from John
   Buzzard to John Barriger on Buffalow Creek, bk 11, pg
   125.
   Children: David, John
   Samuel died in Orangeburgh Dist., SC in 1788.
Swann, John
   1779 - grant for 94 acres on Swan's branch, a branch of
   McCalpin's Creek, bk 10, pg 532 or 533.
   1790 - 402 01 - twp 20
Swann, Joseph & Kezia(2)
   1781 - witnessed a deed, with Hugh Rodgers, from Francis
   & Margaret Johnston to Alexander Johnston, bk 12, pg
   228.
   1790 - 143 00 - twp 2
   1800 - Mecklenburg County
   Joseph died 1827 at the age of 81.
   Kezia died 1824, age 76.
Swann, Moses, Jr. & Ann(2)
   Moses died Nov 5, 1780 at age 28.
   1780 - Loose estate papers
   Son of Moses Swann of PA.
Swann, Moses & Jane M. Bigham(2)
   1780 - witnessed a deed, with David Hayns, from James
   Sawyer to John Farris on Sugar Creek, bk 11, pg 122.
   Mosess died July 1839 at the age of 61.

Son of Moses and Ann.
Jane died March 22, 1875 age 94.
Swanson, Andrew
   1799 - Loose estate papers
Swink, Adam
   1774 - Loose estate papers
Swink, Jacob
   1773 - deed to Peter Bogar for 122 acres on Shenawolf Creek, a branch of Rocky or Johnston River, Test: James Killpatrick, Michael Goodnight, bk 10, pg 106.
Swink, Michael
   1781 -
Taft, Jacob
   1779 - deed from Michael Liggett for 103 acres on Clear Creek, Test: Adam Alexander, Sam Martin, bk 10, pg 321.
Taggart, James(2)
   Children: John ? (Eleanor Russell), James ?, Joseph ?
   James was born 1722, died Dec 14, 1771 at age 49.
Taggart, James(2) & Nancy
   1773 - witnessed a deed, with Joseph Tagert, from James & Margaret Boyer to John McDowel on Sugar Creek, bk 10, pg 319.
   1778 - witnessed a deed, with Hezekiah Alexander, for lots 69, 70, 77, and 78 on the south side of Tryon Street in Charlotte, bk 10, pg 211.
   1783 - witnessed a deed, with Samuel McCombs and Thomas Henderson, from Joseph Nicholson to William Hutchison on Sugar Creek, bk 11, pg 209.
   1784 - named as adjoining land owner to John & Jane Sloan, Jesse Clark, Isaac Williams, Robert Walker, David Hayes, and Alexander McKee on Sugar Creek, bk 12, pg 466.
   1784 - witnessed a bill of sale, and a deed, from Robert Walker, Jr. to John Green, bk 12, pgs 331 & 337.
   1784 - witnessed a deed, with William McCafferty, from Isaac & Eleanor Williams to George Hutchison on a branch of Sugar Creek, bk 12, pgs 430 & 437.
   1790 - 202 00 - twp 1
   1800 - Mecklenburg County
   James was born 1745, died Sept 22, 1815 at age 70.
   Wife - Nancy
   Pension denied July 7, 1838 for proof of his commission and identity with the officer who served.
Taggert, Joseph
   1773 - witnessed a deed, with James Tagert, from James & Margaret Boyer to John McDowel on Sugar Creek, bk 10, pg 319.
Talley, Priar
   1790 - 103 00 - twp 14
Tanner, James
   1790 - 133 00 - twp 8
   1800 - Cabarrus County

Tanner, John
    1773 - witnessed a deed, with Witt Carragin, from John
    McConey to James Kergin, bk 10, pg 182.
    1781 - witnessed a deed, with Hugh Rodgers, from John
    Houston to Archibald Gilmore on Coddle Creek, bk 10, pg
    444.
    1781 - deed from Archibald & Jean Ramsey for 214 acres
    on Coddle Creek joining Zebulon Brevard, Test: William
    Ramsey, Isabel Robison, bk 11, pg 85.
Tanner, Joseph & Ann
    1779 - Joseph's will was probated in Mecklenburg Co.
    Children: John, James
Tanner, Thomas & (Mary Moore ?)
    1790 - 114 00 - twp 16
    1800 - Mecklenburg County
Tasey, Alexander
    1790 - 112 00 - twp 4
    1798 - Loose estate papers
Tate, Adam
    1778 - deed from Mathew Tate of Lancaster Co., PA to
    Adam Tate, also of Lancaster Co., PA, for 600 acres in
    Anson Co., NC on the south fork of Rocky River, Test:
    James Bayly, James Karr, bk 12, pg 414.
    1779 - deed to Joseph Lata for tracts on both sides of
    the south fork of Rocky River in Anson Co., Test: Ruth
    Bayly, Alexander Lawrey, bk 12, pgs 407 & 408.
    Of Donegal township in Lancaster Co., PA in 1779.
    Son of Joseph Tate.
Tate, James
    1765
    1772 - witnessed a deed, with Henry Downs, from James
    McClure to James Potts on the Flat Branch of Twelve Mile
    Creek, bk 10, pg 257.
    1774 - witnessed a deed, with Brace Miller, and John
    McGoin, from Archibald & Mary Crockett to John Willson
    on Six Mile Creek, bk 10, pg 130.
    1775 - witnessed a deed, with Robert Maxwell, and John
    Bigham, from Samuel Knox to Thomas Ferguson on Steel
    Creek, bk 10, pg 251.
    1777 - deed to Hugh McClelland for 450 acres on Six Mile
    Creek, Test Samuel & Elizabeth Lusk, bk 10, pg 265.
Tate, Joseph
    1756 - both sides of the south fork of Rocky River in
    Anson Co., land conveyed from Joseph to Matthew Tate,
    from Mattew Tate to Adam Tate, bk 12, pg 408.
    Matthew Tate of Lancaster Co., PA. In 1778.
Taub, Gotlieb
    1793 - Account ledger of John Melchor's store.
Tawns, Elijah
    1790 - 202 00 - twp 19
Taylor, Abraham & Mary
    1778 - Abraham's will was probated in Mecklenburg Co.

1778 - Loose estate papers
Taylor, Archibald A.
   1801 - Loose estate papers
Taylor, Conarod
   1767 - Loose estate papers
Taylor, David
   1790 - 101 00 - twp 13
Taylor, Elijah
   1790 - 133 00 - twp 7
Taylor, John
   1777 - John's will was probated in Mecklenburg Co.
   Children: Mary, Margaret
Taylor, John
   1784 - Loose estate papers
Taylor, John
   1781 - named as adjoining land owner to Samuel Bigham, Hugh Bigham, William Bowman, and William Porter on Sugar Creek, bk 11, pg 155.
   1781 - deed from Samuel Bigham for 158 acres on Sugar Creek, Test: Will Reed, William Bigham, bk 11, pg 160.
   1782 - deed from Thomas Spencer for 332 acres on the north fork of Steel Creek joining Robert Wilfon (Wilson), and Robert Irwin, Test: Robert Irwin, James McKee, bk 11, pg 177.
   1790 - 242 04 - twp 2
   1800 - Mecklenburg County (widow)
   1800 - Loose estate papers
Taylor, John & Mary
   1790 - 132 00 - twp 9
   John died before 1830
   Unnamed daughter buried in Steel Creek Cemetery in 1814.
Taylor, Mary(2)
   Mary died Sept 27, 1796 at the age of 22.
Taylor, William
   1778 - Signer of 1778 Petition.
   1790 - 123 00 - twp 13
Tedford, James
   1790 - 000 10 - twp 10
Teem/Dean, Adam
   1790 - 142 00 - twp 12
   1800 - Chesterfield Co., SC
Teem/Jeem/Dean, Jacob
   1784 - grant for 31 acres on Hamby's Run of Rockey River, adjoining Peter Ross, Jacob Faget, Michael Fogleman, Charles Barnheart, bk 12, pgs 137 & 145.
   1790 - 201 00 - twp 12
Tellery, Isaac
   1778 - Signer of 1778 Petition.
Temple, Major
   1782 - named as a previous adjoining land owner on Sugar Creek, bk 11, pg 207.
Templeton, Archibald

1761 - named as previous land owner in a 1784 deed from
William Penny to Martain Phifer, bk 12, pg 311.
1777 - named as adjoining land owner to John & Catherine
Phifer, Robert Morton, and John Frohock on Coddle Creek,
bk 10, pg 69.
1782 - named as adjoining land owner to Francis Lock, bk
12, pg 64.
Templeton, David, Jr.
1783 - witnessed a deed, with John Houston, and Robert
Scott, from William Penny to Robert Penny on Coddle
Creek, bk 12, pg 259.
1784 - witnessed a deed, with John Thompson, from
William Penny to Martain Phifer on Coddle Creek, bk 12,
pg 311.
1784 - witnessed a bill of sale, with Robert Scott, from
William Penny to Martain Phifer, Sr., bk 12, pg 241.
1784 - named as adjoining land owner to Martin Phifer,
Sr., and Ephraim Farr, on Caudle(Coddle) Creek, bk 12,
pg 366.
1790 - 143 02 - twp 8
1800 - Cabarrus County
Templeton, David, Sr.
David died before 1761
Children: Archibald, David
Templeton, James
1781 - named as adjoining land owner to John Houston,
and Archibald Gilmore on a branch of Coddle Creek called
Hugh Parks Creek, bk 10, pg 444.
Templeton, Samuel
1778 - deed to William Penny for 67 acres on Coddle
Creek, Test: John Houston, Hugh Park, Jr., and John
Park, bk 11, pg 278.
1784 - named as adjoining land owner to William &
Elizabeth Penny, Lewis Meredith, and John Purner on
Coddle Creek, bk 12, pg 421.
Tenant, William, Rev.
1777 - deed from John & Catherine Biggar for 300 acres
on the Catawba River opposite the mouth of Crowder's
Creek, Test: Samuel Chambers, William Kerr, and Joseph
McKinley, bk 10, pg 84 & 97.
Terrence, Adam
1783 - named as adjoining land owner to Joseph Wilson,
and Gilbert McNear on Dowel's Creek, bk 12, pg 166.
Tetter, George
1790 - 232 00 - twp 14
1800 - Cabarrus County
Thomas, Alexander
1778 - trustee of Liberty Hall, bk 10, pg 211.
Thomas, Benjamin. & Rebecca(2)
1790 - 202 09 - twp 2
Benjamin died Oct 16, 1793, his will was probated in
Mecklenburg Co.

Thomas, John
    1767 - Militia, Mecklenburgh Regiment (Captain)
Thomas, Joseph
    1782 - Joseph's will was probated in Mecklenburg Co.
    Children: Allen, Joseph, Lucy, Sarah
Thompson, Alexander
    1790 - 105 00 - twp 17
    1800 - Mecklenburg County
Thompson, Drury & Martha
    1785 - deed to Charles Cook for 195 acres on both sides
    of Little Richardson Creek, Test: John Belk, John
    Thompson, Darsen Belk, bk 12, pg 600.
    Drury and Martha of Camden District, SC in 1785.
Thompson, Elijah
    1790 - 312 00 - twp 16
Thompson, Gideion
    1781 - named as adjoining land owner to Peter Johnston,
    Andrew McKee, William Lawing, and John Anderson, bk 12,
    pg 444.
    1784 - named as adjoining land owner to Thomas Polk,
    Andrew Dune, and William Lawing on Long Creek, bk 12, pg
    283.
    1790 - 202 02 - twp 6
    1800 - Mecklenburg County
Thompson, Jennings
    1785 - Jennings' will was probated in Mecklenburg Co.
    Children: Joseph, Benjamin, Moses
Thompson, John & Martha
    1778 - Loose estate papers
Thomson, John
    1778 - Signer of 1778 Petition
    1784 - witnessed a deed, with David Templeton, from
    William Penny to Martain Phifer on Coddle Creek, bk 12,
    pg 311.
    1790 - 116 00 - twp 6
    1799 - Loose estate papers
Thomson, John & Ann
    1780 - grant for 300 acres on Richardson Creek, bk 12,
    pg 47.
    1782 - named as adjoining land owner to Rees Shelby on
    Richardson's Creek, bk 12, pg 7.
    1783 - deed from Charles Calhoon for a tract on both
    sides of Benet's fork of Ritcheson's Creek, about half a
    mile above the old Indian path, Test: Robert Irwin,
    Thomas Greer, George Calhoon, bk 11, pg 257.
    1783 - deed to Charles Cook for 150 acres on Little
    Ritcheson Creek, a fork of Big Ritcheson Creek, Test:
    John Belk, Sr., John Libley, bk 11, pg 292.
    1785 - witnessed a deed, with John and Darsen Belk, from
    Drury & Martha Thompson of Camden Dist., SC, to Charles
    Cook on Richardson Creek, bk 12, pg 600.

Residents of Mecklenburg County, North Carolina   347
1762-1790

1786 - deed to Caleb Aledge for 300 acres on Richardson
Creek, Test: John Belk, Obed Thomson, bk 12, pg 602.
1790 - 125 00 - twp 16
1800 - Mecklenburg County
A John Thompson bought land on both sides of Benet's
fork of Ritcheson's Creek about half a mile above the
old Indian path in 1783.
Thompson, Moses
   1779 - witnessed a bill of sale, with Joseph Douglas,
   and William Haggons, from William Killingsworth to
   Archibald Alexander, bk 12, pg 381.
   1781 - Loose estate papers
Thompson, Obediah
   1786 - witnessed a deed, with John Belk, from John &
   Ann Thomson to Caleb Aledge for 300 acres on Richardson
   Creek, adjoining Charles Cook, bk 12, pg 602.
   1790 - 113 00 - twp 17
   1800 - Mecklenburg County
   died before 1825
Thompson, Samuel
   1766 - listed in the militia company of Capt. Adam
   Alexander of Clear Creek.
Thompson, Sham
   1780 - grant for 150 acres on both sides of Onion
   branch, a branch of Richardson's Creek joining Joshua
   Yarbrough, bk 12, pg 13.
Thomson, Thomas & Mary
   Of Rowan Co., NC in 1778.
   1778 - deed to Samuel Brown for 240 acres on the head of
   Rocky River, Test: John Brown, Richard Aubin, bk 10, pg
   365.
   1781 - Thomas' will was probated in Mecklenburg Co.
   Children: John
Thompson, Thomas
   1783 - named as adjoining land owner to William Lawing,
   Justice Beech, Samuel Ziklagg, William Flenniken, and
   Edward Debreel on the Catawba River, bk 12, pg 208.
Thompson, Widow
   1790 - 413 00 - twp 6
Thorn, James & Sarah
   1778 - deed to John Johnston for 200 acres on the Barren
   Ridge between Long Creek and Thomason's Branch beginning
   on the north edge of the wagon road, Test: William
   Lawing, bk 10, pg 58.
   Children: James, Joseph, Margaret, Robert, William.
Titus, Dennis
   1780 - deed from George & Elizabeth McWhirter for two
   tracts, one containing 517 acres, the other 323 acres,
   on Warshaw Creek, Test: Alexander Cairns, Henry Foster,
   bk 10, pg 447.

1780 - deed from George & Elizabeth McWhorter for 19
acres on the north side of Wawhaw Creek, Test: Henry
Foster, Alexander Cairn, bk 11, pg 307.
1790 - 117 00 - twp 17
Children: John
1794 - Loose estate papers
Titus, John
   1801 - Loose estate papers
Tobe/Tove/Taub, George
   1789 - Loose estate papers
Todd, Adam H. & Mary
   1784 - deed to William Todd for 200 acres on the head
waters of Paw Creek, Test: Robert Allison, Joseph Seed,
bk 12, pg 503.
   1790 - 121 00 - twp 6
   1800 - Mecklenburg County
   Children: Mary
Todd, George(8)
   George was born in 1769, died Nov 25, 1838.
Todd, Hugh
   1787 - Loose estate papers
Todd, James & Martha
   1776 - deed to John Todd for 120 acres on the head
branches of Sugar Creek, Test: Thomas Allison, Joseph
Moore, William Todd, James McCafferty, bk 10, pg 21.
Todd, James & Nancy(8)
   Children: James N. (Mary Saddler)
   Wife: Mary Saddler, daughter of P. & J. Saddler
   James died March 12, 1839 at the age of 67.
   Nancy died July 30, 1852 at the age of 85.
Todd, John, Jr.
   1776 - deed from James Todd for 120 acres on the head
branches of Sugar Creek, Test: Thomas Allison, Joseph
Moore, William Todd, James McCafferty, bk 10, pg 21.
   1778 - deed to John Cannon for 120 acres on the head
branches of Sugar Creek, Test: Samuel Martin, John
Alexander, bk 10, pg 346.
   1780 - named as adjoining land owner to James Brown, and
William Blackwood on Gum Branch of Long Creek, bk 11, pg
103.
   1790 - 216 00 - twp 6
   1800 - Mecklenburg County
   John died before 1813
Todd, Joseph
   1790 - 020 01 - twp 66
   1800 - Mecklenburg County
   Joseph died before 1825.
Todd, William
   1776 - witnessed a deed, with Thomas Allison, Joseph
Moore, and James McCafferty, from James & Martha Todd to
John Todd on the head branches of Sugar Creek, bk 10, pg
21.

Residents of Mecklenburg County, North Carolina 349
1762-1790

    1784 - deed from Adam Todd for 200 acres on the head
    waters of Paw Creek, Test: Robert Allison, Joseph Seed,
    bk 12, pg 503.
    1790 - 304 00 - twp 6
    1800 - Mecklenburg County
Tool, John
    1779 - deed to David Alexander for 400 acres on the
    south side of the North Branch of the Catawba River
    joining Samuel Coburn, and ? Leeper, Test: John Smith,
    Aron Alexander, Thomas Shields, bk 11, pg 174.
    Son of Matthew & Eleanor Cathey Toole.
Tool, Matthew
    1776 Indian Camp Creek, south side of the north branch
    of the Cataba River
    Wife - Eleanor Cathey, dau of George Cathey
    Children: John
Tomison, George
    1778 - Signer of 1778 Petition
Torrance, Abraham
    1768 - Abraham's will was probated in Mecklenburg Co.
    1768 - Loose estate papers
    Children: Hugh, Paul, George, William
Torrence, Hugh
    1790 - 115 012 - twp 7
    1800 - Mecklenburg County
    Wife - Isabella Kerr Falls, widow of Galbreath Falls
    Children: James Galbreath Torrance, only child.
    born in 1743, died in 1816.
    Son of Abraham Torrance.
Townsend, Charles
    1783 - named as adjoining land owner to Walter Smiley,
    William Boyett, John Chamberlain, and George Townsend on
    Buffalow Creek, bk 12, pg 118.
Townsand, Dudley
    1790 - 122 00 - twp 10
    1800 - Cabarrus County
Townsand, George
    1783 - named as adjoining land owner to Walter Smiley,
    William Boyett, John Chamberlain, and Charles Townsend
    on Buffalow Creek, bk 12, pg 118.
    1790 - 143 00 - twp 10
    1793 - Account ledger of John Melchor's store.
Townsand, Henry
    1790 - 121 00 - twp 10
Townsend, James
    1778 - Signer of 1778 Petition
    1781 - Loose estate papers
Townsend, James
    1804 - Loose estate papers
Townsend, Sarah
    1806 - Loose estate papers
Townsand, William

1790 - 114 00 - twp 10
1792 - Account ledger of John Melchor's store.
1800 - Cabarrus County
Townsand, William Red.
1790 - 112 00 - twp 14
1800 - Cabarrus County
Tradewall, Stephen, Jr.
1793 - Account ledger of John Melchor's store.
Trot, Andrew
1778 - named as adjoining land owner to John & Jean Wear, John Provane, Ebenezer Newton, Alexander Herrel, William Wilson, and John McEwell on Abraham Alexander's Mill Creek, bk 10, pg 283.
Trotter, Archibald
1783 - witnessed a deed, with Joseph Graham, and Arthur McCree, from William Penny to Martin Phifer, bk 12, pg 320.
Trotter, Richard
1780 - witnessed a deed, with Martin Orr, from John & Catherine McCoy to Jacob Croner on Three Mile Creek, bk 11, pg 66.
1784 - witnessed a deed, with Archibald Houston, and William Fraser, from Martin Phifer, Sr. to Ephraim Farr on Caudle(Coddle) Creek joining David Templeton, bk 12, pg 366.
Troy, Matt
1781 - witnessed a deed, with Hugh Colloden Boyd, from Peter Johnston to Andrew McKee, bk 12, pg 444.
Tryon, William
1767 - named as the previous owner of a tract on Steel Creek, bk 11, pg 252.
Tucker, George, Jur.
1784 - grant for 300 acres on both sides of Rocky River joining Henry Smith, the widow Ciser, and Joseph Howel, bk 12, pg 174.
1790 - 113 00 - twp 12
1800 - Cabarrus County
Tucker, George, Sr.
1775 - named as adjoining land owner to Christian Goodman on Dutch Buffelow Creek, bk 10, pg 26.
1790 - 335 00 - twp 12
1800 - Cabarrus County
Tucker, William
1790 - 211 00 - twp 7
Turner, James
1775 - witnessed a deed, with Robert Wilson, from William (Will) & Sarah Bigham on the north part of Steel Creek, bk 10, pg 171.
Turner, John
1777 - deed from John & Catherine Bigger for 220 acres joining Adam Calhoon, and David McMickan, Test: William Harris, Samuel Chambers, Joseph Waddle, bk 11, pg 141.

Turner, John
    1779 - Loose estate papers
Turner, Robert
    1792 - Loose estate papers
    1782 - grant for 160 acres on Calwell's Creek joining
    James Morrow, John Cromwell, William Taylor, and William
    Spears, bk 12, pg 78.
Uans, Robert
Udy, Bernard
    1794 - Account ledger of John Melchor's store.
Ury, George & Elizabeth
    1793 - Account ledger of John Melchor's store.
    Wife - Elizabeth Hartsell, 2nd wife - Elizabeth   ?
    Children: Levy ? (Elizabeth   ?), Israel ?
    Elizabeth Hartsell Ury was born July 12, 1789, died May
    24, 1829, buried in St John's Evangelical Lutheran
    Church Cemetery.
    George was born Sept 1788, died Nov 10, 1855, buried in
    St John's Evangelical Lutheran Church Cemetery.
    2nd wife, Elizabeth was born Oct 8, 1790, died April 7,
    1855, buried in St John's Evangelical Lutheran Church
    Cemetery.
Ury/Ourey/Aurey, Martin
    1790 - 123 00 - twp 11
    Children: George (Elizabeth Hartsell)
    Buried in St John's Evangelical Lutheran Church
    Cemetery, bur dates and location have been lost.
Urich, George
    1778 - Loose estate papers
Vaich, William
    1790 - 143 00 - twp 19
    1800 - Cabarrus County
Van Pelt, Simon, Sr.
    1790 - 255 00 - twp 1
    1799 - Simon's will was probated in Mecklenburg Co.
    1799 - Loose estate papers
    Children: Simon
Van Pelt, Simeon & Margaret(8)
    1800 - Mecklenburg County
    Simeon died April 30, 1851 at the age of 84.
    Margaret died Dec 25, 1833 at the age of 70.
    Son of Simon Van Pelt.
Vance, Andrew
    1790 - 106 00 - twp 15
Vance, David(2)
    1790 - 333 00 - twp 2
    1800 - Mecklenburg County (widow)
    David died Feb 28, 1800 at age 64.
Vance, Valentine
    1790 - 101 00 - twp 15
Varner, Henry

1779 - named as adjoining land owner to David Reed, Nicholas Gibbony, Samuel Kearh, and John Carson on Sugar Creek, bk 10, pg 412.
1784 - Loose estate papers
Varner, Henry, Sr.
    1783 - deed from Walter Carruth for 215 acres on Paw Creek, Test: John Green, James Sloan, bk 12, pg 387.
    1788 - Loose estate papers
Varner, James
    1778 - James' will was probated in Mecklenburg Co.
    1778 - Loose estate papers
    Children: Robert
Verner, John(2)
    1790 - 105 00 - twp 1
    1800 - Mecklenburg County
    John died Feb 16, 1806 at age 40.
    1806 - Loose estate papers
    Son of Henry & Rebecca Varner
Vernon, Henry
    1783 Sugar Creek
Vernor, Henry & Rebecca
    1783 Paw Creek, of Lincoln Co., NC in 1783 buying land on Paw Creek
    Children: Robert, John
Varner, Robert(2)
    Robert died March 19, 1800, at the age of 29.
    Son of Henry & Rebecca Varner
Vinan, Thomas
    1790 - 153 00 - twp 17
Vinan, William
    1790 - 103 00 - twp 17
Vinen, Drury
    1790 - 153 04 - twp 18
Vines, David
    1778 - Signer of 1778 Petition
Vinson, William
    1797 - William's will was probated in Mecklenburg Co.
    1798 - Loose estate papers
    Children: Thomas, David, Penelope, Penina
Voyls, James
    1784 - named as adjoining land owner to John Chamberlain, James McCraw, and Philip Wise on Coldwater Creek, bk 12, pg 187.
    1790 - 132 00 - twp 10
Voyls, Thomas
    1790 - 223 00 - twp 12
    1794 - Account ledger of John Melchor's store.
    1800 - Cabarrus County
Voyls, William
    1784 - named as adjoining land owner to John Chamberlain on Voil Branch of Coldwater Creek, bk 12, pg 184.
    1790 - 252 00 - twp 10

Residents of Mecklenburg County, North Carolina 1762-1790

1800 - Cabarrus County (widow)
Waddington, William & Polly McLarty
    1782 - grant for 50 acres joining James Love, bk 12, pg 49.
    1782 - named as adjoining land owner to Robert Davies on Rockey River, bk 12, pg 66.
    1789 - Loose estate papers
Waddington, William
    1771 - William's will was probated in Mecklenburg Co.
    Children: John, Samuel, Robert, Frances
Waddell, Hugh & Mary
    1772 - Hugh's will was probated in Mecklenburg Co.
    Children: John, Hugh, Burgwyn
    Brother-in-law: John Burgwyn
    Sister: Hannah
Waddie, William
    1784 - witnessed a deed, with Sam Davidson, and John Wier, from John Davidson to Robert Martin, bk 12, pg 308.
Waddle, Joseph
    1777 - witnessed a deed, with William Harris, and Samuel Chambers, from John & Catherine Bigger, bk 11, pg 141.
Waddell, Mary Burgwyn
    1766 - Mary's will was probated in Mecklenburg Co.
    Children: Hugh, Haynes, John Burgwyn
    Brother: John Burgwyn
Waddle, Robert
    1773 - witnessed a deed, with William Graham, and Abel Duckworth, from John Jackson & Mary Moore to John Criswell, bk 10, pg 90.
Waddle, William
    1778 - witnessed a deed, with Ephraim Bravard, from Thomas Polk to Samuel Lusk on the northwest branch of Twelve Mile Creek, bk 10, pg 202.
    1779 - grant for 380 acres joining ? Miller, and John Cathey, bk 12, pg 4
Waddle, William
    1783 - witnessed a deed, with John Belk, from Denis & Mary McFall to Joseph Wilson on McDowell's Creek, bk 12, pg 497.
    1790 - 134 01 - twp 7
    1800 - Mecklenburg County
Wade, Thomas
    1787 - Loose estate papers
Wagginor/Waggoner, William
    1784 - named as adjoininig land owner to Frederick Cerlock, joining Isaac Loftin on Coldwater Creek, bk 12, pg 196.
    1790 - 152 00 - twp 12
    1800 - Cabarrus County
    Children: Phillip ? (Catherine Lyerly)
Wahaub, James

1790 - 323 09 - twp 18
Waits, Andrew
    1774 - Mentioned in the estate papers of Nicholson Ross.
Walbert, Christopher & Mary
    1774 - deed to John Phifer for 164 acres on Coldwater
    Creek, Test: Thomas Polk, John Barringer, bk 10, pg 141.
Walker, Adam
    1790 - 212 00 - twp 12
    Adam died 1791, buried in St John's Evangelical Lutheran
    Church Cemetery.
Walker, Adam
    Adam was born May 16, 1722, died Oct 7, 1807, buried in
    St John's Evangelical Lutheran Church Cemetery.
Walker, Ambrose & Magdalen
    1783 - deed to John McCain for 330 acres on both sides
    of Cane Creek, Test: John Ramsey, John Shelby, bk 12, pg
    230.
    Son of Thomas Walker.
Walker, Andrew, Capt. & Sarah
    1779 - Indenture of Mary Barns, daughter of Sarah Barns.
    Mary not yet 18. Test: John Drennan, John Walker, bk 10,
    pg 310.
    1779 - deed from Nathaniel & Elizabeth Walker for 400
    acres on a branch of Cane Creek in the Waxhaus
    Settlement joining Hugh McCain, Test: Elizabeth Walker,
    Philip Walker, bk 11, pg 76.
    1782 - deed from James Cook for 200 acres on the north
    fork of Waxhaw Creek joining William McCorlis, Test:
    William Cry, John McCullah, bk 11, pg 126.
    1782 - witnessed a deed, with William Cry, from Henry
    Hurst to John Galaspy of Guilford Co., NC, bk 12, pg
    220.
    1790 - 116 03 - twp 18
    1800 - Mecklenburg County
    Wife - Sarah Morrison, daughter of Robert & Sarah
    Morrison.
    Pension denied June 7, 1832 - was a teamster.
Walker, Archabeld, Capt.
    1790 - 211 00 - twp 15
    1800 - Mecklenburg County
Walker, Elizabeth
    1779 - witnessed a deed, with Philip Walker, from
    Nathaniel & Elizabeth Walker to Andrew Walker on Cane
    Creek in the Waxhaw Settlement, bk 11, pg 76.
Walker, Fredrick
    1790 - 112 00 - twp 11
Walker, James & Esther
    Wife - Esther Black, daughter of John & Mary Black
    1782 - witnessed a deed, with Robert Donalson, from
    George Buckalow to Tunas Hogland on McCalpin's Creek,
    joining James McLure, and James Clark, bk 12, pg 508.
Walker, James

1776 - deed from Hezekiah James & Martha Batch for 88
acres on the ridges between English Buffalow Creek and
Cauddle's Creek, Test: William Scott, John White, bk 10,
pg 221.
1779 - judgement obtained against the administrators of
William Walker, Test: Andrew McCombs, John Queen, bk 10,
pg 356.
1781 - James' will was probated in Mecklenburg Co.
Children: Henry, Mary, James
Walker, James
    1782 - named as adjoining land owner to William Scott,
David Purvine, John Rodgers, and Hugh Caruthers on
Buffalow Creek, bk 12, pg 71.
Walker, John
    1779 - near Twelve Mile Creek
    1790 - 301 00 - twp 18
    1800 - Mecklenburg County
    1804 - Loose estate papers
Walker, John
    1790 - 124 00 - twp 2
    1806 - Loose estate papers
Walker, John
    1790 - 234 00 - twp 1
    1800 - Mecklenburg County
Walker, John & Rosannah
    1790 - 111 00 - twp 20
    1800 - Mecklenburg County
    Wife - Rosannah Black, daughter of John & Mary Black
Walker, John Frederick & Anna Margaret
    John was born March 5, 1758 in VA, died April 11, 1822,
buried in St John's Evangelical Lutheran Church
Cemetery.
    Anna was born March 1, 1768, died Jan 10, 1844, buried
in St John's Evangelical Lutheran Church Cemetery.
Walker, Margaret
    Margaret was born Aug 1, 1777, died Aug 27, 1800, buried
in St John's Evangelical Lutheran Church Cemetery.
Walker, Mathew
    1790 - 120 00 - twp 15
Walker, Michael
    1790 - 101 00 - twp 12
    1800 - Cabarrus County
Walker, Moses
    1790 - 101 00 - twp 15
Walker, Nathaniel & Elizabeth
    1767 - Militia, Mecklenburgh Regiment (Ensign)
    1769 - named as the original grantee of a tract on Cane
Creek in the Waxhaus Settlement in a deed to Andrew
Walker for 400 acres, bk 11, pg 76.
Walker, Phillip

1779 - witnessed a deed, with Elizabeth Walker, from
Nathaniel & Elizabeth Walker to Andrew Walker, bk 11, pg
76.
Walker, Robert & Mary
1773 - named as adjoining land owner to Alexander McKee,
and William Berryhill on Sugar Creek, bk 11, pg 129.
1783 - witnessed a deed, with Samuel Martin, from Jonas
Clark to Jesse Clark on Sugar Creek, bk 11, pg 254.
1784 - bill of sale to John Green for a horse, and 150
acres joining Jesse Clark, William Clark, and John
Walker, Test: James Tagert, bk 12, pg 331.
1784 - named as adjoining land owner to John & Jane
Sloane, Jesse Clark, Isaac Williams, James Tagert, David
Hayes, and Alexander McKee on Sugar Creek, bk 12, pg
466.
1784 - deed to John Green for 150 acres on Sugar Creek,
Test: George Graham, James Tagert, bk 12, pg 337.
1785 - witnessed a deed, with Moses Sharpley, and John
Stinson, from William Stinson to John Welch on Sugar
Creek, bk 12, pg 455.
1790 - 112 00 - twp 20
1800 - Mecklenburg County
Children: Robert, William, James, Conny (? Reed),
Mary (? Rea), Jane (? Reed)
Walker, Robert
1793 - Account ledger of John Melchor's store.
1794 - Loose estate papers
Walker, Sylvanus
1801 - Loose estate papers
Walker, Thomas & Elizabeth
1783 - mentioned in a deed from Ambrose Walker to John
McCain as the grantee of a tract in 1775 on both sides
of Cane Creek, bk 12, pg 230.
1790 - 111 00 - twp 18
1800 - Mecklenburg County
Wife - Elizabeth McCall, daughter of Francis McCall.
Children: Ambrose
Walker, Thomas & Mary Blythe
1778 - witnessed a deed, with Robert Philips, from John
& Jean Wear to John Provane on Abraham Alexander's Mill
Creek, bk 10, pg 283.
1780 - deed from John & Jean Wear for 185 acres
adjoining James Blythe & William Graham, Test: Hugh
Lucas, William Graham, bk 10, pg 456.
Wife - Mary Blythe, daughter of Samuel & Elizabeth
Blythe.
Children: Davina, Mary, Agness, Joseph, G. Smith,
Robert, Thomas, Samuel, Richard, James, Ezekiel, John.
Walker, William
William died before 1773.
1779 - judgement obtained by James Walker, against the
administrators of William Walker, tract on Sugar Creek

sold to Robert Graham to satisfy judgement, Test: Andrew McCombs, John Queen, bk 10, pg 356.

Walker, William
  1790 - 202 00 - twp 15
Walker, William
  1790 - 124 00 - twp 1
Walker, William
  1773 - Loose estate papers
Wall, Henry & Rachel
  1776 - Henry's will was probated in Mecklenburg Co.
Wallace, Alexander
  1771 - witnessed a deed, with John Farr, from John McLilley to John McKnitt Alexander on Mallard Creek, bk 11, pg 192.
  1779 - deed to William Goforth for a tract on a branch of Mallard Creek, Test: Nathaniel Irwin, William Hemphill, bk 11, pg 305.
  1780 - named as adjoining land owner to John Cook, and Alexander Wallace on Mallard Creek, bk 12, pg 138.
  1780 - grant for 156 acres on Mallard Creek joining John Cook, Michael Henderson, Mathew Robison, William Hemphill, and Thomas Frohock, bk 12, pg 120.
  1785 - grant for 25 acres on Mallard Creek(by William McClure), bk 12, pg 517.
  1790 - 301 00 - twp 4
  1800 - Mecklenburg County
Wallace, Aron
  1790 - 102 00 - twp 13
  1800 - Cabarrus County
Wallace, Benjamin
  1773 - deed from Robert Kerr for 125 acres on Long Creek, Test: Robert Carr, Joseph Kerr, bk 10, pg 124.
  1775 - witnessed a deed, with Robert Dowel, from John & Elinor McDowel to Joseph Wallace, bk 10, pg 286.
  1778 - witnessed a deed, with John Walace from William & Sarah Givens to John Thompson, bk 10, pg 285.
Wallace/Wallis, Ezekel
  1779 - named as adjoining land owner to Margaret Wilson, Garrett Wilson, and Alexander Campbell, bk 10, pg 512.
  1790 - 203 04 - twp 4
  1800 - Mecklenburg County
Wallace, George
  1790 - 113 00 - 4
  1800 - Mecklenburg County
  George died before 1803
Wallace, George
  1790 - 103 00 - twp 20
Wallace, James
  1769 - deed from John & Elizabeth Mitchell for 184 acres beginning on the barony line, Test: Adam Alexander, Robert Harrison, bk 10, pg 128.
Wallace, James & Jean

1778 - Signer of 1778 Petition
1778 - named as adjoining land owner to Andrew & Sarah Burns, Robert Smith, Jr., and William Gardner on Rockey River, bk 10, pg 82.
1780 - deed to Martin Phifer, Jr. for 62 acres on Coddle Creek, Test: David Wilson, Zaccheus Wilson, bk 11, pg 142.
1790 - 203 06 - twp 5
Wallace, Jediah
    1790 - 111 00 - twp 9
    1800 - Cabarrus County
Wallace, John
    1778 - witnessed a deed, with Benjamin Walace from William & Sarah Givens to John Thompson, bk 10, pg 285.
    1784 - named as adjoining land owner to William Hayes, and Adam Kess on Wolf Meadow Branch, bk 12, pg 125.
    1784 - grant for 300 acres on Wolf Meadow Branch joining Robert Archibald, bk 12, pg 183.
    1790 - 101 00 - twp 9
Wallace, John
    1790 - 122 01 - twp 5
    1800 - Mecklenburg County
Wallace, Joseph & Margaret
    Carpenter.
    1775 - deed from John & Elinor McDowel for 200 acres, joining John Bravard, and Robert Jennings, Test: Benjamin Walace, Robert Dowel, bk 10, pg 286.
    1775 - Rockey River beginning on the Baroney line.
    1778 - Signer of 1778 Petition.
    1781 - Joseph's will was probated in Mecklenburg Co. Children: William, Edward, Samuel
    1781 - deed from Margaret Wallace and James Barr to John Levison for 200 acres on Rockey River joining james Dysart, Test: Robert Harris, John Davidson, Thomas Mitchel, bk 11, pg 79.
    1781 - Loose estate papers
Wallace, Ludwick
    1783 - between Coddle Creek and Wolf Meadow Branch
    1790 - 119 00 - twp 9
    1800 - Cabarrus County
Wallace, Mathew
    1790 - 113 01 - twp 4
Wallace, Mathew
    1790 - 122 00 - twp 20
Wallace, Moses
    1790 - 112 00 - twp 13
Wallace, William
    1778 - Signer of 1778 Petition
    1786 - named as adjoining land owner to John & Mary Sconnel, and Rachel Sconnel, bk 12, pg 606.
    1790 - 111 00 - twp 4
Wallace, William

Residents of Mecklenburg County, North Carolina 1762-1790

1790 - 123 00 - twp 20
Walls, Abin/Alin
   1790 - 001 00 - twp 7
Walls/Watts, Andrew
   1784 - Mentioned in the estate papers of Nicholson Ross
   1790 - 202 00 - twp 14
   1800 - Cabarrus County
Walter, Nicholas
   1775 - Loose estate papers
Walter, Nicholas
   1783 - Coldwater Creek.
   1790 - 103 00 - twp 10
Walter, Paul
   1783 - grant for 40 acres on Coldwater Creek joining Nicholas Cook, and Jacob Cook, bk 12, pg 139.
   1790 - 123 00 - twp 10
Walten, Nicholas
   1783 - named as an adjoining land owner to Mathias Mitchel on Coldwater Creek, bk 12, pg 124.
   1783 - grant for 176 acres on Coldwater Creek joining Nicholas Coon, Paul Walters, John Ross, and Mathias Mitchel, bk 12, pg 126.
Walten, Paul
   1783 - named as an adjoining land owner to Mathias Mitchel on Coldwater Creek, bk 12, pg 124.
Warden, John
   1779 - named as adjoining land owner to Thomas Smith on Duck Creek, bk 11, pg 6.
Warden, Samuel
   1790 - 122 00 - twp 14
   1794 - Account ledger of John Melchor's store.
Warner, Hardin
   1779 Muddy Creek
Washam, Jeremiah
   1790 - 213 00 - twp 18
Washington, John
   1790 - 000 10 - twp 20
Watkins, James
   1790 - 122 00 - twp 6
Watson/Wahon, Thomas
   1766 - listed in the militia company of Capt. Adam Alexander of Clear Creek.
   1790 - 423 00 - twp 13
Watson, William & Mary
   1779 - deed to James Dickson for 75 acres on Clear Creek, Test: John Jackson, David Moore, Andrew Moore, and Joseph Robbs, bk 11, pg 191.
Watson, William & Sarah Rogers
   1790 - 114 00 - twp 4
Watts/Walls, Andrew (see Andrew Walls)
Waugh, James

1779 - named as adjoining land owner to Alexander Cairn, and George McWhorter on the north side of Waxhaw Creek, bk 10, pg 524.

Waughess, James
1780 - grant for 139 acres on Cane Creek and Waxhaw River, bk 12, pg 29.

Waughup, James
1795 - James' will was probated in Mecklenburg Co. Children: Israel, William, Joseph

Way, James
1778 - deed to Robert Arthur for 227 acres on Four Mile Creek, joining Henry Downs, and Thomas Harris, Test: John Stuart, Benjamin B. Allet, bk 10, pg 73.
1780 - named as adjoining land owner to Thomas Coughran, Sr., and William Houston on Soder Branch of Twelve Mile Creek, bk 12, pg 162.
1783 - named as adjoining land owner to Thomas & Mary Harris, and William Means, bk 12, pg 255.

Wear/Wier, John & Jean
1777 -
1778 - deed to John Provane for 257 acres on Abraham Alexander's Mill Creek, joining Ebenezer Newton, Andrew Trot, Alexander Herrel, William Wilson, and John McEwell, Test: Robert Philips, Thomas Walker, bk 10, pg 283.
1780 - deed to Thomas Walker for 185 acres on Abraham Alexander's Mill Creek, joining James Blyth, and William Graham, Test: Hugh Lucas, William Graham, bk 10, pg 456.
1784 - witnessed a deed, with William Waddie, and Sam Davidson, from John Davidson to Robert Martin on Rockey River, bk 12, pg 308.

Weathers, Reuben
1806 - Loose estate papers

Weathersbee, Cade & Elizabeth ?
1793 - Cade's will was probated in Mecklenburg Co. Children: Absalom, Oliver, Jane Isham, Owen, Shadrach, Martha (? Hollingsworth), Mary (? Sikes), Lucy (? McLean)

Weber, Henry
Henry died 1791, buried in St John's Evangelical Lutheran Church Cemetery

Weigler, John
1783 - witnessed a deed, with James Rodes, from James & Elizabeth Hewit to Joseph Shinn on Three Mile Branch, bk 12, pg 335.

Weir, Thomas
1779 head branch of Reedy Creek.

Weaver, Henry
1790 - 134 00 - twp 12
1794 - Account ledger of John Melchor's store.
Sister: Rosina

Weaver, Jacob

Residents of Mecklenburg County, North Carolina 1762-1790

1790 - 111 00 - twp 12
1793 - Account ledger of John Melchor's store.
Weaver, Michael
   1792 - Account ledger of John Melchor's store.
Weaver, Peter
   1790 - 102 00 - twp 12
   1793 - Account ledger of John Melchor's store.
   1800 - Cabarrus County
Weaver, Valentine
   1772 - Loose estate papers
Weaver, William
   1793 - Account ledger of John Melchor's store.
Weddington, William
   Wife - Polly McClarty, daughter of Alexander & Jenny Morrison McClartey.
Weeks, David
   1777 - witnessed a deed, with John Jack, from John Philip Weeks to John McGivert on Rockey River, bk 10, pg 243.
   1782 - grant for 42 acres on Sugar Creek, bk 12, pg 73.
Weeks, John Phillip
   1777 - deed to John McGivert for 48 acres on Rockey River, Test: David Weeks, John Jack, bk 10, pg 243.
Weeks, Phillip & Elizabeth
   1790 - 203 00 - twp 20
   1800 - Mecklenburg County
Welch, John
   1785 - deed from William Stinson for 10 acres on Sugar Creek joining Robert Walker, and William Barnet, Test: Moses Sharpley, Robert Walker, John Stinson, bk 12, pg 455.
Welch, Joseph
   1790 - 114 00 - twp 13
   1800 - Cabarrus County
Welsh, Thomas
   1767 - Militia, Mecklenburgh Regiment (Lieutenant)
   1779 - grant for 100 acres on the head branch of Reedy Creek, joining Nathan Orr, and Thomas Neiley, bk 10, pg 490.
Wells, William
   1790 - 121 00 - twp 8
West, Benjamin
   1790 - 123 00 - twp 16
West, Martin
   1790 - 152 00 - twp 2
   Mentioned in the will of Samuel Knox.
Wetherspoon, William
   1790 - 111 00 - twp 20
Weymouth, Corbin
   1803 - Loose estate papers
Whipple, David

1782 - deed from William & Margaret Query for 78 acres on the middle fork of Goose Creek joining Robert Glass, Test: John McGinty, Joseph Galbreath, bk 11, pg 151.

White/Wiete, Archabeld, Sr.
   1777 - witnessed a deed, with John White, from John & Margaret Farr to William White on English Buffalo Creek, bk 10, pg 210.
   1778 - witnessed a deed, with Hugh McCree, and Martin Phifer, from Caleb Phifer to Andrew Carothers, bk 10, pg 462.
   1782 - grant for 128 acres on Anderson Creek beginning on the south side of the first hill, bk 12, pg 60.

White, Archibald
   1782 - grant for 300 acres on Anderson Creek joining John Calwell, bk 12, pg 59.
   1783 - witnessed a deed, with John Hagler, from James & Margaret Fleming to Paul Fifer on Meadow Branch, bk 12, pg 216.
   1784 - witnessed a deed, with Samuel White, from John & Elizabeth Caldwell to William and Adam Edgar on Anderson Creek, bk 12, pg 401.
   1785 - witnessed a deed, with William McAnulty, and John White, from James & Elizabeth Love to Archiblad McCordy on Rocky River, bk 12, pg 560.
   1790 - 312 00 - twp 13
   1800 - Cabarrus County

White, David
   1790 - 123 04 - twp 13
   1800 - Cabarrus County

White, Henrietta
   1785 - Henrietta's will was probated in Mecklenburg Co. Children: William, Lucy (? Brown)

White, Hugh
   1775 - deed from Robert Crawford, to Hugh, both of Craven Co., SC, for 127 acres on Warsaw Creek, joining William Beard, John Currey, and William Beard, Test: Nathan Barr, Charles Miller, Jr., Thomas Crawford, bk 10, pg 33.
   1782 - Loose estate papers
Hugh White from Craven Co., SC at the time of the sale.

White, James & Mary
   1766 - listed in the militia company of Capt. Adam Alexander of Clear Creek.
   1771 - James was one of the Cabarrus Black Boys with his brothers, William and John in 1771.
   1771 - deed from Charles & Sarah McCarmon for 77 acres on on a ridge known as Poplar Ridge between English Buffalo and Caddle Creek, Test: William White, bk 10, pg 224.
   1780 - named as adjoining land owner to John Means, Martin Phifer, Walter Farr, James Baker, and William McWhirter on Wolf Meador Branch, bk 12, pg 77.

Residents of Mecklenburg County, North Carolina
1762-1790

    1782 - named as adjoining land owner to John McEachion on Bake(Back) Creek joining James White, bk 12, pg 37.
    1782 - named as adjoining land owner to James Russle, George Masters, Michael Winecoff, and William Erwin near a draft of the three mile branches, bk 12, pg 86.
    1782 - grant for 42 acres on Rockey River, bk 12, pg 28.
    1784 - deed to Paul Barringer for 178 acres on Dutch Buffalow Creek, joining Mathias Beaver, Test: Adolph Niesmann, Philip Littigar, bk 12, pg 395.
    1774 - Mentioned in the estate papers of Nicholson Ross.
    1776 - witnessed a deed, with William Scott, from Hezekiah James & Martha Batch on English Buffalow Creek, bk 10, pg 223.
    1790 - 201 00 - twp 13
    Son of James White.

White, John & Mary
    1770 - John's will was probated in Mecklenburg Co. Children: Griffith, John, William, David, Mary, Ann, Matthew, Jane (James Kemp)

White/Wiete, John
    1766 - listed in the militia company of Capt. Adam Alexander of Clear Creek.
    1771 - John was one of the Cabarrus Black Boys with his brothers, William and James in 1771.
    1774 - Mentioned in the estate papers of Nicholson Ross. Son of James White.
    1777 - witnessed a deed, with Archibald White, from John & Margaret Farr to William White on English Buffalo Creek, bk 10, pg 210.
    1785 - witnessed a deed, with William McAnulty, and Archibald White, from James & Elizabeth Love to Archibald McCordy on Rockey River, bk 12, pg 560.

White, Joseph & Henrietta
    1784 - Joseph's will was probated in Mecklenburg Co. Legatees: Sarah McRee (neice), William Jones (son-in-law), Mary Winslow (sister)

White, Joseph & Frances(5)
    1790 - 103 00 - twp 13
    Joseph died Oct 6, 1842 at the age of 80.
    Frances died Sept 7, 1823 at the age of 58.

White, Moses & Margaret Givens
    1775 - mentioned in a deed from Joseph Rodgers and David Russell to Michael Shaver for 144 acres they conveyed by virtue of a will executed by Margaret White, deceased, on the 6th day of July 1773, bk 10, pg 185.
    1766 - mentioned in the above stated deed. His will dated the 10th day of March 1766.
    1767 - Loose estate papers
    Margaret was the daughter of Edward, Jr. & Agness Gibbons.

White, Samuel

1777 - deed from Robert Harris and Nathaniel Alexander,
trustees for the Presbyterial Congregation of Rockey
River, for 15 acres, Test: Robert Harris, Jr., Adam
Edger, bk 10, pg 206.
1782 - grant for 80 acres on the middle fork of Anderson
Creek, bk 12, pg 62.
1784 - witnessed a deed, with Archibald White, from John
& Elizbeth Caldwell to William and Adam Edgar on
Anderson Creek

White, Thomas & Ann
1768 - Thomas' will was probated in Mecklenburg Co.
Children: Joseph, Sarah, Mary

White, Thomas W. & Margaret(5)
1790 - 121 00 - twp 16
1800 - Mecklenburg County
Margaret died July 18, 1809

White, Thomas
1790 - 132 01 - twp 13
1800 - Cabarrus County

White, William
1774 - Loose estate papers

White, William & Mary
1783 - William's will was probated in Mecklenburg Co.

White, William
1762 - named in a 1782 deed as the original owner of a
tract on Rockey River, bk 11, pg 89.
William died before 1774.

White, William
William was a signer of the petition to pardon the
Cabarrus Black Boys in 1775.
1783 - named as adjoining land owner to Seth Rodgers,
William & Jane Ross, and William Hays, bk 11, pg 290.
1790 - 123 01 - twp 10

White, William
1771 - William was one of the Cabarrus Black Boys with
his brothers, James and John in 1771.
1777 - deed from John & Margaret Farr for 152 acres on
English Buffalo Creek, bk 10, pg 210.
1784 - witnessed a deed, with Seth Rodgers, from
Frederick & Clary Kerlock on English Buffellow Creek, bk
12, pg 564.
1785 - witnessed a bill of sale, with Seth Rodgers, from
Frederick Kerlock to Rachel Williams, bk 12, pg 557.
1790 - 135 00 - twp 13
Son of James White.

White, William W. & Jane(5)
1771 - William was one of the Cabarrus Black Boys with
his cousins, William, James, John White.
Children: Jean, Sarah, William, female (? Scott),
James, Robert, Thomas
William was born March 12, 1751, died July 10, 1794.
Jane died May 18, 1837 at the age of 83.

Whiteside, Dorcas K.T.
  Dorcas died July 31, 1819, age 31.
Whiteside, James & Polly(2)
  Polly died Sept 4, 1802 age 32.
Whiteside, James & Sally
Whiteside, John & Rachel Bigham(2)
  1774 - deed from Samuel Bigham for 217 acres on
  Stell(Steel) Creek, joining Dinnes McCormick, Test:
  Thomas McGee, William Reed, bk 10, pg 411.
  John died March 6, 1824 at age 83.
  Rachel, dau of William Bigham, died Feb 4, 1826 age 74.
Whiteside, Joseph & Elizabeth(2)
  Elizabeth died Oct 15, 1847 age 70.
Whiteside, Joseph & Mary C.(2)
  Joseph died June 23, 1821 at age 31.
Whiteside, Mary J.
  Mary died Nov 7, 1827, age 70, buried in Blackstock
  Cemetery.
Whiteside, Samuel(2)
  1772 -
  Samuel died Oct 22, 1772 at age 22.
Whiteside, William & Rachel Ann Bigham(2)
  Rachel died Nov 26, 1798, age 27, daughter of Samuel &
  Elizabeth Berryhill Bigham.
Whiteside, William(2)
  William died Nov 14, 1780, age 22.
  1780 - Loose estate papers
  Son of John & Rachel Whiteside.
Whitfield, John
  1781 - named as adjoining land owner to Francis &
  Margaret Johnston, Alexander Johnston, Mathew Knox,
  Thomas Nealy, and Hugh Herron, bk 12, pg 228.
Whitley, Exodus
  1796 - Account ledger of John Melchor's store.
Whitley, George
  1794 - Account ledger of John Melchor's store.
Whitley, Titus
  1794 - Account ledger of John Melchor's store.
Whitlow, Nicholas
  Pension denied July 7, 1832 - for further proof and
  specification.
Whitsitt, John
  1790 - 243 02 - twp 2
  1800 - Mecklenburg County
Widington/Weddington, Samuel
  1790 - 112 00 - twp 13
  1800 - Cabarrus County
Wier   (See Wear/Weir)
Wiete/White, John
  1781 - witnessed a deed, with Samuel Blyth, from David
  Davis to John Beel, bk 11, pg 102.
Wiley, Alexander

1775 - witnessed a deed of gift, with Evan Shelby, James Harris, Thomas Shelby, from Moses Shelby to his granddaughter, Mary Carruthers, bk 11, pg 61.

Wiley/Wyley, James
1768 - mentioned in a 1779 deed, from Henry Shute to Joseph Ross, as the previous land owner in 1768, bk 10, pg 354.
James was mentioned in the estate settlement of Wm. Sample.
1771 - James' will was probated in Mecklenburg Co. Children: John, Thomas, Martha, James, Robert
1772 - Loose estate papers
1779 - judgement against the administrators of James' estate for a tract joining James Wylie, bk 10, pg 426.

Wiley/Wylie, James
1784 - deed to William Johnston on both sides of Neal's branch and Reedy Creek adjoining Thomas and James McCawl (McCall), John Parks, John Neel, bk 12, pg 619.
Mentioned in this deed that James was late of New River, VA.
1790 - 102 01 - twp 19
1800 - Mecklenburg County

Wiley/Wilie/Weyle, John
1783 - named as adjoining land owner to John Setsinger, George Crozine, Alexander Ferguson, James Morrison, and John Shaver on Coldwater and Buffalow Creek, bk 12, pg 150.
1786 - named as adjoining land owner to Robert Smith, John Letsinger(Setsinger), George Cozine, Alexander Ferguson, and James Morrison on Coldwater Creek, bk 12, pg 616.
1790 - 211 00 - twp 10
1800 - Cabarrus County
Brother: James Wiley who lived in New River, VA prior to 1784.

Wiley, John
1772 - Neal's branch of Reedy Creek and Rockey River before 1779.
1776 - in Capt. Charles Polk's Light Horse Company.
1778 - witnessed a deed, with Samuel Montgomery, from John & Jane McCall to James Dickson on Clear Creek, bk 11, pg 56.
1790 - 143 00 - twp 4
Oldest brother of James Wiley of New River, VA.

Wiley/Wylie, John
John died before July 1779. Loose estate papers are extant for a John Wylie, but there is no date.

Wiley/Wylie, John
1784 - John's will was probated in Mecklenburg Co. Children: John, Janet, Jane ?

Wiley, Joseph
1790 - 101 00 - twp 4

Residents of Mecklenburg County, North Carolina
1762-1790

Wiley/Wyley, Moses & Mary(5)
   1767 - Loose estate papers
   Mary died June 7, 1818.
Wiley/Wylie, Moses & Ann
   Wife - Ann Jack, daughter of John & Mary Barnett Jack.
   Children: Leroy M., Mary (Thomas Baxter), Thomas, Eliza
   (? Carnes), Sarah Ann (John R. Hays), Laird, Jack
Wiley, Oliver & Mary(5)
   1772 - witnessed a deed of gift, with Adam Alexander,
   from John Carruthers to his daughter, Mary Carruthers,
   bk 11, pg 109.
   1782 - witnessed a deed of gift, with Adam Alexander,
   from John Carruthers to his daughter Isobel Carruthers,
   bk 11, pg 115.
   1782 - witnessed a deed of gift, with Adam Alexander,
   from John Carruthers to his daughter Elinor Carruthers,
   bk 11, pg 117.
   1782 - witnessed a deed of gift, with Adam Alexander,
   from John Carruthers to his daughter Mary Carruthers, bk
   11, pg 118.
   1783 - deed to Jacob Self for 12 acres on the south side
   of Clear Creek, Test: Adam Alexander, Evan Alexander,
   Isack Alexander, bk 12, pg 214.
   Oliver was a signer of the petition to pardon the
   Cabarrus Black Boys in 1775.
   1784 - witnessed a deed, with Adam Alexander, from
   Mathew Miller to John Karr on Meadow Branch, bk 12, pg
   371.
   1790 - 146 04 - twp 13
   1800 - Cabarrus County
   Children: Mary (? Carruthers),
   Oliver died Dec 1802 at the age of 61.
   Mary died Aug 21, 1822 at the age of 78.
Wiley/Wylie, Samuel
   1780 - indenture between George McWherter and Dennis
   Titus for 323-1/2 acres on Warshaw Creek, agreeable to a
   division between Samuel Wylie and Robert Caldwell, bk
   10, pg 447.
Wiley/Wilie/Wylie, William & Martha
   1766 - listed in the militia company of Capt. Adam
   Alexander of Clear Creek.
   1778 - witnessed a deed, with Samuel McComb, from
   William Simmond to James McComb for a tract known as the
   No. Two Tract, bk 10, pg 335.
   1785 - deed to Nehemiah Harison for 150 acres on McKee
   Creek joining Samuel Harris, and William Harris, Test:
   Davis Harrison, Samuel Harris, bk 12, pg 548.
   1790 - 303 02 - twp 4
Wilhelm, George & Eve
   1790 - 141 00 - twp 12
   1800 - Cabarrus County
Wilham, Lewis

1785 - witnessed a deed, with Qudray Wilonlee, and Paul
Farrow, from George & Susan Karriker to John George
Williams on Rockey River, bk 12, pg 592.

Wilkerson, William & Charity
1795 - William's will was probated in Mecklenburg Co.
Children: Charles

Wilkeson, George
1790 - 102 00 - twp 1
1800 - Mecklenburg County

Wilkins, Samuel
1763 - Samuel's will was probated in Mecklenburg Co.
Children: John

Williams, Billy
1790 - 122 00 - twp 6

Williams, Daniel
1782 - named as adjoining land owner to Joseph &
Elizabeth McKinley, John Carruthers, and James McCall,
bk 11, pg 149.

Williams, David(2) & Phebe ?
David died Dec 3, 1777 at the age of 41. His will was
probated in Mecklenburg Co.
Children: John, George, Robert

Williams, David
1787 - Loose estate papers

Williams, Edward
1775 - named as adjoining land owner to Samuel Knox,
Thomas Ferguson, William Barnett, George Cahoon, and
John Henry on Steel Creek, bk 10, pg 251.

Williams, Isaac & Elenor
1784 - deed to George Hutchison for 100 acres near a
branch of Sugar Creek, Test: William McCafferty, James
Tagert, bk 12, pgs 430 & 437.
1784 - named as adjoining land owner to John & Jane
Sloan, Jesse Clark, Robert Walker, James Tagart, David
Hayes, and Alexander McKee on Sugar Creek, bk 12, pg
466.

Williams, Ishmael
1790 - 122 00 - twp 18

Williams, James
1774 - witnessed a deed, from Hugh Montgomery, of Rowan
Co., NC, to John Richey, bk 10, pg 120.

Williams, Jas L.
1790 - 000 10 - twp 7

Williams, Job & Ann ?
1779 - grant for 100 acres on Stoney Creek, joining John
Desard, bk 10, pg 497.
1782 - grant for 73 acres on Mallard Creek joining
Robert Craighead, bk 12, pg 92.
1783 - deed from Robert & Hannah Craighead for 108 acres
on Stoney Creek, Test: Samuel Patton, Thomas Faulkner,
bk 12, pg 224.
1786 - Job's will was probated in Mecklenburg Co.

1786 - Loose estate papers
Children: John, Joseph, Janet, Sarah
Williams, John
    1777 - Loose estate papers
Williams, John & Margaret
    1790 - 121 00 - twp 18
    1800 - Mecklenburg County
    Wife - Margaret McCorkle, daughter of John & Margaret
    Evans McCorkle
William, John George
    1784 - deed from Frederick & Clary Kerlock for 91 acres
    on English Buffellow Creek joining Martin Phifer, bk 12,
    pg 564.
    1785 - deed from George & Susan Karriker for 100 acres
    on a branch of Rockey River, joining Peter Reas, James
    Beatchey, and James Cuntress, Test: Lewis Wilham, Qudray
    Wilonlee, Paul Farrow, bk 12, pg 592.
Williams, Joshua
    1792 - Account ledger of John Melchor's store.
William, Lewis & Mary
    1795 - Lewis' will was probated in Mecklenburg Co.
    Children: Rebecca, Richard, Joshua, Seth, Nancy, Peggy
Williams, Phebe
    1784 - named as adjoining land owner to James McCall,
    and John Carothers, bk 12, pg 177.
Williams, Rachel
    1785 - bill of sale from Frederick Kerlock for natural
    love and affection, Test: Seth Rodgers, William White,
    bk 12, pg 557.
Williams, Thomas
    1782 - Loose estate papers
Williamson, Benjamin
    1790 - 113 00 - twp 4
Williamson, James
    1784 - deed from John & Jean Brevard of Rowan Co., NC,
    for a tract on Rockey River, Test: Thomas Alexander,
    John Gillespie, bk 12, pg 547.
    1785 - deed to Thomas Harris for 52 acres on a branch of
    Rockey River, Test: Robert Potts, bk 12, pg 584.
    1790 - 112 00 - twp 16
    1800 - Mecklenburg County
Willis, Betty
    1792 - Betty's will was probated in Mecklenburg Co.
    Children: Jacob, Ann, Sarah, Diana, Elizabeth, Daniel,
    John
Willis, Daniel & Elizabeth
    1784 - Daniel's will was probated in Mecklenburg Co.
    Children: Daniel, John
Willis, John
    1784 - deed to Absalom Baker for 200 acres on Buffalow
    Creek joining Martin Phifer, John Baker, and Samuel
    Sewell, Test: Joseph Shinn, Jacob Criden, bk 12, pg 449.

1778 - Signer of 1778 Petition.
Willis, Josiah
    1772 - Josiah's will was probated in Mecklenburg Co.
    Children: George, John, Ambrose
Willis, Robert & Ann
    1787 - Robert's will was probated in Mecklenburg Co.
Wilonlee, Qudrey
    1785 - witnessed a deed, with Lewis Wilham, and Paul
    Farrow on Rockey River, bk 12, pg 592.
Wilson, Aaron
    1778 - witnessed a deed from Mary McDowel to John
    McDowel for 350 acres on Sugar Creek, bk 10, pg 29.
    1779 - witnessed a deed, with John McDowell, from Robert
    Wilson to Joseph Wilson on Sugar Creek, bk 10, pg 366.
Wilson, Benjn. & Mary
    1779 - witnessed a deed, with Richard Berry, and William
    Henderson, bk 12, pg 429.
    1790 - 112 03 - twp 7
    Wife - Mary Wilson, daughter of Samuel & Hannah Knox
    Wilson.
    1800 - Loose estate papers
    Son of David Wilson.
Wilson, David(2)
    1771 David died Aug 27, 1771 at age 22.
Wilson, David
    1773 - witnessed a deed from James Dysart to Ephraim
    Farr on Rockey River, bk 11, pg 169.
    1776 - deed from John McLiley for 50 acres on both sides
    of the Tinker Branch, Test: Archibald Houston, James
    Humphrey, bk 10, pg 35.
    1779 - grant for 83 acres joining John Farr, Ephraim
    Farr, Nathaniel Erwin, and James Dickey, bk 10, pg 503.
    1779 - grant for 110 acres joining Nathaniel Erwin's old
    corner, bk 10, pg 504.
    1780 - witnessed a deed, with Zaccheus Wilson, from
    James & Jean Wallace to Martin Phifer, Jr. on Coddle
    Creek, bk 11, pg 142.
    1785 - witnessed a deed from Ephraim Farr to Archibald
    Houston, bk 12, pg 481.
    1785 - deed to John Alison for 83 acres joining Ephraim
    Farr, John Farr, and Nathaniel Ervin, Test: Thomas
    Donnall, Thomas Harris, bk 12, pg 520.
    1785 - witnessed a deed, with Joseph Sharp, from Ephraim
    Farr to John and William Hamilton on Rockey River, bk
    12, pg 531.
Wilson, David
    1790 - 142 01 - twp 7
    1800 - Mecklenburg County
Wilson, Garrett
    1769 -
    1771
    1775 - Loose estate papers

Mentioned in estate settlement of Wm. Sample.
Wilson, Garrett
   1779 - named as adjoining land owner to Margaret Wilson,
   Ezekiel Wilson, and Alexander Campbell, bk 10, pg 512.
Wilson, Isaac
   1785 - witnessed a deed, with Robert Smith, on Coddle
   Creek, bk 12, pg 533.
   1790 - 111 02 - twp 2
   1800 - Mecklenburg County
Wilson, James
   1764 - Loose estate papers
Wilson, James
   1776 - James' will was probated in Mecklenburg Co.
   1777 - Loose estate papers
   Children: John
Wilson, James
   1779 - named as adjoining land owner to Robert Graham,
   Robert Hays, William Wilson, and John McCluer on Sugar
   Creek, bk 10, pg 340.
   1783 - witnessed a deed, with John Bigham on Sugar
   Creek, bk 12, pg 218.
   1790 - 100 00 - twp 2
   1801 - Loose estate papers
Wilson, James
   1778 - Signer of 1778 Petition
   1779 - named as adjoining land owner to Joseph
   Alexander, Stephen Alexander, and Charles Caldwell on
   Coddle Creek, bk 10, pg 523.
   1780 - grant for 93 acres on Coddle Creek and crossing
   at the mouth of Fulmer's Branch, joining Moses Andrews,
   and Hezekiah Alexander, bk 12, pg 193.
   1785 - deed to Martha Moffitte for 93 acres on Coddle
   Creek, joining Hezekiah Alexander, and Stephen
   Alexander, Test: Anthony Ross, Henry Short, bk 12, pg
   558.
   1790 - 314 00 - twp 15
   1800 - Mecklenburg County
Wilson, John & Elizabeth
   1782 - John's will was probated in Mecklenburg Co.
   1782 - Loose estate papers
Wilson, John, Jr.
   1779 - grant for 70 acres on Coddle Creek joining
   Charles Caldwell, bk 12, pg 68.
   1785 - deed to Dr. Thomas Donnell for 3 tracts on Coddle
   Creek, Test: Robert Smith, Isaac Wilson, bk 12, pg 533.
   1790 - 115 00 - twp 8
   1800 - Cabarrus County
Wilson, John
   1776 - deed from Augustine Culp for 50 acres on
   McMichael's Creek joining Samuel Jack, Test: William
   Reed, Elijah Alexander, Abner Alexander, bk 11, pg 222.

1776 - deed from John Dermond for 133 acres on
McMichael's Creek, Test: John Barett, Charles Alexander,
Will Reed, bk 11, pg 246.
1778 - witnessed a deed, with Peter Roland, and William
Smith, from Aaron & Fannie McWhorter to John Smith on
Twelve Mile Creek, bk 10, pg 16.
1779 - grant for 2 ½ acres and 4 poles on McMichael's
Creek joining John Dermond, bk 12, pg 27.
1781 - deed from Andrew McCorkle for 202 acres on
Pickens Creek, a branch of Twelve Mile Creek, Test: John
Nutt, William McMurry, bk 12, pg 274.

Wilson, John
1779 - deed from Nathaniel Cook for 43 acres on Sugar
Creek, joining Thomas Polk, Test: Ezekiel Polk, John
Bitty, bk 10, pg 301.
1790 - 122 00 - twp 20
1795 - Loose estate papers

Wilson, John(2)
1779 - witnessed a deed, with Archibald Crockett, and
John McCulloh, from William & Rachel Robison to John
Gibbins on Four Mile Creek near Providence, bk 11, pg
298.
1780 - named as adjoining land owner to Joseph Douglas,
? Nelson, Robert Crocket, and Michael Ligget on Twelve
Mile Creek, bk 12, pg 95.
1783 - deed from William McCulloh for 190 acres on
McCalpin's Creek joining Robert Parks, Test: William
Polk, John M. Powel, bk 11, pg 241.
1790 - 322 05 - twp 1
1800 - Mecklenburg County
John died Sept 22, 1806 at age 41.
1806 - Loose estate papers

Wilson, John
1790 - 100 01 - twp 7
John died before 1815

Wilson, John & Elizabeth McCrum
1790 - 244 00 - twp 7

Wilson, John
1766 - listed in the militia company of Capt. Adam
Alexander of Clear Creek.
1779 - John's will was probated in Mecklenburg Co.
Children: John, Andrew, Agnes

Wilson, John, Jr.
1790 - 101 00 - twp 7

Wilson, John, Jr.
1794 - Loose estate papers

Wilson, Joseph
1779 - deed from Robert Wilson for 170 acres on Sugar
Creek on the east side of William Bigham's land, Test:
John McDowell, Aaron Wilson, bk 10, pg 366.
1780 - deed from Zaccheus Wilson for 160 acres on Sugar
Creek, Test Dun Ochiltree, Thomas Spencer, bk 11, pg 39.

Residents of Mecklenburg County, North Carolina 1762-1790

1790 - 133 00 - twp 2
1800 - Mecklenburg County
Wife -   ?   Ferguson
Children: Eleanor, Martha, Thomas, David, Robert
Wilson, Joseph
    1779 - witnessed a deed, with William Idglie, from Gilbert McNarr to Francis Nixon on the head branches of Rockey River, bk 12, pg 490.
    1783 - grant for 134 acres on Dowel's Creek joining Gilber McNear, bk 12, pg 166.
    1783 - deed from Denis McFall for 260 acres on McDowell's Creek, Test: William Waddle, John Belk, bk 12, pg 497.
    1790 - 100 00 - twp 7
    1795 - Loose estate papers
Wilson, Margaret
    1779 - deed from George Nicklson for lots 129 and 137 in Charlotte, Test: Samuel Knox, Hugh Barnet, bk 11, pg 28.
    1780 near Garrett Wilson & Ezekile Wallace, Campbell's Creek-a branch of McCalpin's Creek (twp 15).
Wilson, Robert & Jane McDowell(2)
    1775 - witnessed a deed, with James Turner, from William(Will) & Sarah Bigham to Thomas Spencer on the north part of Sugar Creek, bk 10, pg 171.
    1779 - deed to Joseph Wilson for 170 acres on Sugar Creek on the east side of William Bigham's land, Test: John McDowell, Aaron Wilson, bk 10, pg 366.
    1782 - named as adjoining land owner to Thomas & Mary Spencer, John Taylor, John Bigham, and Robert Irwin, bk 11, pg 177.
    1783 - grant for 70 acres on Sugar Creek joining William Bigham, John McDowel, and Thomas Barnet, bk 12, pg 107.
    1790 - 122 00 - twp 20
Wife - Jane McDowell, dau of William & Ellen McDowell of York Co., SC
Robert died March 17, 1816 at age 57.
Wilson, Robert & Eleanor
    1780 - named as adjoining land owner to Samuel Bigham, Sr., Thomas Spencer, and William Bigham on the north fork of Steel Creek, bk 11, pg 1.
    1790 - 602 00 - twp 2
Wife - Eleanor Carruther
Children: Joseph, John, James, Aaron, Robert, Samuel, Zaccheus (Margaret Russell), Josiah, Moses, Thomas
Brother: Zaccheus
    1794 - Loose estate papers for Robert
    1802 - Loose estate papers for Eleanor
Wilson, Samuel, Jur.
    1790 - 102 09 - twp 7
Revolutionary Soldier - died Feb 10, 1843, age 92 yrs & 8 mos. according to The Charlotte Journal dated Feb. 23, 1843.

Wilson, Samuel, Senr. & Hannah
    1783 - grant for 50 acres on Clark's Creek, joining
    Robert Hope, bk 12, pg 121.
    1779 - guardian bond between David McCree and Ezekiel
    Polk whereas Ezekiel Polk is appointed guardian of
    Samuel Polk and Samuel Wilson, providing for them out of
    the estate of Samuel Wilson, bk 10, pg 455.
    Wife - Hannah Knox, daughter of Capt. Patrick Knox.
    Samuel was the son of Samuel & Mary Wilson.
    He was under age at the time of his father's death.
    1790 - 113 00 - twp 7
Wilson, Samuel & Mary
    1767 - Militia, Mecklenburgh Regiment
    1769 - witnessed a deed, with Patrick Carr, from John &
    Elizabeth Mitchell to Jonathan Newman on Clark's Creek,
    bk 10, pg 169.
    Wife - Mary Winslow, daughter of Moses Winslow; the
    widow Potts, Margaret Jack, daughter of Patrick & Lillis
    McAdoo Jack
    1778 - Samuel's will was probated in Mecklenburg Co.
    1778 - Loose estate papers
    Children: Mary (Ezekiel Polk), Violet (John Davidson),
    Samuel (Hannah Knox), John, Benjamin, Robert, Margaret,
    Rebecca (John Henderson), Moses Winslow, 2nd marriage -
    Margaret (John Davidson), 3rd marriage - Sarah (Ben
    McConnell), Charity, Robert (Margaret Alexander), Lillis
    (James Conner), William Jack (Rocinda Winslow)
Wilson, Thomas
    1790 - 143 00 - twp 15
    1800 - Mecklenburg County
Wilson, Thomas, Senr. & Margaret
    1771 - bond between Thomas and James Wilson, Test:
    Robert and Francis Glass, bk 10, pg 209.
    1782 - named as adjoining land owner to Charles McCammon
    on the south side of Rockey River, bk 12, pg 96.
    1790 - 101 00 - twp 15
    1798 - Loose estate papers
Wilson, William
    1778 - named as adjoining land owner to John & Jean
    Wear, Ebenezer Newton, Andrew Trot, Alexander Herrel,
    and John McEwell on Abraham Alexander's Mill Creek, bk
    10, pg 283.
    1779 - named as adjoining land owner to Robert Graham,
    Robert Hays, James Wilson, and John McCluer on Sugar
    Creek, bk 10, pg 340.
    1779 - grant for 109 acres on Starret's Creek and Sugar
    Creek, joining James Larver(Carver), bk 10, pg 491.
    1790 - 223 01 - twp 20
    Children: John, Jeremiah(moved to Livingston Co., KY),
    Joseph(moved to Livingston Co., KY)
    William died before 1807.
Wilson, William & Martha

1778 - named as adjoining land owner to Moses Steel,
William & James McCafferty, James W. Sawyer, and
Alexander Starret on Sugar Creek, bk 10, pg 20.
1779 - grant for 150 acres on a branch of McCulloch
Creek, joining James McCord, bk 10, pg 505.
1779 - grant for 130 acres on Sugar Creek, bk 10, pg
506.
1782 - named as adjoining land owner to John McKoy, John
Springs, Robert Phillips, Andrew Sprott, Alexander
Starret, and John McEwus, bk 12, pgs 244 & 245.
1790 - 111 00 - twp 2
1800 - Mecklenburg County

Wilson, William
1790 - 000 10 - twp 7

Wilson, Zaccheus & Margaret
1780 - witnessed a deed, with David Wilson, from James &
Jean Wallace to Martin Phifer, Jr. on Coddle Creek, bk
11, pg 142.
1780 - deed to Joseph Wilson for 160 acres on Sugar
Creek, Test: Dun Ochiltree, Thomas Spencer, bk 11, pg
39.
1783 - named as adjoining land owner to George &
Margaret Calhoon, James Green, and Robert Wilson, bk 12,
pg 218.
1790 - 204 00 - twp 2
Wife - Margaret Russell, daughter of David Russell.
Zaccheus moved to Sumner Co., TN.

Wilson, Zaccheus, Senr. & Keziah
1775 - Zaccheus was one of the signers of the
Mecklenburg Declaration of Independence on May 20, 1775.
1777 - witnessed a deed, with Martin Fifer, from John
McCoy to Martain Phifer, Sr. on the north side of
Buffalo Creek, bk 11, pg 34.
1778 - witnessed a deed, with Robert McCleary for lot 65
in Charlotte to Ezekiel Polk, bk 10, pg 216.
1778 - Signer of 1778 Petition.
1781 - deed from Nathaniel & Jane Gilmore for 227 acres,
Test: John Smith, Robert Harris, bk 12, pg 317.
1783 - deed from Robert & Catherine Hope, Test: Robert
Harris, Andrew Alexander, bk 12, pg 303.
1790 - 111 00 - twp 5
Zaccheus was a member of Poplar Tent Presbyterian
Church.

Winchester, Daniel
1778 - Signer of 1778 Petition.
1793 - Account ledger of John Melchor's store.

Winchester, Dugles
1790 - 233 00 - twp 12
1800 - Cabarrus County

Winchester, Thomas
1785 - Loose estate papers

Winchester, William

1778 - Signer of 1778 Petition
1782 - named as adjoining land owner to Isaac Breden, and Charles Dacton on Rockey River near the head of Meadow Spring, bk 12, pg 171.
1790 - 224 00 - twp 12
1795 - Loose estate papers
Wines, Abner
   1796 - Loose estate papers
Winesaugh/Winecoff, Michael
   1790 - 101 03 - twp 10
Winesaugh/Winecoff, Michael, Junr.
   1782 - named as adjoining land owner to James Russle, James White, George Masters, and William Erwin near a draft of the three mile branches, bk 12, pg 86.
   1782 - grant for 235 acres on Three Mile Branch, joining William Irwin, James Russell, and George Conder, bk 12, pg 113.
   1790 - 143 00 - twp 10
   1800 - Cabarrus County
Winings, Peter
   1790 - 112 01 - twp 5
   1800 - Mecklenburg County (widow)
Wirtenberg, Frederick
   1767 - Loose estate papers
Wise, Benjamin
   1790 - 000 10 - twp 14
Wise, John
Wise, Phillip
   1784 - named as adjoining land owner to John Chamberlain, James Vorly, and James McCraw on Coldwater Creek, bk 12, pg 187.
Wise, Thomas
   1790 - 225 00 - twp 4
Wise, William
   1790 - 101 00 - twp 7
Wisehart/Wishart, Joseph & Elizabeth
   1773 - deed from Ezekiel Polk for 2 lots in Charlotte on the west side of Tryon Street containing 6 acres, Test: Thomas Polk, Thomas Harris, bk 10, pg 36.
   1777 - deed for lot 67 in Charlotte, Test: Robert Scott, Hugh Pollock, bk 11, pg 62.
   1780 - witnessed a deed, with Francis Herron, for lot 68 in Charlotte, kb 11, pg 244.
   1790 - 102 01 - twp 3
   1796 - Loose estate papers
Wisel/Wiser, Michael & Elizabeth
   1790 - 213 00 - twp 11
   1800 - Cabarrus County
   Children: Polly (Matthias B.Boem), Batsy (Henry Furr, George Barringer), Catherine (Henry Furr)
Wiser, Phillip, Jur.
   1790 - 102 00 - twp 12

Wiser, Phillip, Senr.
   1790 - 301 00 - twp 12
Wite, John
   1790 - 243 02 - twp 13
   1800 - Cabarrus County
Wite, John
   1790 - 104 00 - twp 7
Wite, William
   1790 - 123 00 - twp 7
Witenhouse, Martin/Nathan
   1790 - 000 10 - twp 12
   1792 - Account ledger of John Melchor's store.
Witherford, Wilka
   1790 - 332 00 - twp 14
Witherford, William
   1790 - 113 00 - twp 14
Withers/Wethers, Reuben
   1790 - 215 04 - twp 2
   1800 - Mecklenburg County
Witherspoon, James
   1782 - deed for lots 115 and 123 in Charlotte, Test:
   Hugh Harris, Robert McCleary, bk 11, pg 143.
Wodington/Weddington, John
   1790 - 112 00 - twp 9
   1800 - Cabarrus County
Wolfe, John
   1796 - Loose estate papers
Wolf, Phillip
   1790 - 353 00 - twp 11
   Phillip died before 1817.
Wolfe, Phillip Jr.
   Phillip died before 1806
Woods, John
   1790 - 101 00 - twp 5
Woods, Mathew
   1790 - 211 00 - twp 6
   1795 - Loose estate papers
Woods, Robert
   1790 - 123 00 - twp 6
   1791 - Loose estate papers
Woodside, Archibald
   1778 - Signer of 1778 Petition.
Worke, John
   1774 - deed for lot 156 in Charlotte, Test: David McKee,
   David Byars, bk 10, pg 217.
   Of Rowan Co., NC in 1774
   1793 - Loose estate papers
Wrenn, Alexander
   1796 - Loose estate papers
Wright/Rite, John

1782 - witnessed a deed, with Frederick Kizer, from
George & Mary Kizer to Coonrad Hardwick on Meadoe Creek
and Canada's Branch, bk 12, pg 482.
Wright, William
1790 - 000 10 - twp 3
Wyatt, Sylvester
1790 - 122 00 - twp 19
1800 - Mecklenburg County
Wynchaster, Thomas
1766 - listed in the militia company of Capt. Adam
Alexander of Clear Creek.
Wynchaster, William
1766 - listed in the militia company of Capt. Adam
Alexander of Clear Creek.
Wynens, Peter
1800 - Loose estate papers
Yandel, Andrew
1779 - grant for 48 acres on McMichal's Creek joining
William Yandell, Peter Johnston, William Manson, and
Thomas Polk, bk 10, pg 513.
1790 - 143 00 - twp 20
Yandel, William
1770
1777 - named as adjoining land owner to Peter Johnston,
Isaiah Fitten, Zebulon Alexander, Thomas Alexander,
James Yandel, and Charles Alexander on Sugar Creek, bk
10, pg 94.
1784 - named as adjoining land owner to Peter Johnston,
and Hadawick Davies on McMichal's Creek, bk 12, pg 404.
1790 - 447 00 - twp 20
1800 - Mecklenburg County
Mentioned in estate settlement of Wm. Sample.
Yandell, James
1777 - named as adjoining land owner to Peter Johnston,
Isaiah Fitten, Zebulon Alexander, Thomas Alexander,
William Yandel, and Charles Alexander on Sugar Creek, bk
10, pg 94.
1790 - 134 00 - twp 20
1797 - Loose estate papers
Mentioned in estate settlement of Wm. Sample.
Yarbrough, Ambrose
1792 - Account ledger of John Melchor's store.
Yarbrough, Humphrey
1793 - Account ledger of John Melchor's store.
Yarbrough, Joshua
1780 - grant for 200 acres on Philip's Spring Branch, a
branch of Richardson Creek, bk 12, pg 20.
1780 - grant for 400 acres on Merchion Fork of
Richardson Creek, bk 12, pg 16.
1784 - witnessed a deed, with Sylvanus Phillips, from
Benjamin Cook to Jack Liget on a branch of Two Mile
Creek, bk 12, pg 443.

Residents of Mecklenburg County, North Carolina 1762-1790

1790 - 331 00 - twp 16
1800 - Mecklenburg County
Yearly, James
    Pension denied July 7, 1832 - no evidence of service.
Yerbey, Avent
    1790 - 132 00 - twp 17
    1800 - Mecklenburg County
Yewman/Yeoman, John
    1790 - 102 00 - twp 10
    1800 - Cabarrus County
Yeoman, Jonas, Jr.
    1793 - Account ledger of John Melchor's store.
Yeoman, Stokes
    1793 - Account ledger of John Melchor's store.
Yost, Christina
    1775 - Loose estate papers
Yost/Jost, Phillip
    Children: Catherine (Christopher Luis/Lewis)
Young, James & Jane
    James died Jan 31, 1835 at age 66.
    Buried in Rice Cemetery.
Young, John
    1777 - named as adjoining land owner to Adam & Cathey Moyer, and Mathias Boston on Little Coldwater Creek, bk 10, pg 421.
    1790 - 103 00 - twp 10
    1790 - Loose estate papers
Young, Joseph
    1763 - deed from Daniel & Martha England for 214 acres on Lodle(Coddle) Creek, joining John Alexander, Test: John Griffee, John Whitt Alexander, bk 10, pg 126.
    1773 - witnessed a deed, with Hezekiah Alexander, from James Alexander, of Cecil Co., MD, to John McKnitt Alexander for 5 acres of part of Jeremiah Joy's barony, bk 10, pg 190.
    1782 - named as adjoining land owner to William Young on Coddle Creek, bk 12, pg 35.
    1784 - grant for 80 acres on Coddle Creek, joining John Alexander, and William Young, bk 12, pg 155.
    1790 - 207 05 - twp 5
    1800 - Cabarrus County
Young, Martin
    1790 - 113 00 - twp 10
Young, Mary
    Mary died Dec 25, 1806, age 77, buried in Blackstock Cemetery.
Young, Robert
    Robert died Sept 5, 1811 at the age of 45.
    Buried in Rice Cemetery
Young, Samuel

1774 - named as adjoining land owner to John & Jean
Brevard (of Rowan Co. in 1774), and Andrew Downes, bk
10, pg 183.

Young, William
    1778 - Signer of 1778 Petition
    1782 - grant for 237 acres on Coddle Creek joining
Joseph Young, bk 12, pg 35.
    1782 - named as adjoining land owner to Robert Leviston,
and James Means on Coddle Creek, bk 12, pg 72.
    1784 - witnessed a deed, with Benjamin Patten, from John
Alexander, Sr., to James Smith on Coddle Creek, bk 12,
pg 457.
    1784 - named as adjoining land owner to Joseph Young,
and John Alexander on Coddle Creek, bk 12, pg 155.
    1785 - witnessed a deed, with James Smith, from John
Alexander to Abraham Alexander on Coddle Creek, bk 12,
pg 538.
    1790 - 138 02 - twp 5
    1800 - Cabarrus County

Yurce, Francis
    1790 - 132 00 - twp 2

Ziklagg, Samuel
    1783 - named as the previous owner to a tract joining
William Flenniken, Edward Debreel, and Justice Beach, bk
12, pg 208.
    1784 - named as adjoining land owner to Walter Bell,
George Davies, and William Hall on Caudle Creek, bk 12,
pg 351.

www.ingramcontent.com/pod-product-compliance
Lightning Source LLC
Chambersburg PA
CBHW071232290426
44108CB00013B/1384